JOURNAL FOR THE STUDY OF THE OLD TESTAMENT
SUPPLEMENT SERIES
154

JSOT Press
Sheffield

Nahum M. Sarna

Minḥah le-Naḥum

Biblical and Other Studies Presented to Nahum M. Sarna in Honour of his 70th Birthday

edited by
Marc Brettler
and
Michael Fishbane

Journal for the Study of the Old Testament
Supplement Series 154

Published by JSOT Press
JSOT Press is an imprint of
Sheffield Academic Press Ltd
343 Fulwood Road
Sheffield S10 3BP
England

Typeset by Sheffield Academic Press
and
Printed on acid-free paper in Great Britain
by Biddles Ltd
Guildford

British Library Cataloguing in Publication Data

Minḥah le-Naḥum: Biblical and Other
Studies Presented to Nahum M. Sarna in Honour
of his 70th Birthday. - (JSOT Supplement Series,
ISSN 0309-0787; No. 154)
I. Fishbane, Michael
II. Brettler, Marc Zvi III. Series
221.6

ISBN 1-85075-419-5

Contents

EDITORS' PREFACE

It is with much pleasure, Nahum, that we celebrate you on your 70th birthday, and offer these studies in friendship and respect. As your colleagues, students and friends spanning three generations, we have been the grateful recipients of your careful scholarship in many areas of Biblical Studies. As you shall see, many of the following essays are strongly indebted to your work and interests. Their range is further tribute to your wide-ranging contributions to our field.

Over 40 years ago you came to America equipped with a broad secular and Jewish education, received in the rigorous atmosphere of the English school system and in the bounty of your own home. This combination of cultures, absorbed deeply, formed your vision as scholar and teacher. The scholars who taught you at University College of London University, and at Jews College, are the luminaries of a past generation—mentors such as Isidore Epstein, Arthur Marmorstein, and Cecil Roth. In London you mastered the range of Jewish Studies, specializing in Rabbinics, Semitics and Biblical Studies. The scope of study these teachers offered and demanded influenced your own large view of the field. Equally influential was the strong Zionist vision which shaped your childhood, and the Jewish leaders and scholars who regularly visited your home in connection with 'The Order of Ancient Maccabees' and other matters. Here you came to meet Chaim Weizmann and Nahum Sokolow, along with such savants as Moses Gaster and Simon Rawidowicz. Their lives and example made a deep impression upon you—and stories of your experiences have held many friends in thrall.

After a brief stay in Israel, your deepening interests in Biblical Studies and Semitic languages brought you to the United States for PhD studies with Cyrus Gordon at Dropsie College. Your work in the language of the book of Job grew out of your philological passions—which you combined with a passion for the ideas and literary aspects of this and other biblical books. Your ongoing studies in Jewish literature more generally helped earn you your earliest academic positions as librarian and Assistant Professor of Bible at the Jewish Theological Seminary of America. The great faculty assembled at that institution in the 1950s gave a broad context to your many interests, and provided warm and enduring friendships over the years. In addition, your innovative and dedicated teaching was received by an eager and grateful student body. But for all that, we dare say you could not have been more appreciated than you were as the Dora Golding Professor of Bible at Brandeis University, from 1965 to your retirement, and as longtime Chairman of the Department of Near Eastern and Judaic Studies. Students came to your courses in droves—for to take a 'Sarna course' was an ongoing challenge and intellectual treat. Graduate students marvelled at the clarity, order and range of your knowledge—not to mention the constant readiness to discuss every new idea and proposal. Your frequent acknowledgments in class of observations made by students in previous years was an important lesson in humility. You were and remain for us a model of pedagogical excellence. The 'oral Torah' we heard from you in class and in your office exceeded the bounds of the 'written Torah' that was published—and this was considerable, and has earned you a distinguished and honorable place among the Bible scholars of this generation.

The wide range of your training and interests certainly contributed to your many projects and insights. We think of your lifetime of labor in the book of Genesis and the Psalms, studied in their own right, and in the light of ancient Near Eastern literature and the medieval Jewish Bible commentators. For this reason you could discover the literary devices of the medievals and show their contributions to the biblical text; or see the living link between the medievals and modern Bible Studies; or even the links between ancient Near Eastern literature and rabbinic sources. Similarly, your rabbinic studies and interest in librarianship produced penetrating studies on ancient archival matters, the guilds that contributed to the Psalms, and the nature of the canon more generally. And who will forget your illuminating comments on ancient mythology, or the wide mastery of the text that produced a path-breaking essay on inner-biblical exegesis? In all these ways you contributed to your colleagues' knowledge, and ever encouraged your students to undertake new work. Nothing was discouraged; every hint was supported—and we are grateful.

And not only we few, but surely both the wider scholarly world and the Jewish community at large must rise up and call itself blessed for your vision to produce a Jewish Bible commentary for our generation. The massive energy and effort that went into the project will vivify generations to come; and for those who take the time to look, your pedagogical skills and methodological care are everywhere in evidence. These too can instruct and delight. Equally important is the work you put in over 15 years—often at the expense of your own projects—on producing a faithful but felicitous English translation of the Ketuvim of the Bible for our generation. Any one of these projects would ennoble a lifetime. To have done all of them with devotion and skill is to put us and future generations in your debt.

In all these ways you have been our consummate teacher, friend and mentor—counselling with unfailing humor and wit, but always with caring and concern. We wish you good health in the company of your beloved Helen, and the strength to complete your many scholarly projects. In their completion is our blessing.

Michael Fishbane
Marc Brettler

Abbreviations

AB	Anchor Bible
AbB	Altbabylonische Briefe in Umschrift und Übersetzung
AJS	Association for Jewish Studies
ANET	J.B. Pritchard (ed.), *Ancient Near Eastern Texts*
AnOr	Analecta orientalia
AnSt	*Anatolian Studies*
AOAT	Alter Orient und Altes Testament
AOS	American Oriental Series
ARM	Archives royales de Mari
AS	Assyriological Studies
AsJ	*Acta Sumerologica*
ASTI	*Annual of the Swedish Theological Institute*
ATANT	Abhandlungen zur Theologie des Alten und Neuen Testaments
AUCT	Andrews University Cuneiform Texts
BA	*Biblical Archaeologist*
BaM	*Baghdader Mitteilungen*
BARev	*Biblical Archaeology Review*
BASOR	*Bulletin of the American Schools of Oriental Research*
Bib	*Biblica*
BiOr	Bibliotheca Orientalis
BKAT	Biblischer Kommentar: Altes Testament
BSO(A)S	*Bulletin of the School of Oriental (and African) Studies*
BZAW	Beihefte zur *ZAW*
CAD	*The Assyrian Dictionary of the Oriental Institute of the University of Chicago*
CBQ	*Catholic Biblical Quarterly*
ConBOT	Coniectanea biblica, Old Testament
CT	Cuneiform Texts from Babylonian Tablets
CTA	A. Herdner, *Corpus des tablettes en cunéiformes alphabétiques*
DJD	Discoveries in the Judaean Desert
EncBib	*Encyclopaedia Biblica* (= Hebrew אנציקלופדיה מקראית)
EncJud	*Encyclopaedia Judaica* (1971)
HAR	*Hebrew Annual Review*
HAT	Handbuch zum Alten Testament
HSS	Harvard Semitic Studies
HTR	*Harvard Theological Review*
HUCA	*Hebrew Union College Annual*

ICC	International Critical Commentary
IDB	G.A. Buttrick (ed.), *Interpreter's Dictionary of the Bible*
IDBSup	*IDB*, Supplementary Volume
IEJ	*Israel Exploration Journal*
Int	*Interpretation*
JANESCU	*Journal of the Ancient Near Eastern Society of Columbia Universi*
JAOS	*Journal of the American Oriental Society*
JBL	*Journal of Biblical Literature*
JCS	*Journal of Cuneiform Studies*
JJS	*Journal of Jewish Studies*
JNES	*Journal of Near Eastern Studies*
JPS	Jewish Publication Society
JQR	*Jewish Quarterly Review*
JR	*Journal of Religion*
JSOT	*Journal for the Study of the Old Testament*
JSOTSup	*Journal for the Study of the Old Testament* Supplement Series
JSS	*Journal of Semitic Studies*
JTS	*Journal of Theological Studies*
Judaica	*Judaica: Beiträge zum Verständnis . . .*
KAI	H. Donner and W. Röllig, *Kanaanäische und aramäische Inschriften*
KAR	Keilschrifttexte aus Assur religiösen Inhalts
KAT	Kommentar zum A.T.
Leš	*Lešonénu*
MCS	Manchester Cuneiform Studies
MSL	Materialien zum sumerischen Lexikon
NABU	Nouvelles Assyriollogiques Brèves et Utilitaires
NCB	New Century Bible
NEB	New English Bible
NJPSV	New Jewish Publication Version (*Tanakh*)
OBO	Orbis biblicus et orientalis
OBT	Overtures to Biblical Theology
OIP	Oriental Institute Publications
Or	*Orientalia* (Rome)
OTL	Old Testament Library
OTS	*Oudtestamentische Studiën*
PAAJR	*Proceedings of the American Academy of Jewish Research*
PAPhS	*Proceedings of the American Philosophical Society*
RB	*Revue biblique*
RBén	*Revue bénédictine*
RCB	*Revista de cultura biblica*
RE	*Realencyklopädie für protestantische Theologie und Kirche*
REJ	*Revue des études juives*
RevQ	*Revue de Qumran*
RevSém	*Revue sémitique*

RIM	Royal Inscriptions of Mesopotamia
RLA	*Reallexikon der Assyriologie*
SAA	State Archives of Assyria
SBLDS	SBL Dissertation Series
SBLSBS	SBL Sources for Biblical Study
ScrHier	*Scripta Hierosolymitana*
Sem	*Semitica*
SJLA	Studies in Judaism in Late Antiquity
SOAS	School of Oriental and African Studies
TCL	Textes cunéiformes du Louvre
TZ	*Theologische Zeitschrift*
UET	Ur Excavations, Texts
VAB	Vorderasiatische Bibliothek
VT	*Vetus Testamentun*
VTSup	*Vetus Testamentum*, Supplements
WZKM	*Wiener Zeitschrift für die Kunde des Morgenlandes*
YNER	Yale Near Eastern Researches
YOS	Yale Oriental Series, Researches
ZA	*Zeitschrift für Assyriologie*
ZAW	*Zeitschrift für die alttestamentliche Wissenschaft*

LIST OF CONTRIBUTORS

Professor Marc Brettler, Department of Near Eastern and Judaic Studies, Brandeis University, Waltham, MA.

Professor Gerson Cohen (deceased), Chancellor Emeritus, Jewish Theological Seminary of America, New York.

Professor Aaron Demsky, Department of Biblical History, Bar Ilan University, Ramat Gan.

Professor Michael Fishbane, The Divinity School, University of Chicago, Chicago, IL.

Professor Marvin Fox, Department of Near Eastern and Judaic Studies, Brandeis University, Waltham, MA.

Professor Mordecai Friedman, Department of Talmud, Tel-Aviv University, Tel-Aviv.

Doctor Shamma Friedman, Department of Talmud, Jewish Theological Seminary of America, New York.

Professor Judah Goldin, Department of Oriental Studies, University of Pennsylvania, Philadelphia, PA.

Professor Cyrus Gordon, Professor Emeritus, New York University, New York.

Professor Moshe Greenberg, Department of Bible, Hebrew University, Jerusalem.

Professor Jonas Greenfield, Department of Ancient Semitic Languages, Hebrew University, Jerusalem.

Professor Frederick Greenspahn, Center for Jewish Studies, College of Arts and Sciences, University of Denver, Denver, CO.

Professor William Hallo, Department of Near Eastern Languages and Literatures, Yale University, New Haven, CT.

Professor Menahem Haran, Department of Bible, Hebrew University, Jerusalem.

Professor Baruch Levine, Department of Near Eastern Languages, New York University, New York.

Professor Martin Lockshin, Department of Modern Languages, York University, Downsview, Ontario.

Professor Shalom Paul, Department of Bible, Hebrew University, Jerusalem.

Professor Bezalel Porten, Department of Jewish History, Hebrew University, Jerusalem.

Professor Lawrence Schiffman, Department of Near Eastern Languages, New York University, New York.

Professor Menahem Schmelzer, Jewish Theological Seminary of America, New York.

Professor Uriel Simon, Department of Bible, Bar Ilan University, Ramat Gan.

Professor Shemaryahu Talmon, Department of Bible, Hebrew University, Jerusalem.

Professor Jeffrey Tigay, Department of Oriental Studies, University of Pennsylvania, Philadelphia, PA.

INTERPRETATION AND PRAYER: NOTES ON THE COMPOSITION OF 1 KINGS 8.15-53

Marc Brettler

Some biblical passages, such as the prayer of Hannah for a child in 1 Samuel 1, reflect impulsive, personal prayer, while others, such as Hannah's prayer of thanksgiving in 1 Samuel 2, are learned, stereotyped composition.[1] The prayer of Solomon in 1 Kings 8 certainly belongs in the latter category—it is far from a spontaneous outcry to YHWH. In the following pages, I will attempt to explore certain aspects of Solomon's prayer, one of the central Deuteronomistic texts;[2] I will concentrate on those features which distinguish it as the work of a learned author, who copied and revised other biblical compositions. I thus attempt to dwell on the intersection of two areas that have been of interest to Nahum throughout his productive scholarly career: biblical prayer and inner-biblical interpretation. This venture is not only important for understanding the prayer itself, but for determining how the book of Kings was edited.[3]

The prayer comprises 1 Kgs 8.12-61; due to space limitations, I will only treat vv. 12-53. Within this large section, two relatively

1. On the distinction between spontaneous and formulaic prayer, see Y. Kaufmann, *The History of Israelite Religion*, II (Jerusalem: Mosad Bialik, 1972), pp. 504-506 (Hebrew) and M. Greenberg, *Biblical Prose Prayer as a Window to the Popular Religion of Ancient Israel* (Berkeley: University of California Press, 1983), pp. 38-57 ('Spontaneity Versus Prescription').

2. M. Noth, *The Deuteronomistic History* (JSOTSup, 15; Sheffield: JSOT Press, 1981), pp. 5-6.

3. For discussions concerning the editing of Dtr, see the commentaries and esp. the recent studies of M.A. O'Brien, *The Deuteronomistic History Hypothesis: A Reassessment* (OBO, 92; Göttingen: Vandenhoeck & Ruprecht, 1989) and S.L. McKenzie, *The Trouble with Kings: The Composition of the Books of Kings in the Deuteronomistic History* (VTSup, 42; Leiden: Brill, 1991).

objective factors combine to suggest that 1 Kgs 8.12-13, which I call section A, 14-21, which I call section B, and 22-53, which I call C, are separate units, as is generally recognized.[1] Each set of verses begins with an introductory formula: v. 12 with אז אמר שלמה, 'Then Solomon said'; vv. 14-15 aα reads

> ויסב המלך את־פניו ויברך את כל־קהל ישראל וכל־קהל ישראל עמד: 15 ויאמר
>
> The king turned around and blessed the entire congregation of Israel, while the entire congregation of Israel was standing, and he said;

while vv. 22-23aα states

> ויעמד שלמה לפני מזבח יהוה נגד כל־קהל ישראל ויפרש כפיו השמים: 23 ויאמר
>
> Solomon stood before the altar of YHWH opposite the entire congregation of Israel; he spread his hands heavenward and he said.

In themselves, these formulae might simply introduce three successive speeches of Solomon, but each of the sections that follow presumes a different notion of where YHWH dwells and/or what the function of the newly completed Temple is. In unit A, YHWH himself resides in the Temple—it is (v. 13) מכון לשבתך עולמים, 'an established place for your enthronement in perpetuity'. In unit B, YHWH's *name* resides in the Temple, as in v. 17, בית לשם יהוה אלהי ישראל, 'a house for the name of YHWH, God of Israel'. Unit C frequently emphasizes that YHWH's dwelling place is in heaven, as in v. 30: אל מקום שבתך אל־השמים , 'to the place of your enthronement, to the heaven'. The overlap between the opening formulae and the different notions of where YHWH dwells convincingly suggests that vv. 12-13, 14-21 and 22-53 are from separate hands.

I agree with the scholarly consensus that vv. 12-13, whether we follow the MT or the LXX, are a pre-Dtr source which has been preserved by Dtr.[2] Most scholars consider unit B, on the other hand, to be Dtr, and suggest that 1 Kings 8 has utilized some form of 2 Samuel

1. For a summary, see J.D. Levenson, 'From Temple to Synagogue: 1 Kings 8', in *Traditions in Transformation: Turning Points in Biblical Faith* (ed. B. Halpern and J.D. Levenson; Winona Lake, IN: Eisenbrauns, 1981), pp. 143-66.

2. Compare the pre-Dtr material preserved in 1 Kgs 3.4ff., which, like our source, has been preserved even though it contains elements that are anti-Dtr; see H.A. Kenik, *Design for Kingship: The Deuteronomistic Narrative Technique in 1 Kings 3.4-15* (SBLDS, 69; Chico, CA: Scholars Press, 1983).

7;[1] the similarity between these texts is generally recognized because of the shared phrases between 1 Kgs 8.16-21 and 2 Sam. 7.3-13.[2]

But these two texts do not agree in all respects. The first difference concerns a seemingly insignificant addition in 1 Kgs 8.16:

מן־היום אשר הוצאתי את־עמי את־ישראל ממצרים לא־בחרתי בעיר מכל שבטי
ישראל לבנות בית להיות שמי שם ואבחר בדוד להיות על־עמי ישראל:

> Ever since I took my nation Israel out of Egypt I have not chosen a *city* from all of the tribes of Israel to build a Temple so that my name may be there; but I have chosen David to be over my nation Israel.

The phrase עיר מכל שבטי ישראל, 'a city from all of the tribes of Israel', is surprising; it mixes geographical and clan terminology. The base text in 2 Sam. 7.6-7 mentions only the tribes. It contains no reference to the choosing of a particular city.[3]

1 Kings 8 shows a second deviation from its source. A *Leitwort* of unit B is שם, 'name'. It is reflected, for example, in v. 16 לבנות בית להיות שמי שם , 'to build a house so that my name may be there'. The word is used again in vv. 17, 18, 19 and 20. Even in v. 21, where it is absent, we find the words שָׁם ('there', twice) and ואשם ('I placed'), which pun on שם. This terminology clearly reflects the so-called '*shem* theology', which has been studied by Mettinger.[4] By contrast, 2 Sam. 7.5-6 says

לך ואמרת אל־עבדי אל־דוד כה אמר יהוה האתה תבנה־לי בית לשבתי:
6 כי לא ישבתי בבית

> Go and say to my servant David, 'Thus says the LORD: Are you the one to build a house for me to *reside* in? For I have not *resided* in a house . . .'

1. See the summary in Levenson, 'From Temple to Synagogue', pp. 153-54.
2. For a partial list of these shared phrases, see C.F. Burney, *Notes on the Hebrew Text of the Book of Kings* (Oxford: Clarendon Press, 1903), p. 115.
3. On the Dtr ideology of Jerusalem as a chosen city, see M. Cogan, '"The City that I Chose"—The Deuteronomistic View of Jerusalem', *Tarbiz* 55 (1985–86), pp. 301-309 (Hebrew), English summary p. 1. More generally, on Jerusalem in the biblical ideology, see M. Weinfeld, 'Zion and Jerusalem as Religious and Political Capital: Ideology and Utopia', in *The Poet and the Historian: Essays in Literary and Historical Biblical Criticism* (HSS, 26; ed. R.E. Friedman; Chico, CA: Scholars Press, 1983), pp. 75-115.
4. T.D. Mettinger, *The Dethronement of Sabaoth: Studies in the Shem and Kabod Theologies* (ConBOT, 18; Lund: Gleerup, 1982), pp. 11-79.

Both לשבתי, 'for my residence' in v. 5 and ישבתי, 'I resided' in v. 6 indicate that the author of 2 Samuel 7 felt that the deity actually resides in the Temple.[1] This contrasts with 1 Kgs 8.14-21, our unit B, but agrees with the old pre-Dtr poem in unit A, מכון לשבתך עולמים, 'an established place for your enthronement in perpetuity'. The disagreement between the sources is not merely terminological, but of central theological significance—unit A and 2 Samuel 7 see the Temple as YHWH's dwelling place, following a pattern well attested throughout the ancient Near East, while B, rejecting this notion, suggests that it is only YHWH's name which dwells there.[2]

The two changes of 2 Samuel 7 reflected in B are most simply explained by supposing that the author of B integrated (some form of) 2 Samuel 7 with a section of Deuteronomy 12 or a similar tradition. The theme of Deuteronomy 12, a complex chapter with a long history, is the centralization of worship.[3] According to this chapter, only one place is appropriate for worship; it is (12.11) המקום אשר־יבחר יהוה אלהיכם בו לשכן שמו שם, 'the place which the LORD your God will choose to establish his name'. Deut. 12.11 uses the verb בחר, 'to choose', which is also used in 1 Kgs 8.16 in reference to the choice of a city. In fact, the verb בחר is used frequently throughout Deuteronomy to refer to the chosen place.[4] This verb is missing from 2 Samuel 7 and it is likely that the author of B in 1 Kings 8 reworked the material in 2 Samuel 7 in light of this common phrase of

1. For the various texts concerning YHWH residing in the Temple, see S. Terrien, *The Elusive Presence: Toward a New Biblical Theology* (San Francisco: Harper & Row, 1978), pp. 167-213.

2. 2 Sam. 7.13 contains the phrase הוא יבנה־בית לשמי, but this is probably a secondary development in that text, which otherwise emphasizes the Temple as the place where YHWH will physically dwell. For a different view, see A. Caquot, 'Brève explication de la prophétie de Natan (2 Sam 7.1-17)', in *Mélanges bibliques et orientaux en l'honneur de M. Henri Cazelles* (AOAT, 212; ed. A. Caquot and M. Delcor; Neukirchen–Vluyn: Neukirchener Verlag, 1981), pp. 65-66.

3. On the redaction of Deuteronomy 12, see B.M. Levinson, 'The Hermeneutics of Innovation: The Impact of Centralization upon the Structure, Sequence, and Reformation of Legal Material in Dueteronomy' (PhD dissertation, Brandeis University, 1991).

4. M. Weinfeld, *Deuteronomy and the Deuteronomic School* (Oxford: Oxford University Press, 1972), pp. 324-25, numbers 1, 1a, 3; T.C. Vriezen, *Die Erwählung Israels nach dem Alten Testament* (ATANT, 24; Zürich: Zwingli-Verlag, 1953).

Deuteronomy, in order to suggest that the choosing of David and of the central city were two events that transpired simultaneously. This point has been recently recognized by O'Brien, who notes that the rephrasing of 2 Samuel 7 by our author 'directly associates Yahweh's choice of David with that of Jerusalem'.[1]

The addition of the B section of the שם theology to the ideas of 2 Samuel 7 is similarly explained by the mention of לשכן שמו שם, '(the place which the LORD your God will choose) to establish his name' in Deut. 12.11. This notion is central to Deuteronomy.[2] The author of B adhered to the '*shem* theology' and reworked his source, (some form of) 2 Samuel 7, accordingly.

This model for the composition of unit B suggests that its author was faced with a problem: he had two equally authoritative texts or traditions. One was that of Deut. 12.11, which concerned centralization; the other was that of 2 Samuel 7, concerning the dynastic promise.[3] The dynastic promise tradition referred to the Temple as YHWH's dwelling place and was silent on the matter of the chosen city, while the centralization tradition was concerned with the place which YHWH would בחר, 'choose', and said that only YHWH's name would dwell there. The author of B has blended these two by rewriting the 2 Samuel 7 tradition in light of the one found in Deut. 12.11.

The process of reinterpretation of the Davidic oracle of 2 Samuel 7 should come as no surprise. This is a central theological-historical text, which has been interpreted elsewhere in the Bible as well.[4] In fact Nahum Sarna has shown how sections of Psalm 89 reinterpret the Davidic oracle.[5] The purpose of our author's revision of the David oracle is much the same as that of the psalmist. To apply Nahum's observations concerning 2 Samuel 7 and Psalm 89 to 2 Samuel 7 and

1. *History Hypothesis*, p. 154.

2. E.g. 12.21; see Weinfeld, *Deuteronomy*, p. 225, numbers 2-7, and Y. Zakovitch, '"To Cause His Name to Dwell There"—"To Put His Name There"', *Tarbiz* 41 (1972), pp. 338-40 (Hebrew), English summary pp. v-vi.

3. 2 Sam. 7 has a complex history, and it is difficult to know what form of that chapter the author of 2 Kgs 8 might have known. For a short discussion with bibliography, see O'Brien, *History Hypothesis*, pp. 132-39.

4. M. Fishbane, *Biblical Interpretation in Ancient Israel* (Oxford: Oxford University Press, 1985), pp. 386, 466-67.

5. 'Psalm 89: A Study in Inner Biblical Exegesis', in *Biblical and Other Studies* (ed. A. Altmann; Cambridge, MA: Harvard University Press, 1963), pp. 29-46.

1 Kings 8: they 'do not represent a different, independent recension of Nathan's oracle to David...[but] constitute an exegetical adaptation. . . to fit a specific historic situation'.[1]

The differences outlined between 2 Samuel 7 and 1 Kgs 8.14-21 have important implications for determining the number of Deuteronomistic redactions we must posit for the Deuteronomistic History. 2 Samuel 7 and 1 Kgs 8.14-21 are often considered to be central Dtr texts from the same redactional layer because they are thought to share similar conceptions concerning the Temple and the unconditional Davidic covenant.[2] However, several ideas that are central to Deuteronomy are absent from 2 Samuel 7, specifically that the Temple is being built in the chosen city, and that it is where YHWH's *name* resides. This suggest that 2 Samuel 7 comes from a different level of redaction than Deut. 12.11 and 1 Kgs 8.14-21. To phrase it differently, the contention emanating from the Cross school's understanding of the history of DtrH that '1 Kgs 8.15-21 does not dwell upon 2 Sam. 7.8-16 so much as it recreates it, or most of it, without deviation or innovation'[3] misses the essential difference between different Dtr sources, and cannot be upheld.

1 Kgs 8.22-53, unit C, is especially complex. Some scholars view the unit in its entirety as a unified pre-exilic work, others see it as having a pre-exilic core which was supplemented in the exile, while still others see it as an exilic composition or a set of exilic compositions.[4] Levenson has recognized that many of the stylistic criteria used by scholars to uncover sources within C are problematic.[5] There are, however, several criteria which have not been noted which suggest a new understanding of this unit's structure. Once its structure is

1. 'Psalm 89', p. 39.

2. So, for example, F.M. Cross, *Canaanite Myth and Hebrew Epic: Essays in the History of the Religion of Israel* (Cambridge, MA: Harvard University Press, 1973), pp. 274-89, which is the starting point for most American studies of Dtr redaction. It is interesting to note the observation of Cross on p. 275: 'Oddly, Noth ignores the oracle of Nathan [in discussing central texts composed by Dtr]'. My analysis indicates that Noth correctly understood that 2 Sam. 7 is not as Dtr as many Dtr texts, such as 1 Kgs 8. For a view that dissents from Cross and is more similar to mine, see J. Gray, *I and II Kings* (OTL; Philadelphia: Westminster, 1970), p. 215.

3. Levenson, 'From Temple to Synagogue', p. 154.

4. For a summary, see the works adduced above in on pp. 17 n. 3, 18 n. 1.

5. 'From Temple to Synagogue', pp. 155-56.

properly understood, it is possible to evaluate how various parts of this section have reused earlier biblical materials.

From a thematic perspective, C can be divided into at least two sections: vv. 22-26, concerning covenants, and vv. 27-53, concerning prayer. Although my main focus will be on vv. 27-53, I would like to point out one feature of vv. 22-26 which has not been adequately appreciated, namely the way in which the section *as a whole* equates the Davidic covenant with the covenant to Israel, thereby advocating a conditional Davidic covenant. Verse 23 speaks of a God who

שמר הברית והחסד לעבדיך ההלכים לפניך בכל־לבם:

> *keeps* the gracious covenant for your *servants* who *walk* before you wholeheartedly.

Verse 24 notes that YHWH has

שמרת לעבדך דוד אבי את אשר־דברת לו

> *kept* what you have promised to your *servant* David, my father.

The next verse continues, saying that a Davidic king will always sit on the throne

רק אם־ישמרו בניך את־דרכם ללכת לפני כאשר הלכת לפני

> only if your descendents *keep*/watch their ways to *walk* before me as you have.

The words שמר, 'keep', עבד, 'servant', and הלכ, 'walk' join vv. 23 through 25, and equate Israel as a whole and the Davidic kings. The unit argues that the Davidic covenant is conditional, just like the relationship between YHWH and Israel.[1] This contrasts sharply with 2 Samuel 7, in which the covenant with David is unconditional.[2] The

1. On different covenant types in ancient Israel, see M. Weinfeld, 'The Covenant of Grant in the Old Testament and in the Ancient Near East', *JAOS* 90 (1970), pp. 184-203. For a different type of equation of the Davidic and Abrahamic covenants, see Isa. 55.3 and O. Eissfeldt, 'The Promise of Grace to David in Isaiah 55.1-5', in *Israel's Prophetic Heritage* (ed. B.W. Anderson and W. Harrelson; New York: Harper & Row, 1962), pp. 197-207. Despite recent challenges (e.g. W.C. Kaiser, Jr, 'The Unfailing Kindness Promised to David: Isaiah 55.3', *JSOT* 45 [1989], pp. 91-98), Eissfeldt's interpretation remains compelling.

2. Several scholars (e.g. R.E. Friedman, 'From Egypt to Egypt: Dtr^1 and Dtr^2', in Halpern and Levenson [eds.], *Traditions in Transformation*, pp. 175-76, and R.D. Nelson, *The Double Redaction of the Deuteronomistic History* [JSOTSup, 18;

correspondences between v. 23 and vv. 24-25 are extensive enough to suggest that the author intended to equate the Davidic and Abrahamic covenants.[1] This terminological similarity suggests, contra Cross and others, that v. 25b, which mentions the conditional Davidic covenant, is not a gloss, but is an original part of a conditional covenant text.[2] Thus, the different conceptions of promise in 2 Samuel 7 and 1 Kgs 8.23-25 suggest that these verses are not from the same redactional level.

The remainder of C, vv. 27-53, has prayer as its *Leitmotiv*. This is reflected by the repeated use of words from the roots חנן, 'to plead' and פלל, 'to pray'.[3] The section emphasizes the efficacy of prayer and the importance of the Temple as a conduit for prayer.[4] Although this was an important exilic and postexilic notion,[5] there is no *a priori* reason to assume that this conception first developed in the exile. The exact role of prayer in the First Temple is unclear since most of our sources on that Temple are concerned with sacrifice. It is certain,

Sheffield: JSOT Press, 1981], pp. 100-105), do not view 1 Kgs 2.4, 8.25 and 9.4-5 as conditional promise texts, since they only threaten Solomon with the loss of כסא ישׂראל, 'the throne of Israel', which they understand to be dominion over the Northern kingdom. This position, however, has been vigorously criticized by I.W. Provan, *Hezekiah and the Book of Kings: A Contribution to the Debate about the Composition of the Deuteronomistic History* (BZAW, 172; Berlin: de Gruyter, 1988), pp. 106-11. If Nelson and Friedman's position is correct, then a more nuanced terminology of 'conditions' needs to be imposed upon the Davidic covenant texts. We must then distinguish between totally unconditional grace (e.g. 1 Chron. 17.13) and three different levels of punishment for violating the covenant: physical punishment of the king with no loss of royal realm (e.g. 2 Sam. 7.14-16), loss of some of the royal realm (e.g. 1 Kgs 2.4 and our unit according to Nelson and Friedman) and complete loss of royal realm (Ps. 132.12). Once these distinctions are noted, there is a clear difference between the conception of 2 Sam. 7 and that of a 'partially' conditional covenant in our unit, and it is therefore unlikely that they come from the same redactional layer.

1. For a similar argument, see J.D. Levenson, *Sinai & Zion: An Entry into the Jewish Bible* (Minneapolis, MN: Winston, 1985), pp. 210-11.

2. Contrast Cross, *Canaanite Myth*, p. 287. For a more complete discussion, see Provan, *Hezekiah*, p. 112.

3. This section contains the largest concentration of these roots in the Bible, cf. vv. 28, 29, 30, 33, 35, 38, 42, 44, 45, 47, 48, 49, 52.

4. Cf. esp. vv. 30, 33, 34, 35, 36, 38, 39, 42, 43, 44, 45, 48, 49.

5. Cf. e.g. Isa. 56.7.

however, that prayers were recited at the First Temple.[1] Thus, the centrality of prayer reflected in this section need not imply authorship by an exilic Deuteronomistic historian (Dtr^2).

Scholars have noted that 8.27-53 is comprised of an introduction (vv. 27-30), a description of seven circumstances (which I will call 'cases 1-7') in which YHWH hears in heaven (vv. 31-51) and a conclusion (vv. 52-53).[2] I will concentrate on vv. 31-51, the section dealing with YHWH's sevenfold hearing, and would like to suggest a new understanding of that section's composition and relationship to other biblical traditions.

To anticipate my conclusions, I would suggest that cases 1-4 (vv. 31-40) are a compositional unity, to which case five (vv. 41-43), concerning foreigners, case six (vv. 44-45), concerning war outside of Israel, and case seven (vv. 46-51), concerning repentance, have been added. This conclusion is supported by (1) the structural integrity of vv. 31-40; (2) the relationship of only vv. 31-40 and not 41ff. to material found in Deuteronomy 28; (3) certain similarities between cases 5-7 which are not shared by 1-4; and (4) contradictions and duplications between vv. 31-40 and what follows. These factors converge to suggest that vv. 31-40 are a separate, earlier unit.

Verses 31-40 are structured as a single unit, presenting four cases. The first two cases are of approximately equal length; cases three and four (vv. 35-36 and 37-40) are progressively longer. This pattern of increasing length is broken with case five (vv. 41-43). Cases two, three and four all conclude with a reference to the land (vv. 34, 36, 40); this pattern, which binds them together, changes with the following cases. Furthermore, several features of the fourth case, vv. 37-40, suggest that it originally concluded the unit. It contains the phrase (v. 39) ואתה תשמע . . . וסלחת, 'you will hear and forgive', which mirrors ושמעת וסלחת, 'you will hear and forgive', at the end of v. 30,

1. See the reconstruction of N.M. Sarna, 'The Psalm Superscriptions and the Guilds', in *Studies in Jewish Religious and Intellectual History Presented to Alexander Altmann on the Occasion of his Seventieth Birthday* (ed. S. Stein and R. Loewe; Tuscaloosa, AL: University of Alabama Press, 1979), pp. 281-300. For an additional discussion of prayer and music in the Temple service, see J. Milgrom, *Leviticus 1–16* (AB; New York: Doubleday, 1991), p. 19.

2. It is not certain where the conclusion begins and ends, but this need not concern us here.

the verse which introduces the unit.[1] This phrase binds the unit together. Two features of v. 38 suggest that it is part of a concluding unit: it contains the phrase ופרש כפיו, 'and he spreads his hands out (in prayer)', which recalls the opening of the unit in v. 22, when Solomon spreads out his hands heavenward. In addition, v. 38 is a generalizing verse which goes beyond the specific instances of the previous verses, insisting that כל־תפלה כל־תחנה אשר תהיה לכל־האדם, 'every prayer and every supplication of every person', will be heeded by YHWH. Such generalizations are most suited to conclusions. Finally, the fourth case ends with a motive clause (v. 40).

למען יראוך כל־הימים אשר־הם חיים על־פני האדמה אשר נתתה לאבתינו

> so that they may fear you all the years that they live on the land which you gave to our ancestors.

Such motive clauses beginning with the word למען are frequently used in Dtr literature to conclude a unit.[2] Taken together, these structural features suggest that the four cases of vv. 31-40 should be seen as a unit.

These four cases also cohere from the perspective of their content. The first case, concerning an imprecation (אלה), initially seems out of place—why should this situation be mentioned at all, and especially why is it significant enough to be placed first? It was chosen because in ancient Israel the imprecation was thought to literally come before the altar—as the text says (v. 31)—ובא אלה לפני מזבחך בבית הזה, '... and that imprecation comes before your altar in this house'. This belief raised a theological question for our author, who insisted that YHWH did not reside in the Temple: what is the relation between the Temple altar, where the imprecation settles, and a God who resides in heaven? The answer is given in the following verse (v. 32)—ואתה תשמע השמים, 'and you will hear from the heavens...' In other words, even though the imprecation comes before the Temple altar, YHWH still hears it in the heavens. This case is followed by three examples of calamities, which for Dtr were paradigmatic. These cases reiterate the problem of the relationship between Temple prayer and a deity on high, and

1. A more expanded, different form of the phrase appears in vv. 49-50.

2. E.g. Deut. 12.25; 14.29; 16.3. For a summary of these clauses' use and placement, see R. Soncino, *Motive Clauses in Hebrew Law* (SBLDS, 45; Chico, CA: Scholars Press, 1980).

for all of them the author reassures us that YHWH hears from the heavens (vv. 34, 36, 39).

Already in 1903, Burney noted that Deuteronomy 28 influenced the structure of 1 Kings 8;[1] this would date 1 Kings 8 later than Deuteronomy 28. However, neither Burney nor the scholars who followed him noted that the clear correspondences between the two texts extended only as far as case four. For example, the odd phrase in case four (1 Kgs 8.37 כי יצר־לו איבו בארץ שעריו, 'if an enemy oppresses them in the land of their settlements') is best explained as a reflection of Deut. 28.52 והצר לך בכל־שעריך, 'and he will oppress you in all of your settlements'. Similarly, the phraseology of case two, בהנגף עמך ישראל לפני אויב, 'when your nation Israel is routed by an enemy' (1 Kgs 8.33) agrees with Deut. 28.25, יתנך יהוה נגף לפני איביך, 'the LORD will make you be routed by your enemies'. In contrast the phraseology of war found in unit six, כי־יצא עמך למלחמה על־איבו, 'when your nation goes out to battle its enemy' (v. 44), has no parallel in Deuteronomy 28. The fact that only units 1-4 are patterned after the great rebuke in Deuteronomy 28 further supports the proposition that vv. 41-51 are to be separated from vv. 31-40.

The fifth case opens with וגם, which elsewhere is used to introduce supplementary material.[2] This case, which concerns the foreigner (נכרי), must be understood in relationship to a non-MT form of v. 38. That verse in the MT now reads:

> כל־תפלה כל־תחנה אשר תהיה לכל־האדם לכל עמך ישראל
> אשר ידעון איש נגע לבבו ופרש כפיו אל־הבית הזה:
>
> any prayer or supplication from anyone from all your people Israel, who recognizes the affliction of his heart and spreads his hands toward this house.

The appositional phrase לכל־האדם לכל עמך ישראל, 'from anyone from all your people Israel', is awkward. In addition, the mention of Israelites in this verse conflicts with the universal language of the following verse (v. 39):

> ונתת לאיש ככל־דרכיו אשר תדע את־לבבו כי־אתה ידעת לבדך את־לבב
> כל־בני האדם

1. Burney, *Notes on the Hebrew Text*, p. 113.

2. See Deut. 7.20, which opens וגם, where the case of הצרעה is introduced into the source from Exod. 23.28.

> and you shall render to each person according to his ways for you know his heart; for you alone know the heart of all people.

This verse uses terms for people in general rather than for Israelites, in contrast to the previous cases which use such phrases as עבדיך, 'your servants' (32), עמך ישׂראל, 'your nation Israel' (34) and עבדיך ועמך ישׂראל, 'your servants and your nation Israel' (36). This suggests that the phrase לכל עמך ישׂראל, 'from your people Israel' in v. 38 is a gloss. This is supported by the LXX,[1] which lacks a reflection of לכל עמך ישׂראל, 'from your people Israel'. Thus, grammatical evidence, literary evidence and versional evidence combine to suggest that לכל עמך ישׂראל 'from your people Israel', is secondary to v. 38, which originally concerned לכל־האדם, 'from anyone'. If this reconstruction of case four is correct, then that case assumes that anyone, Israelite or not, may pray toward the Temple. Case four was the original 'universal' conclusion to a unit comprised of four cases. Still, it did not explicitly stress the importance of non-Israelites fearing YHWH and praying to him. This was redressed by a later author through the addition of vv. 41-43, which do stress that the foreigner (נכרי) too may pray toward the Temple. It is quite possible that this idea of case five, emphasizing foreign participation in the cult, originated in the exilic period.[2]

In addition, several structural features of vv. 41-43 suggest that they should be seen as a later addition to the text. The first four cases show a healthy amount of literary variation, as if their author is attempting to avoid the potential monotony of the four parallel cases. In contrast, v. 43 of the fifth case, אתה תשמע השמים מכון שׁבתך, 'and you will hear from the heavens, the established place of your residence', is identical to v. 39 from case four. Furthermore, v. 42, which states of the foreigner ובא והתפלל אל־הבית הזה, 'and he will come and pray toward this house', is odd; is the foreigner actually

1. So Burney, *Notes on the Hebrew Text*, p. 121, following earlier scholars.

2. See my *God is King: Understanding an Israelite Metaphor* (JSOTSup, 76; Sheffield: JSOT Press, 1989), p. 149. It is noteworthy that the biblical book which most clearly emphasizes that YHWH heeds foreign prayers, Jonah, is of exilic or postexilic origin; see J.M. Sasson, *Jonah* (AB; New York: Doubleday, 1990), pp. 26-28. Deut. 23.2-9 is also a central text for understanding this issue; for a discussion of this text and its history of interpretation, see S.J.D. Cohen, 'From the Bible to the Talmud: The Prohibition of Intermarriage', *HAR* 7 (1983), pp. 31-34.

coming to Jerusalem, as in vv. 31 and 33, or is he praying toward (אל) the Temple, as in vv. 35 and 38? The most likely explanation for the odd phrase is that it originated as a conflation of cases one and two, where the individual is praying *in* the Temple (ובא), and cases three and four, where he is praying *toward* the Temple (אל). This type of conflation would later characterize rabbinic midrash, and is found elsewhere in the Bible as well, especially in Chronicles.[1] This conflation suggests that case five, concerning the foreigner, is a later literary creation, based on the earlier cases, and written to supplement the earlier, non-universal version of case four.

Case six, vv. 44-45, is written to supplement case two, vv. 33-34. Verses 33-34 deal with a case where Israel, defeated in battle, prays at the Temple, while case six raises the possibility that Israel, amidst a military defeat, might find itself far from Jerusalem. For such situations, he adds, one may pray דרך העיר אשר בחרת בה והבית אשר־בנתי לשמך, 'by way of the city which you chose and the house which I built for your name'. The phrase דרך העיר אשר בחרת בה, 'by way of the city which you chose', suggests an ideology of Jerusalem as a holy *city*, which was not found in the earlier cases of unit C, which are narrowly Temple-centered, but not Jerusalem-centered.[2] It is found, however, in section B, in v. 16. It is thus reasonably likely that the author of vv. 44-45 based his addition both on unit B and an earlier form of unit C. Additionally, it is odd that case six, which begins with a description of war, ends with the phrase ועשית משפטם, 'and you will uphold their cause', a general phrase which is not especially appropriate to war.[3] Perhaps this indicates that the issue at hand is not only military victory, but the general efficacy of prayer outside of Eretz Israel. The author of this section says that even prayers that originate outside of Israel, probably in the exile, use Jerusalem and the place of the Temple as a conduit for prayers. In this connection, it is worth recalling Jer. 41.5, which notes that the Temple site remained central

1. See esp. 2 Chron. 35.13, and Fishbane, *Biblical Interpretation*, pp. 134-37. This example is especially instructive because the Hebrew text that results from the conflation is problematic, as is 1 Kgs 8.42b.

2. For a discussion of holy city versus holy Temple, see J.Z. Smith, 'Jerusalem: The City as Place', in *Civitas: Religious Interpretation of the City* (ed. P.S. Hawkins; Atlanta: Scholars Press, 1986), pp. 25-38.

3. For the sense of משפט in our verse, see B. Johnson, 'משפט', *ThWAT*, V, p. 100.

after the exile, and Dan. 6.11, which notes that Daniel prayed via his windows that faced Jerusalem.[1] A *beraita* in *b. Ber.* 30a similarly notes that one must pray in the direction of Israel, or if in Israel, in the direction of Jerusalem; the later prescription uses our verse, 1 Kgs 8.44, as its prooftext.

Case seven, vv. 46-51, explicitly addresses the issue of prayer and repentance in exile. As the last and latest case, it builds upon previous sections of unit C as well as other texts. For example, it expands the previous case, which concerns prayer (v. 44) דרך העיר אשר בחרת בה והבית אשר־בנתי לשמך, 'by way of the city which you chose and the house which I built for your name' and increases this to (v. 48)

> דרך ארצם אשר נתתה לאבותם העיר אשר בחרת והבית אשר־בנית [בניתי] לשמך
> by way of their land which you gave to their ancestors, the city which you chose and the house which I built for your name.

In other words it adds the conception of Eretz Israel as a whole as the conduit for prayer. This presumes that YHWH's presence is concentrated in Eretz Israel.[2] The dependence of case seven on parts of Deuteronomy 4 has been developed by Braulik and Nelson.[3] I would add to their observations that the author of Solomon's prayer has revised Deut. 4 in two interesting ways:

1. Deut. 4.29 reads:

> ובקשתם משם את־יהוה אלהיך ומצאת כי תדרשנו בכל־לבבך ובכל־נפשך
> and you will seek from there YHWH your God and find him, when you seek him with all of your heart and soul

while 1 Kgs 8.48 reads

1. Ps. 28.2, בנשאי ידי אל־דביר קדשך, may convey the same idea though it is unclear whether the psalmist there is at the Temple already, and facing the דביר, or is praying outside of the Temple.

2. On this notion, see A. Rofé, *The Prophetical Stories: The Narratives about the Prophets in the Hebrew Bible, their Literary Types and History* (Jerusalem: Magnes, 1988), pp. 130-31. Compared to the holiness of YHWH or the people Israel, the notion of holy land has been largely overlooked; cf. e.g. J.G. Gammie, *Holiness in Israel* (OBT; Minneapolis, MN: Fortress Press, 1989). For obvious reasons, this topic is of more interest to Israeli scholars, cf. e.g. E. Schweid, *Homeland and a Land of Promise* (Tel-Aviv: Am Oved, 1979), pp. 27-31.

3. Nelson, *Double Redaction*, p. 72 and G. Braulik, 'Spuren einer Neubearbeitung des deuteronomistischen Geschichtswerk in 1 Kön. 8,52-53,59-60', *Bib* 52 (1971), pp. 20-33.

ושבו אליך בכל־לבבם ובכל־נפשם בארץ איביהם אשר־שבו אתם

and they return to you with all of their heart and soul in the land of their enemies who carried them off.

Although the theme of Deut. 4.25-31 is repentance or תשובה, the root שוב is not used in Deut. 4.29, which our author is paraphrasing. In contrast, that root and other similar sounding roots are overabundant here in case seven.[1] Thus, the author of unit seven rewrote Deuteronomy 4 using different theological terminology.

2. While Deut. 4.29 speaks in general terms of seeking YHWH, 1 Kgs 8.47 states

ושבו והתחננו אליך בארץ שביהם לאמר חטאנו והעוינו רשענו

and they will repent and supplicate to you in the land of their captivity, saying, 'we havc sinned, we have acted perversely, we have acted evilly'.

Deuteronomy merely states that one must seek YHWH intently, but 1 Kings offers a liturgical formula for accomplishing this: חטאנו והעוינו רשענו, 'we have sinned, we have acted perversely, we have acted evilly'. This suggests that at a later stage of the composition of 1 Kings 8, quite likely in the Babylonian exile, this formula existed as part of a penitence ritual. A similar formula is found in Ps. 106.6 חטאנו עם־אבותינו העוינו הרשענו, 'We have sinned like our ancestors, we have acted perversely, have acted evilly'. According to most scholars this psalm is exilic.[2] The author of 1 Kgs 8.47 may have known this psalm, or both the psalm and 1 Kings 8 may reflect a common (exilic) liturgical practice.

It is noteworthy that this final section emphasizes several times the special relationship between YHWH and Israel. In v. 50 Israel is called עמך, 'your [YHWH's] nation', in v. 51 this is expanded to עמך ונחלתך, 'your nation and your inheritance', and in v. 52 they are עמך ישראל, 'your nation Israel'; v. 53, the final verse of the section, con-

1. J.D. Levenson, 'The Paronomasia of Solomon's Seventh Petition', *HAR* 6 (1982), pp. 135-38.

2. See H.-J. Kraus, *Psalms 60–150* (trans. H.C. Oswold; Minneapolis, MN: Augsburg, 1989), p. 317 and A.A. Anderson, *Psalms* (NCB; London: Marshall & Scott, 1972), p. 736. Anderson (p. 738) also calls attention to Dan. 9.5, a longer formula which begins with the three verbs used in Kings, and he notes that 'perhaps they [the verbs חטא, עוי and הרשע] form part of a formula of confession'. Verse 47 of the psalm clearly implies an exilic date; this is further suggested by the placement of the psalm in the last two books of the Psalter, which contain several late psalms. However, the psalm shows no clear signs of late biblical Hebrew.

tains a motive clause which notes Israel's separation from the other nations. The sentiments expressed here contrast sharply with those of case five, vv. 41-43, which states that YHWH heeds the prayers of the נכרי, the non-Israelite. This raises the possibility that this final section has a polemical aim as well, combatting the notion expressed in vv. 41-43 by emphasizing that YHWH as hearer of prayers has a special relationship with Israel only.

In sum, the final three cases are a set of separate additions to the original four cases. Case five supplements the original form of case four, by adding that foreigners may pray at/toward the Temple. The sixth case, Israel defeated in war, supplements the second case in the eventuality that the defeat takes place away from the land of Israel. The seventh and final case supplements the fourth case, which originally concluded the unit; they both are general summaries. Thus six corresponds to two, seven corresponds to four and five corresponds to the original form of case four; this strongly bolsters the suggestion that 5-7 are later, separate additions.

Although these final three cases are not by the same hand, they do share certain common features. The שם or 'name' theology which was so prevalent in unit B is never found explicitly in the first four sections of C. It is found, however, in cases five, six and seven (vv. 43, 44, 48). In addition, cases 5-7 all deal with events outside of Eretz Israel, in contrast to 1-4. These similarities are not specific enough to presume unity of authorship; rather, they probably emanate from the fact that units 5-7 are exilic. This is why they focus on events outside of Israel, and also explains why they concentrate on the שם or 'name' theology—once the Temple was destroyed, this theological notion helped to explain how YHWH continued to dwell at the Temple site in Jerusalem.[1]

This analysis suggests that more than three Deuteronomistic hands are responsible for the authorship of Solomon's prayer. I have intentionally avoided positing dates for these redactions and supplementations; I do not believe that the evidence allows us to date them. Instead, I have attempted to correct the current study of that chapter in two matters. First, I have tried to show that the chapter is too com-

1. The connection between the destruction of the Temple and the rise of the שם theology is emphasized by Mettinger, *The Dethronement*; I cannot, however, agree with his conclusions that this idea only developed in the exile.

plex to be accounted for by only a double redaction. In this instance, I generally agree with Nelson, who also finds multiple levels of redaction in this chapter, although we use different methods, and have reached different understandings of the chapter's development.[1] Secondly, I have shown the intertextual nature of various parts of the chapter. It should not be surprising that this sermonic-style prayer is based on earlier texts which it rephrases and interprets; Rex Mason has already shown that this is an important feature of the sermon-like speeches of the Chronicler.[2] In 1 Kings 8, unit B combines Deuteronomy 12 and 2 Samuel 7. The first few cases of unit C use the great rebuke of Deuteronomy 28. Verses 41-43 incorporate language from earlier parts of 1 Kings 8, and blend them together, creating a problematic phrase. The author of vv. 46-51 knew both some form of Deuteronomy 4 and 1 Kgs 8.12-45, and blended these together with the notion of תשובה and a penitential formula. While accepting some earlier sources as authoritative, he also polemicized against case five, which stressed the efficacy of the prayer of the foreigner. Future studies of the Deuteronomistic History should be more attentive to the possible reuse of earlier Dtr material by later Dtr authors.[3] Deuteronomistic historians reused earlier Deuteronomistic materials in the same way that they used and incorporated earlier non-Deuteronomistic materials.[4] In general, a greater awareness of the exegetical features of the Deuteronomistic History is called for. This should encourage scholars to go beyond lists of Dtr terms which show general similarities of 'school' between texts, and to develop more subtle and complex theories concerning the redaction of certain key Dtr passages.

It should not be surprising that Solomon's prayer has gone through more than two Dtr revisions, because its main theme is the consecra-

1. Nelson, *Double Redaction*, p. 72; cf. the discussions of the chapter in O'Brien, *History Hypothesis*, pp. 153-58 and McKenzie, *Trouble with Kings*, pp. 138-40.

2. *Preaching the Tradition: Homily and Hermeneutics after the Exile* (Cambridge: Cambridge University Press, 1990), index, s.v. 'Inner-biblical exegesis'.

3. An important contribution in this area is by N. Sarna, 'Zedekiah's Emancipation of Slaves and the Sabbatical Year', in *Orient and Occident: Essays Presented to Cyrus H. Gordon on the Occasion of his Sixty-fifth Birthday* (AOAT, 22; Neukichen–Vluyn: Neukirchener Verlag, 1973), pp. 143-49.

4. On the reuse of legal material from Exodus in Deuteronomy, see Levinson, 'The Hermeneutics of Innovation'.

tion of the Temple, which according to the Dtr ideology reflected in Deuteronomy 12 should be a central event. Events such as the Temple dedication function as magnets, attracting multiple texts and causing great reflection, redaction, and re-redaction. These reflections would increase in the exile, when theologians grappled with the relationship between prayer, exile, the Temple site, the holy city and Eretz Israel.[1] The likelihood that 1 Kings 8 was important is further indicated by the unusual presence of post-Dtr, P-like additions throughout the chapter.[2] The solutions offered in 1 Kgs 8.46-53, where Israel, Jerusalem and the Temple are a conduit of prayer, were not accepted by all of exilic Israel; for example, Ezek. 11.16 suggests that YHWH's direct presence in exile serves as מקדש מעט 'a small sanctuary' for them.

An analogy helps to explain why 1 Kings 8 developed in the fashion outlined above, through multiple layers of interpretation and supplementation. Moshe Greensberg has argued that the Sinai pericope in Exodus cannot be handled by traditional source-critical methods; it has too many sources and interpretive fragments. These have accumulated precisely because of the significance of the revelation at Sinai.[3] I have argued elsewhere that the evidence of 2 Kings 17, which concerns the exile of the Northern kingdom, another central point from the perspective of a Judean historiographer, contains too many sources to fit comfortably into a single or double redaction theory.[4] 1 Kings 8, which concerns the dedication of the Temple in the chosen city within a book which greatly emphasizes the place of that city and Temple, is similar.[5] Furthermore, Solomon's prayer is couched in terms of a prayer which contains sermonic elements—these are genres which various Dtr editors were familiar with, and they found it easy

1. On the theological changes effected by the exile, see P.R. Ackroyd, *Exile and Restoration: A Study of Hebrew Thought of the Sixth Century B.C.* (OTL; Philadelphia: Westminster Press, 1975) and R.W. Klein, *Israel in Exile: A Theological Interpretation* (OBT; Philadelphia: Fortress Press, 1979).

2. See the commentaries, e.g. Gray, *I & II Kings*, pp. 201-202.

3. M. Greenberg, 'Exodus, Book of', *EncJud* VI, p. 1056.

4. 'Ideology, History and Theology in 2 Kings XVII 7–23', *VT* 39 (1989), pp. 268-82.

5. See above, p. 19 n. 3.

to introduce new material into such forms.[1] It is certainly easy to add a section to a prayer, just as it is easy to add some new sins to a catalogue of sins, as in 2 Kings 17.

Although I feel that it is impossible to assign dates and sigla to the various redactions of this chapter and other central chapters such as 2 Kings 17, this probably has little bearing on the average Dtr text in Kings. In fact, I would suggest that in studying the redaction of the Deuteronomistic History, we must separate these central texts, which act as magnets, attracting multiple sources, reflection and interpretation. We can then examine the more 'average' material in order to understand the basic outlines of the editing of Kings.

1. On sermons in the exile, see E.W. Nicholson, *Preaching to the Exiles: A Study of the Prose Tradition in the Book of Jeremiah* (New York: Schocken Books, 1970).

THE HEBREW CRUSADE CHRONICLES AND THE ASHKENAZIC TRADITION*

Gerson D. Cohen

I

In the spring of 1096, frenzied mobs of Christian Crusaders attacked a number of renowned Jewish communities of the Rhineland and in most cases succeeded in wreaking havoc on Jewish lives and property. The tragic story of the Jews of Worms, Mainz, Cologne and Regensburg, among others, during the First Crusade is today well-known, thanks, above all, to three medieval Hebrew chronicles which recount the history of the onslaughts with an amplitude of detail that is virtually unparalleled in medieval Jewish historiography.[1] Names of

* This essay was presented as a lecture at the University of Toronto in October, 1979. In the wake of the author's death, it has been edited for stylistic consistency only, with no attempt to update the text or notes in light of recent research.

1. For a bibliography of the textual editions and for references to modern critical analyses, see R. Chazan, 'The Hebrew First-Crusade Chronicles', *REJ* 133 (1974), pp. 235-54; and 'The Hebrew First Crusade Chronicles: Further Reflections', *AJS Review* 3 (1978), pp. 78-98. All references to the Hebrew texts are to the edition of A.M. Habermann, *Sefer Gezerot Ashkenaz we-Sarefat* (Jerusalem, 1945); English translations are taken from S. Eidelberg, *The Jews and the Crusaders* (Madison, WI, 1973). For a highly readable summary of the Crusades, see *A History of the Crusades* (ed. K.M. Setton; 4 vols.; Madison, WI, 2nd edn, 1969–77); as background for this paper, see vol. I, *The First Hundred Years* (ed. M.W. Baldwin). For a reasoned explanation of the varying fates of the Jewish communities of the Rhineland, see S. Schiffmann, 'Heinrichs IV. Verhalten zu den deutschen Juden zur Zeit des ersten Kreuzzuges', *Zeitschrift für die Geschichte der Juden in Deutschland* 3 (1931), pp. 39-58; 'Die deutsche Bischöfe und die Juden zur Zeit des ersten Kreuzzuges', *Zeitschrift für die Geschichte der Juden in Deutschland* 3 (1931), pp. 233-50; and *Heinrich IV und die Bischöfe in ihrem Verhalten zu den deutschen Juden zur Zeit des ersten Kreuzzuges* (Berlin, 1931), which was unavailable to me. Owing to the influence of Schiffmann's conclusions on virtually every subsequent

people and places, specific dates and vivid accounts of resistance, defeat and mass suicide are described with a specificity and fullness, and, what is most important, with sufficient agreement between the various accounts to warrant rating these documents among the finest products of pre-modern Jewish historiography. For all the discrepancies in detail between them, and there are discrepancies, the three chronicles by and large confirm and supplement one another, thus making it evident that however much one may have drawn from, or been influenced by, one of the others or its source, each has a value and merit of its own. Of the three accounts, at least two had access to independent sources of information. Since I shall attempt to analyze some of the unstated motives of these historians, it is important to identify and characterize each of them briefly.

The longest, and perhaps even the oldest, of the chronicles is the account of R. Solomon b. Samson. Whatever its merits or shortcomings, it is patently not complete, for it makes unequivocal reference to other portions of its narrative that are no longer part of the account. This makes any full appraisal of the work in and of itself precarious, but there are things that can be said about it that are independent of its merits and historiography. A second account, which Professor Robert Chazan has cogently demonstrated is based on the Chronicle of Solomon b. Samson, is that of R. Eliezer bar Nathan of Mainz (d. after 1152). In this chronicle, the narrative is interlaced with poetic dirges and patently liturgical memorials for the martyrs. Finally, the briefest but literarily most polished of the chronicles is the so-called 'Mainz Anonymous', possibly entitled by its author, *The Narrative of Earlier Persecutions*. While this account has evidently suffered truncation at its end, it has come down to us without tampering in the body of its text, and is a sophisticated historical essay as far as it goes. Some have preferred to regard it as the most reliable of the accounts. It is, in my view, probably the latest of the three chronicles, as evidenced by the way its author characterizes it ('the narrative of ancient [or earlier] persecutions') and by the clear but

critical-historical analysis of the fates of medieval Jewish communities, it is regrettable that her small but significant book has not been reprinted or translated into English or Hebrew.

hitherto unnoticed influence of Abraham ibn Daud's *Sefer ha-Qabbalah* on his style, thus placing composition after 1161.[1]

Since the chronicles are so full, so congruent, so free of fantasy and yet so different from each other in style and content, they have understandably generated a considerable body of critical study—on the sequence of events, the character of the chronicles as historical sources, the relationship of each to the others and to Crusade historiography generally, the historical perceptions of the writers, the relationship of the chroniclers to their presumed sources, and so on. The one question that does not seem to have exercised modern scholars generally is why the chronicles should have been composed in the first place. The question of course, seems to have occurred to some modern critics, but they make short shrift of the problem by indicating, almost in a subordinate clause, that obviously the chroniclers were motivated by the desire to memorialize and apostrophize the martyrs and Jewish heroes of the events. Also evidently in the minds of the chroniclers was the problem of theodicy which was the medieval way of accounting for the causation of so cataclysmic a turn in the Jewish fate.

With all due allowances for the gratitude of later generations, particularly historically minded ones such as those of the last century and even now, the question must, however, be faced squarely: what motivated the writers of these chronicles of the First and Second Crusades—but most especially of the First Crusade—to compose records of the events that had befallen them? After all, historiography was not one of the more salient genres of literary expression of the time, certainly not of the Ashkenazic community of the eleventh and twelfth centuries. The Book of Jossipon, the Hebrew paraphrase of Josephus, and the chronicle of Ahima'az cannot be invoked as precedents, for they are of quite different literary genres. Ibn Daud's *Sefer ha-Qabbalah* provides no answer even for the chronicler who I believe must have read it, for the thrust of the two works is so different as to make them unrelated to each other. One is a history of the Spanish rabbinate in the context of universal history, and the other a martyrology, pure and simple. And even if any or all of these works had

1. For the title, see Habermann, p. 93; Eidelberg, p. 99. The influence of Abraham ibn Daud, *Sefer ha-Qabbalah*, is evident in the wording in Habermann, pp. 94 (8 lines from bottom), 95 (l. 2).

stimulated these chroniclers, it is still appropriate to ask what the motives and thrust of any particular author are, and this applies to the authors of these works as well.

The question, I must insist, is by no means an idle one. The motives for the composition of a historical memoir may appear to us to be so self-evident as to require no question—but that was decidedly not the case in the Middle Ages. The paucity of historical chronicles on the Almohade persecutions, for example, or the expulsions from England, France, Germany and Spain, and even the Second Crusade should give us pause about taking our three chronicles for granted as perfectly natural products of the first great medieval trauma. I, for one, find the customary silence of my ancestors on many great turning points in Jewish history, sad as well as happy, regrettable but understandable. What engages me is their relative loquacity in this case.

It is particularly appropriate to ask why we should have three chronicles of the First Crusade, especially in the light of the high probability (fairly cogently demonstrated by modern critical analysis) that at least one of the chroniclers was well aware of the work of one or more who had preceded him. Granted that each chronicle provided at least some information that the other two did not, was it necessary to compose a whole account *de novo*? Would the chronicler not have achieved his purpose equally well by appending or inserting his additions to an account that was already available to him? Or was there perhaps some parochial or locally oriented motivation that drew each of the chroniclers to ignore formulations composed by other authors and substitute his own?

Since some such considerations must have apparently been at work, quite apart from the different data offered by each of the accounts, it is appropriate to take note of one factor that all of the chronicles—the three of the First Crusade and the only known one of the Second—share in common, while yet reflecting it differently. I refer to the obvious liturgical cast of each of the historical accounts. Each of the chronicles clearly implies, indeed almost invokes, some kind of liturgical response on the part of the reader audience. This, it seems to me, is significant, for it can hardly be fortuitous. Moreover, it is not a literary device known to us from other medieval prose works.

An example or two from each of our historiographic sources of the phenomenon I have mentioned is warranted. Of the three chronicles of the First Crusade, the liturgical thread is most evident in that of

R. Eliezer bar Nathan. Five times his chronicle is interrupted by poetic dirges, each of which contains at least one stanza with an acrostic of the author's name—a tell-tale sign of pietistic liturgy of Ashkenaz[1]—and each of these poetic passages is capped by a verse from Scripture with the introductory word *ka-amur* (as it is said in Scripture). This alone would suffice to suggest the *Sitz im Leben*, or the functional context, of the Ra'ban's chronicle as a form of *payyetanic* lecture. However, even the Ra'ban's purely prose and narrative portions bear certain marks which, at first blush, might be dismissed as of no major consequence but which, in the light of the other chronicles, turn out, I submit, to be very clear indications of liturgical usage. Thus, several times R. Eliezer uses a plaintive formula taken from Isa. 64.11: 'At such things will You restrain Yourself, O Lord?' To the medieval reader auditor, the quotation of this half of the verse sufficed to evoke in his mind the second half of the verse as well: 'Will You stand idly by and let us suffer so heavily?'[2] Clearly, this cry is not directed in the first instance to the reader auditor, but to God. In other words, this is a liturgical cry, not mere expostulation. What is more, the Ra'ban's chronicle is literally peppered with elegiac verses from the books of Psalms and Lamentations not only bemoaning the calamity but praying for the reward of the martyrs and the vengeance of their suffering. This, too, is good Jewish liturgical form. Finally, the chronicle ends with a paean of praise to the martyrs, assuring the reader auditor that the souls of the martyrs are bound up in the bond of eternal life, each one of them having gained two crowns and eight raiments of the clouds of the divine glory. Since modern editions hasten to add impressive references to obscure midrashim, presumably as a form of explanation of this passage, permit me to add a word indicating what this phrase meant to the medieval. To be cloaked with eight raiments and a diadem meant that each of the martyrs was a high priest who was ministering to God in the innermost sanctum of the divine Glory. Each act of martyrdom was, accordingly, a performance of the supreme liturgy of sacrificial atonement! These ostensible prosaic

1. Cf. I.G. Marcus, *Piety and Society: The Jewish Pietists of Medieval Germany* (Leiden, 1981), pp. 110ff.

2. See Habermann, p. 75 (end of first paragraph); and cf. also p. 80 (3 lines from end of first paragraph, and at end of second paragraph).

characteristics are of particular significance in identifying the liturgical threads of the other two chronicles.

In the shortest of the chronicles, the third in my enumeration, the author notes that the martyrs of Worms willingly gave up their lives 'in sanctification of the Eternally Awesome and Sublime Name of Him Who rules above and below, Who was and will be, Whose Name is Lord of Hosts, and is crowned with the graces of the seventy-two names' and so on.[1] This is not history, not even hagiography; it is a lapse into liturgical frenzy. As we shall have occasion to note later on, such phrases as 'the Holy One of seventy-two names' are not mere inflated rhetoric; they stem from the marrow of Ashkenazic liturgical orientation.[2] Shortly after this point in the Mainz anonymous chronicle, a particularly heart-rending episode of slaughter by the hands of his father of a child significantly named Isaac—the comparison with the *Akedah* is expressly articulated by the father—culminates with the verse from Isaiah that we encountered in R. Eliezer bar Nathan's chronicle: 'At such things will You restrain Yourself, O Lord?' Followed by a stock phrase adapted from Scripture: 'Throughout all this, the Lord did not turn away His great wrath from us' (cf. 2 Kgs 23.26; Jon. 3.9).[3] Then comes another paean:

> What they did had never been witnessed by the eye of man. It is of them and the likes of them that it was said: 'From the righteous who suffer death on this earth, for Your sake, O Lord, who will have their portion in eternal life' (Ps. 17.14 as translated by the Targum). 'Such things no age has seen, O God, but You Who act for those who trust you' (Isa. 64.3). They all fell by the hand of the Lord and returned to their rest, to the Great Light in the Garden of Eden. Behold, their souls are bound up till the time of the end, in the bond of life with the Lord, God, who created them. [4]

A little later, the account of the slaughter of Isaac ben Moses and Rabbi Kalonymos culminates with a dirge and paean to Israel,[5] and again, we get the refrain: 'At such things will You restrain Yourself,

1. Habermann, p. 95; trans. Eidelberg, p. 102.
2. Cf., for example, Jacob b. Asher, *Araba'ah Turim*, Oraḥ Ḥayyim 113.
3. Habermann, p. 96.
4. Habermann, p. 97 (near bottom); I have deviated deliberately from the translation of Eidelberg, p. 105, to convey more precisely the sense intended by the Mainz chronicler.
5. Habermann, p. 100; trans. Eidelberg, p. 109.

O Lord'; 'Avenge the spilt blood of Your servants! Let one and all behold—has the like of this ever occurred?'[1] The attentive reader will not have failed to note that the last phrase, 'Avenge the blood of Your servants', taken from Ps. 79.10, became fixed in the liturgy in the *Av ha-Raḥamim* prayer for vengeance after the First Crusade. In sum, a series of liturgical allusions or liturgical-like threads run through this ostensibly prosaic and matter of fact account as clearly as they do in Eliezer bar Nathan's chronicle, despite the absence of poetry.

The same is easily demonstrated from the longest of the accounts, that of R. Solomon b. Samson. Prooftexts from Scripture, prayers for revenge, and affirmations of the acceptance of the sacrifice of the martyrs by Heaven characterize this chronicle as they do the others. It comes as no surprise that the refrain from Isaiah 64, 'At such things will You restrain Yourself, O Lord', appears here as well as in the other chronicles.[2] Indeed, this chronicle is interrupted by a long didactic prayer that hardly makes sense in a work of pure history. The following excerpt clearly demonstrates that prayer, not history, was being written:

> May He Who by His word caused the world to come into being, avenge the spilt blood of His servants [once again the phrase from Ps. 79.10 that became enshrined in the *Av ha-Raḥamim* prayer]. . . 'God of vengeance, O Lord of vengeance show forth! For Thy sake are we killed all the day. . . O Earth, cover not their blood, and let there be no resting place for our cries. . . May the blood of His devoted one stand us in good stead and be an atonement for us and our posterity after us, and our children's children eternally, like the *Akedah* of our Father Isaac when our Father Abraham bound him upon the altar.'[3]

Moving this may be; pure history it is not.

The liturgical motif in these chronicles, at least two of which are adaptations from another, can hardly be a coincidence. However, before attempting to suggest any explanation, it is appropriate to put these liturgical manifestations into a wider context. After all, the chronicles I have described are only a fraction of the liturgy, emotional and conceptual Jewish deposit generated by the traumatic events of the First Crusade. A considerable body of Hebrew poetry clearly

1. Habermann, p. 101; trans. Eidelberg, p. 110.
2. Habermann, p. 42, l. 4.
3. Habermann, pp. 42ff.; Eidelberg, pp. 47-49.

meant for liturgical recitation and in large measure now readily available alongside the chronicles themselves was inspired by the memory of the unprecedented onslaughts. Apart from original poetry, a string of liturgical innovations, now taken for granted as standard Jewish synagogal practice, was instituted in consequence of the Crusade—lines added in the catena of *Avinu Malkenu* pleading for salvation in the name of the spirit of the martyrs, the memorial services for the dead (*Kaddish Yatom* and *Yizkor* and *El Maleh Raḥamim*), the prayer for divine vengeance, and probably the present form of the midrash on the Ten Martyrs (*Eleh Ezkerah*). The events and their deposit stimulated a parallel body of literary fruits of the Second Crusade, which, as is well known, was far less devastating to the Jews of Europe than the First. However, it, too, inspired a memorial book by R. Ephraim of Bonn and it, too, generated *payyetanic* memorials. Subsequent tragic incidents affecting Jewish communities were then often memorialized in similar ways, although they were largely obscured by the memory of the calamities of 1096. However, all of them left their imprint on local memorial books, the outstanding one of which is the Nurnberg *Memorbuch*, which records the names of community leaders and martyrs of many communities and many generations.

To sum up, if the First Crusade generated a considerable number of liturgical compositions and practices, it is no accident or forced reading of a text to discern a liturgical *leitmotif* even in the purely prose chronicles of the First Crusade, the evident function of which is to memorialize people and events. The chronicles themselves are manifestly not liturgical pieces, and they betray no clear sign of having been intended for synagogal reading. However, since the liturgical bent of mind in these chronicles is indisputable, the question that immediately comes to mind is whether this characteristic is fortuitous, or symptomatic of a far wider phenomenon. To put the question plainly, is the liturgical orientation of the Crusade generation a quirk or is it an aspect of the 'normal' culture of the chronicles? Most important, does this liturgical posture in historical documents bespeak a purpose that we can identify?

II

Anyone who contemplates medieval Franco-German Jewish culture as a whole cannot but be struck by several salient characteristics of Ashkenazic culture—and under the Ashkenazic rubric I include here French, Provençal and even Italian Jewish culture. The first major characteristic of Ashkenazic culture is the centrality of liturgy in the preoccupations of the rabbinic leaders of the community. This concern with liturgy obviously has cognate manifestations in every major medieval community, but it does not require any microscopic analysis to discern and easily identify singular Franco-Ashkenazic orientations to liturgy that are not duplicated elsewhere.

By way of explanation, let me begin by pointing to the disproportionate emphasis placed by Ashkenazic Jewry on liturgical codification, including under that rubric the codification of local liturgical rite and custom. Between the twelfth and fifteenth centuries, Ashkenazic Jewry produced an unparalleled number of codes in which liturgy is the subject of emphasis far beyond that given in the Talmud, the Babylonian codes, Andalusian literature, or even in pre-Crusade Italy. These Ashkenazic codes are renowned, having come out of the schools of Rashi and his disciples and later out of the circle of R. Meir of Rothenberg. One need but recall the *Siddur* of R. Solomon b. Samson, the *Sefer ha-Orah*, the *Sefer ha-Pardes*, the *Siddur Rashi*, the *Maḥzor Vitry*, and so-called *Siddur of Ḥaside Ashkenaz*, *Shibbole ha-Leqet* of Italy, the *Kol Bo*, *Amarkol*, the *Sefer Rabiah*, the *Orḥot Ḥayyim*, *ha-Eshkol*, the *Sefer ha-Roqeaḥ*, the *Minhage Dura*, the *Manhig*, the *Minhage R. Hayyim Paltiel* and the *Minhage R. Abraham Klausner* that was taken from it. This list is only a fraction of the codes that were compiled in the great centers of Ashkenazic concentration in the post-Crusade period. One of their characteristics is that they make no effort at comprehensiveness in covering Jewish law as a whole as do the *Semag*, *Semaq*, the *Sefer Yere'im*, the *Or Zaru'a*, the *'Ittur* and, only a little later, the *Bet ha-Beḥrah*, the *Rosh* and the epoch-making *Arba'ah Turim*. Although the last two are technically Sephardic, they nevertheless reflect the extension of the Ashkenazic influence beyond the Pyrenees.

While these great codes reflect the genre of comprehensive codification that does not require any special explanation, the shorter code with its concentration on liturgy does. To be sure, the codes listed here are not restricted solely to liturgical matters, for they usually cover a variety of ritual topics (e.g. *millah, sheḥitah, yibbum, shabbat, 'eruvin*) that qualified them as handbooks of law, but several qualifications are in order. A glance at the more comprehensive codes, and especially at the responsa literature, will reveal that much more of Jewish law than that encompassed by these liturgical codes was still quite functional in the medieval Jewish community. Moreover, liturgy to the medieval Jew, *'avodah* in the technical sense, was not confined to prayer. Hence these codes with laws on *sheḥitah* and *millah* are still liturgical, even when they go beyond matters dealing with synagogal ritual and prayer. What cannot be denied is that within these codes the problem of liturgy, in the narrow sense of the term, occupies a disproportionate amount of space, especially if one uses the Talmud and its divisions as a yardstick. Prayer is central to them, and along with this concern are coupled discussions of liturgical rites in the broadest sense of the term.[1]

Alongside these codes one must also take into consideration the great *maḥzorim* that were utilized by the *sheliḥe tzibbur* of the great communities such as Nurnberg, Worms and Leipzig. These prayer books constituted compilations of local rites, and unlike the synagogues themselves, whether these were buildings or rooms, prayer books were on occasion preserved, amplified and used by cantor-poets over a period of centuries. *Memorbücher*, such as the renowned one of Nurnberg, and the manuscript *Memorbuch* of Spires

1. V. Aptowitzer, in his epoch-making and exhaustive *Introductio ad Sefer Rabiah* [Hebrew] (Jerusalem, 1938), p. 84, took note of the disproportionate emphasis on liturgical–ritual law in contrast with family, civil and interpersonal law, all of which were operative in the Middle Ages. Aptowitzer explains that the author devoted other works to those subjects. To this we need add only two comments. First, it is significant that the twelfth- or thirteenth-century author saw in Jewish law a natural division between liturgy and ritual, on the one hand, and interpersonal law (including family law), on the other. What this shows is that liturgy–ritual constituted a discrete context in the medieval Jewish mind. Secondly, while it is no longer possible to accept Aptowitzer's contention that the author composed two works—see the introduction of E. Pressman and S.Y. Cohen to *Sefer Rabiah* 4 (Jerusalem, 1965), pp. 13-16—it probably remains true that the ritual–liturgical portion of the work is a thorough piece of original research by the author, while the second part on interpersonal law (the 'Aviasaf') is but a compilation of selected views of other authorities.

must be reckoned as appendices of these *maḥzorim*, and they, too, acquired a sanctity in the great communities of Ashkenaz, giving them the hallmarks of a veritable literary-liturgical genre.

The second feature of Ashkenaz of which we must take note is the uninterrupted tradition of fresh poetical composition for every conceivable liturgical, but only liturgical, occasion. The Ashkenazim did not compose secular lyrics, wine songs, autobiographical or heroic panegyrics. True, they composed panegyrics to patrons, but paeans to people—and incidentally, unlike the habit of the Jews of Spain, even to women—are memorials, and not apostrophizations of living people. In other words, Ashkenazic poetry was purely religious. To put the matter bluntly, however rigidly tradition- and precedent-oriented they were with respect to liturgical rites, however ostensibly unworldly and, indeed, even fundamentalist when compared with their Spanish brethren,[1] in the field of liturgical composition they maintained a fluid, open-ended and innovative tradition. This is no small thing for communities and teachers who were so code- and rite-oriented!

In the final analysis, the most remarkable feature of Ashkenazic poetic activity was the vast corpus of textual commentary on the *piyyutim*. It began no later than with R. Moses ben-Darshan and matured under the inspiration of the great trailblazer (*ha-tayyar ha-gadol*) Rashi himself. This corpus of commentative traditions and works has been studied in the awe-inspiring introduction of Ephraim E. Urbach's edition to R. Abraham ben Azriel's *'Arugat ha-Bosem*. Urbach has unearthed fresh materials and drawn extensively from the various great commentaries of the Middle Ages still in manuscript form. One of the things that emerges quite clearly from his scholarly *tour de force* is that there were various approaches to *piyyut*, even as early as Rashi's day. By the time of the activity of Ḥaside Ashkenaz, liturgical commentary had become diversified and oriented to different religious temperaments. Since the articulation or composition of a commentary to *piyyut* became an established genre of literature in Ashkenaz, and only in Ashkenaz, the question that immediately confronts the historian is 'why?'. What motivated the creation of

1. This is, of course, an image that will not stand up under critical scrutiny; cf., for example, R. Judah he-Ḥasid's commentary on the Pentateuch.

a virtually new genre of Hebrew literature, commentary on non-classical texts, and what special function was commentary on liturgical poetry calculated to fulfill?

Obviously, commentary was to be elucidatory on many levels—on the level of the explanation of the meaning of obscure words, of pointing to a classical rabbinic source for a conception that was not part of the normal religious vocabulary of the worshipper or that was obscurely expressed, or finally, of the elucidation of the esoteric religious meaning of a phrase, line or stanza. Commentary served the function of unravelling what was obscure and hidden. This sounds like tautology, except that an examination of Ashkenazic commentaries in general, and of commentaries on liturgy in particular, will reveal a special effort at the detection and identification of esoteric content even when there appears to be none. On occasion, it would seem that Ashkenazic authors purposely looked for obscurity as a vehicle of expression in their own liturgical expressions. Thus, one and the same author could compose a *piyyut* on one of the Ten Commandments in obscure Aramaic and then proceed to compose a commentary on his own *piyyut*.[1] The Ashkenazic commentators seem bent not only on *dis*covering but on *un*covering and even on *manufacturing* an esoteric level. (While this was especially true in the field of liturgy, it was by no means confined to that area of expression. We may note here that, paradoxically and conversely, the more obscure and esoteric the text to be explicated, the simpler the task of the commentator and the more plainly elucidatory his commentary.)[2] Finally, there is one dimension to medieval commentary that must be stressed above all else: a commentary is a tacit affirmation of the vitality and relevance of the text that is being explicated. A medieval commentary is, in the first instance, an affirmation of the authoritative character of the text being explicated, be it the text of Scripture, the Mishnah, or some later work such as Alfasi's the *Mishneh Torah*, the *Guide of the Perplexed*, or the *Arba'ah Turim*. Further, the commentary reveals what the author of the commentary considers to be the real burden of the text

1. See M.M. Schmelzer, 'Perush Alfabetin by R. Benjamin ben Abraham min Ha-Anavim', in *Texts and Studies: Analecta Judaica* (ed. H.Z. Dimitrovsky; New York, 1977), p. 172 (Hebrew), on R. Jacob b. Samson's *piyyut*, 'Lo Taḥmod'.

2. Cf. the commentary on *Alfabetin* itself, pp. 167ff.

he is elucidating.[1] The commentary of Rabbenu Hananel to the Talmud is qualitatively different from that of Rashi, not only because one was the work of a North African authority and the other the product of a man of Northern France and the Rhineland, but first and foremost because of the different view of what each considered to be the essential burden of the Talmud: to Rabbenu Hananel it was the *halakha*, while to Rashi it was the text of the Talmud itself, the aggadic portions no less than the legal ones.[2]

A medieval commentary served one further function, and that was exegetical. A commentary was first and foremost a midrash, an elucidation of the relevance of the text to the spiritual life of the later student. This was true in the case of rationalist commentaries, whether of Ashkenaz or of Spain, no less than in the case of openly homiletical or mystical ones. A medieval commentary kept the text alive for the reader, so that an ancient text now spoke directly to the student or worshipper.

To keep our eyes fixed on the subject under inquiry, the provision of a commentary to liturgy represented not only an affirmation with Rashi that liturgy embodied 'the mystery of the revelation of the Creator principally through customary usage transmitted by our ancestors, and by official transmission through rabbinic authority',[3] but also an affirmation that liturgy is a pulsating vehicle of special effectiveness, a bearer of a potency not accessible through other channels. To be more specific: Ashkenaz, I submit, placed great emphasis on liturgy because liturgy was the key by which one might open the gates of Heaven. Put differently, the keys to the Kingdom consisted of words, the prayer, properly recited. Accordingly, if liturgy was to be effective, the worshipper had to attribute to each word and phrase the proper *kavvanah*, the proper meaning, for this could make the usage proper and effective. The slightest change in meaning altered the out

1. See my remarks on medieval commentaries on *Pirke Abot* in 'The Soteriology of R. Abraham Maimuni', in *Studies in the Variety of Rabbinic Cultures* (Philadelphia, 1991), pp. 223-26.

2. See C. Tchernowitz, *Toledoth ha-Poskim: History of the Jewish Codes*, II (New York, 1947), esp. 1-14 (Hebrew).

3. Cited in Abraham b. Azriel, *Sefer 'Arugat ha-Bosem* 4 (ed. E.E. Urbach; Jerusalem, 1963), p. 6.

come.[1] From that perspective, commentary was an indispensable tool for effective 'service of the heart' at prayer.

Although these remarks on the implication of commentary seem patently obvious, modern Jewish scholarship has done relatively little in the sociological and ideological analysis of the medieval commentary. Once confronted, however, the question can aid in understanding such disparate and ostensibly discrete phenomena as the Crusade chronicles, Rashi's commentary on the Pentateuch (in contrast with his commentary to the Talmud and other parts of Scripture), the various florilegia of Ashkenazic culture—such as the *Yalqut Shim'oni* and the *Ma'aseh Book*—and, to go beyond the immediate borders of Ashkenaz, the chronicle of Ahima'az. In that setting, light is shed on the Ashkenazic mentality as a whole.

III

To return to the initial point of inquiry, it is a matter of common knowledge that from the First and Second Crusade we have been left with a deposit of memorial poems and lists of martyrs which indeed were read in synagogues at the time of memorial services and locally on the occasion of the memorial of the calamity that struck a particular community. Thus if one finds the *zulat* refrain of *Ha-Shem al domi lakh* in the Ashkenazic rite for the Sabbath before Shavu'ot, or several of the dirges of Kalonymos b. Judah of Mainz in Ashkenazic compilations of *seliḥot*, clearly these poems have not fallen into these complications by sheer coincidence. Thus, the poem *Elohim be-oznenu shama'nu* was preserved in the *seliḥot* of Worms.[2] In attempting to explain some of the textual peculiarities of the Crusade chronicle of Solomon b. Samson, Isaiah Sonne plausibly suggested almost half a century ago that the text that we have received is, on the one hand, truncated, for it lacks the *Memorbuch* or list of names of the city of Mainz that preceded it, and, on the other hand, is, at least with respect to one of its tales of martyrdom, a rendition in prose of

1. See the vehement protest in the *Siddur of R. Solomon ben Samson of Garmaise, Including the Siddur of the Haside Ashkenas* (ed. M. Hershler), p. 107-108, against the Jews of France and England who add to the number of words in one paragraph of the daily *'Amidah*.

2. See S. Bernfeld, *Sefer ha-Dema'ot*, I (Berlin, 1923), pp. 193-97, 207-209.

some lines of poetry available to us in a memorial dirge of R. Kalonymus b. Judah.[1]

Yitzhak Baer, while rejecting Sonne's contention on the dependence of the chronicle on the *piyyut*, affirmed his perception of the strong liturgical thread that permeates all the chronicles and suggested that they originally may have been intended for synagogue reading.[2] I am not concerned, for the moment, with which of the two perceptions is correct, Sonne's or Baer's. What I want to emphasize is that even a scholar like Baer who regards the chronicle as derivative from an Ur-chronicle composed immediately after the events as part of the literature of Jewish heroism cannot avoid seeing that liturgical orientation. The key question then emerges: what liturgical role can a historical chronicle have in a Jewish context? Was prose history ever recited in the synagogue? Baer's suggestion that the chronicles may have been intended for synagogue reading is the kind of safe historical suggestion that risks nothing and, therefore, gets us nowhere. Surely the student of history must at least confront the questions with which we opened our inquiry and suggest some likely *Sitz im Leben* for the chronicles.

I venture to suggest that the liturgical context of Ashkenazic Jewry of the Middle Ages, from which we have extrapolated some hard-core documentary evidence, provides the cogent explanation we have been seeking. Like the somewhat but not much later *'Arugat ha-Bosem* of R. Abraham b. Azriel, and the *Perush Alfabetin* of R. Benjamin b. Abraham min ha-Anavim, or the commentaries on Aramaic *piyyutim* included in the *Maḥzor Vitry*, and the numerous other commentaries cited from manuscript by Urbach in his introduction to *'Arugat ha-Bosem*, the chronicles of the First Crusade, like the *Sefer Zekhirah* by R. Ephraim of Bonn, were originally conceived and committed to writing as hagiographic commentaries to the memorial dirges and martyrologies that had previously been composed for liturgical

1. I. Sonne, 'Nouvel examen des trois rélations hébräiques sur les persécutions de 1096', *REJ* 96 (1933), pp. 116, 133-34; and 'Which Is the Earlier Account of the Persecutions during the First Crusade?', *Zion* 12 (1946), pp. 75-76 (Hebrew). The *piyyut* in question, 'Amarti she'u mimmeni', is not reprinted in Habermann; cf. I. Davidson, *Thesaurus of Medieval Hebrew Poetry*, I (New York, 1970 [1924]), no. 5971 (Hebrew).

2. Y. Baer, 'Gezerot TTN"W', in *Sefer Assaf* (ed. M.D. Cassuto *et al.*; Jerusalem, 1953), p. 134.

recitation. This proposal will account for the liturgical thread that runs through the prose chronicles which are not actually liturgical pieces. Moreover, my proposal provides a structured framework for the chronicles for which we have numerous analogues in other liturgical commentaries. If it should be asked why someone considered it necessary to write a historical commentary to the poetic martyrologies, my answer is that each of these chronicles provides the material from historical reality for the proper *kavvanah* required for these memorial prayers. If it should be asked why proper *kavvanah* is necessary, the answer again is at hand. The martyrs were considered sacrifices whose ashes and souls were offered up daily on the divine altar as soteric atonement for all Israel. For this theological notion, we have explicit evidence from so early a prayerbook as that of Ḥaside Ashkenaz[1] (in other words not only from the chronicles but from actual handbooks on liturgical usage), thus making the prayers of the martyrs in the chronicles that they would be received as sacrifices and bound up in eternal glory a reflection of the atmosphere that actually pervaded their synagogues.

Is this suggestion for the cultural matrix of the chronicles purely inferential and circumstantial, or is there more palpable and direct evidence to support it? Happily, such material is available to support my suggestion. Prayer was explained by what the medievals considered history and historical events. R. Judah ha-Hasid protested vigorously against any changes in the *'Alenu* prayer, for the number of words in that paragraph, he claimed, had been fixed at 152 by Joshua bin Nun. Another pietist, R. Eleazar of Forchheim, ascribed the origin of a paragraph in the *taḥanun* to King Hezekiah.[2] As is well known, the *We-Hu Raḥum* prayer of Mondays and Thursdays was attributed to the miraculous rescue of three shiploads of exiles set adrift by Vespasian after the destruction of the Second Temple[3] (the historical context of a number of prayers for the High Holidays). Thus every school child of the traditional Jewish world of Ashkenaz was taught a number of *piyyutim*. R. Simon bar Isaac b. Abun of Mainz

1. See *Siddur of R. Solomon ben Samson*, p. 109; and the introduction of Urbach to *Sefer 'Arugat ha-Bosem*, 4.67-68 and n. 86.

2. *Sefer 'Arugat ha-Bosem*, 4.98 and n. 64.

3. See my 'The Story of the Four Captives', in *Studies in the Variety of Rabbinic Cultures*, pp. 164-67.

bore the name of his son Elhanan because the latter was said to have been forcibly baptized, rose to become pope and ultimately returned to Judaism. This fanciful story preserved in medieval anecdotal collections came to explain an ostensible anomaly in Ashkenazic *piyyut*. Anything peculiar in the liturgy had to be explained, and as early as 1000 the Ashkenazim were invoking 'history'. Much later the Ashkenazim would appropriate for new martyrology a pre-Ashkenazic *piyyut* known as *U-Netaneh Toqef* and ascribe it to R. Simon of Mainz who taught the poem to Kalonymus b. Meshalla in a dream!

The matter is best summed up by Professor Urbach in his description of R. Eleazar Roqeah's role in the explication of liturgy. R. Eleazar had no hesitation in rationalizing the recitation of certain Psalms in *Pesuqe de-Zimra* of the morning service in consequence of historical events of his own day! Thus Ps. 135.14, 'for the Lord will champion His people', R. Eleazar explained as a prediction of the miraculous rescue of the Jews of Mainz on Friday, the 28th day of Shevat of 1188. Other events from succeeding months of that year of the eve of the Third Crusade were cited by R. Eleazar in legitimization of the recitation of other passages.[1] That Eleazar's was not a totally novel approach to the legitimization of prayers is evident. A glance at the chronicle of Ahima'az will recall how much earlier incidents inspiring certain *piyyutim* were well remembered.[2] Clearly, then, there was well-established precedent for recalling the historical events that generated a certain prayer. What these explanations reflect *au fond* is the wish to fend off the charge of unwarranted religious innovation by the introduction of prayers that do not have the warrant required for their introduction into the synagogue and, as we have indicated, the desire to associate the proper *kavvanah* or meaning with a specific prayer.

Once we view the Crusade chronicles as part of the genre of liturgical commentary, their common properties as well as their singular features quickly become explicable. Each of them came from the pen of a different commentator who, presumably, responded to a need for

1. *Sefer 'Arugat ha-Bosem*, 4.101 and n. 84.

2. Ahima'az ben Paltiel, *Megilat Aḥima'az* (ed. B. Klar), pp. 27, 29, and cf. also pp. 17, 24, 37-39; and see also A. Jellinek (ed.), *Bet ha-Midrash* (6 vols.; Jerusalem, 1938), 5.148ff., 6.137ff., on the *piyyut* of R. Simeon ibn Abun.

explication of local liturgical novelties of various kinds that had emerged as a consequence of the First Crusade. Each synthesized the materials in his own way and in accordance with the information and materials that he had at his disposal.

If my suggestion on Crusade chronicles as part of the genre of liturgical commentary is accepted, perhaps they can provide us with some unexpected insight into the broader cultural matrix as a whole from which they emerged. In the context of medieval literature, generally, the Hebrew chronicles are more closely related to the genre of martyrology and hagiography than to any other form of literature. They rest on four pillars that lie at the source of all martyrology-hagiography: (1) the calendar, that is the dates of trial, tribulation and sanctification of the Divine Name; (2) the martyrs and their deeds; (3) the place where the martyrdom occurred; (4) the glories of the martyrs. These are well-known phenomena in Christian hagiography, where the lives of the saints and the martyrs are all told in the framework of these four pillars. As in the case of the Hebrew Crusade chronicles, Christian hagiography, too, was oriented in the first instance to annual liturgical celebration of the saint. While the Jewish martyrs did not become subjects of a cult quite in the Christian sense of the term, their role as sacrifices puts them in as close to the category of saint as a Jewish pattern of mind would permit its adherents to conceive of. The Hebrew Crusade chronicles are part of the same universe of discourse as Christian hagiography-martyrology.[1]

1. Ra'ban's concluding description (Habermann, p. 82) of the state of the martyrs in heaven brings to mind the medieval Christian iconographic representations of martyrs, with halos or crowns, carried on clouds of glory. The idiom of the Hebrew chronicle is essentially Jewish, since the eight garments make each martyr a high priest, but the picture is a cross-cultural one.

THE ROUTE OF JACOB'S FUNERAL CORTEGE AND THE PROBLEM OF *'EBER HAYYARDEN* (GENESIS 50.10-11)*

Aaron Demsky

The Bible in general, and the book of Genesis in particular, is replete with passages of a geographical nature which are couched in literary formulations that sometimes obscure the original intent.[1] The modern commentator must give them full consideration and apply all skills involving linguistics, literary style, knowledge of Eretz-Israel and the ancient Near Eastern background. Nahum Sarna, in his masterful style, has shown how to integrate literary matters and historic realia so as to achieve a clear and cogent reading of the text. As a small token of my indebtedness to him as one of my first mentors in Bible and for his enduring friendship over the years, I offer this solution to an ancient geographical crux.

At the end of Genesis, we find Joseph and his brothers on their way from the land of Goshen to bury their father Jacob in Hebron. The location and significance of Goren Ha'Atad at Abel Mizraim, which was their main stop on the route, remain unclear. Sarna[2] has translated the passage:

* I wish to thank the members of Kibbutz Sa'ad and particularly Reuven Evron who joined me in visiting Kh. 'Irq and Tell Shihan in order to clarify some of the topographic problems raised in this paper. I am especially grateful to Benjamin Mazar for sharing his thoughts about this topographical problem and other related matters as well as to my colleague Yehoshua Schwartz.

1. Another example is the location of Rachel's tomb; see my summary and suggestion in 'Qeburat Rahel', *EncBib*, VIII, cols. 360-63 (Hebrew); 'The Clans of Ephrath: Their Territory and History', *Tel Aviv* 13–14 (1986–87), p. 51 n. 7

2. N.M. Sarna, *Genesis* (The Jewish Publication Society Torah Commentary; Philadelphia, 1989), pp. 348-69.

> When they came to Goren ha-Atad, which is beyond the Jordan, they held there a very great and solemn lamentation: and he observed a mourning period of seven days for his father. And when the Canaanite inhabitants of the land saw the mourning at Goren ha-Atad, they said, 'This is a solemn mourning on the part of the Egyptians'. That is why it was named Abel-Mizraim, which is beyond the Jordan (Gen. 50.10-11).

Several difficulties arise concerning the otherwise unknown Goren Ha'Atad and Abel Mizraim *'asher be' 'eber hayyarden*. First, it is strange that the location of a minor site, namely a threshing floor protected by briars (*'atad*), should be specified in relation to a much broader regional term like 'beyond the Jordan'. A more precise location is expected, especially since a threshing floor was usually associated with a town or village and situated on its outskirts (cf. *M. B. Bat.* 2.4).[1] Of course, it is possible that Goren Ha'Atad is a place name. Similar toponyms containing the term *grn* are documented in Shishak's victory stele for the northwestern Negeb: *grn 'dm* (nos. 127-29) and *'en grn* (line 11,4).[2]

Secondly, a locale in Transjordan implies that the funeral cortege took an unusually roundabout trek through the Negeb, around the Dead Sea to the mountainous Moabite plateau and then via Jericho back to Hebron in the hill country.[3] Such a circuitous route might have been necessary were the Canaanites hostile and their well-fortified southern border closed to intruders, as at the time of the Exodus (Num. 18.28. 29; 21.1). However, at the time in question, Egypt apparently reigned supreme over Canaan; furthermore, Joseph the vice-regent was leading a funeral party of Egyptian dignitaries and courtiers, accompanied by a heavy military escort. The soldiers played a ceremonial role and were not needed to protect the family once it crossed the border into Canaan (Gen. 50.7, 9). Therefore, it

1. See H.Z. Hirschberg and S.A. Loewenstam, 'Goren', *EncBib*, II, cols. 559-60 (Hebrew).

2. See S. Ahitub, 'The Egyptian Topographical Lists Relating to the History of Palestine in the Biblical Period' (dissertation, Hebrew University, Jerusalem, 1979), pp. 95-96. Note the use of the term מדבר אטד, a pseudonym for Egypt in *y. Sanh* 1.1 (19.1); *y. Ned* 6.13 (40.11).

3. R. de Vaux's adoption of this strange route for the funeral leads him to suggest an 'aberrant transjordanian tradition' regarding Jacob's burial. He also adds that this is the only case of a Canaanite settlement found east of the Jordan (*Histoire Ancienne d'Israël*, I [Paris, 1971], pp. 126, 170).

would have been logical for such a party to take the most direct route from Goshen to Hebron.

The most direct route between Egypt and Canaan is the well-documented coastal road, known from Egyptian sources as *W3t-Ḥr*,'The Ways of Horus', traversed in the northern campaigns of such kings as Thutmose III, Seti I, Rameses II, Shishak I and Necho. In the Bible it is called דרך ארץ פלשתים (Exod. 13.17).[1] Due to a better understanding of biblical geography, some modern scholars[2] (and perhaps one or two medieval Jewish commentators)[3] realized that this should have been the route taken by Jacob's funeral procession into Canaan. This leads them to identify the reference to Jordan with Cisjordan. Be that as it may, the cortege would probably have veered off in a northeasterly direction toward Hebron from some point north of Raphiah. It is along this highway, then, that we seek to locate Goren Ha'atad and Abel Mizraim.

1. Y. Aharoni, *The Land of the Bible* (London, 1979), pp. 446-47.

2. See Y. Schwarz, *Tebu'oth Ha'aretz* (Jerusalem, 1900), pp. 93-94, with A.M. Luncz's comments (Hebrew), where a route through Beer-sheba to Hebron is suggested. I.S. Horowitz (*Palestine and the Adjacent Countries*, I [Vienna, 1923], p. 6 [Hebrew]) identifies Goren Ha'Atad with 'Ard Shokat 'Assufi (080/071), 11 km south of Khan Yunis. F.M. Abel (*Géographie de la Palestine*, II [Paris, 1938], pp. 234, 274) has made the interesting suggestion that Eusebius's identification of Goren Ha'Atad with Βηθάγλα, i.e. Beth Hoglah, near Jericho, (followed by the Madaba Map) and based on the *midrash* that as a sign of respect the nations hung their crowns *around* (עגל) the deceased, may actually preserve an earlier tradition rightly assigning the biblical site to Beth 'Eglaim, i.e. Tell 'Ajjul (098/097), 7 km south of Gaza. See E.Z. Melamed, *The Onomastikon of Eusebius* (Jerusalem, 1966), p. 3 (Hebrew). (It is of interest to note that the author of this *midrash* [*b. Sot.* 1.13a] is Rabbi Abbahu of Caesaria, the contemporary of Eusebius.) In his commentary to Genesis, Sarna concurs with the last identification noting its proximity to Deir el Balah, 'where a large collection of Egyptian-style anthropoid clay coffins have been found in a Late Bronze Age cemetery. The place was a burial ground for high-ranking Egyptians serving in Canaan and for Egyptianized Canaanite rulers and dignitaries. Such an association would explain why the cortege halted at Abel-Mizraim for public homage to Jacob in his own country' (*Genesis*, p. 349).

3. See M.M. Kasher, *Torah Shelemah* 7 (New York, 1950), pp. 1870-71, para. 29, citing the commentaries of Ḥizquni and Sekhel Tov.

Goren Ha'Atad

The biblical description of the incident seems to imply that the solemn lamentation was observed at Goren Ha'Atad because it was located on the Egyptian–Canaanite border. The intent of the episode is to point out the high regard in which Jacob was held by the Egyptians. After stopping at the border to pay their last respects to the deceased, the Egyptian dignitaries parted ways from the other mourners to return home (50.13). Goren Ha'atad was close enough for the Canaanites to take note of the seven-day ceremony. Thus, the locale of the account is at the divide of the two cultures.

Abel Mizraim

It is more than likely that the place name Abel Mizraim is a biform of Nahal Mizraim (cf. Nahal/Abel Shittim, Num. 33.49; Joel 4.18),[1] the well-known boundary between Canaan and Egypt. The term *'abel* indicates a watercourse, or at least a well-watered area.[2] Abel appears twice as a toponym in the second half of the Shishak stele (nos. 72, 122), probably to be found along the major *wadis* of the northern Negeb. The elaborate funeral rites of the Egyptians and their sensitivities regarding death and burial were well known to the Canaanites.[3] Therefore, it seems that this awareness determined the toponym Abel Mizraim, aetiologically (cf. 1 Sam. 6.18-19) derived in the folk etymology from the mourning (*'ebel*) practices of the Egyptians honoring Jacob.

Where is Nahal Mizraim? This crucial question continues to divide historical geographers. The majority maintain a median location at Wadi el-Arish, first documented in the Hellenistic period (cf. LXX Isa. 27.12; see also Rabbi Saadya Gaon on Num. 34.51); the maximalists

1. I. Joffe 'Abel Mizraim', *Mizrah U-Ma'arab* 2 (1938), pp. 363-365 (Hebrew). He locates Abel Mizraim at Nahal el-Arish. I owe this reference to M. Bar Ilan.

2. B. Mazar, ''Abel', *EncBib*, I, cols. 36-37 (Hebrew), and esp. W.F. Albright, *BASOR* 89 (1943), p. 15 n. 44.

3. Note this motif in the Sinuhe story and the reference to burial customs made by Wen Amon in his dialogue with Zakarbaal, king of Byblos, *ANET*, pp. 21-22, 23. See also N.M. Sarna, *Understanding Genesis* (New York, 1988), p. 226.

argue for the Pelusaic arm of the Nile, while the minimalists suggest Wadi Gaza, i.e. Nahal Besor.[1] These different locations are based on Egyptian, Assyrian, Greek and biblical sources reflecting, for almost a 1500 year period, sundry historiographic and literary perspectives. It seems to me that the difficulty lies in the attempt to determine a singular location, instead of viewing Nahal Mizraim as a 'shifting place name', designating a watercourse marking the Egyptian border, but varying according to the political, cultural and demographic perceptions of the different authors at different times.

Therefore, in our case, it would be methodologically more correct to study the problem from the perspective of the book of Genesis. The southern border of Canaan is anticipated[2] in Gen. 10.19, where it is clearly delineated as extending from Gerar (Tell Abu Hureira) as far as Gaza in the west and to the five cities of the plain in the east.[3] Furthermore, the patriarchal narratives, describing the relationship of Abraham and Isaac to the kings of Sodom and Gerar, reflect the southern limits of Canaanite settlement. Their 'walking about the land', their pleas and prayers on behalf of the indigenous kings and inhabitants as well as their claim to water rights in the northern Negeb are acts of suzerainty in preparation of the fulfillment of the divine plan. In other words, the southwestern border of Canaan in Genesis lies in the vicinity of the confluences of Nahal Besor (Wadi Gaza) and its tributaries.

1. N. Na'aman, 'The Brook of Egypt and Assyrian Policy on the Border of Egypt', *Tel Aviv* 6 (1979), pp. 56-90, esp. pp. 74ff. (bibliography cited). But note the critique of this position by A. Rainey, *Tel Aviv* 9 (1982), pp. 131-32 and Ahitub, *Topographical Lists*, ch. 5. Also see N. Na'aman, *TA* 7 (1980), pp. 105-106; *idem*, *Borders and Districts in Biblical Historiography* (Jerusalem, 1986), ch. 7.

2. On this literary device in Genesis, see N.M. Sarna, 'The Anticipatory Use of Information as a Literary Feature of the Genesis Narrative', in R.E. Freedman (ed.), *The Creation of Sacred Literature: Composition and Redaction of the Biblical Text* (Berkeley, 1981), pp. 76-82.

3. On delineating borders in ancient Israel, see A. Demsky, '"From Kzib unto the River *near* Amanah": A Clarification of the Northern Border of the Returnees from Egypt', *Shnaton* 10 (1990), pp. 71-81 (Hebrew).

'Eber Hayyarden

If indeed Abel-Mizraim is Nahal Besor and Goren Ha'atad lies on its southern (Egyptian) bank, then what is the meaning of *'asher be'eber hayyarden*? Some scholars have suggested that Jordan refers here to Cisjordan, as is the case in Num. 32.19; Deut. 3.21, 25; Josh. 9.1. However, these references are all from a vantage point in Transjordan, that is necessarily north of the Dead Sea, an area outside Canaan and some 200 km from Nahal Besor. Therefore, it seems far-fetched in this context that a minor site in the northwestern Negeb should be referred to as 'beyond the Jordan'. Moreover, our passage reflects a view from *within* Canaan, so that comparison with the above-mentioned passages is invalid.

The key to understanding *'asher be'aber hayyarden* in the Jacob story is identifying (ה)ירדן with the site *y-w-r-w-d-n*, no. 150 in Shishak's victory stele.[1] Assuming close proximity of the sites mentioned in lines 10 and 11, this *Yrdn* (l. 10) must have been in the general vicinity of Raphiah (l. 11.2), Laban (11.3) and other cities in the northwestern Negeb connected by the same road system. It is also plausible to identify ירדן with the Ἰαρδάν mentioned by Josephus as a point marking the southwestern corner of Judea, 'a village on the Arabian frontier which the local Jews call Ἰαρδάν' (*War* 3.3.5 [51]; one manuscript actually has Ἰορδάν).[2]

Can this Jordan be located? Mazar has identified Josephus's Ἰαρδάν with Yursa, which he locates at Tell Jemmeh on the southern bank of Nahal Besor.[3] However, the fact that Shishak's stele features both Yursa (no. 133) and *Yrdn* (no. 150) precludes their being the same, regardless of the Yurza–Tell Jemmeh equation.[4]

---

1. As pointed out to me by B. Mazar, this equation has already been made in a popular publication by Y. Ziv, 'Yrdn-Lebo Mizraim', *Teva' Va-'Aretz* 2 (1960), pp. 412-13 (Hebrew).

2. *Josephus*, II (Loeb Classical Library; Cambridge, MA/London, 1976), p. 590. See also *War* 7.6.5 as explained by G. Dalman, *Arbeit und Sitte*, I (Gütersloh, 1928), p. 78 and accepted by S. Klein, *Eretz Yehudah* (Tel Aviv, 1939), p. 246 (Hebrew).

3. B. Mazar, 'Yurza–Tel Jemmeh', in *Cities and Districts in Eretz-Israel* (Jerusalem, 1975), pp. 141-48 (Hebrew).

4. Mazar has identified both Ἰαρδά[ν] and Orda (see below) with Yursa ('Yurza' p. 145); in another paper, 'Harrekem Ve Haheger', he entertained the

Since *Yrdn*/Jordan does not appear in the city lists of southern Judah and Simeon, it follows that it was not located at one of the prominent tells but was rather, as Josephus states, 'a village' (κωρη). Its occasional appearance in our sources might be explained by assuming that while it was a relatively small settlement it was noteworthy for its demarcation of the extreme point on the southern border of Canaan and, later, Judea.

The place name *Yrdn*//Jordan seems to have been preserved in the sixth century CE name ῎Ορδα, ῎Οραων, ῎Ορδων, ᾿Αρδων, the capital of the bishopric of Gerar.[1] In the Madaba Map, Orda lies between Seana (Kh. Shihan–105/095) and Photis (Kh. Futeis–114/081): the latter is already mentioned in Shishak's stele (nos. 68-69). Alt and Aharoni place Orda at Kh. 'Irq (108/086), at the junction of Nahal

possibility that ᾿Ιαρδάν is the same as *Yrdn* (no. 150) of the Shishak list (p. 136 n. 17) (Prof. Mazar has informed me that he has retracted this last identification); see also Ahitub, *Topographical Lists*, pp. 113, 220 n. 3. Mazar hesitantly (p. 146) and later Na'aman ('Brook', p. 73, n. 9) emphatically added Arza, near Nahal Mizraim, conquered by Esarhaddon to the equation. However, Na'aman suggests that Shishak's *Yrdn* should be located elsewhere. Ahitub, basically following Mazar, now identifies Yursa with Josephus's ᾿Ιαρδα and with Orda (*Canaanite Toponyms in Ancient Egyptian Documents* [Jerusalem, 1984], p. 203). Regarding *Yurd(a)n* (no. 150), he states that it 'is an unidentified settlement, most probably situated on the southern edge of the route from the Land of Israel to Egypt' (p. 202), 'Not to be confused with Yursa, as done by Mazar and others' (n. 630).

It seems to me that for the sake of sounder linguistics and greater clarity, we should remove the whole issue of Yursa and its supposed cognates. In fact, A.F. Rainey's proposal placing Yursa at Tell el-Hesi may be correct (*Tel Aviv* 7 [1980], p. 197). It certainly fits my view of Canaan being north of Nahal Besor.

1. A. Alt, 'Das Bistrum Orda' (1931), in *Kleine Schriften zur Geschichte des Volkes Israel*, III (Munich, 1968), pp. 382-91; Mazar, 'Yurza'. It is possible that the shorter form Orda might be a backformation of the Greek-speaking local population, taking the final *n* of Ordan as a case ending. See also M. Avi-Yonah, *Mapat Madaba* (Jerusalem, 1953), p. 24 no. 105 (Hebrew); *idem*, *Gazetteer of Roman Palestine* (Jerusalem, 1976), p. 85. For a more recent and fuller discussion of the boundary in the Roman and Byzantine periods, see Y. Tzafrir, 'The Provinces in Eretz-Israel–Names, Borders and Administrative Districts', in Z. Baras *et al.* (eds.), *Eretz Israel from the Destruction of the Second Temple to the Muslim Conquest*, I (Jerusalem, 1982), pp. 350-86, esp. pp. 359ff. (Hebrew); esp. cf. D. Barag, 'The Borders of Syria-Palaestina on An Inscription from the Raphia Area', *IEJ* 23 (1973), pp. 50-52.

Gerar and Nahal Pattish (Photis), six km southwest of Tell Gerar (112/087).[1]

A still later reference to Jordan, whose importance for the history of this area has not been appreciated, may be found in a Syriac chronicle describing the Muslim victory over the Christians on February 4, 534 CE.[2] The battle took place some 18 km (12 Roman miles) east of Gaza. The fleeing Christians left their wounded leader (Lat. *patricius*) in Jordan,[3] where he was killed together with some 4000 Christians, Jewish and Samaritan villagers by the invading Arabs, who then went on to destroy the local settlements.[4] It was probably in this conflagration that Jordan/Orda was obliterated.

Since this document has been almost completely overlooked in this

1. A. Alt, 'Das Ende des Limes Palaestinae' (1938), in *Kleine Schriften*, III, p. 457; Y. Aharoni, 'The Land of Gerar', *IEJ* 6 (1956), p. 29. Kh. 'Irq remains to be excavated. Archaeological surveys have turned up artifacts dating only to the Roman and Byzantine periods; see now M. Cohen, 'Distribution of Settlement Between the Besor and the Shiqmah during the Roman and Byzantine Periods' (masters dissertation, Bar Ilan University, Ramat Gan, 1988), pp. 108, 161, 170, 172 (Hebrew). One might also note that there is an Amoraic tradition that placed Nahal Mizraim in the vicinity of Gerar, *y. Sheb.* 5.1; (36.3).

2. J.P.N. Land, *Anecdota Syriaca*, I (Leiden, 1862), p. 17 (Syriac text), p. 116 (Latin translation). This text is also mentioned by Alt, 'Das Ende'.

3. Assuming this to be part of the fallen leader's name, Alt overlooked the possible reference to Orda in the Syriac *Yrdn* ('sein name ist nicht sicher ueberliefert' 'Das Ende', p. 457 n. 5). The problem is that the Syriac text originally read *lptryqys bryrdn* (so Alt and Klein), but the first *r* in *bryrdn* was a scribal slip and was erased, see Land, *Anecdota*. Similarly, S. Klein missed this point when citing this source in connection with Gaza (*Sefer Hayyishub*, I [Jerusalem, 1939], p. 114) (Syriac text in Hebrew letters with a Hebrew translation). Both Alt and Klein follow E. Brooks, *Corpus Scriptorum Christianorum Orientalium, Scriptures Syri* (3.4; Leipzig, 1903), pp. 147-48 (Latin translation, p. 114). According to Klein, the text dates from the reign of Hisham 724–743.

4. According to the Arabic sources, the battle took place at the otherwise unknown site of Dathin, a village near Gaza; cf. P.K. Hitti, *The Origin of the Islamic State-Kitab Futuh Al Buldan* (London, 1916), pp. 167-68; but see R. Hartmann, 'Gillik', *OLZ* 18 (1915), cols. 235-40. See now M. Gil, *Palestine During the First Muslim Period (634-1099)* (Tel Aviv, 1983), pp. 31-32 (Hebrew). Gil brings the Syriac text in Hebrew translation under the exploits of the Arab general Amru ibn El'as. He also identifies the Byzantine 'commander' ('the *patricius*', in Arabic: *bitriq*) as Sergius, the governor of Gaza. However, Gil suggests that the Syriac chronicler must have identified *Yrdn* with *Jund 'Urdan*, i.e. northern Eretz-Israel (n. 50).

context, I will bring it in its original and then in Hebrew characters and in English translation:

ܒܫܢܬ ܬܫܥܡܐܐ ܘܐܪܒܥܝܢ
ܘܚܡܫ ܗܢܕܩܛܝܘܢܐ ܕܐܒܕܡܐ. ܒܫܒܛ ܒܐܪܒܥܐ ܒܗ. ܒܥܪܘܒܬܐ
ܒܬܫܥ ܫܥܝܢ. ܗܘܐ ܩܪܒܐ ܕܪܗܘܡܝܐ ܘܕܛܝܝܐ ܕܡܚܡܛ
ܒܦܠܣܛܝܢܐ ܡܢ ܡܕܢܚܐ ܠܓܙܐ ܬܪܥܣܪ ܡܝܠܐ. ܘܥܪܩܘ
ܪܗܘܡܝܐ. ܘܫܒܩܘܗܝ ܠܦܛܪܝܩܝܣ ܒܪ ܝܪܕܢ (¹ ܘܩܛܠܘܗܝ ܛܝܝܐ.
ܘܐܬܩܛܠܘ ܬܡܢ ܐܝܟ ܐܪܒܥܐ ܐܠܦܝܢ ܩܘܪܝܐ ܡܣܟܢܐ
ܕܦܠܣܛܝܢܐ. ܟܪܣܛܝܢܐ ܘܝܗܘܕܝܐ ܘܫܡܪܝܐ. ܘܚܪܒܘ ܛܝܝܐ ܠܟܠܗ
ܐܬܪܐ ...

בשנת תשעמאא וארבעין וחמש הנדקטיונא דאבדמא בשבט בארבעא בה
בערובתא בתשע שעין הוא קרבא דרהומיא ודטייא דמחמט בפלסטינא מן
מדנהא לגזא תרעסר מילא. וערקשן רהומיא ושבקוהי לפטריקיס
ב(ר)ירדן וקטלוהי טייא. ואתקטלו תמן איך ארבעא אלפין קורייא
מסכנא מנה דפלסטינא כרסטינא ויהודיא ושמריא וחרבון טייא לכלה
אתרא.

In the year 945, in the seventh Index on the fourth day of Shevat on Friday in the ninth hour, there was a battle between the Romans (i.e. Byzantines) and the Arabs of Mohammad in Palestine twelve (Roman) miles east of Gaza. And the Romans fled and left a patrician in Jordan and the Arabs killed him. And 4000 impoverished villagers of Palestine were killed there: Christians, Jews and Samaritans: and the Arabs destroyed the whole area.

Once we recognize that this text is referring to a place by the name of *Yrdn*/Jordan, located not far from a battlefield some 18 miles east of Gaza, its significance becomes apparent. It is the same name, preserved here in a Semitic script and identical with the Hebrew spelling. Secondly, the above description emphasizes the fact that Jordan was a border town in the northwestern corner of the Negeb. Furthermore, the almost precise mileage brings us close to Kh. ʻIrq, the suggested site of Jordan.

Finally, the choice of the preposition and definite article in the place name ʻEber Hayyarden was obviously influenced by the better-known eastern border of Canaan and might be another type of word-play on toponyms that we find in this passage. The problem would not have been so acute had a preposition like *mul, neged* or *negeb* been used. The term *ʻeber* is commonly used in relation to a river, i.e. ʻa riverside, bank', as may be the case here at Abel Mizraim. B. Gemser[1] has shown the basic meaning of *'eber* in these cases is 'to cross or pass-over', which suggests that the above place name might be better translated 'The Jordan Pass/Crossing'. Indeed, it was here that the funeral procession entered Canaan.

To sum up, the common denominator of the obviously related ירדן in Genesis, *y-w-r-w-d-n* in Shishak's list, Josephus' Ἰαρδάν and *Yrdn* in the Syriac chronicle is the fact that all four are located on the southwestern border of Canaan/Judea. If they are indeed the same and can be identified with Orda(n), in the vicinity of Tell Gerar near the tributaries of Nahal Besor, the geographical route of Jacob's funeral cortege becomes clear (see map overleaf). Veering off the Coastal Road near Raphiah, the party probably proceeded to the Egyptian fortress at Tell Jemmeh and then continued on and encamped on the southern bank of Nahal Besor. Somewhere along this border, a spectator viewing the procession from a vantage point within Canaan would see a seven-day mourning period being observed at a place called Goren Ha'Atad on the other side of the *wadi*, i.e. Nahal/Abel Mizraim, in what was regarded as Egyptian territory. Naturally, this site was identified in relation to a point on the southern border of Canaan, in this case, we believe the village of Jordan, perhaps Kh. 'Irq. Crossing over into Canaan proper, the family took one of the main routes from Tell Gerar to their destination in Hebron.

1. B. Gemser, 'Be'Eber Hajjarden: In Jordan's Borderland', *VT* 2 (1952), pp. 349-55, esp. p. 352.

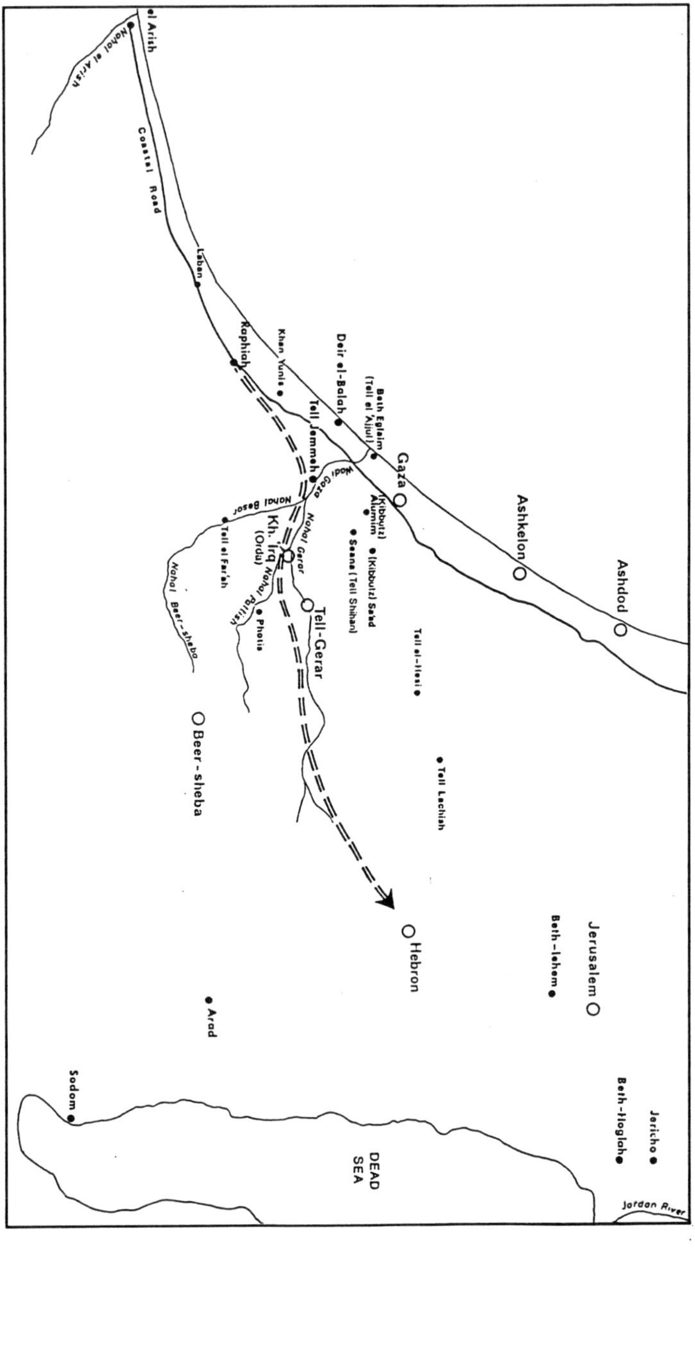

Map showing the route of Jacob's funeral cortege.

LAW TO CANON: SOME 'IDEAL-TYPICAL' STAGES OF DEVELOPMENT

Michael Fishbane

Canon, we may say, is the 'measure' of a culture's facts and artifacts. Indeed, from the perspective of the earliest Jewish movements towards canon and canonicity, it is clear that what is involved are such cultural issues as textual boundaries (what is and is not a legitimate text), authorial checks (who is and who is not an authoritative author), and cultural checks (when is a person or text or phenomenon part of the in-group, and when not). Gradually a fixed and explicit terminology emerges, and the criteria of inclusion and exclusion become sacred and binding. The available sources indicate how the emergent classical culture of Judaism came to deal with such issues as textual closure and acceptance, or scriptural inspiration and sacrality—and how considerations of political and social power invariably affect the process.[1] For in the final analysis the hierarchies and boundaries in question are maintained by principles of regulation which must be imposed so long as they are not freely accepted. Within Jewish antiquity, among the most culturally fateful of boundaries is that of scriptural closure; and among the most fateful consequences of this phenomenon is the recontextualization of legitimate interpretation. No longer is exegesis embedded within the canon of the Hebrew Bible, but comes to constitute a canonical phenomenon in its own right.[2]

1. For a close review of the question of canonization within the framework of early rabbinic Judaism, see S.Z. Leiman, *The Canonization of Hebrew Scripture—The Talmudic and Midrashic Evidence* (Transactions of the Connecticut Academy of Arts & Sciences; Hamden, 1976). See also the considerations recently advanced by D. Kraemer, 'The Formation of Rabbinic Canon: Authority and Boundaries', *JBL* 110 (1991), pp. 613-30.

2. I have dealt with the biblical origins of this phenomenon in my *Biblical Interpretation in Ancient Israel* (Oxford: Clarendon Press, 1985).

It would, of course, be both arbitrary and anachronistic to import later Jewish notions of canonicity into a discussion of canon-formation in ancient Israel—and I have no intention of doing that. I shall rather attempt a more empirical exploration of the biblical evidence, and try to suggest something of the movement towards such canon-formation to the extent that it can be reconstructed from legal traditions and formal features preserved in the Pentateuch. Towards this end I shall focus, first, on how specific rules or regulations have been supplemented, and then on how larger collections of these rules have been both expanded and incorporated into wider narrative settings. Only then will some attention be given to the emergence of the Pentateuch as a whole—built as it is out of a variety of legal corpora set within a historical narrative. Several distinct stages of recontextualization shall therefore be considered: (1) the supplementation of older rules; (2) the supplementation of legal series and their inclusion within narrative sequences; and (3) the collation of legal corpora into a comprehensive literary history. In the process, the principal techniques whereby the ancient Israelite legal rules grew into the received canonical framework will be considered. Accordingly, the examples chosen here are merely intended to suggest some of the typical trajectories of growth of the biblical legal canon—no more. Their value is proportionate to the light they shed on how the 'biblical canon' assumed its present shape.

It is a very great pleasure to offer these reflections in honor of my dear teacher, colleague and friend, Nahum Sarna. Over many years, his exacting exegesis of biblical sources has set a high standard for emulation; and his concern for questions large and small has had an equally formative impact upon me. One early encounter, some twenty-five years ago, was in the context of a course examining the rabbinic sources bearing on the canon. Many of his insights subsequently found their way into his own seminal study on the biblical canon.[1] I offer these new considerations with warm memories and life-long thanks.

1. S.v. 'Bible', *EncJud*, IV, pp. 816-36.

1. *Torah-Instructions and their Expansion*

A close examination of the technical conclusions found at the end of many priestly rules suggest that they serve to provide a concise resumption of the preceding instructions.[1] The terse summary of the rules of male and female effluxes (Lev. 15.1-31) in Lev. 15.32-33, or of post-partum purifications (Lev. 12.1-7a) in Lev. 12.7b are cases in point. In these and other cases the standard formula introducing these subscripts is *zo't torat ha-*, 'this is the *torah*-instruction concerning (thus and so)'. So precise, in fact, is this scribal convention that it may also serve as an index of the inner growth of the rules at hand.[2] In this regard, the complex traditions concerning leprosy and related miasmic discolorations in Leviticus 13–14 may provide a particularly instructive source for consideration; for the structure of this entire unit is notably marked by several 'colophons' which purport to indicate the subsets of the legal teaching. Now while this is not an entirely false description of the phenomenon, a closer examination shows that it somewhat simplifies the literary reality at hand. Indeed, in this collection of rules the relationships between content, structure and summary are neither direct nor symmetrical. A valuable internal witness to the historical stratification of the leprosy laws in Leviticus 13–14 can therefore be had through a close review of the several summary lines involved. Let me briefly summarize the pertinent facts. Four basic units may be isolated.

1. Lev. 13.1-46. This section deals with human leprosy, its prognostication, features and variations—all depending on the aetiology and initial condition. There is no summary to this part of the text.
2. Lev. 13.47-58. This sub-unit follows directly upon the preceding one with no separate introduction, and deals with the

1. See my 'Accusations of Adultery: A Study of Law and Scribal Practice in Numbers 5.11-31', *HUCA* 45 (1974), pp. 25-44. The phenomenon is also found in non-pentateuchal genres which borrow from priestly, scribal techniques; cf. M. Fishbane and S. Talmon, 'The Structuring of Biblical Books—Studies in the Book of Ezekiel', *ASTI* 15 (1976), pp. 129-53; and see n. 2 below.

2. In addition to the following example, see my discussion of Joshua 20 in 'Biblical Colophons, Textual Criticism and Legal Analogies', *CBQ* 42 (1980), pp. 443-46.

entirely separate matter of comparable diagnostic features in the warp and woof of flax or wool, or in skins and tooled leather. The summary in v. 59 echoes vv. 47-58 and the contents of this law.

3. Lev. 14.1-32. This section deals with the purification rituals for persons whose leprosy has run its course. The text opens with a *torah*-formula (v. 2) dealing with normal sacrificial procedure. Verses 21-32 deal with permissible substitutions due to indigency. A concluding summary refers to the latter subset alone.[1]
4. Lev. 14.33-35. This last subsection begins a new unit that deals with leprosy features found in buildings, as well as the appropriate fumigations and purifications. This section ends with a summary referring to buildings (v. 55) and other matters dealt with (vv. 54-57).

This condensation of the contents of the instruction reveals several structural matters. First, not all the units have summary-lines. Thus, while unit 1 deals with leprosy on human skin, the first summary in 2 does not refer to it. Moreover, while unit 2 deals with objects and does have a summary, the purification rites detailed in 3 only deal with persons—not with the fumigation or decontamination of garments. It thus appear that 2 breaks the logical nexus between 1 and 3 and is intrusive. Not only that, but unit 4 like 2 also deals with objects; so that following the purification rites for persons in 3, 4 strikes one as a legal *addendum*. In sum, then: units 2 and 4 deal with objects, not persons, and are not joined either before or after 3;[2] while the latter unit, 3, contains a purification rite for persons, and is thematically continuous with the contents of unit 1. Units 1 and 3, dealing with

1. This unit begins *zo't torat*. . . in 14.1, Similar introits are found in Lev. 6.2, 7, 18 and 7.1, 11, which A. Rainey has classified as a series of prescriptive ritual texts which provide an 'administrative' order to the sacrifices vs. the 'didactic' one in Lev. 1–5. See his 'The Order of Sacrifices in Old Testament Ritual Texts', *Bib* 51 (1970), pp. 307-18.

2. Some structural problems were noted by D.Z. Hoffman, *Das Buch Leviticus übersetzt und eklärt* (Jerusalem: Mosad haRav Kook, 1962), I, pp. 253, 286 (in Hebrew). His solutions, however, are weak and apologetic. The older critical argument that the underlying problem is one of different sources has been mostly fostered by M. Noth, *Leviticus* (OTL; Philadelphia: Westminster Press, 1965), p. 104.

leprous manifestations and their purification in persons, are thus arguably disconnected by the addition of units 2 and 4, which deal with objects.

These literary-historical conclusions, derived from a structural analysis of the content of Leviticus 13–14, are confirmed by an analysis of the final colophon in Lev. 14.54-57. This conclusion reads:[1]

54. This is the *torah*-instruction for all malignant skin-diseases, and for scurf,
55. for mold in cloths and fungus in houses,
56. for discoloration of the skin, scab, and inflammation—
57. to declare when[2] these are pronounced unclean and when clean. This is the *torah*-instruction for skin-diseases, mold and fungus.

It is obvious that this summary contains all the contents of Leviticus 13–14. However, the sequence bears scrutiny. While vv. 54 and 56 summarize the contents of unit 1, the consecution is broken by v. 55 which combines the contents of units 2 and 4. That is to say, the contents dealing with human skin eruptions are disrupted by reference to comparable discolorations in objects. The interpolated nature of v. 55 thus corroborates the preceding analysis of Leviticus 13–14. It may therefore be proposed that an original rule dealing with human skin disease was doubly supplemented when unit 2 and 4 entered, with the result that the original colophon to 1 was displaced to the end of the entire text. Significantly, the inclusion of these additions to the older instruction maintains the authoritative voice of a divine instruction—though in different ways: for 2 is absorbed into the divine command (to Moses and Aaron) at Lev. 13.1, while 3 is given its own introit (but only to Moses) in 14.1. The accumulative growth of the instruction is also marked in the colophon itself by the repetition of the formulary 'this is the *torah*-instruction' in 14.54 and 57. Such a bracketing resumption or *Wiederaufnahme* regularly signals the

1. The translation follows NEB, for the sake of consistency. One will easily note that NJPSV translated v. 56 differently. I have chosen NEB primarily because I think the translation of NJPSV to v. 54 more seriously obscures the complicated text-history of the unit (see below). By the same token, NEB in v. 57 is tendentious in that it lists separate diseases when the MT uses only one general term.

2. *Targ. Jer.* reads *byn* for MT *bywm*. This variation is likely due to the influence of Lev. 10.10.

incorporation of new materials into the ancient tradition.[1]

The rules of festival sacrifices in Leviticus 23 provide proof of the preceding phenomenon on a wider scale, and thus expand the horizon of our inquiry beyond a specific *torah*-instruction to small series of rules on one topic. The thematic unity of this text is indicated by even the briefest review of its language and content. Overall, Leviticus 23 is a highly stylized priestly instruction in which each of the festivals (beginning with the paschal-offering in the first month and concluding with the Tabernacles ritual in the seventh) are introduced by a double introit ('And YHWH spoke to Moses saying: Speak to the Israelites. . .'; 23.1-2, 9-10, 23-24, 33-34) and followed by pertinent sacrificial instructions and the refrain that 'you shall not work at your occupations' (*kal melekhet 'avodah lo' ta'aśu*; vv. 8, 21, 28, 35, 36)[2] on the holy convocations (*miqra' qodesh*). The list of instructions is concluded by the following summary,

> These are the festival-times of YHWH which you shall convoke as holy convocations (*'eleh mo'adey YHWH 'asher tiqre'u 'otam miqra'ey qodesh)*, bringing offerings by fire to YHWH—burnt offerings, meals offerings, sacrifices and libations, on each day what is proper to it' (v. 37),

and by the immediate disclaimer that neither Sabbath sacrifices, nor gifts, nor votive offerings, nor freewill offerings are dealt with in this context (v. 38). It would thus appear that this conclusion at once provides a summary of the preceding contents and resumes the title of the text found just prior to the first festival instruction (the paschal offering): 'These are the festival-times of YHWH, holy convocations, which you shall convoke on their appointed times' (*'eleh mo'adey YHWH miqra'ey qodesh tiqre'u 'otam bemo'adam*; v. 4). The stylistic

1. On this literary and redactional technique, see the earlier considerations of H. Wiener, *The Composition of Judges II, 11 to 1 Kings II, 46* (Leipzig: Hinrichs, 1929); and C. Kuhl, 'Die "*Wiederaufnahme*"—Ein literar-kritisches Prinzip?', *ZAW* 65 (1952), pp. 1-11. More recently, see I.L. Seeligman, 'Hebraïsche Erzählung und biblische Geschichtsschreibung', *TZ* 18 (1962), pp. 302-25; and S. Talmon, 'The Presentation of Synchroneity and Simultaneity in Biblical Narrative', *Scripta Hierosolymitana* 27 (1978), pp. 9-26.

2. On *melekhet 'avodah* as referring to occupational work, see J. Milgrom, *Studies in Levitical Terminology* (University of California Near Eastern Studies, 14; Berkeley: University of California Press, 1970), I, pp. 80-81 n. 297; and see the discussion in my *Biblical Interpretation*, pp. 197-99.

variation between vv. 4 and 37 is inconsequential.

Two problems remain. The first is that the introduction ('And YHWH spoke') does not immediately precede the instruction on the paschal offering (at v. 5), as one might expect, but comes at vv. 1-2—before an instruction about the Sabbath (v. 3) which, it will be recalled, was formally excluded by the concluding summary in v. 38. Add to this the fact that the prohibition of labor on the day of holy convocation is formulated differently here than elsewhere in the list ('You shall do no work'; *kol melakhah lo' ta'aśu*),[1] with the fact that the introductory 'And YHWH spoke' in vv. 1-2 is also followed by the title of the whole piece ('these are the festival times of YHWH which you shall convoke as holy convocations; these are My festival times'—*mo'adey YHWH 'asher tiqre'u 'otam miqra'ey qodesh 'eleh hem mo'aday*), and there are strong grounds to suppose: (1) that the Sabbath regulation is a supplement to the beginning of the list (being separated from it by the *Wiederaufnahme* of the title-line in vv. 2 and 4), and (2) that the original title (v. 2 or v. 4) was originally linked to the initial divine command in v. 1 and the first ritual instruction in v. 5.[2]

An indirect benefit of this analysis is that it suggests a solution to the redundant and awkward formulation of v. 2. For if it be readily seen that both the title in v. 4 and the summary in v. 37 begin *'eleh mo'adey YHWH* ('These are the festival-times of YHWH'), it will also be observed that the first reference to the title (in v. 2) simply follows the standard phrase 'and you shall say to them (*ve'amarta 'alehem*)' with the words *mo'adey YHWH* ('festival times of YHWH')—i.e., minus the demonstrative pronoun *'eleh*; while at the end of the line the title occurs with the demonstrative pronoun but in the apocopated form *'eleh hem mo'aday* ('these are My festival times'). In the light of

1. For the striking switch to the second person singular, see the comments of Abarbanel, *ad loc.*

2. I formulated this idea in December 1987, and presented an earlier version of this paper at a conference on the 'Biblical Canon' held at the National Humanities Center, April 1988. I subsequently received the Hebrew dissertation of Israel Knohl, 'The Conception of God and the Cult in the Priestly and the Holiness School' (PhD, Hebrew University, 1988). The author deals there with this and other texts treated here in similar ways and with similar results. His important study is now a book, *The Sanctuary of Silence: A Study of the Priestly Strata in the Pentateuch* (Jerusalem: Magnes, 1993), in Hebrew.

the full titular phrase *'eleh mo'adey YHWH* in vv. 4 and 37 it may therefore be proposed that, following the indirect object *'alehem* ('to them') in v. 2a, the word *'eleh* of that title was lost (by haplography) and only the words *mo'adey YHWH* were preserved. The ancient tradents, however, realized the awkwardness of this formula and offered the marginal gloss (now in the text, at v. 2b), so that the words *'alehem mo'adey YHWH* of v. 2a stand for the original full reading *'alehem; 'eleh hem mo'adey YHWH* (viz., 'to them: these are the festivals of YHWH'). Once this clarification was incorporated into the text (at v. 2b), it was repointed in order to make contextual sense. Accordingly, we now have *mo'aday*, 'My festival times', instead of *mo'adey [YHWH]*, 'festivals of YHWH'.

This is not the only addition to the text. For it will be further noted that, after the summary statement in v. 37, another summary (with introduction) concludes the entire document (before a new divine introit at Lev. 24.1): 'and Moses declared the festival times of YHWH to the Israelites' (v. 44). Indeed, this compliance formula is entirely unexpected and, in fact, merely serves to bracket-off the other addition of rules pertaining to the festival gathering of species in the seventh month (vv. 39-43). The secondary nature of this paragraph is certain. First of all, the unit begins after the summary and employs the qualifying adverb *'akh*, 'however';[1] secondly, the ensuing injunction is not formulated in the style of vv. 5-36, which deals with festival offerings and holy convocations, but as part of a command to gather the seasonal species as part of the pilgrimage celebrations;[2] and finally, the paragraph ends with a historical aetiology about the custom of booths (vv. 42-43), though none of the other festivals have national or historical explanations. Thus, an original collection of rules of festival offerings (Lev. 23.1-2, 4-38) has been supplemented by *addenda* at the end (vv. 39-43) and at the beginning (v. 3), and each has been incorporated into the received document by the stylistic device of a bracketing resumption (cf. vv. 2 and 4; and vv. 38 and 44).

The concluding supplement may be due less to a need to specify the

1. For the use of *'akh* introducing exegetical qualifications, see *Biblical Interpretation*, pp. 184-85 and 197-99.

2. On uses of the species in antiquity, see my remarks in *Biblical Interpretation*, pp. 111-12 and the notes there.

requisite species of the festival than to mark an additional eighth day of rest after the ritual week of ingathering (v. 39). Such a day is not noted in Deut. 16.15, but is mentioned in the priestly list of sacrifice for festivals as a day of 'assembly' (Num. 29.35). The *addendum* in Leviticus 23 may thus be a harmonizing expansion.[1] By contrast, the Sabbath supplement at the beginning of the calendar may be best understood as part of the theological up-grading of the Sabbath in the postexilic period.[2] By virtue of an editorial act, it is now proclaimed as the appointed holy day of YHWH *par excellence*—one of the *mo'adey YHWH*.

If the result of these procedures is, for the modern reader, a somewhat conflated congery of legislative authority (divine, Mosaic and editorial), it bears note that the ancient redactor does attempt to preserve the authority of the received divine instruction before him—and this in two ways: first, by virtue of the fact that the second addition was not incorporated into the block of rules on Tabernacles (i.e. at vv. 33-36), but joined to the summary as a *clausula finalis*; secondly, insofar as the addition of the Sabbath rule in v. 3 did not displace the (now contradictory) remark about the Sabbath in the summarizing conclusion (v. 39), even though its privileged position at the beginning of the instruction effectively neutralizes the original postscript. Canon formation thus proceeded cumulatively, but decisively, through the incorporation of supplementary material into a fixed corpus of teachings. Indeed, both these examples and the earlier one dealing with the rules of leprosy exemplify one of the paradoxes of the growth of a traditional literature under the sign of an authoritative divine voice: the paradox of closure. Perhaps we may mark this as the 'fiction of closure', insofar as the older document absorbs the (legitimately) new material while simultaneously disguising its own growth. If fixity is the outer norm of tradition, enterprising expansions constitute its inner life.

A final example must be taken up at this point, for its shows how legal supplements may not only add rules of a related type but

1. For the ritual on the eighth day, and some legal-ritual complications, see *Biblical Interpretation*, pp. 151-53.

2. See the comments of M. Greenberg, '*Parashat Ha-Shabbat Be-Yirmiyahu*', in *Iyyunim Be-Sepher Yirmiyahu* (ed. B.Z. Luria; Israel Bible Society, 1971), II, pp. 27-37; and in *Biblical Interpretation*, pp. 478-79.

effectively introduce an entirely new theology and praxis. The result can be a regulation somewhat unfollowable in its consecution, and requires a reader of the rule tacitly to comply with Quine's hermeneutical principle of 'charity' in order to save the text as a meaningful expression; that is, one tries to follow the shifts of subject and focus in the text as if they were sensible and deliberate, and not the result of conflation or interpolation. Be this as it may, the process of unraveling the various strands of the document can be most instructive from the perspective of cultural and canonical developments. The textual case I have in mind concludes the priestly regulation of atonement (or purgation) in Leviticus 16. Following the account of the ritual to be performed by Aaron (for himself, his family and the nation) and his assistant (designated to dispose of the scapegoat) in Lev. 16.2-28, the text seems to draw to a final point in vv. 29-34.

> (v. 29) And (this) shall be for you permanent statute (*ḥuqqat 'olam*): In the seventh month, on the tenth day of the month, you shall afflict yourselves; and you shall do no manner of work, neither the native nor alien dwelling among you. (v. 30) For on this day atonement shall be effected for you, to purify you of all your sins; you shall (thus) become pure before YHWH. (v. 31) It shall be a sabbath of complete rest for you, and you shall afflict yourselves; (it is) a permanent statute (*ḥuqqat 'olam*). (v. 32) And the priest who shall be anointed and ordained to serve as priest in place of his father shall effect the atonement. He shall wear linen garments, the sacral vestment. (v. 33) And he shall effect atonement for the sacred sanctuary, and the Tent of Meeting and the altar; and he shall effect atonement for all the priests and all the people of the congregation. (v. 34) This shall be for you a permanent statute (*ḥuqqat 'olam*), to effect annual atonement for the Israelites for all their sins. And he (Aaron) did as YHWH commended Moses.

It will be immediately observed that the rule not only moves from an unspecified time to a designated annual rite but from a third person singular rule (which the priest Aaron must learn to perform) to a formulation in the second person plural (concerning the whole nation). The introit and conclusion are marked by the phrase *ḥuqqat 'olam*, and this seems to set the boundary of the paragraph—the compliance formula at the end being a ritual tag, indicating the performance of the rite. Recent commentators thus tend to regard vv. 29-34a (minus the compliance) as a whole, even though the stylistics of vv. 29-31 are readily regarded as a rhetorical unit, and the priestly praxis (in v. 33) is easily seen to repeat earlier formulations.[1] The latter thus seems a necessary redundancy serving to underscore the permanent performance of the rite on a special day, as announced to 'you'—the people. But matters are more complex.

To begin with, one should note the triple repetition of the idiom *ḥuqqat 'olam* (in vv. 29a, 31b and 34a). In the first and third case the formulation is part of the larger Mosaic rhetoric to the priests (the second instance is more sparse, and part of an instruction to the people), and thus stands out from the indirect phraseology in vv. 32-33, which concerns priests (and their descendants) alone—as also in the Mosaic instruction of vv. 2-28. Accordingly, and in light of the editorial principle of repetitive resumption enunciated above, the following reconstruction may be proposed. An original rule directed to Aaron for purgation on special (but unspecified) occasions (vv. 2-28), to be performed by priests alone, concluded with a notice that insured perpetual priestly performance of the rite and summarized its basic features (vv. 32-34a). This transfer of the praxis to future Aaronids has particular poignancy here, given the fact that the rule now follows the death of Aaron's two sons for improper sacral encroachment (see vv. 1-2). It was presumably placed at this point in order to serve as an *exemplum* of proper access to the *sanctum*;[2] but this does not change the original meaning and purpose of the rule.

The second phase of the rule fixed the date of atonement (see v. 29; cf. v. 34) and commanded the people to afflict themselves and refrain from all manner of work. This instruction begins after the formulation 'And (this) shall be for you a *ḥuqqat 'olam*' (v. 29a), and is concluded in v. 31b by the *Wiederaufnahme*, 'a *ḥuqqat 'olam*'. The latter clause is clearly disjunctive, and merely serves to separate the peoples' praxis from the ensuing priestly regulation. This concluded, a repetitive resumption of the phrase 'this shall be for you a *ḥuqqat 'olam*' follows in v. 34a, as part of a concluding summation. As now formulated, this verse is addressed to the priestly hierocracy—even as they are the original addressees in v. 29a. But due to the larger redaction of the rule, v. 29a *now* introduces the instruction to the people

1. Both Knohl, *Sanctuary*, pp. 38-39, and J. Milgrom *Leviticus 1–16* (AB, 3; New York: Doubleday, 1991), pp. 1057, 1064-65, note the whole unit as an appendix and see the special quality of vv. 29-31.

2. On this editorial matter, see the discussion in Part 2, below.

(vv. 29b-31a). Thus vv. 2-29a + 31b-34a emphasize the priestly praxis, as against the parallel rite of affliction and cessation of work which the people are bidden to perform in vv. 29b-31a. The overall result is to institute permanent rituals of purgation and involve the people in the 'effectuation' of their atonement. One may thus see here a move to supplement the seemingly automatic praxis of priestly purgation with the obligations of private penitentials and personal participation. Whether or not vv. 29b-31a were first formulated after the destruction of the Temple, and before the renewal of priestly practices cannot be determined. But the intrusion here of a more popular strain into a divine instruction signals the complementarity of canonical and cultural processes. That the people's rite is now part of the divine law certainly serves to authorize the new ritual—or re-authorize an older, customary performance.

In this context, it may be further proposed that this penitential ritual was already in place by exilic times—a point which suggests a yet earlier redaction of vv. 29b-31a into the priestly corpus. We may argue thus because of the exegetical reapplication of just these verses in Isaiah 58. I have analyzed the case at length elsewhere, and so will now only underscore the point that the people believed their penitentials to be performative actions effectuating no less then the redemptive advent of God.[1] But they were harshly rebuked and instructed anew. As a further point in the canonical process, therefore, the prophet reuses the authoritative priestly rule of Lev. 16.29-31 to teach true penitential abstinence: the giving of food and clothes to the poor. Such moral action is now the effective rite for the exiles, the penance God prefers (Isa. 58.5-7).

2. *The Expansion of Torah-Instructions into New Contexts*

The agglutinative nature of traditions results in topical series of various types. A notable example of this trend is the collection of priestly rules in Leviticus 11–15, a compilation of *torah*-instructions on permissible foods, post-partum purifications, the detection and treatment of skin eruptions and fungi, and matters dealing with bodily dis-

1. See *Biblical Interpretation*, pp. 305-306. The influence of Lev. 23.27-29 cannot be excluded, of course. This would not effect the exegetical point made, but would qualify any discussion as to the editing of Lev. 16.29-34.

charges or effluxes. On the one hand, each of these rules is a distinct instruction marked by individual summaries. On the other, a double thematic of impurities and purifications links all the materials together. Indeed these several *torah*-instructions exemplify the priestly duty to clarify the differences between pure and impure matters. This task is stated explicitly in two of the colophons (cf. Lev. 11.47, *lehavdiyl beyn haṭṭame' vehaṭṭahor*, 'to distinguish between the impure and the pure'; and 14.57, *lehorot,* 'to instruct' on these matters), and to my mind explains the inclusion of the entire series (chs. 11–15) at this point. For though there is no independent title to this priestly collection, it will be observed that it follows the divine commandment (to Aaron) that priests must 'distinguish between (*lehavdiyl beyn*) the sacred and the profane and between the pure and the impure (*haṭṭame' u-veyn hatṭṭahor*), and to instruct (*lehorot*) the Israelites. . . ' in the Mosaic rules (Lev. 10.10-11). Still, the question remains just why this latter commandment appears where it does, attracting to it (after a brief interruption, vv. 12-20) the series of rules in Leviticus 11–15. The answer is instructive for the present inquiry into the relationships between the growth of laws and process of canon formation.

An examination of the wider literary context of Leviticus 11–15 (and its 'heading' in 10.8-11) points to the fact that the whole complex opens with a reference to the illegitimate incense offering of Aaron's sons (who employed an improper, or 'foreign fire': *'esh zarah*, Lev. 10.1) and their punishment 'measure for measure': 'Then a fire descended from before YHWH and consumed them (*vatteṣe' 'esh millifney YHWH vatto'kal 'otam*) so that they died' (v. 2). Following this catastrophe Moses immediately enjoins various regulations bearing on the exigencies of the occasion upon Aaron and his sons—in order that they 'not die' (vv. 3-7). These restrictions are continued in vv. 12-20 (along with various exegetical considerations of older rules),[1] but they occur only *after* the cluster of priestly teachings found in vv. 8-11. It would thus appear that this latter instruction, being of a general import unrelated to the exigencies of the disaster, was added to the specific rules preceding (and following) it because of the regulation there regarding priestly behavior within the Tabernacle: 'so that you [viz., Aaron and his sons] shall not die' (v. 9a). This catch phrase concerning not dying because of a ritual

1. See my discussion in *Biblical Interpretation*, pp. 226-27.

fault thus drew the unit of vv. 8-11 into the episode of Nadab and Abihu's transgression, even though the latter deals with an improper incense offering and has nothing to do with the prohibition of priestly praxis while intoxicated—the specific concern of v. 9. Moreover, since the ruling in vv. 8-11 also included a reference to distinguishing purities and impurities, this further led to the inclusion of chs. 11–15 into the present framework.

If further proof be needed that the materials in Lev. 10.8ff. and Leviticus 11–15 were secondarily linked to the narrative hook in 10.1-2, one need only look to the end of the priestly series—where Lev. 16.1 resumes (the narrative thread of) 10.1-2 with the words: 'And YHWH spoke to Moses after the death of the two sons of Aaron, when they came before YHWH [or: 'when they brought a false fire before YHWH'] and died'. It is significant that after this bracketing resumption a new introit follows in 16.2 ('And YHWH said to Moses', etc.), which provides a regulation concerning when Aaron might come into the innermost sanctum 'and not die'.

The literary theme of death due to the improper performance of a ritual thus led to the incorporation of diverse priestly instructions, informing the priests what to do in order that they (also) not die when serving the Lord in the shrine (10.9, 16.2). Indeed, precisely these literary considerations further suggest that the very episode of Aaron's sons is itself a secondary intrusion within the received complex of traditions. For at the conclusion of the ceremony describing Aaron's investitute, just prior to the episode of Aaron's sons and just after Moses and Aaron blessed the people (Lev. 9.23), it is recorded that 'then a fire descended from before YHWH and consumed (*vatteṣe' 'esh millifney YHWH vatto'kal*)' the various offerings upon the altar (v. 24). This expression of a positive theophany by fire recalls the similar description of the punishment of Aaron's sons (in Lev. 10.1). It was presumably because of the associative link between these two formulations that the exemplary event of a priestly fault was included here—interrupting the more natural nexus of Leviticus 1–9 and 17.

It is thus a paradox of the growth of the canonical traditions that the 'anti-canonical' behavior of Nadab and Abihu served to generate the recontextualization of a variety of priestly regulations. That the resultant stitches should be so blatant to the eye is only further testimony that it was the texture of tradition that was most important—and not the production of a seamless narrative. Indeed one of the features repeatedly noted so far is that traditional materials absorbed newer ones, and were not rewritten or eliminated by them. The result often leads to what may be regarded as the frequently unfollowable narrative sequence of the Pentateuch, or at least to the compilation within it of contradictory and redundant materials. Typical expressions of this include the various *addenda* to Leviticus 23, discussed earlier, and the inclusion of assorted ritual rules (Lev. 10.3-7, 8-11, 12-20; Leviticus 11–15) into the narrative context of Lev. 10.1-2 and 16.1. When one turns to the more epic portions of the Pentateuch, even more conglomerate combinations of traditions abound, and even more blatant displacements mark the inclusion of diverse legal traditions within the narrative. In some cases, there is only a temporary disruption of the reported action; in others, the narrative complex produced is almost entirely unfollowable—and only a traditional reading (which is to say, a reading of the text from the perspective of its canonical reformulations) saves the day. What one 'follows' in such cases is less the narrative thread of a specific discourse than the discourse of a culture's narrative formation. An example of the first type is found in Leviticus 24. The complex of traditions at the end of Exodus 12 exemplifies the second type.

The legal narrative found in Lev. 24.10ff. follows a pattern of other episodes, in which a case occurs whose resolution is beyond the ken of Moses and requires him to resort to divine adjudication. A mantic procedure is followed, an *ad hoc* ruling enunciated and, thereafter, a more formal statement of the rule.[1] The case at hand, dealing with a situation wherein a blasphemer (of mixed parentage) was caught *in flagrante delicto*, follows this basic form: the case is presented in vv. 10-11; a divine ruling is sought and received in vv. 12-14; and a general rule for such situations is formulated in vv. 15-16. Finally, Moses complies with the adjudication in v. 23.[2] From the perspective of the history of legal decision-making, we can observe several types: *ad hoc* situations requiring the ruling of a judge; a mantic appeal for divine adjudication where human jurisprudence does not suffice; and a legally formulated rule—here divinely dictated. From the perspective of canon-formation and redaction

1. For these cases and their forms, see *Biblical Interpretation*, pp. 98-106.
2. See the specific discussion, *Biblical Interpretation*, pp. 100-102.

history we can further observe how this case was supplemented by others, based on certain similarities. The result is to incorporate an extraneous legal collection (vv. 17-21) into a divinely authorized dictum bearing on an *ad hoc* case.

A closer look at the complex shows how the new collection became part of the desert narrative and its divine rulings. As noted, the general rule on the blasphemer concludes at v. 16—with the penalty of stoning and the words 'both an alien and a native-born who blasphemes the Name (of God) shall be put to death (*yumat*)'. Before Moses administers the sentence in v. 23, a different complex of rules intervenes. It opens at v. 17 with the statement that 'if anyone kills a human being, he shall be put to death (*yumat*)'. The common penalty of court-administered death thus links the first rule of the legal complex to the prior ruling about the blasphemer. Other rules follow in vv. 18-21, concerning slaying animals and causing damages to humans and animals. The unit concludes with a restatement (in slightly altered form) of the principle that 'one who kills a human being shall be put to death'. This resumption of v. 16 thus frames the legal pericope and sets it off as a distinct unit. The ensuing extension (v. 22), stating that 'You shall have one ordinance for the alien and native-born alike', provides a *Wiederaufnahme* with v. 16 (the conclusion of the law of the blasphemer) and provides further proof that the legists who redacted the complex wanted to link the legal series on physical injury with the case of the blasphemer, and to set the new material within a double frame (capital punishment for killing a person; and one ordinance for all) that would distinguish it as a special string of rules. Despite the hiatus, the punishment for the original case follow in v. 23. The *Wiederufnahme* at v. 22 (with v. 16) helps guide the reader back to the principle case and overcome any problems of coherence. Canon-formation thus gives new authority to a set series (vv. 17-22) and shows how the larger drive towards legal-cultural coherence comes somewhat at the expense of local coherence in a given narrative. The problems of 'followability' are aggravated as the narrative scope expands. The exodus epic provides a case in point.

Following diverse accounts of the ritual paschal ceremony (Exod. 12.1-19, 20-28), which concludes with a compliance formula (v. 28; 'Then the Israelites went and did so; as YHWH had commanded Moses and Aaron, so they did'), the historical narrative continues with an account of the death of all the Egyptian firstborn, of the despoliation of the Egyptians, and of the command of Pharaoh ordering the Israelites to leave (12.29-36)—thereby recalling the divine forecast of these three episodes in Exod. 11.1-8, prior to the incorporation of the Israelite paschal ritual into the plague cycle. The narrative then naturally continues with a report of the Israelite journey from Ramses, along with a concluding historical notice of the people's 430-year sojourn in Egypt (vv. 37-40). This point is re-emphasized by the comment: 'And it was (*vayehi*) after 430 years on that very day (*be'eṣem hayyom hazzeh*), that all the armies of YHWH departed from the land of Egypt (*yaṣe'u kal ṣiv'ot YHWH me'ereṣ miṣrayim*; v. 41)'. The entire account closes with an injunction that that night of vigil should be remembered for all future generations (v. 42).

Though this would appear to be the end of the legal-historical account of the Egyptian sojourn, another piece of legislation regarding the paschal offering appears in vv. 43-49. Among its provisions is the rule that only non-Israelite slaves and strangers may eat of its meat, and then only after they are circumcised (vv. 44, 48), as well as the injunction that no bone (*'eṣem*) of the sacrifice might be broken in the home ceremony (v. 46). This ruling was presumably attracted here as a *clausula finalis* on two accounts: thematic and textual. The thematic association between this rule and the earlier material is the immediately preceding notice that a 'mixed multitude' departed Egypt with the Israelites (v. 38). This point, together with the repeated injunction to observe the rules of the paschal offering and the unleavened bread in future generations (12.14, 17, 24, 42), inevitably raised questions as to the legitimate participation of foreigners in native Israelite ceremonies. The rules in vv. 43-49 provide clarification on such matters. The textual reason for the incorporation of the material here may be explained by the verbal nexus linking the notice of the Israelite departure from Egypt 'on that very (*'eṣem*) day' with the paschal ruling that no bone (*'eṣem*) of the offering might be broken during the rite. In any event, the secondary nature of the regulations in vv. 43-49 is established by the bracketing resumption of the concluding historical notice from v. 41 at v. 51 (where it states in a slightly variant formulation): 'And it was on that very day (*vayehi be'eṣem hayyom hazzeh*) that YHWH brought out the Israelites from the land of Egypt by their armies (*hoṣi' YHWH 'et beney yisrael me'ereṣ miṣrayim 'al ṣiv'otam*)'.

A final consideration reinforces these observations regarding the agglutination of legal traditions in Exodus 12 and their incorporation into the received narrative framework—and that is the comment at v. 50, just after the final statement of the new law ('You shall have one *torah*-instruction for the native and stranger dwelling among you', v. 49), and just before the resumptive historical notice of the exodus 'on that very day' (v. 51). That remark is the compliance formula 'And the Israelites did so; as YHWH commanded Moses and Aaron, so they did'. Its occurrence here is problematic since, first, the paschal ruling in vv. 43-49 was addressed to Moses and Aaron only and not to the people generally; and secondly, the very issue of compliance is out of place in this setting. However, since this phrase is virtually an exact repetition of the compliance language found in v. 28, just after the earlier rulings in 12.1-27, one should see here a further attempt by ancient Israelite tradents to locate new materials in the expanding blocks of authoritative tradition. The resumption of v. 28 at v. 50 thus marks the incorporation of the materials in vv. 29-49 into the wider framework of the chapter. It is arguable moreover, that the compliance formula in v. 49 follows a ruling dealing with the paschal rite precisely because the language of compliance in v. 28 comes just after the paschal ruling in 12.1-27.[1] As noted, such repetitions produce complications for the reader. But textual 'followability' is not the mainstay of canon-formation. The goal of tradition is rather to preserve authentic traditions from whatever quarter they come and to contextualize them within the received formulations at hand. In the biblical canon this governing form is a narrative history—the *Heilsgeschichte* of Israel.

3. *The Grand Context of the Laws*

Up to this point the growth of the 'canon' has been viewed form the perspective of diverse legal expansions—beginning with brief and more extensive *torah*-instructions (cf. Lev. 14.54 and 23.2-3) including the development of series and their narrative emplacement (cf. the material incorporated between Lev. 10.1-2 and 16.1); and going on to consider the inclusion of laws (Exod. 12.1-28, into the forecast–fulfillment framework of the exodus cycle (Exod. 11.1-8 and 12.29-

1. Verses 21-23 and 25-26 are disjunctive matters added to expand upon v. 24—a formula also found at v. 18 in connection with the rite of unleavened food.

36), as well as the further addition of a cluster of narrative and legal pericopes (12.37-42 and 12.43-51). In this latter case the narrative sequence of the exodus clearly provides the overarching framework to the additions. On a wider scale, the more expansive literary sequence of desert wanderings provides the setting for the full-scale legal collections embedded within it. For present purposes let us simply recall here the well-known facts that the marching sequence that begins in Exod. 15.22–19.2 is literally suspended by an assortment of legal materials: the Sinai theophany and its laws in Exodus 19–24; the Tabernacle text in Exodus 25–31 and 35–40; the sacrificial and other priestly rules in the book of Leviticus; the assorted priestly lists and rules in Numbers 1–6; the dedication of the Tabernacle in Numbers 7–8; and a revised law concerning the paschal rite and rules pertaining to the wilderness journey, Num. 9.1–10.10. The trek sequence is only resumed at Num. 10.11. What is particularly striking for our present analysis is the less obvious fact that the very sequence of episodes found in Exod. 15.22–18.27 recurs (with variations) in Numbers 11 and 20. Thus before the gathering at Sinai there is the tradition of testing in conjunction with water (Exod. 15.22-26), the report of food from heaven (Exodus 16), another tradition of testing over water in conjunction with Moses' use of a staff (Exod. 17.1-7), and an account of the appointment of judges to assist Moses (Exodus 18). In a strikingly parallel way, quite similar events are repeated after the legal intermezzo of Exodus 19–Numbers 10: an account of the gift of food from heaven (Num. 11.1-15, 31-35), an account of the appointment of judges (Num. 11.16-30), and an account of the testing over water in conjunction with Moses' use of a staff (Num. 20.1-12). There is no doubt that the repeated traditions vary in small and large degrees; but their repetition around the large legal complex of Exodus 19–Numbers 10 shows that this repetition was due to a concern by the tradents to preserve all known historical traditions (however similar or diverse), while at the same time incorporating authoritative civil and priestly regulations within them. It is altogether likely that the narratives and rules once circulated separately among priests and legists. Their collation and recontextualization in this form—which recapitulates on a grand scale the framing device noted earlier with regard to the agglutination of smaller legal units—is thus a powerful expression of the presence of canon-formation in ancient Israel. Nothing is lost. To the contrary: everything is preserved and intertwined, despite the textual repetitions and narrative dislocations that result.

The same principle of incorporation through bracketing resumptions also marks the most daring move toward the contextualization of laws into a narrative: the inclusion of assorted legal traditions from the end of Numbers (chs. 28–36) as well as the entire book of Deuteronomy into the narrative history of Moses and the early history of Israel. This may be appreciated by focusing on what appears to be the natural terminus to the pentateuchal traditions about Moses. He is first commanded by God to ascend Mount Abarim (*'aleh 'el har ha'abarim*) and behold the land before he dies, since he cannot enter it because of his and Aaron's sin at the site of Meribah (Num. 20.1-12)—'when you rebelled against My command. . . to "sanctify Me" through the water' (Num. 27.12-14); and he is thereafter commanded to invest Joshua as his successor, to lead the nation along with Eleazar the priest (vv. 15-23). Generally speaking, the death of a leader and the transfer of rulership is a thematic hinge of the ancient historical narratives (cf. Joshua 1 and 24.29-31 with Judges 2.7-10; 1 Samuel 1; 1 Samuel 31–2 Samuel 1; and 1 Kings 1–2). Accordingly, one would expect that this account of Moses' impending death would immediately precede a notice of his death and Joshua's succession. But this is not the case. Instead, a series of rules interrupt this sequence: first by the laws in Numbers 28–36 (which end with the totalizing summary, 'These are the laws and statutes which YHWH commanded Moses for the Israelites on the Plains of Moab by Jericho-on-Jordan', 36.13), and then by the repetition of divine teachings by Moses (Deuteronomy 1–30). Only thereafter does the subject revert to Moses' imminent death—in actual fact, to a resumption of the topics first treated at the end of Numbers 27. Much like the bracketing repetitions discussed earlier, Deut. 32.48-52 is formulated along the very same lines as Num. 27.12-14. There is thus the divine command that Moses ascend the mountain (*'aleh el har ha'abarim*) to see the land before he dies, and the reference to his (and Aaron's) sin at the waters of Meribah—when 'you sinned against Me. . . (and) did not "sanctify Me" among the Israelites'. After a final testimony (ch.33), Moses complies with this command and ascends the mountain to view the land before he dies (34.1-6). The episode concludes with a reference to Joshua's succession (v. 9) and an assertion of the incomparability of Moses (vv. 10-12).

The repetition of these references to Moses' death and Joshua's succession at the end of the book of Deuteronomy thus resumes the earlier notice of these facts in Numbers 27—and therewith draws the entire cycle of deuteronomic traditions into the 'canonical' Mosaic framework. For it is decisive that these teachings were not repeated by Joshua, but by Moses himself. Whatever is said therein thus bears the stamp of his authoritative pronouncement—however much the repetition of these traditions may seem to vary from the comparable regulations found in the Book of the Covenant and elsewhere. It also seems strategic that Joshua, who is described as 'a man with the spirit (of God)' in Num. 27.18 is referred to as a person 'filled with the spirit of *wisdom*' in Deut. 34.9. This new attribute marks him as a wise interpreter of the teachings of Moses, which he is bidden to study in order to succeed and be wise (Josh. 1.7-8). Unlike Moses who knows God face to face (Deut. 34.10), Joshua is a disciple—a man of implementation, of application and of transmission.

By so bracketing the deuteronomic teachings with the notice of Moses' death and Joshua's succession the tradents did more than preserve ancient traditions and give them Mosaic sanction. They also closed off the main period of revelation and set it apart from all future teaching (divine or otherwise). In this way, a hierarchy of sanctity and significance is introduced that distinguishes the Mosaic corpus—the product of a 'prophet... whom YHWH knew face to face'—from the instructions of wise and inspired disciples to come. One may even perceive in this death-and-succession notice a strong concern to nullify future charismatic pretenders to Mosaic authority. The frequent revisions of Mosaic legislation in the mouth of later prophets, and the likelihood that messianic expectations challenged the abiding authority of old rulings, made this no idle matter. In this regard, it is not insignificant that the entire prophetic collection also closes with an emphasis on the teachings of Moses (at Mal. 3.22, after statements of an imminent messianic advent). One may confidently suppose that both codas (the pentateuch and the prophetic) mark a political point as much as they signal the prestige of the Mosaic corpus as a canonical collection for the entire community.

In the preceding pages, I have tried not to speculate abstractly on the meaning or development of the biblical canon. Rather, starting from the concrete reality of ancient rules, I have attempted to suggest several 'ideal-typical' stages of its development—on the basis of diverse modes of legal expansion, on the one hand, and on the basis of the incorporation of legal units into larger narrative complexes. The analysis thus proceeded from the expansion of summary lines and prescriptions to the expansion of larger series on related themes, and from there to the incorporation of legal complexes into narrative sequences of diverse types. In almost all of the examples discussed, moreover, the editorial-authorial technique of a bracketing resumption was utilized. The strategy of inclusion has the merit of displaying in clear and factual terms how traditional material was variously supplemented while retaining its original patterns of authority. Presumably this and the other editorial strategies whereby this dynamic was operative recurred at different times and in different temporal sequences. I therefore make no case for the restriction of smaller *addenda* to the early stages of canon-formation. The trajectory presented here merely serves as a heuristic model whereby the latter-day investigator may perceive something of the agglutinative nature of legal traditions, as well as their 'movement' towards the full pentateuchal context in which they now stand. For prior to the meager comments of the early rabbinic sages in the post-biblical period, the seams left by the tradents of ancient Israel provide our only certain measure of how the ancient legal traditions were textualized. It is to their work—both deftly wrought and deftly obscured—that we must repeatedly return if we would ever know something of how the final texture of biblical tradition was spun.[1]

1. See *Biblical Interpretation*, p. 524.

R. Isaac Arama's Philosophical Exegesis of the Golden Calf Episode

Marvin Fox

The episode of the making and worshipping of the golden calf by the Israelites in the Sinai desert preoccupied both Jewish and Christian exegetes in antiquity and throughout the Middle Ages. The puzzles are immediately apparent even to the most casual reader. How can we account for the faithlessness of a people that had witnessed so many divine miracles? How could the people who had been liberated from slavery in Egypt, who saw the sea split open before them, who were fed manna from heaven, and who experienced the great theophany at Sinai—how could this people exchange their God for a golden calf? And how could Aaron, the divinely inspired prophet and future high priest, co-operate in such a venture? Why, if Aaron and the people were guilty of so grave a sin, was God ready to forgive them?

A vast literature of commentary has been generated over the centuries in the effort to deal with these and similar problems so as to provide some intelligible account of the episode. On the Jewish side, rabbinic *aggadot* and *midrashim* abound, and these were followed by the work of the exegetes through the end of the medieval period. On the Christian side the golden calf episode is a recurrent theme in the New Testament, and occupies a prominent place in patristic literature and in the work of the Christian exegetes. For the most part the Christian literature uses the episode as a polemical tool to discredit the validity of Jewish claims to religious legitimacy. The Jewish literature, on the other hand tends to be apologetic, seeking to explain the episode in such a way as to exonerate Aaron and to reduce the apparent guilt of the people.[1]

1. For extended discussions see L. Smolar and M. Aberbach. 'The Golden Calf Episode in Postbiblical Literature', *HUCA* 39 (1968), pp. 91-116, and most

Relatively little attention has been given in the literature to the work of the medieval Jewish exegetes in their account of the making and worship of the golden calf. Among the most interesting and most neglected of these exegetical works is the *Akedat Yitzhak* of R. Isaac Arama,[1] which takes a strikingly original approach to the exposition of the golden calf episode. In order to see the full significance and originality of Arama's treatment, I propose first to summarize briefly the approach of three of the most familiar Jewish commentators of the Middle Ages, and then to concentrate on an analysis and exposition of Arama's commentary. My aim is to show that while Arama's philosophical exegesis shares certain of the common concerns of the more standard non-philosophical exegetes, he nevertheless has his own program and his own way of addressing and interpreting the text. My summary of the earlier commentators will present their conclusions rather than a full account of their exegetical methods and techniques.

In the history of Jewish exegesis, Rashi (1040–1105) occupies a place of undisputed pre-eminence. His Bible commentaries, to say nothing of his indispensable commentary to the Babylonian Talmud, are among the most widespread and the most popular of all Jewish exegetical works In his commentary to Exodus 32, Rashi largely follows selected *aggadot* and *midrashim* whose main burden is to reduce the apparent guilt of the people and of Aaron. Using a standard argument, he reads the statement that Moses was late in returning as an explanation of the despair of the people. They had been told to expect Moses on the fortieth day, and erred by one day in their count. In their anxiety that Moses had abandoned them, they were tempted by Satan who created darkness and confusion so that the people were convinced that Moses had died. In addition Satan generated for them a vision of what appeared to be the bier of Moses. Under these

recently, P.C. Bori, *The Golden Calf and the Origins of the Anti-Jewish Controversy* (Atlanta: Scholars Press, 1990). The latter work has an extensive bibliography of studies on this subject.

1. Arama lived in Spain through most of the fifteenth century (c. 1420–1494). He was a rabbi and philosopher. *Akedat Yitzhak* was first published in 1522 in Salonika and has appeared since in many printings and editions. It consists of philosophical sermons and commentaries on the weekly readings in the Pentateuch. For the most comprehensive study of the thought of Arama see S. Heller-Wilensky, *Rabbi Yitzhak Arama u-Mishnato ha-Filosofit* (Jerusalem: Bialik Institute and Devir, 1956) (Hebrew).

conditions they were terrified at being left in the desert without a leader to protect them, and responded to their terror by seeking a new power that would guide them. Thus it would seem that their actions, although regrettable, were understandable and merited some sympathy. The defense is strengthened, moreover, by the claim that the real culprits were not the true Israelites, but the mixed multitude of Egyptians who accompanied them and now reverted to their familiar idolatrous practices. In this way, Rashi uses midrashic sources to explain and exonerate the Israelites.

Rashi also does much to exonerate Aaron. According to his account, the entire episode occurred in the course of less than a day. Aaron used every possible tactic to delay the making and the subsequent worship of the golden calf in the confident expectation that Moses would soon return and restore order to the community. The calf itself, according to this account was not Aaron's work, but resulted from the intervention of magicians from among the mixed multitude. In Rashi's version, even Moses shows sympathetic understanding for the plight of Aaron. In the biblical text Moses asks Aaron. 'What did this people do to you that you have brought such great sin upon them?' (Exod. 32.21). Rashi construes this as an expression of sympathy for the situation in which Aaron found himself. He has Moses saying, 'How much pain this people must have caused you to suffer so that you were finally forced to bring this sin upon them!' From all of this emerges a picture of Aaron and the Israelites as more or less innocent victims of circumstances beyond their control. In a final protective gesture, Rashi even has Moses blame God for the defection of the people. Commenting on Moses' statement to God, 'Alas, this people is guilty of a great sin in making for themselves a god of gold' (32.31), Rashi paraphrases a talmudic passage. Moses accuses God in strong language. 'You are the one who caused them to commit this sin because you gave them large quantities of gold and all else that they desired. How could one expect them not to sin?[1]

Abraham ibn Ezra (1089–1164), like Rashi before him, also largely exonerates both Aaron and the people. He first builds up the case against them by listing and rejecting many of the conventional lines of defense. The theory is offered in some rabbinic sources that Hur, Aaron's nephew, had already been put to death by the mob because he

1. For the talmudic source, see *b. Ber.* 32a and *b. Yom.* 86b and *b. Sanh.* 102a.

opposed them. As a result, Aaron was understandably concerned to protect his own life so he went along with the demands of the people. Ibn Ezra dismisses this theory contemptuously, saying that through all the subsequent generations of Jewish history even ordinary Jews gave their lives in acts of martyrdom rather than compromise with the worship of false gods. How then is it possible to expect less of Aaron, a prophet and saint? Surely, God would not have chosen as his messenger a person who was destined to commit the worst of all sins. Nor can one defend Aaron on the ground that he was deceived by the people who made the form of a calf without his being aware of what was happening. Ibn Ezra asks how it is possible to think that God would have chosen such a simpleton as his special messenger.

His exculpation of Aaron and the people begins from the premise that it is utterly unthinkable that Aaron would have made an idol or that the people of Israel would have demanded such an idol. What then actually occurred? The people were convinced that Moses had died because they did not believe that any human being could survive so long a time on a mountain without food and drink. They knew that it was Moses who led them on their journey and that he did so by divine inspiration. What they sought was a power that would lead them as Moses did, a physical form into which divine power would be poured. This is the meaning of the expression *elohim* in Exod. 32.1 when they ask Aaron, 'Come make us *elohim* who shall go before us'. It refers not to a god, but to a leader, physical in form, who will draw down the overflow of divine guidance. What went wrong is that the mixed multitude mistakenly treated the calf as a god and influenced some of the Israelites to follow them. We know from the text that only 3000 Israelites sinned and were put to death. This constitutes just one-half of one percent of the 600,000 adult male Israelites, certainly not grounds for condemning the entire nation. Aaron was in no way guilty of co-operating in a venture involving idol worship, nor was this what the people wanted. Their desire for a leader was legitimate, as were their fears about Moses.

If Aaron had made an idol, Moses would have been required to put him to death. Yet we find that Moses prayed for him, rather than condemning him. God is justified in his anger with Aaron, not because he did anything wrong, but because he was the indirect cause of the shameful events. Similarly, at the waters of Meribah, both Moses and Aaron were punished although neither of them sinned deliberately.

This supports Ibn Ezra's view that a great man may arouse God's wrath even if he is merely the indirect and unintended occasion for sin.

We see here how Ibn Ezra has gone beyond purely textual exegesis in several respects. First, he introduces common-sense considerations. Aaron could not have been a divinely chosen leader if he were lacking either in courage or intelligence. Secondly, Ibn Ezra offers a quasi-scientific account of the nature of the golden calf. It is meant to be a physical vehicle for the divine overflow, a notion which was fully comprehensible to his contemporary readership. Thirdly, he minimizes the range of guilt by restricting it to the 3000 who were put to death. Finally, he introduces the principle that great men are culpable for even the indirect consequences of their actions, and he defends this principle by references to another biblical text.

R. Moses ben Nahman (1194–1270) follows the general lines of Ibn Ezra's defense although he differs with him on some points. He exonerates both Aaron and the people of the charge of idolatry on the ground that what they sought was an inspired figure to replace the leadership given them until now by the absent Moses. This is the clear implication of their reference to 'that man Moses, who brought us from the land of Egypt' (Exod. 32.1). They seek a replacement for 'that man Moses', not for some presumed divine being. The best evidence that this was the request of the people is that as soon as Moses returned, they abandoned the golden calf. 'They could not have considered it a god, since it is not the way of men to abandon a divine king to be burned in fire.' Moses could not have destroyed the calf without arousing the wrath of the people if they considered it to be a god. Yet he destroyed it completely and the text records no opposition whatsoever on the part of the people. When they said, 'This is *elohekha,* O Israel' (32.4), they could only be referring to a concretization of a divinely inspired figure of leadership, not to an actual divine being. Nahmanides argues that 'in the whole world there is no one so stupid as to believe that the gold which had just recently ornamented their ears was the divine power that had brought them out of Egypt'. It was, in their view, simply an earthly symbol of the heavenly powers under which they believed themselves to have been led. To reinforce this stance Aaron built the altar and proclaimed, 'Tomorrow shall be a festival of the Lord' (Exod. 32.5). He stressed that this was to be a festival of the Lord in order to make certain that they would worship the one true God of Israel, and not make the grievous error of ascribing divinity to the newly fashioned golden calf. When the following morning they brought their offerings the verse reads, 'Early next day, the people offered up burnt offerings and brought sacrifices of well-being' (Exod. 32.6). Nahmanides notes that the text does not specify to whom they offered these sacrifices, because, he says, most offered them up to God, while only a few offered them to the golden calf.

Nahmanides sees two levels of sin in the entire episode. One was evil intention, the other was the public act of making and venerating the calf. Many of the people sinned in the act of making the calf, as is evident in the fact that they so readily gave their golden jewelry to be used. It is for this reason that the divine wrath was directed generally to the entire people. However, only small numbers actually worshipped the calf with evil intention. God, who sees into the hearts of men, knew who they were, and it was against them that the death penalty was imposed. Like his predecessors, Nahmanides limits severely the range and number of the truly guilty, and largely exonerates both Aaron and the people of any major wrong-doing.

Among the later medieval commentators, Levi ben Gershom (1288–1344) stands out as a major philosophical exegete of great power and originality. Yet, in his treatment of the golden calf episode he largely follows the lines of his predecessors with some added insights of his own. He, too, is concerned to exonerate Aaron and the people by finding some justification for their action, reducing significantly its most offensive aspects, and limiting the true sinners to a small number. Gersonides argues that the fear of the people that Moses would not return was fully legitimate, since they had no advance information about how long he would be gone. Forty days understandably seemed to them an inordinately long time, so that it was not unreasonable for them to be concerned with finding new leadership.

Aaron is represented by Gersonides as essentially blameless. His only concern was to protect the people from acting on their own worst impulses and to save them from the consequences of grave sin. To begin with, Aaron knew that if he openly opposed the people, they would kill him. His interest, however, was not in protecting his own life, but in saving the people from the terrible punishment that they would suffer for putting him to death. This alone determined all of his strategy. He decided to act as if he were in agreement with them and shared their plans. Having won their trust, he was able to pursue a variety of delaying tactics in the expectation that Moses would return and all would then be resolved favorably. When he could no longer delay, he deliberately made a calf, not a lamb. The Egyptians lived under the sign of Aries (ram), so Aaron invoked instead the sign of Taurus (the bull) to prevent the people from falling back into the Egyptian form of idolatry. Since Taurus follows Aries and is, therefore, in ascendancy over Aries, the people readily trusted Aaron because they could see that he sought to connect them with higher and more effective powers. Thus, the choice of the form of a calf was also a calculated move by Aaron to win the confidence of the people so that, if necessary, he could pursue further delaying tactics effectively. We see here how Gersonides, the accomplished astronomer, explains the actions of Aaron as resulting from his own knowledge and the knowledge that the people had of astrological forces and phenomena.

Thus, it seems that although the people behaved foolishly, they were not guilty of the sin of idolatry. Like Ibn Ezra and Nahmanides, Gersonides also holds that when they asked Aaron to make *elohim* who would lead them, they did not mean a god, but a talisman that would draw down divine inspiration. When Moses still did not arrive, only a small number of the people presented offerings and turned the calf into a god. This is evident from the fact that only 3000 were put to death for this sin. The others were saved because having seen the process by which the calf was made, they were not so foolish as to ascribe to it divine powers. Those who worshipped the golden calf showed, above all, the depth of their idiocy. As Gersonides puts it, this was not an action that should be understood as stemming from intelligent understanding and careful thought. Even the guilty parties were more nearly guilty of stupid and immature action than of deliberate sin.

Aaron, on the other hand, emerges in Gersonides' account as something of a hero. True, God was angry with him, because despite his good intentions he was still, in some respect, the cause of the entire dreadful event. At the same time, Gersonides stresses that God rewarded Aaron and his descendants with the priesthood. As he puts it, 'Because Aaron played the role of the priest to false gods, but did so only for the honor of the true God so that the Israelites would not turn away from Him, God rewarded him by making him and his descendants the priests who would serve Him'.[1] So we find that, in his reading of the biblical text, Gersonides follows lines similar to some of his predecessors in order to provide a plausible account of the golden calf episode, and one which removes serious blame from the shoulders of both Aaron and the people. Despite his standing as a major philosopher and scientist, very little of his philosophical and scientific learning enters into his exegesis of the passage before us.

Arama was thoroughly familiar with the exegetical work of his predecessors. In the course of his essay on the golden calf episode he makes reference to all four of the commentators whom we have discussed. He takes some points from them, explicitly rejects some others, but basically develops his own approach to an understanding of this difficult scriptural section. The basic framework is set by his use of a talmudic passage as a prologue which he then treats as the key to a correct understanding of the events as they are recorded in the Bible. The passage from the Talmud reads as follows:

> R. Joshua ben Levi taught: Israel made the calf only in order to provide an opening for sinners to repent (ליתן פתחון פה לבעלי תשובה). As we read in Scripture, 'May they always be of such mind, to revere Me always [and follow all My commandments]' (Deut. 5.26). It was this that R. Johanan had in mind when he taught that, 'David was not such as to perform that deed [the sin with Bathsheba], nor was Israel such as to have performed that deed [the making and worship of the golden calf]. David was not such as to perform that deed, as Scripture teaches, David said, '[For I am poor and needy,] and my heart is pierced within me.' (Ps. 109.22) Israel was not such as to perform that deed, as Scripture teaches, 'May they always be of such minds, to revere Me always, etc.' Why then did they do these acts? So that when an individual sins, we can say to him.'Follow in the way of that individual [David, who sinned and repented].' And if a community sins, we can say to them, 'Follow in the way of the community [that sinned and repented].'[2]

The simple sense of this passage seems to be that the golden calf episode occurred only to show all future generations that a community that sins can repent successfully and restore their broken relationship with God. Arama does not accept this conventional reading, finding it theologically unsound. If it means that God deliberately caused the people to sin so as to establish for future generations the possibility of

1. Based on *Exod. R.* 37.2.
2. *B. Av. Zar.* 4b-5a.

teshuvah, then the Israelites in the desert did not choose freely to build and worship the calf, but they were coerced. In that case there would have been no sin, no *teshuvah* and no forgiveness by God. Thus, the entire event would have been pointless.

Alternatively, it might be understood that the people chose deliberately to commit a grave sin in order to teach the effectiveness of *teshuvah*. Arama rejects this option as well, since it directly contradicts the rabbinic principle that, 'One who says, "I will sin and then repent", is denied the opportunity of repentance.'[1] He further expresses grave doubt that it would ever be wise or appropriate to commit a deliberate sin, even if the possibility of repentance were assured. He then undertakes to produce what he takes to be a sound exposition of the talmudic passages so that it can be used as the exegetical framework for the golden calf episode.

The essential background for such an exposition is his account of the nature of idolatry and how it comes about. Looking at the story of the golden calf, it strikes Arama that, considered at a superficial level, the people seem to be guilty of sheer stupidity. He asks how any person of normal intelligence who experienced the presence of God from the exodus through Sinai could turn away from faith in him? How could anyone who saw the process by which the calf was made attribute divinity to an inert piece of gold? Clearly, something more was happening, and it is to this that Arama turns.

He argues that idolatry is the result of a deficiency of intellectual power and philosophical understanding. He cites the verse, 'They exchanged their glory for the image of a bull that feeds on grass' (Ps. 106.20). His exposition makes the point that the idolator is a person who has abandoned his rational soul for those material things that man shares in common with the other animals. Such men do not understand what is essential to their own humanity, and reduce themselves to the animal level. In so doing they abandon what is most precious and distinctive in human nature. The question that Arama now faces is how does it come about that men who are endowed with the power of reason should choose to behave in ways which are so irrational. His explanation flows from his reading of the text of the golden calf episode.

In a summary statement near the end of the essay, Arama dwells on

1. *M. Yom.* 8.9.

Moses' plea for the people. 'But Moses implored the Lord his God, saying, "Let not your anger, O Lord, blaze forth against Your people, whom You delivered from the land of Egypt. . . " ' (Exod. 32.11). As Arama interprets the verse, the critical stress is not just on their having been saved, but specifically on their having been delivered from Egypt. The significance of this point lies in his account of the philosophical problem which faith in the one true God poses for most people. Men are so deeply rooted in knowledge which comes from the senses that they find it inordinately difficult to maintain a steady faith in a God who is absolutely incorporeal. Non-material existence is difficult to conceive, above all the non-material existence of the ultimate being who is the ground of all existence. Even the community of Israel, which should be able to affirm such faith with relative ease, vacillates and is filled with uncertainty. Philosophers have always known that the idea of a purely metaphysical being transcends the intellectual capacity of most men. This, according to Arama, was the problem which confronted the newly liberated Israelites. They were asked to put their trust in a God whom they could not see or touch, and this was more than could reasonably be expected of them.

This general problem, which confronts anyone who is required to believe in an invisible incorporeal God, was made much more acute by virtue of the fact that, as Moses points out, this people had dwelt for a very long time in Egypt. This seemingly high culture was in actuality, according to Arama, the ultimate in corruption and degradation. The Israelites were exposed there to an elaborate idolatrous cult whose gods were visible in concrete forms. They grew accustomed to the modes of worship in which the Egyptians engaged. In Arama's view, this resulted in the Egyptian style of worship becoming deeply imprinted on the Israelite mind to the point where it was inescapable habit and second nature. In effect, they were coerced by their circumstances to develop an idolatrous cast of mind. No one could reasonably expect them to escape completely the effects of their long residence in Egypt. 'One who is coerced in this way,' says Arama, 'has some ground for justifying his backsliding into idolatrous practices.' This is the explanation and defense that Moses offers for their grievous sin.

The specific explanation that the making and worship of the golden calf was not merely stupidity, but the result of a philosophical/theological problem, is now deepened by Arama by an account of how idolatry arose. Given the biblical story of the creation of man, it is puzzling that the early generations turned away from God so quickly and in such a categorical fashion. One might have expected that Adam and Eve and their immediate descendants would have found it relatively easy to know and trust God. Arama argued that these generations suffered from the metaphysical problem that we have already discussed and this led them to a further conclusion. They held that the world was eternal rather than created, from which it seemed to follow that there is a fixed order of nature dependent on necessary causes. This fixed natural order cannot accommodate an independent ultimate cause which controls, through its will and purpose, the realms of both nature and history. That is to say, there is no room in the universe for the biblical God who is Creator of the world, and who controls the destiny of man and the cosmos.[1]

Natural causation, as they understood it, operates through the force of the heavenly bodies. Human virtue or vice has no effect on the forces flowing from the stars. However, it is possible to invent devices for drawing the power of particular constellations down into the world, and thus to benefit from that power. Given this picture of how the world works, it is easy to understand how it happened that an elaborate ritual of worship of the heavenly bodies developed and won the loyalty of large segments of mankind. Through concrete representations of the various heavenly bodies, and through the rituals which were developed to worship these bodies, it was assumed that their power could be channelled and controlled for the benefit of those who had deified them.

Abraham brought back to the world the knowledge of the one true God, and this knowledge was preserved by his descendants. It was restored again and reinforced by Moses who did not rest with abstract theological instruction, but exhibited publicly the works of God in history. The plagues, the exodus, the splitting of the sea, the manna and the quail, the miraculous well, and above all the theophany at Sinai should have been more than enough to convince even the most skeptical, but it clearly was insufficient. So rooted were the people in the corruption which had been implanted in them in Egypt that they

1. Arama's account of the origins of idolatry seems to depend considerably on the account set forth by Maimonides. See *H. Avodat Kokhavim* 1.1, 2 and *Guide of the Perplexed* 1.36; 3.29, 30, 37.

continued to be confused and uncertain. They needed to test God repeatedly in order to help confirm their faith.

The two types which emerged at this point are embodied in Moses, on the one hand, and the Israelite people, on the other. Moses has no doubt about the reality and power of the God whom he serves in perfect faith. His deepest desire is to acquire the fullest possible knowledge of that God, to complete and deepen his love of God through a full apprehension of the divine reality. Thus, he prays, 'Now if I have truly gained Your favor, pray let me know Your ways, that I may know You and continue in Your favor' (Exod. 33.13). Again, shortly after, Moses pleads with God, 'Oh, let me behold Your presence' (Exod. 33.18). His need is not for evidence that God exists or that he is the Lord of both nature and history. What Moses desires in order to achieve the highest level of personal religious fulfillment is to know God in his true essential nature, to penetrate the inner mysteries of the divine being. As we know from the text, Moses learns that such ultimate knowledge of God transcends all human capacity, even that of this greatest of the prophets. His desire is satisfied as fully as his finite humanity allows. He cannot see the 'face' of God, but he is permitted to see his 'back'. This metaphorical language teaches us that Moses grasped as much of the inner divine reality as is possible for man.[1]

Arama explains that the Israelite people, meanwhile, are on a totally different plane. They are far from being concerned with a metaphysical understanding of the divine being. They still have to be convinced that there really is an incorporeal God who is above the forces of nature, that the world is controlled by him, not by the stars and the planets. They are at the level of Pharaoh who proclaimed, 'Who is this Lord that I should heed Him and let Israel go? I do not know the Lord, nor will I let Israel go' (Exod. 5.2). Pharaoh cannot conceive of an absolutely powerful transcendent God who intervenes in the order of history. Like him, the Israelites who were inescapably influenced by the culture and religious thought of Egypt needed repeated convincing. They were driven by an inner need to subject God to repeated tests, and no body of evidence seemed sufficient to overcome the religious and intellectual deficiencies which they brought with them when they were liberated from their bondage in Egypt.

1. Arama's account reflects the influence of talmudic sources and of Maimonides. See *Guide of the Perplexed* 1.54.

As Arama understands it, the most intensely skeptical segment of the Israelite people already had a fully formed theory of their own. In their view, it was the power of Moses that had liberated them from Egypt and led them through the various trials which they had endured up to this point. Moses had, after all, been trained in the royal palace and was a master of all the arcane learning and esoteric arts that could influence the higher spheres. They believed that Moses had even exceeded his Egyptian teachers in his mastery of these subjects and consequently in the power that this knowledge conferred. The notion that it was not Moses using theurgic secrets, but rather God who liberated them and guided them, was totally alien to their way of thinking.

So long as Moses was with them and repeatedly demonstrated his capacity to serve and protect them, they were prepared to trust him. Moreover, they had no opportunity in his presence to test their own independent powers. Once they saw that Moses had left them for a very extended period and they had no knowledge as to when or whether he would return, they seized the opportunity to test their own powers. They expected that they could do what they believed Moses had been doing all along, that is, draw down the influence of the heavenly bodies to lead them, serve them, and protect them. The strategy behind the making of the golden calf was, as Gersonides had suggested earlier, to engage the power of Taurus to overcome Aries. This is what they were certain Moses had done, and now that Moses was gone they were determined to achieve the same ascendancy on their own. They were not so much defying God, about whom they remained in doubt in any case, but imitating what they believed to be the method of the absent Moses. They would create anew a connection with the power that had led them out of Egypt. We can see that, when viewed this way, the people might well be considered victims of their mistaken doctrine. They were not so much rebellious and faithless as they were sufferers from the effects on their thinking of their long residence in Egypt. They did not yet truly know and understand the nature of the God who had redeemed them from bondage, nor could they comprehend the role of Moses as servant and spokesman of that God. That is to say, they were intellectually and philosophically deficient.

Arama is now able to define Aaron's actions in a way which leaves him free of blame. As he understands it, when Aaron realized that he could not prevent the people from carrying out their plan, he deliberately acted as if he were fully allied with them and shared their purposes. His strategy was to make the golden calf in the best possible way so as to forestall the criticism that it did not work because it had been improperly fashioned. He wanted to be certain that they could not account for the failure of the idol to exhibit any power by finding some defects in the way it was fashioned. It was his expectation that when they confronted the empirical evidence that this gold figure had no power whatsoever and could do nothing for them, they would be ashamed and would feel degraded by their own stupidity. They would be forced to recognize that it was not planetary power conveyed through the concrete image by the artifice of Moses that had saved them. Then they would finally come to know and trust God, forming that depth of loyalty and faithfulness which would save them from ever sinning again in this way.

In considerable measure Aaron's tactic was successful. The vast majority of the people did not worship the calf. They were wise enough to wait and see whether it would be effective. For this reason they were not condemned to death. Only 3000 people actually worshipped the idol, and having taken this step were condemned to death. We should note that, unlike some other commentators, Arama does not suggest that the blame belongs to the mixed multitude rather than the native Israelites.[1] In turn, Arama holds, with the midrashic passage cited by Gersonides, that Aaron was rewarded by God with the priesthood for himself and his descendants as compensation for having behaved in a way which was intended to protect the people from their own worst impulses and to serve the glory of God.

With this background we can now understand the deeper meaning of Arama's interpretation of the talmudic passage with which he began his exegesis of the golden calf episode. The statement that this event and the sin of David were for the purpose of opening the way to

1. In this exposition, and in what follows, I have not followed the order in which Arama sets forth his exegetical account. His style is a kind of dialectical moving back and forth between themes and arguments, on the one hand, and expositions of particular details of the text, on the other. I have tried to provide an accurate account of his views while giving a more modern order and structure to the presentation. At certain points I have filled in explanations of some of Arama's teaching in order to make statements which are terse and allusive in the original more readily accessible to the reader.

repentance for later sinners should not be dismissed with the criticisms that Arama originally made. The point that the Sages were making is that no man, however elevated in stature, can avoid sinning. The issue is not whether we will sin, but rather what we can do about it. The aim of Satan and all forces of evil in the world is to convince us that once we have sinned there is no turning back and all is lost. In that case, man might just as well continue to sin, since he has no opportunity of redeeming himself and finding favor in the eyes of God.

The talmudic passage comes to teach us otherwise. It addresses the problem of collective sin and of individual sin. It informs us that neither the most exalted community, nor one of the most exalted of individuals can hope to escape all sin. In the tradition, the children of Israel who stood at Sinai are considered, as a community, to have been nearer to intellectual and spiritual perfection than any subsequent generation in history. Similarly, David is considered to be an individual who stood near the summit of such perfection, rarely matched before or after. Yet, both were guilty of gross violations.

In the previous discussion I set forth Arama's explanation of how it is that gross sinfulness, such as that of the worshippers of the golden calf, comes about. What we learn from the talmudic passage is that no person should lose hope because he has sinned. The gates of repentance are open to all. If even the best of us are transgressors, what can be expected of those of us who are ordinary people? The Talmud teaches that the way to reconciliation with God is always open, no matter how grave the transgression.

The models of the effective repentance of the Israelites and of David provide a paradigm for all future sinners.

> They provide all sinners with an effective weapon to overcome Satan and the *yetzer ha-ra'* who encourage us to sin even more, because once one has sinned, there is no possibility of repairing the damage which has been done. Indeed, those who understand the teaching of the Sages will be encouraged to return to God. This is the purpose of this biblical story, and others similar to it, however ugly they may be. They are the model that teaches us that God wants sinful men to repent their sins [and thereby restore themselves to a state of proper relationship with him]. It is important to recognize that, however great the shame and disgrace of

confronting our sins, they are far outweighed by the benefit we gain through sincere repentance.[1]

There is a final point of particular interest in Arama's discussion of the value of repentance. It serves as a useful tool in protecting the Jews against the polemical attacks of their enemies. In recording both the episode of the golden calf and the fact of God's acceptance of the repentance of the people, the Torah closed the door against those who would use this sin as a ground for permanently condemning the people of Israel. The Torah did not suppress the story, but showed us both its negative and positive aspects. In this way, the Torah provided a refutation in advance of all those who might argue that Israel abandoned their God, and that he, in turn, abandoned them.

There are numerous specific points in Arama's exegesis of the golden calf section which are worthy of attention, but which I cannot deal with here. In his treatment of details of the text, he often shows himself to be acute and original, just as he is in building the larger framework of exegesis which we have set forth. The specific account of the details which Arama offers is only possible in the context of his theoretical framework which we have set forth here.

1. *Akedat Yitzhak* (Pressburg, 1849; photo-offset, Jerusalem, 1961), II, Sec. 35, pp. 174b-175a.

Menaḥem ben Aaron ibn Ẓemaḥ's Anti-Polygyny Torah Commentary from the Geniza

Mordechai A. Friedman

I

The Cairo Geniza documents have proven that polygyny was a fairly common phenomenon among the Jews living under Islam during the High Middle Ages. Recently edited documents from the classical period of Geniza research (approximately the 10th–13th centuries) describe dozens of cases of polygynous marriages. Polygyny often occurred in families in which the first wife had borne no children or in which there were other peculiar circumstances, but in many cases there is no indication of any special reason for plural marriages. Moreover, society in general seems to have been relatively tolerant of polygyny. There is hardly any evidence that the religious leadership of the community disparaged the practice.[1]

Attitudes of the religious luminaries towards polygyny seem to have changed with Moses Maimonides and his son Abraham. At least they are outspoken in finding fault with the institution. Moses Maimonides, for example, lists polygyny among the marriages and sexual relations considered reprehensible by the sages.[2] Abraham was the leader of a pietist movement in Egypt in the early thirteenth century. His commentary to Genesis is significant in this context because, as with the text edited below, it too explains the presence and absence of polygyny

1. See M.A. Friedman, *Jewish Polygyny in the Middle Ages: New Documents from the Cairo Geniza* (Jerusalem and Tel Aviv, 1986) (Hebrew).

2. Mishna Commentary (ed. J. Qāfiḥ), IV, p. 182 (*Sanh.* 7.4). See the sources and discussion in Friedman, *Polygyny*, pp. 25-26; *idem*, 'Tamar, A Symbol of Life: The "Killer Wife" Superstition in the Bible and in Jewish Tradition', *AJS Review* 15 (1990), p. 53.

among the patriarchs. As a ruler Joseph might have been expected to practice polygyny, but because of his asceticism he married only one woman. The narrative singles out Rachel as Jacob's wife (Gen. 44.27 and 46.19) since he had intended to marry her as his only wife; he took Leah as well as Bilhah and Zilpah only because the circumstances dictated doing so.[1]

The Pentateuch commentary, a portion of which is edited below, is from a large folio from the Geniza found in the Taylor–Schechter (TS) Collection of Cambridge University Library. Sides a and b interpret the end of the Torah portion Emor (Leviticus 24) and the beginning of Behar (Leviticus 25). These are identified not by their content, which does not refer to any specific verse in these portions, but by the heading פרשת בהר סיני in letters almost one cm high on the last line of b. Sides c and d evidently come from the commentary to Ki-Tetse (Deut. 21.10ff.). We are concerned here exclusively with the latter. The commentary is written in Hebrew. Both the handwriting and the Hebrew style are clearly from the post-classical Geniza period. The text exhibits no influence of the Arabic language or of the Islamic milieu (see below).

The first portion of the commentary to Ki-Tetse, dealing with the captive woman in Deut. 21.10-14, has not been preserved. Side c opens in the middle of v. 15 ('If a man has two wives', etc.) and continues through side d discussing the disloyal and defiant son (vv. 18-21). Side d concludes with a discussion on the necessity of one distancing himself from his menstrual wife.

The work consists of a verbose homiletic and moralistic commentary rather than a line by line exposition. Its discussion (on sides c and d) is ultimately based on the familiar midrash concerning the juxtaposition of the passages that begin with the captive woman and conclude with the disloyal and defiant son. As part of their campaign to delegitimate the taking of a captive woman, the rabbis suggest a cause and effect relationship: if one takes home a woman captured in war, she will bear him a disloyal and defiant son.[2]

The middle link, on primogeniture in the family of the bigamist with an unloved wife (vv. 15-17), or rather its opening clause (15a)

1. *Perush R. Avraham b. Ha-Rambam z"l 'al Bereshit u-Shemot* (ed. E.J. Weisenberg; London, 1958), pp. 164-65, 176-67 and 214-15.

2. *B. Sanh.* 107a and parallels.

'If a man has two wives, one loved and the other unloved', produced two separate midrashim. According to R. Simeon/Ishmael, 'The verse speaks of the natural order of things: in the end he will hate her and love another'.[1] Contrary to the suggestion of some modern commentators, the antecedent of 'her' is obviously the captive woman and not one of the wives of any bigamist. This complements both R. Akiva's interpretation of v. 12, according to which, as with the trimming of her hair, the captive woman must let her nails grow long 'in order to make herself repulsive',[2] and the anonymous midrash on v. 14, 'should you no longer want her': 'Scripture informs you that you will hate her.'[3] Similarly, according to R. Simeon/Ishmael, a captive woman will be rejected in the end; her captor will love and marry another woman. Verse 15 is construed to read: when a man has an unloved wife, he will love and marry another woman.

R. Simeon/Ishmael's statement disparages taking a captive woman but not polygyny as such. The latter is done in an anonymous midrash found in the *Tanḥuma*:

> Our sages taught, 'One commandment leads to a second: one transgression leads to a second' (*M. Avot* 4.2). 'And you see among the captives a beautiful woman. . . and she trims her hair' (Deut. 21.11-12). In order that he not find her attractive. What is written after this? 'If a man has two wives' (v. 15). If there are two wives in the home, there is contention in the home. Moreover, 'one (is) loved and the other unloved' (ib.) or both are unloved. What is written after this? 'If a man has a disloyal and defiant son' (v. 18). If one marries a captive woman, they will have a disloyal and defiant son.[4]

While the unattractiveness of the captive woman is the reason for the second marriage, v. 15a is rendered: if a man has two wives, one is loved and the other unloved.

Our Torah commentary condemns polygyny in general but does so as an independent elaboration of R. Simeon/Ishmael's midrash, not of the *Tanḥuma* passage. Our author considers polygyny opposed to the

1. *Sifre on Deuteronomy* (ed. L. Finkelstein; New York, 1969), sect. 215, p. 248; see variant readings and notes.
2. *B. Yev*. 48a and parallels.
3. *Sifre on Deuteronomy*, sect. 214, p. 247.
4. *Tanḥuma* (ed. M. Buber), Tetse, no. 1, p. 33; cf. printed edition of *Tanḥuma*, ibid.

natural order of the world as elucidated in the narrative of the creation story in Gen. 2.21-24. One woman was created, not two: 'and he clings to his wife, so that they become one flesh' (v. 24).

The creation of one woman rather than two or more as proof of the Torah's intention that man be monogamous is found in a midrash attributed to R. Judah b. Betera on Job 31.1-2: 'I have covenanted with my eyes not to gaze on a maiden. What portion is decreed by God above? What lot by Shaddai in the heights?'

> Job expounded the verse to himself. 'What portion is decreed by God above? (What lot by Shaddai in the heights?)' Had it been fit for the first man to have been given ten wives, He would have given them to him. It was not fitting to give him more than one wife. Also for me my wife is sufficient; my portion is adequate.[1]

Gen. 2.24, on the other hand, was not interpreted by the talmudic rabbis as implying man's monogamous nature.

> 'When evil men assail me to devour my flesh' (Ps. 27.2). These are (David's) *wives* whom he saved, as it is written 'and he clings to his wife, so that they become one flesh' (Gen. 22.24).[2]

Polygyny counters man's intelligence according to our Torah commentary. The commendation of monogamy and the condemnation of polygyny having been woven into the Torah narrative, it was unnecessary explicitly to forbid plural marriages. Such a restriction was required only in reference to kings (Deut. 17.17). The patriarchs engaged in polygyny as the result of special circumstances.

The talmudic rabbis explain the exclusivity of the law of the king in the opposite direction. An ancient halakha (presumably known already to the author of 2 Chronicles) restricts the king to 18 wives.[3] But no

1. *Aboth de Rabbi Nathan* (ed. S. Schechter; New York, 1967), version B, ch. 2, p. 9. The midrash vocalizes *she-dai* (which is sufficient) for *Shaddai*. Here and in the continuation biblical passages are translated as in *NJPS* except where another understanding was intended in the source quoted.

2. *Pesiqta Rabbati* (ed. M. Ish Shalom; Vienna, 1880), sect. 8, p. 31a.

3. The meaning of the rule in *m. Sanh.* 2.4 is debated there by the sages of the mid-second century CE. *J. Sanh.* 2.6, 20c and *b. Sanh.* 21a associate the number with a midrash on 2 Sam. 12.8. 2 Chron. 11.21 has Rehoboam marrying 18 wives. There is no basis for this in 1 Kings. The Chronicler probably attributed the number of wives accepted as normative by the midrash/halakha to the first king descended from David the number of whose wives had not been specified.

restriction applies to the commoner who may marry as many women as he can support.[1]

The Torah commentary's approach is comparable to that of the Judean Desert sect. There strict monogamy was the rule for king and commoner, and marriage of a second wife was considered adultery. Presumably the explicit commandment in Deut. 17.17 prohibiting the king from taking a second(!) wife was considered necessary lest one think that he be exempted from the general prohibition.

> They are caught in fornication by marrying two women during their lifetime. The principle of creation is 'male and female He created them' (Gen. 1.27). Those who came into the ark: 'two of each (male and female) came into the ark' (Gen. 7.9). Concerning the king it says 'he shall not have many (wives)' (Deut. 17.17).[2]

Likewise Jesus cites Gen. 1.27 and Gen. 2.24 in equating second marriages with adultery.[3]

The Palestinian tradition illuminated by Geniza sources defined marriage as a partnership and empowered a man's first wife to demand divorce if her husband married a second.[4] The author of our commentary, contrariwise, did not associate the monogamous principle of creation with partnership or equality of the sexes. The opposite is the case. It is the trouble caused by women that makes monogamy a rule of common sense. Only one woman was created because women usually cause pain and damage. A man has more than enough difficulty putting up with one wife and her children. His superiority and dominion over her is defined by Gen. 3.16. A woman is more often than not a nuisance. She has the intelligence of a child. It is the benevolent discipline and instruction of children and a wife to which most of the remainder of the commentary is devoted.

1. The prohibitions listed in the king's law do not apply to the commoner: *Tos. San.* 4.5. See *b. Yev.* 65a and the discussion in Friedman, *Polygyny*, pp. 7ff.

2. Damascus Covenant 4.19ff. In the continuation an explanation is offered for King David's practice of polygyny. See the discussion in G. Vermes, 'Sectarian Matrimonial Halakhah in the Damascus Rule', *JJS* 25 (1974), pp. 197-202. Cf. the Temple Scroll 57.17-18 and Yadin's discussion: Y. Yadin, *The Temple Scroll*, I (Jerusalem, 1977), pp. 272-74 (Hebrew edition).

3. Mk 10.2ff. and Mt. 19.3ff. For a recent study of these passages with references to other scholarly literature, see E. Lövestam, 'Divorce and Remarriage in the New Testament', *The Jewish Law Annual* 4 (1981), pp. 47-65.

4. See Friedman, *Polygyny*, pp. 7ff., 53 and references cited there.

With this commentary the attitudes towards monogamy and polygamy as conveyed in the Geniza seem to come full circle, from a relatively enlightened polygyny in the pre-classical and classical periods to a somewhat misogynous monogamy in the post-classical period. The identification of the author of the commentary and his provenance, to which we now turn, support the impression that the attitudes expressed in it are foreign to the corpus of Geniza documents. Separated chronologically and geographically, they attest a divergent religious and social milieu.

II

Menaḥem ben Aaron ibn Ẓemah (c. 1310–1385) was born in Estella, Navarre. After the riots of 1328 he moved to Toledo where he studied with Joseph b. Shu'ayb and Judah b. Asher b. Jehiel. It was there that he compiled his magnum opus *Ẓeidah la-Derekh*, a code mainly concerning daily life. Three small works preserved in manuscript are also attributed to him. It is possible that they are abridgments of *Ẓeidah la-Derekh.*[1]

A comparison of the Geniza manuscript (sides c and d) and *Ẓeidah la-Derekh* reveals that our commentary is in fact a slightly different edition of a portion of that code. The extant 'commentary' parallels about one fifth of the opening chapter of the division concerning the Laws of Women (IIIA1). This serves as an introduction to the division and is entitled 'On the Merit of Marriage and the Meaning of the Benedictions'.

The Torah commentary contains several lines and clauses that are absent in *Ẓeidah la-Derekh* as well as variants in wording. Based on their style both versions appear to come from the same hand, and as a working hypothesis I suggest that Menaḥem edited suitable portions of his code as a Torah commentary. (The identification of the relationship of sides a and b of the Geniza manuscript to *Ẓeidah la-Derekh* will help clarify this issue.) The literary and bibliographical questions merit a separate investigation. Nevertheless, I note here that the entire commentary is likely to have been relatively short, as evidenced by the discussions to the (Emor) Behar and Ki-Tetse portions on the same

1. See A. Freimann, 'Menahem Ben Zerach', *Annuario di Studi Ebraici* 1 (1934), pp. 147-67.

folio. The attribution to Menaḥem of a brief Torah commentary entitled *Or Torah* published in 1626 has been rejected by later scholarship.[1] Our manuscript gives cause to reconsider his authorship of that work.

The extant section of the commentary edited below is a version of the middle portion of the aforementioned *Ẓeidah la-Derekh* chapter. I doubt if the entire chapter was brought here, and Menaḥem probably selected only that passage which could be seen as relevant as a commentary to the Ki-Tetse Torah reading. Side d, l. 2, if not a scribal error, contains what may be a notation ('which is not in it') from the editing process, referring to a portion of the *Ẓeidah la-Derekh* chapter not copied in the commentary; see the note to the text below. In the following translation the missing portions of the first and last paragraphs are restored in order to clarify the context.

TS K 27.68[2]

[Whoever wants to sustain the species in the manner of perfection will seek an efficient[3] wife, not a 'beautiful woman'.[4] Because the most attractive woman who has no good sense and intelligence will disparage and humiliate her husband. This conflicts with the intention of the Torah which stated 'and he shall rule over you' (Gen. 3.16). Concerning her the (most) wise man said, 'Like a gold ring in the snout of a pig is a beautiful woman bereft of sense' (Prov. 11.22). Accordingly, the Torah spoke addressing the evil inclination: 'and you are seeing among the captives a beautiful woman' (Deut. 21.11). And the Torah commanded that she spend time making herself repulsive. Perhaps his perverted inclination will cool off.

To this was juxtaposed 'If a man has]

(Side c.) two wives, one loved and the other unloved', etc. (Deut. 21.15). Because in the end this man will hate his wife and marry a second

1. See Freimann, 'Menaham', p. 167, and the literature cited there. I have been unable to locate a copy of the work in question. (It is not one of the three abridgements referred to above.)

2. Thanks are hereby extended to the Syndics of the Cambridge University Library and to Dr S.C. Reif. Dr Reif informs me that the Genizah Research Unit has no bibliographical information on this manuscript, but that its position in K 27 and an accompanying notation show that Solomon Schechter was interested in it.

3. Or intelligent (משכלה).

4. The words יפת תואר are an allusion to Deut. 21.11.

wife.[1] For the proper conduct of the species it is not the intention of the Torah that a man have two wives. According to the narrative one woman was created from man's rib to serve as a fitting helper.[2] Two were not created, because they usually cause pain and damage. Thus it says, 'and he clings to his wife, so that they become one flesh' (Gen. 2.24).

Although two or more wives are not forbidden by the Torah, we have already seen that it is sufficient for the Torah to prevent through its narrative those things which are excluded by the intellect. Just as the Torah did not explicitly prohibit intoxication, the suggestion in its narratives being adequate for this, so the Torah did not forbid polygyny. For who would dare do this? Would that one could satisfy one woman and her children!

True, the kings, whose rule is grand with wealth and property, had to be cautioned not to take [many] wives. But there is no need to caution other men. Because they are heedful of this by themselves. Even though the narrative states that the patriarchs Abraham (Isaac!)[3] and Jacob did not find one wife sufficient, the narrative already stated the reason which caused each of them to marry a second wife. But Rebekah was enough for Isaac, because she was 'an efficient wife'. Concerning her it was stated, 'and let her be a wife to your master's son, as the Lord has spoken' (Gen. 24.51). Similarly the (most) wise man said, 'a[n efficient] wife comes from the Lord' (Prov. 19.14).[4]

An efficient woman is the one who knows her standing with her husband and conducts herself as was intended for her: her urge shall be for her husband, and he shall rule over her (Gen. 3.16) with befitting dominion.[5] Namely, her husband shall love her and respect her; and she shall love, respect and serve him the service due a king. In this way their love will grow, domestic harmony will increase and they will have the merit of having virtuous children.

Accordingly, the narrative states that woman was created from one of man's limbs from which the body is built, in order that she be attracted to his service and he have compassion over her and cling to her as the limbs cling one to another, as one. Because one of them cannot survive, if he removes his supervision and assistance from the others. And if. . . one of them over the others, like his supervision over himself,[6] then the body

1. The aforementioned midrash of R. Simeon/Ishmael.
2. Gen. 2.18.
3. 'Isaac' is an error here.
4. 'As the Lord has spoken' thus suggests both the efficiency of Rebekah and the divine plan of monogamy. See note to text.
5. Cf. *Bereshit Rabba* 20.7 (ed. Theodor-Albeck), p. 191: 'Could it mean all kinds of dominion. . . ?'
6. Cf. R. David Kimḥi's commentary to Gen. 2.18.

is whole.[1] Likewise, when a man and his wife constantly pay proper attention to this, they will succeed in conducting themselves and in raising and teaching their children.

(Side d.) The opposite occurs when the wife lords it over her husband and acts as his equal.[2] This applies to a woman who has no intelligence and no reason. [Concerning this] scripture prefaced, 'a stupid son is calamities (pl.) for his father; the nagging of a wife is like the endless dripping of water' (Prov. 19.13). The verse says that the stupid son is 'calamities' for his father, not just one calamity. Because a poor [father] wearies his body and distresses his soul in order to raise his son and instruct him. And when he h[opes] to have pleasure from his wisdom and his fine intelligence, his body and soul pain him because of his stupidity and wickedness.

Similarly a wife who stands aloof[3] from her husband is like 'an endless dripping on a rainy day' (Prov. 27.15). For the rain, intended for a man's benefit and subsistence, aggravates and irritates him in that place (his home) which is set aside for his rest. And when such occurs in a woman, it causes the son to become a [disloyal] and defiant son and the wife to be unloved.

Consequently, that portion was juxtaposed to the portion concerning [the disloyal] and defiant [son]. And the commandment is to eliminate him from this world when his father and [mother] cannot control him.[4] [For] they are obligated to discipline him, and he is obligated to accept their discipline and their instruction. [This is implied] in the passage 'This son of ours is disloyal and defiant; he does not heed us. He is a glutton and a drunkard' (Deut. 21.20). This passage shows that the Torah commanded that even for excessive eating or drinking they should discipline him and that he should heed them, how much more so concerning other excesses.

[But] the discipline should be moderate. That is, the left hand should push away, and the right hand draw near.[5] This was the intention of the (most) wise man when he said, 'Discipline your son while there is still hope, and do not set your heart on his destruction' (Prov. 19.18). The meaning is explicit in the verse.

Since a woman's intelligence is like the intelligence of minors. . .

1. Cf. *b. Yev.* 63a and parallels.

2. Or, and estranges herself from him. See the note to the text.

3. The phrase עומדת מנגד is probably to be associated with the midrash on Gen. 2.18: 'If he merits—a helper; otherwise—against him' (*Bereshit Rabba* 17.3, p. 152).

4. Deut. 21.21.

5. *B. Sot.* 47a and parallels cited in *The Babylonian Talmud with Variant Readings. . . Tractate Sotah* (ed. A. Liss; Jerusalem, 1979), II, p. 303; see there references to rabbinic literature.

especially during her adolescence and youth, our sages cautioned concerning her. . . 'let the left hand push away, and the right hand draw near'.[1] This is of the best of their advice.[2] [The intention of] this statement is that they should not be entirely drawn near, nor should the pushing away be made equal to the drawing near. They rather attributed the pushing away to the left hand and the drawing near to the right hand.[3]

This is the best way for a man to conduct his house and to conduct himself in receiving his natural pleasures. [Therefore they compared] in this context the evil inclination to a child and a woman.[4]

Because of our Torah's perfection it instructs [man to distance] himself from his wife, some of the(ir) time. And it made the punishment in this time like the punishment of incestuous relations. The result is that the people of Israel have been more sanctified than all the nations through this way about which no one disagrees except for the obstinate who loves discord. Furthermore, from [distancing himself from her a man will find his wife attractive, as a groom who has pleasure from his bride. Because when the bodies are constantly one with another they grow to loathe each other. This is why the (most) wise man said, 'Visit your neighbor sparingly, lest he have his surfeit of you and loathe you' (Prov. 25.17). Similarly R. Meir said, 'Since whoever is too familiar with something loathes it, the Torah commanded that a menstrual woman should wait seven days, in order to endear her to her husband on the day of her immersion like the day of her marriage.']'[5]

1. *B. Sot.* 47a and parallels. Cf. Rashi.
2. Literally 'whisper'.
3. The obvious intention is that the right hand is stronger than the left. Cf. Maharsha to *b. Sanh.* 107b: 'The left always indicates compassion and the right strict justice'. See Abraham b. David of Posquieres, *Ba'ale ha-Nefesh* (ed. J. Qāfiḥ; Jerusalem, 1964), pp. 123ff. where the left hand seems dominant.
4. The aforementioned passage in *b. Sot.* 47a. Cf. *Ba'ale ha-Nefesh*, pp. 123-24.
5. *b. Nid.* 31b. Although it forms an integral part of the *Ẓeidah la-Derekh* chapter, it is difficult to see how this paragraph can be construed as belonging to a commentary to Ki-Tetse. It is associated by extension with the theme 'let the left hand push away'.

TS K 27.68 (SIDES C & D). TEXT.[1]

1 [וסמך לו כי תהיין לאיש] שת[י] נשים האחת אהובה והאחת שנואה וג.
כי זה סוף האיש ההוא שישנא
2 את אשתו ויקח אשה אחרת עליה[2] מה שאין כונת התורה בשתי נשים
3 לפי הנהגת המין הזה על דרך ישרה כי כ[ך ב]א הספור שאשה[3] אחת נבראה
4 מצלע האדם להיות עזר כנגדו ולא נבר[או][4] שתים כי הן על הרב לצער
5 ולנזק והוא שאמ׳ ודבק באשתו והיו לבשר אחד.[5] ואע״פ שלא
6 נאסרו בתורה שתים נשים או יותר כבר קדם לנו כי הדברים[6] שירחיקם
7 השכל יספיק לתורה במניעתם בדרך ספור וכמו שלא אסרה תורה
8 השכרות בפירוש והספיק לה ברמיזה ב[ס]פורים כן לא אסרה התורה
9 לקחת נשים רבות כי[7] מי זה אשר [מלא]ו לבו לעשות כן ולואי שישיג
10 ספוק האחת ובניה אמנם המלכים שממשלתם רבה בעשר ובנכסים
11 הם שהיה הצרך[8] להזהירם שלא [ירבו] להם נשים אבל שאר אנשים
12 אין צריך להזהירם כי נזהרים הם מעצמם על זה[9] ואע״פ שהאבות
13 אברהם יצחק(!) ויעקב בא הספור שלא הספיקה להם אשה אחת כבר
14 בא בספור [10] בסבה שגרמה לכל אחד מהם לקחת אשה על אשתו [11]
15 אבל יצחק הספיק לו ברבקה שהיתה אשה משכלת ונאמר עליה[12] ותהי
16 אשה לבן אדניך כאשר דבר יי׳ וכמו כן אמר החכם ומיי׳ אשה.[13]

1. Each page measures approximately 22.5 × 30 cm and contains wide margins. The difficult handwriting, poor state of preservation and scribal errors make the decipherment uncertain at places; but the reading can be established in many of these when there is a parallel in *Ẓeidah la-Derekh* (below *ZL*). Variants from *ẒL* are cited from the second edition, Sabyonita, 1567; the first edition was not available to me.
2. *ẒL*: שסופו לשנאותה וליקח אחרת.
3. *ẒL*: ישרה שהרי.
4. *ẒL* (from l. 3): נבראת ולא.
5. *ẒL*: אחד וגו׳.
6. *ẒL*: נאסרו שתי נשים כבר אמרנו שהדברים
7. *ẒL* (from l. 7): יספיק הסיפור בתורה בהם כי.
8. *ẒL* (from l. 10): ובניה אבל המלכים היה צורך התורה.
9. From l. 11 (אבל) to here not in *ẒL*.
10. Read הספור as in *ẒL*.
11. *ẒL* (from l. 11): ירבו נשים ואעצפ שהאבות בא הספור בהם שלקחו יותר מאחת גם בא הספור בסבה למה לקחום.
12. *ẒL*: רבקה שנאמר בה.
13. *ẒL* adds here משכלת. In our manuscript there is a blank space which could accommodate it, but in the photograph there is no trace of any writing there. It is not clear whether the word was written or omitted, and if the latter whether or not

17 והמשכלת היא שיודעת ערכה אצל בעלה ומתנהגת עמו כפי המכון
18 בה להיות אל אשה[1] תשוקתה והוא ימשול בה הממשלה הראויה
19 והוא שהבעל יאהב אותה ויכבדנה והיא תאהב[נו ותכבד]נו ותעבוד
20 אותו עבדת מלך ובזה תגדל חבתם ויגדל שלום ה[בי]ת[2] ויזכו לבנים
21 הגונים ולפי׳ בא הספור שהאשה נבראה מאחד איברי האדם שבהם
22 יבנה הגוף לפי שתהיה נמשכת לעבודתו והוא יחמול עליה וידבק[3]
23 בה כדבקות אברי הגוף לפי אחד זה בז[ה שאין[4] קיום] לאחד מהם אם
24 יסלק השגחתו ועזרו מחבריו[5] וכא[שר . . .] אחד מהם על האחרים
25 כהשגחתו[6] על עצמו אז ישלם הגוף וכמו כן כשתהיה השגחת איש ואשתו
26 על זה מתמדת כראוי יצליחו בהנהגת עצמם ובגבול[7] בניהם ולמודם ע״ב
1 והפך זה כשתהיה האשה משתררת על בתלה ומשתנה[8] אליו וזה נמשך
לפי[9]
2 האשה בלא שכל ובלא טעם הוא [שה]קדים הכתו׳ שאין בו[10] הוות לאביו בן
3 כסיל ודלף טורד מדיני אשה. . .אמ׳ הכתו׳ כי הבן הכסיל הוא לאב
4 הוות לא הווה אחת בלבד כי [האב] העני ייגע גופו[11] ויטריד נפשו כדי
5 לגדל בנו וללמדו וכאשר יק[וה] לשמוח בו לחכמתו ולטוב שכלו[12] יכאב
6 גופו ונפשו בסכלותו וכמו כן האשה כשהיא עומדת מנגד אל בעלה[13] היא

intentionally. (*Ẓ̣L* refers to the verse earlier, but this may not have appeared in our commentary; see side d, 1.2).

1. An error for אישה. *ẒL*: ומתנהגת במאמר התורה ואל אישך . . .
2. *ẒL* (from l. 18): ימשול בך גם הוא יכבדנה ויאהבנה ובזה יגדל שלום בבית.
3. *ẒL*: בנין גופו . . . והוא ידבק.
4. *ẒL*: הגוף שאין.
5. *ẒL*: יסתלק . . . ועזרתו מחברו. The continuation through the end of l. 26 is not in *ẒL*.
6. Or בהשגחתו.
7. Read ובגדול.
8. Read ומשתוה?
9. See E. Ben Yehuda, *A Complete Dictionary of Ancient and Modern Hebrew*, p. 3379.
10. *ẒL*: והפך זה כשתשתרר האשה על בעלה והוא שקדם לפסוק בית והון. The words שאין בו (the latter word could also be read כי) bear no resemblance to בית והון, and it is difficult to see them as a regular scribal error. As a working hypothesis, I suggest that they are an editorial note from the process by which the *ẒL* passage was adapted for the Torah commentary. Since the latter presumably began the excerpt from *ẒL* after the citation, at the beginning of the chapter, of Prov. 19.14 (where בית והון appear), the comment 'which is not in it' was noted.
11. *ẒL*: שתי הוות כי האב יטרח בגופו.
12. *ẒL*: לשמוח בטורחו ובחכמתו ושכלו ויהיה הפך זה.
13. *ẒL*: נפשו וגופו בסכלותו וכן האשה כשהיא משתררת עליו.

7 כדלף טורד על ראשו ביום סגריר שהמטר המכון לתועלת האדם

8 ולחייו יצערנו ויכאיבנו במקום המיוחד למנוחתו וכשיהיה זה הענין[1]

9 באשה הוא סבה שיהיה הבן בן [סורר] ומורה וכשתהיה[2] האשה שנואה[3]

10 ולפי׳ סמך לפרשה ההיא[4] פרשת [בן סורר] ומורה ובאה המצוה לבערו

11 מן העולם כשלא יוכלו לו האב וה[אם כי מו]טל עליהם מוסרו ולמודו [ו]על

12 הבן מוטל לקבל מוסרם ולמודם והוא שנראה[5] במאמר בננו זה זולל

13 וסובא איננו שומע בקולנו [ש]הכתו׳ הראה שאפי׳ על יתרון[6] אכילה

14 ושתיה צותה התורה שייסרו אותו וישמע הוא אליהם [כל] [7] שכן בשאר יתרונות [8]

15 [אבל] צריך שיהיה המוסר בדרך בינונית והוא שיהא [9] שמאל דוחה וימין

16 מקרבת ו[כן ר]צה [10] החכם באמרו [11] יסר בנך כי יש תקוה ואל המיתו אל תשא

17 נפשך כפי[רוש] הנגל[ה] בכתוב ולפי שדעת האשה אל הרב היא

18 כדעת הקטנים. . .ים כל שכן בימי נעוריה ובחרותה הזהירו

19 רבותי׳ עליה. . .שתהא שמאל דוחה וימין מקרבת וזה

20 מטוב לחשם ש[. . .]ו במאמרם זה שלא לקרבם לגמרי גם לא להשוות [12]

21 הריחוק אל הקרוב אלא יחסו הדחיה אל השמאל והקרוב אל הימין [13] זה

22 מטוב הנהגת הבית ומטוב הנהגת האדם בעצמו [14] בקבלת הנאותיו

23 הנמשכות אחר הט[בע ולפי׳ השו]ו בזה היצר אל תינוק ואשה ומתמימות [15]

24 תורתינו ש[ציות]ה על [האדם לרחק] ממנו [16] מאשתו קצת זמנם [17] ושם

1. *Ẓ**L*: יצערנו במקום. . . הענין הזה.
2. Read ושתהיה or וכן שתהיה.
3. *Ẓ**L*: לפיכך סמך לאשה השנואה.
4. *Ẓ**L*: הבן סורר ומורה (without the continuation).
5. Reading uncertain.
6. *ZL* (from l. 11): העולם ואפי׳ על יתרון מעט.
7. *Ẓ**L*: ושתיה כל. The word כל was mistakenly omitted in our manuscript.
8. The word can be read only by comparing *Ẓ**L*.
9. *Ẓ**L*: אבל המוסר על הקו האמצעי כמו שאמרו יצר אשה וקטן תהא.
10. Reading uncertain.
11. *Ẓ**L*: וכן אמר שלמה.
12. *Ẓ**L* (from l. 17): נפשך ולא השוה.
13. *Ẓ**L*: לשמאל והקריבה לימין.
14. *Ẓ**L*: הבית וכן האדם עצמו.
15. *Ẓ**L*: הטבע ומתמימות.
16. The word ממנו is probably a scribal error for עצמו.
17. *Ẓ**L*: לאדם להתרחק מן האשה קצת זמן. In the Geniza manuscript זמנם may be an error for זמניו.

25 עונשם <ב>זמן [1] ההוא כעונש ער[יות] עד שנקדשו בני ישראל[2] מכל האמות

26 בדרך שאין חולק עליה אלא מעקש אוהב מחלוקת מצורף על זה כי מן
[רחוק זה תמצא חן בעיני בעלה [3] . . .]

ADDENDA

Menaḥem ben Aaron ibn Ẓemaḥ's attitude towards polygyny, the subject of the passage edited in this article, should be seen in the perspective of that of his contemporary countrymen as reflected elsewhere in his own writings and beyond. In Ẓeidah la-Derekh III1B he comments: 'There are a custom and an enactment in most of the land not to marry a second wife; and if one does so, his first wife can demand her divorce settlement'. See Friedman, *Polygyny*, p. 43. For a recent discussion of Spanish Jewry's attitude towards polygyny during this period with references to the pertinent literature, see E. Westreich, *Grounds for Permitting a Man to Marry Bigamously in Jewish Law* (Thesis submitted for the degree Doctor of Law, Hebrew University, Jerusalem, 1990), pp. 122ff.

Attention should be called to a responsum by a Spanish predecessor of Menaḥem, Solomon b. Abraham Adret (c. 1235–1310), who on the basis of the same midrash on Deut. 21.10ff. vigorously condemns one (the specific case refers to a man already married) who purchased a slave girl, converted her and kept her as his concubine. See S.Z. Havlin, 'The Takkanot of Rabbenu Gershon Ma'or Hagola in Family Law in Spain and Provence', *Shenaton ha-Mishpat ha-Ivri* 2 (1975), pp. 237-38.

As we have seen, Gen. 2.24 was held by the midrash as being consonant with polygyny. It is curious to note that Telypolygamus, the proponent of polygyny in Bernardino Ochino's Basel 1563 Dialogue on Polygamy, similarly argues that one can cling to and become one flesh with many wives, an argument that was later taken up by John Milton (references in J. Cairncross, *After Polygamy Was Made a Sin: The Social History of Christian Polygamy* [London, 1974], pp. 68, 128-29, 133).

1. The *bet* is added between the lines.
2. *ẒL:* עונשם כענש...שנתקדשנו בזה:
3. *ẒL:* חולק על זה...מחלוקת ובסבת זה תמצא. . . .

The Holy Scriptures Defile the Hands—The Transformation of a Biblical Concept in Rabbinic Theology

Shamma Friedman

The rabbinic decree that the holy scriptures defile the hands has long been a famous *crux criticorum*. All agree only to the fact that no satisfactory explanation that is demonstrable has been offered. This impasse justifies an attempt to retrace some steps of scholarly analysis to see if their derailment can be repaired.

The pertinent talmudic sources[1] suggest nothing of sinister or negative quality surrounding the 'impurity' of the holy scriptures. On the contrary, this status is unhesitatingly associated with their *sanctity*, both in explicit statements—'Did they not decree that Scriptural books defile the hands *because they are sacred?*'[2]—and implicitly through the deep structure of legal conceptualization surrounding these laws. Defilement of hands pertains only to scrolls prepared according to the exact halakhic prescriptive,[3] and only to those containing divinely inspired texts![4] Furthermore, *not* defiling the hands is the mark and

1. See S.Z. Leiman, *The Canonization of Hebrew Scripture: The Talmudic and Misrashic Evidence* (Hamden, CT, 1976), pp. 104-20. I have made some use of his translations below. See pp. 110-20, for a critical review of scholarly opinion.

2. *Y. Sot.* 2.4, 18a כלום גזרו על הספרים שיטמאו את הידים לא מפני קדשותן. In *m. Yad.* 3.5, R. Akiba argues that the Song of Songs 'makes the hands impure because כל הכתובים קדש ושיר השירים קדש קדשים—All of Scripture is holy, but the Song of Songs is holy of holies'.

3. 'They do not defile the hands unless they are written in Assyrian characters, on parchment, and in ink' (*m. Yad.* 4.5) לעולם אינו מטמא עד שיכתבנו אשורית, על העור ובדיו. Regarding a historical context for parchment and the other requirements, see M. Haran, 'Book-Scrolls at the Beginning of the Second Temple Period', *HUCA* 54 (1983), pp. 112-14, 122.

4. 'R. Simeon b. Menasia says: The Song of Songs defiles the hands *because it*

measure of the non-inspired work, or the non-halakhically executed scroll.[1]

The unconvincing nature of the talmudic explanations for this impurity led scholars to conclude that its roots are ancient and pre-rabbinic, no longer comprehended by the rabbis themselves; they are, according to M. Haran, 'a vestige of folk-ritual from the pre-Talmudic period'.[2] Accordingly, records of debates between Pharisees and Sadducees on this very issue seem to indicate that the ancients themselves had no authentic explanation available for these *halakhot,* and that those explanations appearing in this debate-context were polemical and *ad hominem.*[3] How much more so are the later talmudic explanations (so that scrolls would not be stored with *terumah*, which could lead to their deterioration)[4] to be considered rationalizations.[5]

was composed under divine inspiration. Ecclesiastes does not defile the hands because it is only the wisdom of Solomon' (*t. Yad.* 2.14) ר שמעון בן מנסיא אומר שיר השירים מטמא את הידים מפני שנאמרה ברוח הקדש קהלת אינה מטמא את הידים מפני שהיא מחכמתו של שלמה

1. 'The Gospels and heretical books do not defile the hands' (*t. Yad.* 2.13) הגליונים וספרי המינין אינן מטמאות אתהידים.

2. *Tarbiz* 25 (1956), English summary, p. 11; Hebrew, p. 260 = S.Z. Leiman (ed.), *The Canon and Masorah of the Hebrew Bible* (New York, 1974), pp. 225, 242.

3. 'Rabban Johanan ben Zakkai replied: The preciousness of Holy Scripture accounts for their uncleanness, so that they may not be made into spreads for beasts' (*t. Yad.* 2.19; see *m. Yad.* 4.6) אמר להן רבן יוחנן בן זכאי כתבי הקדש חבתן טומאתן, שלא יעשה אותן שטיחין לבהמה:

This evaluation (that the debate was *ad hominem*) was offered by Maimonides in his Commentary to the Mishnah (*ibid.*) 'Rabbi Johanan's answer was said in ridicule and derision' וג׳ ואב רבן יוחנן להם ג׳ אבה פי מערץ׳ אלהזל ואלהזו בהם

Concerning formal introductory language of polemical flavor in sectarian disputes recorded in rabbinic literature, see Y. Sussman, 'The History of Halakhah and the Dead Sea Scrolls—Preliminary Observations on Miqsat Ma'ase Ha-Torah', *Tarbiz* 59 (1990), p. 29 n. 75, and literature cited there. The problem of assigning the various sentences of the *mishnah* in *Yadayim* to the correct speakers has been addressed by D. Daube, 'Three Notes Having to Do with Johanan ben Zaccai', *JTS* 11 (1960), pp. 53-56; J.M. Baumgarten, 'The Pharisaic Sadducean Controversies about Purity and the Qumran Texts', *JJS* 31 (1980), pp. 162-63.

4. *Shabbat* 14a, See Rashi *ad loc.,* and Maimonides to Zavim, end: *Avot Ha-tum'ot* 9.5.

5. Z. Falk has dealt with these explanations recently, taking them as reflections of actual concerns, the 'deterioration' explanation being more realistic and the 'spreads'

In the Bible, impurity and holiness are two parallel realms, both operating on a principle of contagion by physical contact, with the holy being the realm of true power, and impurity taking on a shadowy existence, in contrast to the pagan 'separate but equal' impurity.[1] Several biblical prohibitions mandate against physical contact with the holy by those not qualified. Such contact is improper and even dangerous, due to the contagious effect and its consequences; 'it [holiness] is conceived as being virtually tangible, a physical entity'; 'material in quality'.[2]

Scholarship has already considered a type of contagious Levitical holiness as being the reason for the *halakhot* requiring washing the hands after contact with the holy scriptures.[3] However, this approach

explanation phrased with premeditated exaggeration, for pedagogic purposes ('The Holy Scriptures Defile the Hands', *Sinai* 106 [5750], pp. 94-95). He further rationalized the 'deterioration' theory as reflecting a practice by priests of using worn parchment sheets from scrolls as tablecloths for eating *terumah*, and the 'spreads' explanation pedagogically exaggerating this concern. I would surmise the actual literary relationship of these talmudic explanations to be in the opposite direction. The harsh language of 'spreads for beasts' was converted to a more refined explanation, thus becoming even further removed historically from the first. Elsewhere, I have discussed 'refinement of jarring language' among characteristic features of editorially reworked texts. For an early rationalization on the 'protection' theme, see L. Blau, *Studien zum althebräischen Buchwesen* (Strassburg, 1902), p. 112.

1. See Y. Kaufmann, *The Religion of Israel* (trans. and ed. M. Greenberg; Chicago, 1960), pp. 103-105, 74, 55-56; J. Milgrom, 'Israel's Sanctuary: The Priestly "Picture of Dorian Gray"', *RB* 83 (1976), pp. 392, 397; *idem*, 'The Graduated Ḥaṭṭā't of Leviticus 5.1-13', *JAOS* 10 (1983), p. 252.

2. M. Haran, 'The Priestly Image of the Tabernacle—IV. The Graduated Taboo', *HUCA* 36 (1965), pp. 216-26; *idem*, *Temples and Temple-Service in Ancient Israel* (Winona Lake, IN, 1985 [1978]), pp. 175-81; J. Milgrom, 'Sancta Contagion and Altar/City Asylum', *Congress Volume, Vienna* (VTSup, 32; 1980), pp. 278-320; see also *idem*, 'Graduated', *idem*, 'The Priestly Laws of Sancta Contamination', in *Sha'rei Talmon* (ed. M. Fishbane and E. Tov; Winona Lake, 1992), p. 139. For earlier literature, see especially W. Robertson Smith, *The Religion of the Semites* (1884; New York 1957), pp. 146, 161, 451; A. Geiger, *Urschrift* (Frankfurt a. M., 2nd edn, 1928), pp. 171-75 (= Heb. trans., pp. 110-12); cf. C. Tchernowitz, *Toledoth Ha-Halakah* (New York, 1936), I, b, pp. 284-86.

3. In its original form, a neutral taboo was usually considered, an area where holiness and impurity meet, thus differing from the concept I will present below. For some of the early literature, or references to it, see Smith, *Semites*, p. 452; F. Buhl, *Canon and Text of the Old Testament* (trans. J. Macperson; Edinburgh, 1892), p. 7;

has been criticized regarding the lack of rabbinic documentation for this type of washing of the hands.[1] It was rejected by Segal, and similarly by Haran, in that the talmudic sources specifically indicate 'defile', and not 'sanctify'.[2]

Is it reasonable to expect that talmudic sources would use appropriate terminology regarding the washing required for hands after touching the holy scriptures if the historical function of the act was the washing away of contagious holiness? I think not. They do not use such terminology in treating clear *biblical* examples of contagious holiness. In fact, the rabbinic sources exhibit studied denial and rejection of the very concept, in a development parallel to the one Kaufmann described regarding the biblical concept of impurity, but more extreme.

The interchangeability of the realms (in the opposite direction), appears in the rabbinic interpretation of Deut. 22.9. The verse reads:

לא תזרע כרמך כלאים פן תקדש המלאה הזרע אשר תזרע ותבואת הכרם:

The *peshat* of פן תבדש, 'lest it be made holy',[3] is circumvented in talmudic interpretation through a *notariqon*. אמר ר' חנינה פן תקדש פן תוקד אש Rabbi Hanina said, '*lest it be sanctified*, lest fire break out'.[4] The obverse of the usual meaning of תקדש was also obtained through

K. Budde, *Der Kanon des Alten Testaments* (Giessen, 1900), pp. 4-5; D.B. Stade, *Biblische Theologie des Alten Testaments* (Tübingen, 1905), p. 136; E. Schürer, *Geschichte des Jüdischen Volkes* (Leipzig, 1907), II, p. 371 n. 18 (= *The History of the Jewish People in the Age of Jesus Christ* [rev. and ed. G. Vermes, F. Millar and M. Black; Edinburgh, 1979], II, pp. 320-21 n. 8; Tchernowitz *Toledoth Ha-Halakah*, p. 286; see below, p. 132 n. 1. G. Lisowsky, *Die Mischna. . . Jadajim*, (Berlin, 1956), p. 50. Cf. Segal, *Introduction to the Bible* (Jerusalem, 1967), p. 821 (Hebrew), n. 26; Haran, 'Canonization', p. 259 (= 241), and n. 37. Louis Finkelstein wrote, 'Just as the Pharisees required the priest to wash away the holiness of the sacrificial meat and the heave-offering before using his hands for mundane affairs, so they washed their own hands after touching a sacred book, to prevent the contamination of the holy with the profane' (*The Pharisees* [Philadelphia, 3rd edn, 1962], I, pp. 278-79).

1. For priests after the Temple service, see Leiman, *Canonization*, p. 193 n. 549.
2. 'Canonization'. Cf. Leiman, *Canonization*, p. 118.
3. See Haran, *HUCA* 36, p. 202 and n. 25. Cf. Geiger, *Urschrift*, pp. 171-72 (trans., p. 110).
4. *J. Pes*. 2.1. 28c; *j. Kil*. 8.15, 31b; *b. Qid*. 56b (Hizqiah), *b. Hul*. 115a.

comparison with *qadeš*, 'cult prostitute' (Deut. 23.18), functionally yielding a neutral '*prohibited* for any use':

ואית דבעי מימר נאמר כאן פן תקדש, ונאמר להלן ולא יהיה קדש מבני ישר׳
מה קדש שנ׳ להלן אסור בהנייה, אף כאן אסור בהנייה,[1]

Onkelos and Rashi carry this line of interpretation even further, and achieve the polar opposite. Onkelos: דילמא תסתאב, 'lest it become *defiled*'! Rashi:

פן תקדש: כתרגומו תסתאב: כל דבר הנתעב על האדם בין לשבח כגון הקדש בין
לגנאי כגון איסור, נופל בו ל׳ קדש כמו אל תגש בי כי לקדשתיך,

Lest it be made holy. Like its Targum 'lest it become defiled'. Any object under taboo (lit. 'abomination') whether in the positive sense, like *heqdeš* (consecrated temple property), or in the negative sense, such as through a prohibition, can be designated by *qdš* as 'Don't come closer, for I would render you *qdš*' (Isa. 65.5).[2]

The new JPS translation of Deut. 22.9 chose more neutral ground in defusing this crux: 'may not be *used*'. This can hardly be considered a literal translation of פן תקדש. The root *qdš* is still used in Tannaitic literature in this context (e.g. *m. Kil.* 4.5).

Regarding the sin offering, the Torah warns, 'Anything that touches its flesh shall become holy',[3] namely, will receive holiness through

1. *J. Kil.* (*ibid.*) Rashbam comments: 'lest it become prohibited like holy sacrifices'. A third interpretation in the Palestinian Talmud may come closer to the heart of the matter, were we to accept Penei Moshe's redirection (even by paraphrase and not emendation) to Exod. 29.37! מניין שהוא אסור בהנייה, נאמר כאן פן תקדש ונאמר להלן פן תוקדש בו מה פן האמור להלן אסור בהנייה אף פן שנ׳ כאן אסור. בהנייה פני משה: פן תוקדש בו לא נמצא זה בפסוק וטעות הוא וצ״ל כל הנוגע במזבח יקדש. However, *Cod. Vat.* reads ונא׳ להלן פן תוקד בו correct to פן תוקש בו, Deut. 7.25 which is acceptable at least in terms of meaning. Also, see *Sifre Devarim*, par. 230 (ed. Finkelstein), p. 263 and notes.

2. Compare Rashi, *b. Shev.* 18b, s.v. *qerav* קרב אליך, עמוד בעצמך. ליצני הדור היו אומרים לנביא עמוד בעצמך אל תגע בי שלא אטמאך, שאתה קדוש, ואני טמא, קדשתיך, טמאתיך, כמו (חגי ב) הן ישא איש בשר קדש, וכמו (דברים כב) פן תקדש in contrast to Rashi, Isaiah, *ad. loc*. An intense reaction to the rabbinic interpretation is found in Mahberet Menahem, along with an intricate original interpretation by the author, based on the concept of intermingling of irretrievable Levitical tithes ([ed. H. Filipowsky; London and Edinburgh, 1854], pp. 105-106). Ibn Ezra presents a brief synthesis of Menahem, which, in his commentary to Hag. 2.12 approaches communicable holiness (see below, p. 126 n. 5).

3. Lev. 6.20 כל אשר יגע בבשרה יקדש.

contact with the holy sacrifice. Similarly Ezek. 46.20, 'This is the place where the priests shall boil the guilt offerings and the sin offerings, so as not to take them into the outer court and make the people consecrated'.[1]

Sifra *ad loc.* is most instructive:

> *Anything that touches its flesh shall become holy.* One might think, even if it had not absorbed; Scripture instructs, *its flesh*, only if it absorbs. One might think that even if part of it touched, all of it will become invalid; Scripture instructs, *that touches shall become holy*, what touches is invalid. How (should one act)? Cut off the place of the absorption. *Its flesh*, and not bones, sinews, horns or hoofs. *Will become holy*, to be like it. If it is invalid, it will become invalid, and if it is valid, it will be eaten, according to the most stringent status it possesses.[2]

This remarkable pericope exemplifies a thorough rejection of the concept of contagious holiness. Rather than an electricity-like quality that is conducted through all matter by contact, holiness is limited to the very substance of the original sacrifice, and transfers to another object *only if that object absorbs some of the fluid of the sin offering*![3] The extent of contamination is limited to the physical area of actual liquid absorption.

Even more astounding is the fact that according to this passage, it is not *holiness* at all that transfers, but rather the *halakhic status* of the sin offering, namely, either validity or invalidity to be consumed by

1. לבלתי הוציא אל החצר החיצונה לקדש את העם
Ezekiel would probably have translated the above verse in Leviticus: 'Any *one who* touches its flesh. . . '; cf. Num. 19.16, 22, etc. Compare Milgrom, 'Sancta Contagion'.

2. כל אשר יגע בבשרה יקדש: יכול אעפ׳ שלא בלע, תלמוד לומר בבשרה, לד שיבלע: יכול אף נגע במקצתו יהיה כולו פסול, תלמוד לומר, אשר יגע יקדש, הנוגע פסול: הא כיצד, חותך מקום הבלע: בבשרה ולא בעצמות ולא בגידים ולא בקרנים ולא בטלפיים: יקדש, להיות כמוה, ואם פסולה תפסל, ואם כשירה: יאכל כחמור שבה. *Sifra*, *Ẓav*. 3.5, 32b; *b. Pes*. 45a; *b. Zev*. 97a-b; *b. Naz*. 37b. Cf. *Sifra*, *ibid*., 3.6, 31a, to Lev. 6.11.

3. See Rashi *ad b. Zev* 97b, top. Rashi's position is that absorption of taste would not be sufficient, and here it is actual substance שאין זה טעם אלא ממש. This figured centrally and controversially in the famous halakhic discussions טעם כעיקר, היתר מצטרף לאיסור

the priests, the actual language of the Tannaitic law emphasizing *invalidity*.

Similarly, Exod. 29.37, regarding the altar, 'whatever touches the altar shall become holy'[1] generated *m. Zev.* 9, entirely devoted to validity or invalidity of becoming potential sacrifices, for animals or objects touching the altar. Its functional import is that an object that is potentially valid for becoming a sacrifice, or even bearing a minor invalidity, if placed upon the altar, shall not be removed (אם עלה לא ירד). It is a type of propriety, similar to rules like מעלין בקדש ואין מורידין. But sacrifices bearing a greater level of invalidity are simply removed, without becoming 'holy'. At most, 'consecration', but hardly 'sanctification', and certainly not contagious holiness, automatic, 'material in quality'.[2] In fact, the talmudic *halakhah* actually allows non-priests to *touch* the altar.[3]

Regarding Exod. 30.29, which indicates holiness by touch for the table (שלחן), lampstead (מנורה), altars, and other vessels, there is little rabbinic material. *M. Zev.* 9.7 applies the same law we have discussed for the altar to all of these. In this context it may be most suggestive to quote *m. Hag.* 3.7 '. . . and they say to them, "take heed least ye touch the table and lampstead"'! Even though existing rabbinic interpretation is otherwise, it would be interesting to speculate whether this

1. כל הנגע במזבח יקדש *NJPSV*: 'Shall become *consecrated*'. I have unified the translation with Lev 6.20. The discrepancy in *JPS* ('holy'/'consecrated') may have to do with unedited divergencies of different translators, or the acceptance of the Talmudic interpretation here, see below. Regarding a reponsum by R. Sherira Gaon on the entire *sugya*, see S. Abramson, *R. Nissim Gaon* (Jerusalem, 1965), p. 254 n. 38.

2. Cf. *Sifra*, beg. *Ẓav.*, 29a-b; *b. Zev.* 83b; *b. Sanh.* 34b. Pseudo–Jonathan (and glosses) correctly expanding the import of Onkelos, sidesteps this tradition in taking כל הנשע more literally as referring to people: כל דיקרב במדבחא יתקדש מן בני אהרן ברם משאר עמא לית אפשר להן למיקרב דילמא יתוקדון באישא מצלהבא דנפיק מן קודשיא reflecting the above-cited interpretations to Deut. 22.9. Cf. Exod. 30.29. The indebtedness of this language in Pseudo-Jonathan to the talmudic sources can be added to Milgrom, 'Sancta Contagion', pp. 280-81. On the rabbinic redefinition of the altar's power, cf. J. Neusner, 'From Scripture to Mishnah: The Origins of Mishnah's Fifth Division', *JBL* 98 (1979), pp. 274-75.

3. אך אל כלי הקדש ואל המזבח לא יקרבו: יכול אם נגעו יהו חייבין אמרת אך, משום עבודה זר הן חייבין, אין חייבין משום מגע. (*Sifre Zutta* to Num. 18.3, p. 291); לא יקרבו לעבודה, אבל ליגע מותרין. (Maimonides, Klei ham-Miqdaš 3.9).

quote represents an early concern reflecting the very biblical prohibition quoted above.[1]

Holiness through contact was still a clear and expressed concept in Ezekiel's description of the Temple (chs. 40–48), for example, the requirement for the priests to deposit the garments used in the divine service before exiting to the outer court, 'Lest they make the people consecrated by (contact with) their vestments' (44.19).

In Hag. 2.11-13 it figures in a halakhic question (*torah*) that the prophet poses to the priests, their answer serving as the text upon which he bases his exhortative homily.

> Thus said the Lord of Hosts: Seek a ruling from the priests, as follows: If a man is carrying sacrificial flesh in a fold of his garment, and with that fold touches bread, stew, wine, oil, or any other food, will the latter become holy? In reply, the priests said, 'No'. Haggai went on, 'If someone defiled by a corpse touches any of these, will it be defiled?' And the priests responded 'Yes'.[2]

1. The actual wording (in Danby's translation) is: 'Take heed lest ye touch the table *and render it unclean*', based on the standard editions. E.g., Albeck: הזהרו שלא תגעו בשלחן (ובמנורה) ותטמאוהו. However, the Kaufmann Codex has היזהרו ומא תגעו בשלחן ובמנורה. Other conservative textual witnesses also lack ותטמאוהו (see J.N. Epstein, *Mavo L'Nosah Ha-Mishnah*, p. 145 n. 4; cf. R. Hananel), and consequently it must be viewed as an explanatory gloss. Even the exact meaning of this gloss was disputed. The general context of this passage, purification of the holy vessels which became defiled during the festival (itself a worthy subject for comparison with the biblical laws, which are summarized and interpreted in Milgrom, 'Sancta Contamination'; cf. *idem*, 'Sanctuary'; 'Graduated', pp. 253-54) was clearly the inspiration for the explanatory gloss. However, the very idea that the menorah and table might be defiled by touch during the actual purification ritual (the simple sense, cf. R. Hananel *contra* Rashi) is most surprising, especially if this warning was made to priests (cf. R. Rabbinovicz *ad loc.*, p. 92 n. 8; concerning an ancient concern about *seeing* these Temple vessels, cf. A. Büchler, *JQR* 20 [1908], pp. 330-46). Our Mishna passage has recently been discussed in the context of sectarian disagreement on the role of the populace in the Temple; see Y. Sussman, 'The History of the Halakha and the Dead Sea Scrolls', *Tarbiz* 59 (1990), p. 68; I. Knohl, 'Participation of the People in the Temple Worship', *Tarbiz* 60 (1991), p. 141. Although the Second Temple period was marked by preoccupation with *purity and defilement* it is possible that the wording of this 'warning' harks back to the (forgotten?) *biblical* concern for *holiness*, and the mandatory avoidance of contact with the vessels embodying it.

2. כה אמר ה׳ צבאות שאל־נא את הכהנים תורה לאמר הן ישא־איש בשר־קדש בכנף בגדו ונגע בכנפו אל־הלחם ואל־הנזיד ואל־היין ואל־השמן ואל־כל־מאכל היקדש, ויענו הכ הנים

The first question deals with transferable holiness, Haggai's 'sacrificial flesh', corresponding to contact with flesh of the sin offering mentioned in Lev. 6.20, the second with transferable impurity. Both are still clear and valid concepts, though it would appear that holiness is not as readily transferable as impurity.[1] However, talmudic discussion, attributed to first generation Amoraim, construes both of Haggai's questions as being issues of *Levitical impurity only*.[2] Thus Rashi, in his Talmud commentary *ad loc.*, explains 'sacrificial flesh' (בשר קדש) as 'flesh of an unclean thing' (שרץ);[3] 'will the latter become *holy*' as 'will it become *impure*'.[4] We shall see that this interpretation by Rashi is completely warranted by the talmudic discussions.

In an intricate discussion, the talmudic *sugyot* envision several possibilities as to what Haggai asked the priests in his first question. *None* of these considers the simple meaning, communicable holiness, thus demonstrating how far the sages had distanced themselves from this biblical concept. It is true that they suggested that the query concerned 'a fourth stage transmission in holiness'.[5] However, this concept has nothing to do with contagious *holiness* but rather the law that *impurity* (!) communicates through three stages only, except if the object

ויאמרו לא. ויאמר חגי אם יגע טמא נפש בכל־אלה היטמא, ויענו הכהנים ואמרו יטמא

Prophetic oration based upon a halakhic question is also found in Jeremiah 3. The same style—opening of the 'if' clause of the question with הן, is also found there, where the question is posed rhetorically (cf. Lev. 10.19-20). Jer. 3.1 opens with לאמר, which precedes הן in Haggai also. However the occurrence in Jeremiah, where it stands alone, is a famous crux. The truncated form was caused through loss of text, or is an elliptical style. These explanations seem superior to connecting it artificially and unsuccessfully with 2.37, as Radaq *ad loc.*; see P. Trumer, 'The Infinitive Construct of the Verb 'to Say' לאמר', *Te*ᶜ*uda* 7 (1991), p. 93. One cannot resist comparison with the truncation through ellipsis of a quotation formula at the head of each She'ilta of the She'iltot, producing an abrupt statement of a law (which will be the subject of a homily!) beginning with ד־ (for previous discussion, see J.N. Epstein, *JQR* ns 12 [1921], pp. 305-307; S.K. Mirsky [ed.] *Sheeltot* I [Jerusalem, 1957], intro., p. 20).

1. However, it does, presumably, transfer to the garment.

2. *J. Sot.* 5.2, 20b; *b. Pes.* 17a. ששאלן תחלה על דבר טומאה... וחזר ושאלם עוד בדבר טומאה (R. Hai Gaon).

3. בשר קדש. שרץ, לשון קדש היה בארץ (מלכים א, יד:כד) טומאה. See below, p. 130 n. 4.

4. Cf. *Aruch Completum*, VII p. 208 היקדש. כלום נטמא.

5. (Sotah) וכי יש רביעי בקודש; (Pesahim) רביעי בקדש בעא מינייהו

receiving the impurity is sacred, in which case even a *fourth* stage will be disqualified for its sacrificial functions (*m. Hag.* 3.2).[1] In this scheme, the sacrificial flesh is not the *emanator*, but the *receiver* of the contagious quality, which is the quality of *impurity*.[2] In fact, in PT *ibid.*, R. Yohanan excuses the priest's incorrect answer to the first question, in that 'he asked them (this question) *before* they had decreed a fourth derivative stage (for impurity communicated through) sacred objects'.[3] The other amoraic authorities who considered the priests' first answer incorrect explained this as due to their inferior expertise in a specific type of *impurity*.[4]

The Haggai passage is one of the best examples of the biblical concept of holiness transmittable by contact, in that the application is clear, and the juxtaposition with impurity exemplifies the parallel nature of these two realms.[5] The extended talmudic discussion of this passage, where various interpretations were offered, without one of these acknowledging transferable holiness, or citing a tannaitic tradition that does, shows how completely this belief and its legal impli-

1. הרביעי בקדש פסול, והשלישי בתרומה. Cf. *t. Hag.* 3.18 (ed. Lieberman, p. 390) and parallels. In line with this, the terminology found in R. Hananel and Aruch, 'invalid' and not 'impure,' is more accurate: היקדש, כלו׳ היפסל (*Aruch Completum* VII, p. 245); וטעו והשיבו לא קדש, כלומר, לא נפסל המאכל (R. Hananel).

2. Explicit in the Palestinian Talmud in connection with R. Levi's position that Haggai asked concerning a *fifth* stage כנף תחילה, ובשר קודש שני, ונזיד שלישי וכו׳. Similarly R. Hananel to BT *ibid.*: הן ישא איש בשר קדש בכלנף בגדו שנגע בו שרץ, ונגע הבשר בכנף בגדו הטמא, ונגע עוד הבשר בלחם או בנזיד או ביין... נמצא הכנף של בגדו שנגע בשרץ ולד ראשון כי השרץ הוא אב ונמצא הנוגע בו ולד ראשון והבשר שנגע בכנף שני ואלו הלחם והמיד והמשקין הללו שנגעו בבשר שלישי וכו׳. R. Hai Gaon advanced the sacrificial meat itself to the fourth stage. הן ישא איש בשר קדש, ממש, בכנף בגדו, ונגע אדם בעדו לבוש כנפו אל הלחם ואל הנזיד הכמאין משרץ... והלחם ראשון, האדם שני, הכנף שלישי, הבשר רביעי (*Otzar ha-Gaonim* [ed. B.M. Levin. III, 1930; *Pesahim*, p. 16). Now almost literally הרביעי בקדש!

3. אמר רבי ירמיה רבי חייה בשם רבי יוחנן קודם עד שלא גזרו רביעי בקודש שאלן

4. ר אחא בשם רבי אבא בר כהנא, בקיאין היו בהיסטות ולא היו בקיאין במדפות (Palestinian Talmud) אמר רב נחמן אמר רבה בר אבוה בקיאין הן בטומאת מת ואין בקיאין הן בטמאת שרץ (Babylonian Talmud).

5. This point is successfully recovered by Ibn Ezra in his anti-talmudic polemic: בשר קדש. כמשמעו, קודש ממש, והפך יקדש יטמא. ואם יקדש יטמא, למה ישנה והנה השאלה על בשר קדש שכתוב וכל אשר יגע בבשרה יקדש...

Onkelos (היסתאב), Rashi and Radaq follow the talmudic explanation; also Radaq, *Sefer ha-Shorashim*, pp. 321-22.

cations had disappeared from rabbinic thought. When it became necessary to interpret the legal status concerning this quality transmitted by contact, *the familiar laws and terminology of Levitical impurity were substituted.*

The biblical phenomenon of contagious holiness, clearly expressed in the Torah in priestly passages regarding the altar and sacrifices, in Ezekiel, and Haggai, and also in non-priestly contexts regarding contact with the holy ark, was eliminated in rabbinic tradition, so far as our sources reveal. This represents a theological development in rabbinic Judaism parallel to, and continuing, trends described by Yehezkel Kaufmann. The automatic power of impurity, functioning as an elemental cosmic humor, was reinterpreted as simply a legal status imposed by divine decree, part and parcel of the system of commandments. Similarly regarding impurity: 'The corpse does not defile. . . I have issued it as a decree; you are not permitted to trespass My decree'.[1]

The rub-off type of holiness underwent an even greater transformation.[2] Touching the altar imposes sacrificial status upon objects that touch it only if they are halakhically qualified; otherwise nothing happens. Sacrificial flesh does not transfer its status by touch; the biblical law is interpreted as actual absorption of the sacrificial liquid, so that the first object is actually contained in the second. Where this type of transformation does not fit, since the details of the transfer-by-contact laws are too explicit, the entire complex of the the laws of *impurity*, terminology and functional superstructure are substituted for holiness through contact.

This presentation of the thorough transformation of the biblical concept of contagious holiness in rabbinic sources goes beyond Milgrom's description of a gradual evolution of this concept within the Bible, and extending through the Tannaitic literature.[3] He writes: 'Haggai attests a further reduction. . . The final reduction in sancta contagion is posited in the Tannaitic sources. . . '.[4] This change from

1. *Pes. K.* 4.7 (ed. Mandelbaum; New York, 1962), I, p. 74. See Rom. 14.14

2. Geiger has noted that the halakha attempted to resist the idea of transfer of holiness by touch (*Urschrift*, pp. 172-73 = trans. p. 111).

3. Milgrom's seminal study came to my attention after the body of this article had been written. I am grateful to Dr Baruch Schwartz for pointing it out to me.

4. 'Sancta Contagion', p. 297.

the position of Haggai, the final stage of the biblical evolution, to that of the Tannaim, 'is minuscule',[1] according to Milgrom. In my mind, in fact, it was too great an evolution to be viewed in quantitative terms alone,[2] and the rabbinic concept must be considered qualitatively different.

Indeed, it would appear from the rabbinic sources that holiness was no longer considered a substance-like quality which acts automatically, the very two characteristics which justify the use of the term 'contagion' regarding holiness in the Bible. In passages where this concept does figure, it is instead a halakhic category, determined by God's decree,[3] no more and no less. In other contexts it is completely removed by rabbinic interpretation.

I have tried to demonstrate this with respect to three categories of rabbinic style. In the first, terminology somewhat similar to that of the Bible is used, and therefore, it is more difficult to demonstrate my contention. המזבח מקדש את הראוי לו—'The Altar makes holy whatsoever is prescribed as its due' (*m. Zev.* 9.1)—does overlap כל הנוגע במזבח יקדש —'Whatever touches the altar shall become holy'

1. 'Sancta Contagion', p. 298.

2. 'Reduce the compass' (Milgrom, 'Sancta Contagion', p. 282); 'the rabbinic reduction of the sancta's powers of contagion' (p. 282 n. 15); 'the rabbis restrict its meaning further' (p. 282 n. 16); 'the rabbis impose further restrictions' (p. 283 n. 17); 'the rabbis restrict the power of the altar even further'; 'the rabbis reduce the power of all the sancta' (p. 290 n. 39).

3. Milgrom writes, 'The fact is that impurity retains its lethal potency all during the biblical period and into rabbinic times. . . Why then does the power of impurity remain undiminished whereas the power of holiness is successively reduced?' ('Sancta Contagion', pp. 298-99). I would prefer to alter both of these evaluations, as far as rabbinic theology is concerned. The *power* of impurity is *much* diminished. Milgrom himself has referred to the rabbinic 'reduction in the power of impurity' ('Graduated', p. 253). According to the above-cited statement of Rabban Yochanan ben Zakkai, it has in fact entirely disappeared, and impurity has been redefined as a halakhic status: 'The corpse *does not defile*'. I have presented this in literal translation, and departed from the Braude-Kapstein translation, 'The corpse does not have the power by itself to defile' (Philadelphia 1975, p. 83, used for the rest of the text above), although it can convey the same idea. The kernel style is reminiscent of *m. Roš. Haš.* 3,8. See also J. Neusner, *The Idea of Purity in Ancient Judaism* (Leiden, 1973), p. 105. The 'power of *holiness*' is not simply reduced, but similarly transformed. It is no longer automatic, and therefore does not operate on its own. God and his decrees are the only independent realm.

(Exod. 29.37). But the automatic quality implied in the biblical language is set aside by את הראוי לו of the Mishnah, which carries a flavor of *propriety*. If objects qualified to be sacrificed on the altar are placed on the altar, it is not *proper* to remove them אם עלו לא ירדו.[1] However, did the mistaken placing of an object upon the altar automatically impose upon it an irrevocable holiness, such as in the Bible?[2] I think not. Consequently, כשם שאם עלו לא ירדו, כך אם ירדו לא יעלו—Just as what goes up may not come down again, *so what comes down may not go up again.* (*m. Zev.* 9.4)![3]

The basic thrust of these laws is the fact that contact does *not* impart automatic holiness. אותו ואת בנו שעלו ולשבי מזבח ירדו שאין המזבח מקדיש אלא את הראוי לו '"It and its young" (Lev. 22.28) which went up the altar *must come down*, for the altar sanctifies only what is fit for it' (*Tos. Zev.* 9.4). The power of halakha has vanquished the power of the holiness of the altar!

Furthermore, we have seen that contact with the sin offering is not described in the rabbinic sources as absorption of the holiness, but absorption of its actual liquid. Thus, the sanctity does *not* transfer from one substance to another.

The absence of any explicit description or allusion to physical sancta contagion, and the substitution of other categories—halakhically expressed propriety, and limitation to actual substance of liquid transfer—argue that the former concept was no longer operative in rabbinic thought.

Category two: פן תקדש of Deut. 22.9 was midrashically reinterpreted in such a way that it was removed from the simple meaning of the root *qdš*, and from the very concept of 'holiness'. One may argue that this is an anomaly, in that the rabbis did not preserve

1. Hence, instead of 'makes holy' in Danby's translation cited above, I would prefer 'consecrates', just as I prefer '*become holy*' for the verse in Exodus to *JPS* 'become consecrated'.

2. Num. 17.3.

3. Cf. *m. Zev.* 9.8. In the parallel Tosefta: כשם שאם עלו לא ירדו, כך אם ירדו לא יעלו ואם עלו ירדו. Milgrom ('Sancta Contagion', p. 283 n. 18 and see p. 279 n. 3) explains this source also in terms of sancta contagion, with reference to S. Lieberman, *Tosefet Rishonim* (Jerusalem, 1938), II, pp. 210-11. Indeed, Lieberman does base his explanation upon a concept of holiness by contact. However, his explanation of why the *second* contact is ineffective is completely halakhic.

any tradition that linked this law with the quality of holiness, and, as such, were forced to substitute a midrashic interpretation. Of course, this does not contradict my contention, and may even support it.

However, it is the third category that is most telling. The context in Haggai is absolutely explicit. The parallelism with impurity is abundantly clear. Only a quality that transfers by *contact* can be meant by these verses. The extremely forced doubling of impurity for our passage and imposing upon the word היקדש, already in early rabbinic literature, the meaning היטמא, the diametric opposite of its simple meaning, is the absolute demonstration of the fact that the very concept of contagious holiness was no longer available to these rabbinic sages.[1]

Reverence for the Torah, at the inception of the Second Temple, emerges clearly from Nehemiah 8. The same passage also describes the beginning of the process of the ritualization of the Torah scroll. Undoubtedly much attention was given to scriptures and the proper handling of the scrolls during the Persian and Hellenistic periods; the activity of the *Soferim* was recalled generally by later tradition, but no specific sources regarding their activities survived this period.[2] The scrolls themselves eventually became independent sources of holiness, by virtue of their inspired contents, and by virtue of the sanctified name of God, which they contained.[3] The sanctity of various parts of Scripture is evaluated on a graduated scale.[4]

1. Milgrom address this only obliquely (in a slightly different context): '"*yiqdaš*" in Hag. 2.12 is rendered by the rabbis as yitma. . . but this is due to their *unique interpretation* of this verse' ('Sancta Contagion', p. 281 n. 14, emphasis added). I have tried to expose the root of this unique interpretation. I would like to add that my conclusions are completely compatible with the major thrust of Milgrom's study namely, the gradual and ultimate elimination of the concept of sancta contagion to persons.

2. See S. Lieberman, *Hellenism in Jewish Palestine* (New York, 1962), II, pp. 20-22.

3. See *t. Shab.* 13.5 (ed. Lieberman, p. 58) and parallels. מה אם להטיל שלום בין איש לאשתו אמ׳ המקום ספר שנכתב בקדושה ימחה על המים וכו׳. Cod. Erfurt: שמו, which is the more developed reading, as in the talmudic parallels (*Tosefta Kifshuta*, p. 207). Uninspired, or sectarian use of the name created a conflict (*t. Shab.*). The text can be (or must be) destroyed; the writing of the name must be preserved and guarded: קודר את הזכרותיהן וגונזן, ושורף את השאר.

4. *J. Meg.* 3.1, 73d-74a נותנין תורה ע״ג תור׳. . . אבל לא נביאים וכתובים על גבי תורה וחומשין. . . ר׳ ירמיה בשם ר שמואל בר רב יצחק תור׳ וחומשי׳ קדוש׳ אחת הן

During the early post-Second Temple period, when halakhic literature was finally recorded after a gap of centuries, the touching of Torah scrolls, those of the prophets and the other Sacred Writings, is included within those situations which bring about a necessity to wash the hands ritually (*netilat yadayim*). The terminology and legal-conceptual system appearing with these laws is that of 'impurity'—the holy scriptures defile the hands. We possess no demonstrable explanation for this situation. The only logical hypothesis that has been offered is that the washing of the hands protects one from spreading the sanctified quality of the holy books to non-worthy objects (as the blood of the sacrifices was to be laundered off garments).[1] Indeed the sources themselves connect the 'impurity' of the books with their holiness: 'Did they not decree that Scriptural books defile the hands *because they are sacred?*'[2]

The theory connecting the defilement of the hands by scriptural books with tangible-like transferable holiness was rejected due to the fact that the sources use explicit impurity terminology for this phenomenon. We have seen that this cannot be considered a valid refutation, in that biblical passages clearly dealing with that concept of holiness are also transferred to the legal categories of Levitical *impurity* by Talmudic sources.[3] If anything, therefore, such terminology is a recommendation. An idea originally related to a concept of the transfer of *sanctity* from the holy books to the hands that touched

1. Lev. 6.20. Similarly, in the *Testaments of the Twelve Patriarchs*, the priests are required to wash the blood of the sacrifices from their hands and feet והא באדין תשרא למזרק דמא על כותלי מדבחה ועוד רחע ידיך ורשליך מן דמא 'then begin to sprinkle the blood on the sides of the altar, and again wash thy hands and thy feet from the blood' (*JQR* 19 [1907], pp. 573, 580). Cf. *Jub.* 12.16-17 (Kahana, p. 263), *T. Levi* 9.11 (Kahana, p. 165). Cited by Finkelstein (see above). If precaution against improper spreading of holiness was a special concern of the Persian or Hellenistic periods, but not taken over by the sages, it is not surprising that this practice is not recorded in rabbinic literature. Leiman's criticism of Finkelstein (*Canonization*, p. 193 n. 549) therefore does not apply to our reconstruction.

2. See above. These laws even specify that purity is a required attribute for generating this 'impurity'. *T. Yad.* 2.12 תיק הספרים ותיבה של ספרים ומטפחות של ספר, בזמן שהן טהורין מטמאות את הידים

3. *M. Zav.* 5.12. The entire category of impurity of 'hands' alone, removed by ritual hand-washing, and not related to impurity of the whole body, is an anomaly vis-à-vis biblical law. It must also derive from an early period, with insufficient documentation surviving.

them was ultimately couched in terms of *impurity*, in that this was the only realm in rabbinic theology where such a transfer by contact survived.[1]

1. In contrast to the early approach, which envisioned an actual overlapping of the concepts of holiness and impurity here. Cf. Geiger: 'die Berührung heiliger Gegenstande mache unrein' (*Urschrift*, p. 174, and p. 146; trans., p. 112 and p. 95).

REUBEN*

Judah Goldin

Nothing exhibits the rabbinic awareness of even the tiniest details inside biblical verses studied or taught as do the tannaitic and post-tannaitic exegetical midrashim. The same applies to even the homiletic midrashim on a particular verse or verses invoked as proem, or in the body of the commentary[1] to represent a whole pericope. 'Is not He the Father who created you (*qnk*; root, *qnh*)' (Deut. 32.6b). *Sifre Deuteronomy* 309[2] offers the following:

> Moses said to Israel, 'You are the ones precious to Him, you are the *purchase* (*qnyn*) He made for Himself—you're not merely an inheritance for Him.' By way of parable: Instance someone to whom his father left ten fields as inheritance and then the son *bought*[3] one field of his own. That field the son loved more than all the fields his father gave him as inheritance. . . Similarly, Moses said to Israel: 'You are the ones precious to Him, you are the purchase He made for Himself—you're not merely an inheritance for Him'.[4]

* This paper is concerned only with the narrative as we have inherited it, and midrashic commentary thereon; not in historical or proposed historical reconstruction or sociology Both what a story tells and does not tell are revealing of the author's (or authors') outlook. Except for midrashic need, biblical citations are from NJPSV. *ARN* = *Abot de-Rabbi Natan*, ed. S. Schechter, Vienna, 1887. All references to *Genesis Rabba* are to the edition by J. Theodor (Berlin, 1912)-Ch. Albeck (Berlin, 19287); *Leviticus Rabba* = ed. M. Margulies (Jerusalem, 1954–58). *Sifre Deuteronomy* = ed. L. Finkelstein (New York, 1969).

1. See *Lev. R.*, Part V (Jerusalem, 1960), Xff., and A. Goldberg in *Leshonenu*, 38 (1964), pp. 163-69.

2. Ed. L. Finkelstein, 349.

3. *qnh* not *lqḥ*.

4. I.e., descendants of the patriarchs. Indeed, not till after twenty generations does Abraham appear; *M. Abot* 5.2, *ARN* 46b-47a.

That *qnh* (*qanah*) means 'created', the Rabbis knew from Gen. 14.19: '*qnh* heaven and earth'.[1] (From whom could He possibly have purchased them? Gen. 1.1.) Here, however, they chose 'purchase' (cf. Gen. 49.30). The dual possibilities of *qnh* are hardly the most startling example of rabbinic focus on a specific term and sensitivity to its more than one meaning. There are more examples that can be enlisted; to furnish just one more, *ml'k* can mean both angel and messenger (hence, not improperly also 'prophet').[2] But their attentiveness goes very much further: they do not ignore defective spellings alongside full spellings;[3] kere and kethib idiosyncrasies;[4] 'Read not. . . but' (*'l tqry. . . 'l'*) proposals;[5] perfects in imperfect form[6] (biblical tenses are only hazily connected with time; gematria employed as code.[7] This incomplete choice of their approaches is meant simply as a spelling-out of the summary statement that the Sages ignored hardly a particle of Scripture, that without concordances and auxiliary aids, they knew their Bible inside out,[8] although perhaps some lists were drawn up, as is later reflected, for example, by *Abot*, beginning of chapter 5, and by *ARN*. This is not to imply that there was something miraculous or supernatural about the gifts of these Bible-masters. After all, what else did they read if they were not to follow the lead of an Elisha ben Abuyah?[9] Moreover, without vocalization signs in their scrolls (and later in codexes too; the same true of course of Dead Sea scrolls),

1. See Theodore's comment on *Gen. R.* 43.7, 421, and Rashi and Kimhi on the Genesis verse. JG, *The Song at the Sea* (New Haven, 1971), pp. 228-30 and notes *ad loc.* Cf. the first interpretation in Leqah Tob, 33a.

2, *Lev. R.* 1.1, 3-4 and notes p. 3.

3. On Ephron (Gen. 23.10, 13, 16), *Gen. R.* 23.7, 627. See E.Y. Kutscher, *The Language and Linguistic Background of the Isaiah Scroll* (Jerusalem, 1959), pp. 6-8, 57-65 (Hebrew).

4. E.g., *Tanḥuma*, Meq-qeṣ, ed. Buber, pp. 9, 95b (R. Simon).I have so transliterated this time because such is the primary spelling in *Webster's*. Note John Milton's irritation in his 'Apology for Smectymnus' in F.A. Patterson, *The Student's Milton* (New York, 1934), p. 534, col. a; 'Areopagitica', p. 738, col. b.

5. *Tanḥuma*, *ibid.* (ed. Buber, pp. 13, 99b; or *Pesikta de-Rab Kahana* (ed. Mandelbaum; New York, 1962), p. 1 line 9; etc.

6. Cf. *Mekilta*, Shirta [so!] (beginning), ed. J.Z. Lauterbach, II, 1.

7. E.g., *rdw* = 210 (*Tanḥuma*, ed. Buber, on Gen. 42.2b).

8. *Midrash ha-Gadol, Deut.* (ed. S. Fisch; Jerusalem, 1972), p. 737, and incorporated by D. Hoffmann in *Midrash Tannaim*, p. 205.

9. *b. Hag.* 15b (towards bot.), and note Rashi, s.v., 'noshrin'. (Naturally on the assumption that this is not mere amoraic piling insults on his head.)

despite orally transmitted pronunciation, considerable freedom with wordplay was inevitable. And because they were captivated by the contents of Scripture, saw in its injunctions an immediate imperative,[1] and had accepted that it was divinely revealed (cf. Exod. 20.19 [Eng. 22]; Lev. 26.46; 27.34), they studies it atom by atom (as Greeks did Homer; but the Jewish passion was much more intense)[2] and noticed everything.

This concentration on thoroughness underscores all the more seriously the absence of comment on a puzzle in a biblical narrative, Genesis 34. Here is given the account of the ravishing of Dinah and the brutal vengeance executed by her brothers Simeon and Levi.

Simeon and Levi, who are they? The second and third sons of Jacob and Leah, the unfavored wife, gave birth to. Where was Reuben, the first-born, the oldest son?[3] Simply to say that apparently he did not join his two younger brothers, and therefore the narrator does not speak of him, is no answer. For even if that were the case, it would still call for notice; Reuben did not join Simeon and Levi because of... what? Indifference? He is not given to impulsive or rash behavior. He is as timid as his father (Gen. 34.5, 30).[4] How can it be

1. Cf. *Sifre Deut.* 33, p. 59; *Deut. R.* (ed. Lieberman; Jerusalem, 1974), p. 117.

2. For the Jews, Wisdom = Torah at least from Ben Sira (c. 200 BCE) on, and is to be pursued by all, not just philosophers or their privileged associates. Cf. the anecdote in *Tanna de-be Eliyahu* (ed. Friedmann; Vienna, 1904), pp. 195-96 and *Tanḥuma*, Wa-Yelek 2 (on Deut. 31.1). Everything is in the Torah (Abot 5.22 and *ARN*, 28a). This is not to deny that there were many analphabetics in their society (especially in Galilee; cf. M. Bar-Ilan in *PAAJR* 54 (1987), Hebrew section, pp. 1-12. Cf. Bickerman citation in Eichler-Tigay (next note), p. 281).

3. On the theme of younger son favoritism, cf. B.L. Eichler and J.H. Tigay (eds.), *Studies in Midrash and Related Literature*(Philadelphia, 1988), pp. 121-39; and on the Tamar story (Gen. 38), see M.A. Friedman in *AJS Review* 15 (1990), pp. 23-61 (I'm indebted to Professor Friedman for this reference and a copy of his fascinating study).

4. In Egypt Reuben upbraids his brothers (Gen. 42.22); note how Joseph seats his brothers at the 'banquet' he prepares (Gen. 43.33); Jacob calls Reuben 'my might and first fruit of my vigor, exceeding in rank and exceeding in honor (Gen. 49.3); on the Reubenite city of refuge, *Deut. R.* (ed. Lieberman), p. 60; the first born to be redeemed (Exod. 13.13b, 15b)—but that is tit for tat, as v. 15 says. However, the deuteronomic law (21.15-17) is emphatic on his importance; the *bkwr* of the levir carries on the father's name (Deut. 25.6); even the prophet Samuel assumes at first, mistakenly, that Jesse's firstborn, Eliab, is the one intended by God (1 Sam. 16.6ff.) and it is Eliab, as first-born, who rebukes David for neglecting the flock and

that the oldest son when he hears that his sister has been violated remains far in the background,[1] if there?

Several answers are impossible. We are not told that he was absent when the brothers heard about the outrage; Scripture does not even hint that. Lack of courage? Reuben did not lack it, as his readiness to oppose all his brothers determined to shed blood demonstrates (Gen. 37). They frustrated his intent—even if we prefer to assume that he acted out of self-interest. Perhaps sisters don't matter. Not true even for biblical story-tellers (see 2 Samuel 13; and cf. v. 14b with Gen. 34.2b!—worse than Shechem!). Serah, the daughter of Asher, is merely an item in a genealogical list (Gen. 46.17; Num. 26.46; 1 Chron. 7.30), yet she is individualized more than once. The Rabbis assign to her an important role: she was the one who informed Moses where to find the dead bones of Joseph,[2] without which the Israelites could not advance toward the promised land, or, if they did, they would be breaking the promise (the oath!)[3] originally made.

Fact is that almost everything reported of Reuben by the biblical narrators might be to his credit—even that one shocking action on his part (Gen. 35.22), sleeping with Rachel's handmaiden (Gen. 29.29), Jacob's concubine (Gen. 35.22) may be granted—but not by Scripture—a quasi-positive defense.[4] If the early Palestinian amora, R. Yohanan, can come up with more than a mild apology for Judah's conduct (*Gen. R.* 85.8, 1041f.) with the veiled street-sitter (*wtšb*), one need not feel that it is gauche to act as Reuben's defense attorney. He brings mandrakes he found in the field during wheat harvest to his mother as a gift (Gen. 30.14 and note vv. 15-16). That it is not a small gift is evident from Rachel's desire and from what she was prepared to grant in exchange (Gen. 30.14ff.). Reuben wishes to

appearing at the battle scene (1 Sam. 17.28). God calls 'Israel my first-born son' (Exod. 4.22). See further Num. 3.40-43; Ps. 89.28 of David! A first-born surely has responsibilities. Joseph tries to correct his father (Gen. 48.13, 17-18). And note Reuben in Gen. 37.22, 29-30.

1. Note 'few in number' in Gen. 34.30 and (of Reuben) Deut. 33.6 (see below). Intended as echo?

2. Mekilta, Be-Shallaḥ 1, ed. Lauterbach, I, pp. 176-77. (This version is certainly superior to that of ed. Horovitz-Rabin, p. 78; cf. J. Goldin in E.S. Fiorenza, *Aspects of Religious Propaganda in Judaism and Christianity*, Notre Dame, 1976, pp. 127-29 and notes *ad loc.*) And on Serah, see also *Midrash Mishle* on Prov. 31.26!

3. Gen. 50.25; Exod. 13.19.

4. Cf. above p. 135 n. 3 for reference (pp. 132-34).

protect Joseph from the hideous intentions of all his brothers. he offers extravagantly (foolishly)[1] to be responsible for Benjamin's safe return. But he is out of favor in his father's eyes.

It is customary to assume that Reuben was first discredited because of the Bilhah affair. Scripture itself associates criticism of him with his mounting his father's bed, as can be seen from Jacob's last testament to his sons (Gen. 49.3-34), and much later the Chronicler (1 Chron. 5.1) still refers to it.[2] Is there a faint echo in Moses' blessing, Deut. 33.6b, 'though few be his numbers'? Nevertheless, at least one midrashic comment refers to a Reubenite as 'a well of Torah'.[3] Esau sold his birthright and later regretted it (Gen. 25.31-32; 27.36); Reuben neither sold nor lost his official status as 'first born', *bkwr* (35.23 and repeatedly), and theoretically, perhaps received a 'double portion' legacy (Deut. 21.15-17) although he was regarded unfavorably.

I now wish to propose—despite Scripture's silence (and my being reprimanded likely and properly, as was Akiba by Judah ben Batyra, *Sifre Num.* 113, ed. Horovitz, 122)—that there are early traces of discontent with Reubenites, hence Reuben.

Already in the Song of Deborah, Reubenites were rebuked: 'great searchings of heart' (Judg. 5). 'The historical value of the Song of Deborah can hardly be exaggerated. It is the oldest extant monument of Hebrew literature, and the only contemporaneous monument of Hebrew history before the foundation of the kingdom'.[4] In the rebellion of Korah and his company of 250 sympathizers, only Dathan and Abiram (cf. Ps. 106.17) and On ben Peleth, 'the Reubenites', are mentioned by name and by tribal affiliation;[5] not the tribe of Levi!

1. *Gen. R.* 91.9, 1132.

2. In the *Testament of Reuben* (*The Testament of the Twelve Patriarchs* in Charles, *Pseudepigrapha*, pp. 296ff.) fornication is Reuben's fault; there's no reference to his absence from, or presence at, the Dinah affair. Nor is there allusion to Reuben's absence in the review of the Dinah story in *Jubilees* 30, concerned principally with intermarriage with Gentiles. On which incidentally, cf. R. Hunya in *Gen. R.* 80.11, 966! (And for variety of attributions, cf. Albeck's note.)

3. For a positive view of Reuben, cf. *Deut. R.* 7.5 (Wilna, 114a, top); and note yalqut Shimeoni (offset Salonica, 1527), 1086 (on 1 Chron. 5.6; already noted by A.M. Padua in leqaḥ Ṭob, Wilna, 1884, Deut. 63b, n. 31). *b'rh* is possibly a pun on *b'r*, interpreter. Cf. *Midrash ha-Gadol*, Deut. 761, line 23.

4. G.F. Moore, *Judges* (ICC, 1901), pp. 132-33.

5. On 'On ben Peleth', see *Tanḥuma Korah* 24, ed. Buber, 47a: saved by his

Asking what is not relevant is characteristic of the clod (golem), and that is exemplified by Reuben, according to both versions of *ARN* (56b). The prooftext is Gen. 42.37, the very verse in *Genesis Rabba* (91.9, 1132) that Rabbi (Judah and Prince?) employs to illustrate the expression 'mad first-born' (*bkwr šwṭh*).[1] Such is the rabbinic attitude toward Reuben, and it is an articulated estimate of him along the lines of the biblical attitude. Note also how R. Tarfon used to dismiss incompetent expositors (ARNB, p. 112)! This makes it all the more surprising that the Midrash fails to call attention specifically to Reuben's absence from the violent attack on the Shechemites. He was from the very first slighted (because he was devoted to his mother, who had to bargain for a night with her husband?). Why? I have no suggestion as alternative to what was proposed in 1977: first-born in biblical narrative is displaced by the younger:[2] a folk protest against the presumptions of the Establishment.[3]

And not only in Midrash[4] is there no reference to Reuben's absence from the aggression against the Shechemites, but in the classical medieval commentators also.[5] Not in R. Joseph Bekor Shor's commentary on Genesis; nor in Abarbanel in spite of his eloquence or longwindedness.—And by the way, this possibly (I say tentatively) may illuminate the course adopted by exegetes: Whatever early commentators comment on, later commentators tend to comment on; what the early ones do not, the latter also tend to ignore.[6]

Regardless of what documentary source or sources the Dinah story

wife. Cf. NJPS, 234, note *b-b*. N.b., only in 16.1 is On referred to; thereafter only Dathan and Abiram.

1. Cf. S. Lieberman, *Hellenism in Jewish Palestine* (New York, 1962), p. 12 and n. 50.
2. See reference above in p. 135 n. 3 (p. 139).
3. What the *folk* cherished; cf. Eichler-Tigay, p. 139.
4. Review, for example, all the relevant entries in M.M. Kasher, *Torah Shelemah*, V, 1320-35. On the passage from Mekilta, Shirta 10, II, 52, cf. *Song at the Seat*, 245 f.(nothing on Reuben, only on 'brothers of Dinah', Gen. 34.25), and the theme is 'giving one's life in behalf of someone'.
5. At least those assembled in *Torat Chayim* (Jerusalem, 1987), II, 117-19. Whether Y. Kaufman (in *Toledot ha-Emunah ha-Yisraelit*, I, Tel-Aviv, 1937, very bottom line of n. 17, p. 178) is sensitive to our problem, I cannot make out.
6. Obviously this is no more than impression; perhaps it deserves further research.

may derive from,[1] nowhere in Scripture is there genuine respect for Reuben. He is indeed the *bkwr* of Jacob; the genealogists do not allow us to forget it; he is thoughtful of his mother. He will not collaborate with his vindictive brothers. But there seems to be a sustained prejudice against his tribe and him, and therefore it is not the first-born but Simeon and Levi, the second and third sons of Jacob, 'the brothers of Dinah', who rise against the people of Hamor and Shechem. How come no one care to emphasize this—even among the modern commentators?[2]

Supplementary Note

I regret to disagree entirely with E.A. Speiser's summation of the story although not of course with his suggestion of what may be the historical foundation on which the narrative is ultimately constructed, in the light of ancient Near Eastern developments. S. Yeivin[3] also suggests a historical basis, in terms of the history of *Israel*; and presents a Carta map of the Reubenite territory. 'The story', Speiser says,

> is a tale of sharp contrasts. . . candor and duplicity. There is a marked difference between the generations. Hamor and Jacob are peace-loving and conciliatory; their sons are impetuous and heedless of the consequences that their acts must entail. The lovesick Shechem prevails on his father to extend to the Israelites the freedom of the land—with the requisite consent of his followers. But Dinah's brothers refuse to be far-sighted. After tricking the Shechemites into circumcising their males, and thus stripping the place of its potential defenders, they put the inhabitants to the sword. Jacob is mournful and apprehensive. But his sons remain defiant and oblivious of the future.

I have deliberately quoted almost in full in order to crush any impulse in me toward cantankerousness; we are dealing with the view and words of an important scholar, and he deserves genuine respect.

1. Cf. Speiser, *Genesis* (AB, New York, 1964), pp. 266-67; J. Pedersen, *Israel* (London, 1926), pp. 521-22, note to p. 291; and the commentators in the next note.
2. Of course I have not read all of them. I have checked only Speiser (see preceding note), Dillman (*Genesis*, Edinburgh, 1897, pp. 287ff.); Gunkel (7th edn, and note on p. 377); Skinner (ICC, 1956, pp. 421-22); G. von Rad (1966, pp. 329-30); S.R. Driver (Westminster, 1924, pp. 305-306); Ehrlich (*Mikra Ki-Pheshuto*, 1969, p. 96); Sarna (JPS Commentary, 1988, pp. 237-38).
3. *Encyclopaedia Biblica*, Hebrew (Jerusalem, 1976), VII, pp. 285-94.

But hardly a sentence in this concluding paragraph of his may be tolerated. Fathers and sons do differ, long before Turgenev. That Shechem wants that girl desperately is said in vv. 3 and 8. How long that will last is anybody's guess, but let it pass. He never advised his father how to conciliate Jacob's family: the text never says it. Note the order of names, Hamor first, Shechem second in vv. 20, 24 and 26. True; first father, then son. But the original idea is Hamor's. All his son says is, I want that girl for a wife; get her for me; name whatever high bride-price you want. The Son presumably knows he can depend on his father's cunning. He is right. Hamor is a thorough liar—the author of the narrative never calls him that; if he wishes to report deception, lying speech, he will say it without hesitation of the sons of Jacob (v. 13, *bmrmh*, *be-mirmah*; a literary stroke of genius!).[1] Of Hamor, he simply presents a 'tape recording' of how he speaks to the Jacob family and then speaks to the Shechemites, his own people! And Rashi already called attention to it (in his comment on v. 16)—no wonder Ehrlich in *Mikra Ki-Pheshuto* exclaims in admiration. What is more, in speaking to his own people Hamor never lets on what prompted his geopolitical shrewdness. No surprise therefore that Shechem did not procrastinate and the Shechemites submit without protest: all that property and prosperity, and their women *nochdazu*. (As for our women, we'll decide whom they can have.)

Simeon and Levi behave like savages. And the last verse of ch. 34 informs us why: exactly what Judah (Gen. 38.15, 21, 24), the fourth son later thought that veiled street-sitter was. Whether the crime deserves such devastating punishment, let the legislators or lawyers decide—certainly not Jacob, either in the light of his early capitulation (with fears!) to his mother, his long postponed outburst against his uncle/father-in-law, his fear of a *rencontre* with Esau, or his keeping quiet until his sons returned: and now, what will the neighbors do!

No one in Genesis 34 emerges clean-handed or clean-minded (and in a book full of a number of wonderful stories, the 'Dinah' is especially dramatic: complete objectivity). Compare it with the flat digest thereof by Josephus (*Ant*. 1.337-40). As for Philo, see Loeb Classics, *Philo*, X, index s.v. 'Dinah'—'virgin soul and shameless fool': abstract reflection, philosophizing. All blood has been drained

1. Note Isaac's tone of sadness in Gen. 27.35 (and Esau's outcry in vv. 34 and 36).

out of the scandal, in which all have had a part, and a most human one, though not humane.

The story can still make headlines; see the daily newspaper.

The Aramaic Incantation Bowls in Historic Perspective

Cyrus H. Gordon

Though the Aramaic bowls of talmudic Babylonia are abundant and well known, general awareness of their ancient roots and late survivals lags over a quarter of a century behind the publication of sources pointing in new directions.[1]

The earliest inscribed magic bowls are among the thirteen Egyptian 'Letters to the Dead' chiefly from the Old and Middle Kingdoms. Six of the Letters are written on ceramic bowls. The Letters are requests or threats addressed to deceased relatives for help, on the premise that the dead in the West could exert influence on those they left behind in the land of the living.

In the Letters we find the matronymic personal name Mereri son of Merti. In the Aramaic bowls virtually every personal name is matronymic (contrary to regular Semitic usage). Matronymy is more in keeping with Egyptian than with Semitic sociology. (One's male protector in Egypt was not one's father but one's maternal uncle). There are also other features of the Aramaic bowls that are anticipated in the Egyptian Letters to the Dead.[2]

The magic bowl tradition was modified in the various regions through which it spread. The practice in the Near East and Mediterranean was to deposit the bowls inverted. Two inscribed Minoan incantation bowls were found buried upside down under a

1. For orientation, see J.A. Montgomery, *Aramaic Incantation Texts from Nippur* (Philadelphia: University Museum; 1913); and J. Naveh and S. Shaked, *Aramaic Incantation Texts of Late Antiquity* (Leiden: Brill, 1985).

2. S.R. Keller, 'Ancient Egyptian Letters to the Dead in Relation to the Old Testament and Other Near Eastern Sources' (PhD dissertation, New York University; Ann Arbor, MI: University Microfilms, 1989).

floor of the palace at Knossos.[1] The Linear A texts written on them are in the Northwest Semitic Minoan language which has Aramaic affinities including terminology familiar from the Aramaic incantation bowls.[2] Uninscribed magic bowls of the Mycenaeans have also been discovered; they are regularly found deposited upside down. The significance of inverting the bowls is expressed in the bowl-texts themselves.[3] Inverting the bowls represents the upsetting (annulment or cancellation) of the black magic directed at the clients through the curses (spells) of their enemies. Moreover, the overturning is also often 'symbolic' of the personified curses being sent back to the enemies (who set the curses in motion) so that the enemies are to suffer the woes with which they had hexed the clients. I have used the word 'symbolic' in order to make this practice more easily comprehensible to the modern reader who does not believe in magic. For the ancients, however, the practice was not considered merely symbolic, but was thought to have a genuine effect. Analogously, a liberal adherent to a conservative form of Christianity (such as Roman Catholicism, Eastern Orthodoxy or the Coptic Church) may say that in the sacrament of communion the wafer symbolizes the body and the wine symbolizes the blood of Christ, but to a true believer the wafer and wine become his actual flesh and blood. Until we grasp that for the bowl magicians and their clients their practices were causally effective (and not symbolic), we are not in a frame of mind for understanding the topic under discussion.

Magic is very syncretistic. Various ethnic groups within the community of people who resorted to the incantation bowls are listed on a bowl designed to protect the clients from the spells of 'Aramaeans, Jews, Arabs (?),[4] Persians, Hindus, Greeks and Romans[5]—in any of the seventy languages—by women or men—against them, their

1. The Minoan Linear A texts are collected by L. Godart and J.-P. Olivier in *Recueil des inscriptions en Linéaire A* (5 vols.; Paris: Gauthier, 1976–85). See vol. IV, pp. 118-25, for the two incantations.

2. E.g. C.H. Gordon, *Evidence for the Minoan Language* (Ventnor, NJ: Ventnor, 1966), p. 27 (§119), pl. IX.

3. C.H. Gordon, *Or* 10 (1941), p. 117, text 1, which opens thus: אפיכה אפיכה ארעה אפיכה ארעה. . . אפיכין כל נידרי ולוטתה: 'upset, upset is the earth, upset is the earth. . . are all the vows and curses. . . '

4. C.H. Gordon, 'Correction to D:9', *ArOr* 9 (1937), p. 106.

5. The term is כיחין.

children, camels, horses, oxen, asses—all great and small cattle—and all their possessions'.[1] Note that the text aims at covering everything—all the languages, all the spells from whatever source—to protect the whole family and every species of their livestock. It should be remembered that domestic animals were considered members of the community.[2]

The syncretism appears in many ways. A spell that ends, 'Blessed art thou YHWH, God of Israel. Amen, amen, selah', can scarcely be anything but Jewish. Yet it also invokes the Mandaic Yu-kabar Ziwa son of Rabbē. An ecumenical note is struck by attributing to YHWH a concern for the welfare of all mankind: 'Blessed art thou, O YHWH who heals the ills of all flesh'.[3] Furthermore, one of the bowls,[4] though in the distinctively Jewish Aramaic script, is for Gentile clients: 'Araznish' is Persian, while גריגור, 'Gregory', and בתחדשבה, 'Daughter of Sunday' (cf. 'Domenica / Dominique') are Christian names.

Since pre-Christian times, trilogies have been common in Jewish usage. 'Holy, holy, holy' (Isa. 6.3) is one of the most striking of many examples. Note also familiar formulae such as, 'we have eaten, been satisfied and have left (something) over', 'who has kept us alive, sustained us, and caused us to reach (this happy occasion)', and so on. Note the triplicate invocations of God in the bowl formula, 'YHWH, YHWH, YHWH; 'El Shadday, 'El Shadday, 'El Shadday. In the name of "H "H "H, YH YH YH'.[5]

Against the foregoing background, it is not altogether surprising to find a Jewish (but completely non-Christian) form of the Trinity:[6] 'In his Holy Name. And in the name of Metatron, the Great Prince of the

1. C.H. Gordon, *ArOr* 6 (1934), p. 328, text D.
2. Thus domestic animals belonging to Hebrews are to rest on the Sabbath; in the Tenth Plague, the first-born of Hebrew (but not Egyptian) cattle were spared; the Ninevites who had to fast and wear sack-cloth included the cattle (Jon. 3.7-8; cf. 4.11) and so on.
3. Gordon, *Or* 10, p. 127, text 7.12. Although this incantation is Jewish and Yahwistic and invokes Hebrew Scripture, all the clients are Gentile with no Jewish names. It would have been completely out of place to refer to Yahweh as the healer of his people Israel in this text.
4. C.H. Gordon, *ArOr* 6 (1934), pp. 321, 322, text A.
5. Gordon, *Or* 10, p. 125, text 6.3.
6. C.H. Gordon, *ArOr* 9, p. 94, text L.

Entire Universe. And in the name of Raphael, the Prince of all healings'. The Holy Name corresponds to God the Father. Metatron (μετὰ θρόνον), whose name means 'next to the throne', corresponds to Jesus the Son, who on the Day of Judgment is to sit on God's right, and is the παντοκράτωρ, who rules the world. Raphael corresponds to the Holy Spirit; a prominent manifestation of the Holy Spirit is the ability to heal the sick by casting out demons (for example in the Acts of the Apostles).

A repeated device for ridding clients of female liliths (and also, somewhat whimsically, of male demons) is to serve on them a bill of divorcement formulated by the famous Rabbi Joshua son of Perahiah. This role of R. Joshua is not mentioned in rabbinic literature. Jesus of Nazareth had a wide reputation as an exorcist and wonder-worker. He appears as such in rabbinic literature,[1] where he is associated with Joshua bar Perahiah. The association is historically impossible because the latter lived in the century before Jesus. Joshua bin Nun and Jesus of Nazareth are both called Ἰησοῦς in Greek, for 'Joshua' and 'Jesus' are indeed the same name. Apparently, some Jews in early Christian times felt the need for a master-exorcist 'Joshua' of their own. Joshua bar Perahiah, a reputable rabbi among the 'pairs' in the *Pirke Abot* (1.6), was selected for the role. Such legends are in no need of historic support.

Rabbinic bills of divorcement have to be delivered in letter form. In the bowls the document served on the lilith or demoness is called אגרת שיבוקיכי, 'the letter of thy abandonment'.[2] There is another bowl text[3] in which the spell is specifically called אגרתא, 'the letter', reminding us of the Egyptian Letters to the Dead.

One of the Letters to the Dead is inscribed on a jar-stand, on which refreshments had apparently been placed to gain the good will and assistance of some spirit. In this connection it is interesting to compare a ritual described in an Aramaic bowl, whereby the magician or client goes up on the roof to mollify demons by offering them food. The text[4] reads,

1. The references in rabbinic literature are cited by M. Jastrow, *Dictionary*, p. 599b, sub ישו.
2. Gordon, *ArOr* 6, p. 169, text G.7
3. Gordon, *ArOr* 6, p. 93, text L.4
4. Gordon, *Or* 10, p. 349.

> I went up to the roof at night and said to them [If you are hungry, come], eat; and if you are thirsty, come, drink; and if you are dry, come and be anointed. But if you are not hungry, thirsty or dry, return and go [back] by the road on which you came, and enter the house from which you went out, and enter the mouth from which you went out.

Another bowl[1] refers to a similar ritual thus, 'Enter! Come! Here is meat to eat and here is wine to drink! They opened their mouths and said to us, Who is entering your house?' The clients have thus extended hospitality to the demons which the latter have declined. Therefore they will depart without any grievances.

The Letters to the Dead are all posted in tombs so as to be in the realm of the dead. The Aramaic bowls are usually buried under houses, often at the four corners of the dwelling. However, the Mandaic bowls from Khouabir were found in a cemetery; two of them[2] are labeled on the exterior surface of the bowls דבית קובריא 'of the graves' (a normal Semitic equivalent of Egyptian tombs).

The above should convey an idea of the setting into which the Aramaic incantation bowls fit. I have not considered the rich Mesopotamian background because it is in the process of expanding dramatically.[3]

1. Gordon, *Or* 10, p. 342.

2. E.M. Yamauchi, *Mandaic Magic Texts* (AOS, 49; New Haven, CT: American Oriental Society, 1967), p. 162, (text 4) and p. 208 (text 16).

3. See C.H. Gordon, 'The Ebla Exorcisms', *Eblaitica* 3 (1992), for the bearing of the Ebla Archives (c. 2300–2250) on the background of later magical texts including the Aramaic incantation bowls.

From the Workshop of The New Jewish Publication Society Ketuvim Translators

Moshe Greenberg and Jonas C. Greenfield

Prologue

In 1966, after ten years of intensive labor, the first NJPS translation committee had published only the Torah (1962) and was busy with the Haftarot and the Five Megillot (*Preface to Five Megillot*, 1969). To enhance the chances that the project would be finished within the lifetime of those concerned it was decided to appoint a second committee to work simultaneously on translating Ketuvim (minus the Megillot). The Prophets were the territory of the first committee since they had already made inroads into them in translating the Haftarot (their complete translation of the Prophets appeared in 1978).

The composition of the second committee was modeled on that of the first: three academics—Moshe Greenberg, Jonas C. Greenfield and Nahum Sarna, and three rabbis—Saul Leeman (Conservative), Martin Rozenberg (Reform) and David Shapiro (Orthodox). It was understood that the rabbis would keep in view the place of the Bible in the life and liturgy of the faith community and thus act as a sobering curb on the scholarly hobbies and idiosyncrasies of the academics. The secretary and facilitator of the committee was the JPS editor, Chaim Potok.

A critical experience at the outset of our labor was a visit to a working session of the first committee. Their intense engagement was impressive, and manifest in the high tones of argument. But points seemed to be carried as much by aggressive rhetoric, persistence and assertion of authority as by prooftext. The effect on us was decisive: we drew up a set of guidelines for procedure whose gist was this: any change proposed from the draft had to be supported by documented prooftexts and appeals to standard authorities. If one could not persuade the others within a reasonable time he would retire from the field; if he did not a vote would decide the issue.

Operating procedure was as follows: the task of preparing the first draft was equally divided among the academics, each academic responsible for a third of each book (for example Sarna for the first 50 psalms, Greenberg for the second 50, Greenfield for the last 50). The draft included annotations justifying the renderings. It was circulated by mail among all members for their comments. In accord with the guidelines, any proposal for change had to be justified in writing. The comments were sent to Potok who distributed them by mail to each member. The committee met to fashion the (first) committee draft, having before it all the homework. Every word of the text, Hebrew and English, was weighed, and in the end the consensual rendering was recorded by Potok. The guidelines were faithfully adhered to; there was no pounding on the table and very, very few decisions by vote. If one failed to persuade the others he withdrew his proposal. Occasionally we disagreed over a choice between English expressions; having exhausted argument to no effect, we turned to Potok to break the deadlock. Aside from his administrative task, such arbitration was an important service to the committee.

Since Sarna had done a good deal of study of Psalms, he was entrusted with the pathbreaking task of preparing the draft of the first 50 chapters. In a way it was a thankless task, because the likelihood of divergence of opinion was greatest during this first round of common labor, when we were least attuned to one another. The drafter was never at a later point so likely to miss the consensus, and therefore to witness such a thorough dismantling of his effort. Nor was there at any later point such a volume of comment, as each member gave voice to his thoughtful ruminations on Sarna's drafts. In belated appreciation of Nahum's pioneering work, the good spirit in which he took criticism of the draft, and in pleasurable recall of sixteen years of amicable, harmonious and deeply satisfying cooperation, we offer a small sample of the evolution of our Psalms translation from Sarna's draft to the printed edition.

We have chosen Psalm 39 for our sample because it is among the most richly commented upon—every committee member had a documented part in its fashioning. We have before us the original pages of comment by each member, and have presented the contribution of each to maximal fullness. To simulate something of the dynamic of the work, we have restructured the material in dialogue form, as indeed it was the basis of lively dialogue among us. Editorial comment by us is enclosed in brackets. Moshe Greenberg is largely responsible for this Prologue and vv. 2-5 (the title in v. 1 is not discussed in our notes), Jonas Greenfield for vv. 6 onward and the Epilogue.

39.2 אמרתי אשמרה דרכי מחטוא בלשוני\אשמרה לפי מחסום\בעוד רשע לנגדי

Sarna Draft
I resolved, / I will guard my ways, / Lest I sin with my tongue; / I will keep my mouth curbed, / So long as the wicked man is present.'
['Keep my mouth curbed' renders what is literally 'keep / guard a muzzle for my mouth'—a fusion of 'guard / watch my mouth' and 'put a muzzle to my mouth'.]

Discussion
Greenberg: Direct speech with 'resolve' is un-English. 'Sin with tongue' not immediately clear; one curbs his tongue [as he would an untamed horse] but muzzles [= blocks the opening of] his mouth. Proposal: 'I resolved I would watch (or: to watch) my step / lest I offend by my speech; / I would keep (or: to keep) my mouth muzzled / While the wicked was present'.
Leeman: 'lest I sin with my speech'.
Rozenberg: 'sin with tongue' is stronger than 'speech' for it brings to mind 'evil tongue' [לשון הרע = calumny]. For 'keep my mouth curbed' read 'stifle my speech'. Delete 'man' [wicked man].
Greenfield: My horsemanship is limited, but one curbs (restrains, governs) the tongue (imaged as an animal) but muzzles (literal translation of חסם) the mouth. Technical details in Feliks, החקלאות, 255-57. 'Guard my ways' is too stiff and Greenberg's 'watch my step' too colloquial, though it catches the nuance; perhaps 'watch my ways'?

Committee Draft
I resolved I would watch my step[a] / Lest I offend with my speech; / I would keep my mouth muzzled, / While the wicked was present.
Note a: lit. 'ways'.
['Offend' replaced 'sin' as the context is not specifically theological; throughout NJPS alternatives to 'sin' appear in such contexts. The

committee was unwilling to adopt 'watch my step' without reservation, hence the note. The use of a definite adjective in the singular ('the wicked [= the wicked man] was') appears elsewhere in our translation (e.g. in v. 9. 'the benighted', = נבל preferred for terseness [Jespersen, *A Modern English Grammar*, II, pp. 232-33]); but the courage of the committee failed eventually in this case.]

Printed Version
I resolved I would watch my step, / Lest I offend by my speech; / I would keep my mouth muzzled, / While the wicked man was in my presence.
[Note a. was deemed pedantic; 'by' suits better the act-word 'speech' (bordering on a verbal noun, 'speaking'); 'in my presence' is closer to Hebrew's suffixed form.]

39.3 נאלמתי דומיה\ החשיתי מטוב\ וכאבי נעכר

Sarna Draft
I was dumb, silence itself; / I held back from pleasure, / While my pain was troublesome.

Discussion
3a
Greenberg: דומיה is 'waiting in stillness, quietly expectant'; both notions are present here and in 62.2 [אל אלוהים דומיה נפשי], and in the related verb in 37.3 [דום לה']; 62.6 [לאלוהים דומי נפשי].
[*Greenfield* concurred; see his comment on v. 3b. Notes that Seidel takes the word as 'speech'.]
Rozenberg: 'I waited in utter stillness' [merges the two words].

Committee Draft (= Printed Version).
I was dumb, silent;
[Committee preferred brevity and clear reflection of two words]

3b
Greenfield: The progression in vv. 3-4 is from expectant silence (Greenberg) to an outburst of speech; 3a and 3b are parallel. Aramaic חשי occurs in the *Genesis Apocryphon* 20.16: ובכית וחשית, 'I cried silently'.

Greenberg: 'I said nothing good'. The simplest rendering, whatever it means. Possibly: things went so badly, there was no opportunity for me to say anything good (3a, b, c would then be stages in the deterioration of his condition). Or: my resolution to keep quiet (v. 2) went so far as to exclude even saying a good word about anything (not only a bad one that might have offended).
Rozenberg: 'I shrunk in silence from saying even good'. מטוב contrast with מחטוא בלשוני of v. 2—good versus sinful speech. The psalmist is so afraid of offending he refrains from saying even that which is good.
Shapiro: Draft seems out of context; one suffering greatly wouldn't have to say that he refrained from seeking pleasure. Render either: 'I held back from speaking even good (of God)—lest I arouse the wicked to sarcastic comment on God's allowing his favorites to suffer. Or טוב might equal 'speech'—so M. Seidel in חקרי מקרא (citing Hos. 14.3: קחו עמכם דברים . . . קח טוב . . . שפתינו) and Dahood:
Greenfield: Seidel's suggestion is approved by Yalon (*Quntresim*, p. 23); does Seidel cite Neh. 6.19 where טובותיו \\ דברי? (Löw's reading).

The draft of 3b is very difficult but so is the rendering of מטוב as 'good'. Perhaps it equals Aramaic טובא, 'very much', which Gordis (*JTS* 35, pp. 186-87) finds in לטוב in Jer. 15.11, Mic. 1.12.
Leeman: One has the feeling that החשיתי מטוב continues the theme of being silent ('I was good and quiet')—rather than refraining from pleasure.

Committee Draft
I was exceedingly[b] still.
Note b: cf. use of *ṭwb* in Mic. 1.12, Jer. 15.11, Hos. 10.1, Jon. 4.4.
[The strained interpretations of מטוב yielded to the neat and simple adverbial construal (Greenberg noted later Hebrew adverbial function of -מ as in מעומד, 'while standing'). Lehman's parenthesis gave a happy semantic English parallel for 'good' meaning 'very much'.]

Printed Version
I was very[a] still.
Note a: cf. use of *ṭwb* in Hos. 10.1; Jon. 4.4.
[The briefer word prevailed; the citations were limited to those passages in which the Prophet's committee rendered טוב similarly.]

3c
Greenfield: נעכר with Kissane, 'stirred up'. He kept still though he suffered pain.
Greenberg: 'Troublesome' is too mild. I tried 'was distressing'—but that's unsatisfying too. It seems to mean, 'cast a pall over everything, blot out consciousness of everything else'. The *niphal* form נעכר, like נמרץ ['grievous'], describes that which is alive with or productive of the root idea [עכר = make turbid].

Committee Draft (= Printed Version)
While my pain was intense.
[Committee despaired of finding a semantic parallel.]

39.4 חם־לבי בקרבי\ בהגיגי תבער־אש \ דברתי בלשוני

Sarna Draft
My blood[a] boiled inside me; / At the thought of it[b-] I was in a furor[-b]; / I spoke aloud[c].
Note a: lit. 'heart'. Note b-b: lit. 'a fire blazed'. Note c: lit. 'with my tongue'. Annotation to 'blood boiled': cf. Deut. 19.6 [יחם לבבו, NJPS: 'in hot anger'].
[Multiple notes reflect tension between a desire to render idiomatically and fidelity to the letter of the text.]

Discussion
Leeman: A better parallelism with the first verset would result from rendering the second 'Within my mind (note: lit. 'thought') a fire blazed'.
Rozenberg: Draft misses the progression: 'My feelings grew tense within me / As I reflected they burned as fire / Then I spoke out (or: gave tongue to my speech)'.
Shapiro: 'Blood boiled', 'in a furor' implies great anger—as in Deut. 19.6, but the context indicates that Psalmist is experiencing rather the inability to control his grief and pain. Jer. 10.9 is a more likely parallel (והיה בלבי כאש בערת), NJPS: 'But [his word] was like a raging fire in my heart'.
Greenberg: 'Blood boils' suggests, in the first place, indignation (though it can mean any strong emotion [OED *s.v.* boil]); here frus-

tration and resentment take priority. Proposal: 'My mind heated up inside me / My thoughts were all aflame / I spoke out'.
Greenfield: Draft says more than text; whence 'at the thought of it'? Greenberg makes him sound like an oven. Render the second verset, 'My mind was troubled' (note: lit. 'was aflame'). Note for the pun: Arabic *hğğ* = 'to blaze'.

Committee Draft (= Printed Version)
My mind was in a rage / My thoughts were all aflame; / I spoke out. ['Rage' implies a boiling over of feeling; it often connotes a sense of frustration, a temporary mental derangement, or a determination to take revenge (Webster's *Synonyms*). Notes have gone by the wayside; the Hebrew letter means what we translate.]

39.5. הודיעני ה׳ קצי\ ומדת ימי מה־היא. אדעה מה־חדל אני

Sarna Draft
Lord, let me know when my end will come, / What be the measure of my days, / That I might know how [d-]fleeting is my life[-d].
Note d-d: meaning of Hebrew uncertain. Annotation to 'fleeting חדל': cf. our 17.14 חלד 'fleeting'], taking Heb. as metathesis, with Mezudat Zion ['A transposition of חלד, like כבש / כשב']; cf. Targum ['when I will be gone from the world'.]

Discussion
Shapiro: After 'I spoke aloud' the vocative 'O Lord' is more fitting.
Greenfield: קץ here, as in the Dead Sea Scrolls, means 'appointed time, term'.
Greenberg: Proposal: 'Tell me, O Lord, what my term is [= Hebrew word order] / What is the measure of my days / I would know how short-lived I am (or: fleeting my life is). Taking this, with Saadya and Kraus (*Biblischer Kommentar*), to hold up to God how short-lived he has made man, as a basis for the appeal to his mercy (vv. 8ff.).

Committee Draft
Tell me, O Lord, what my term is / What is the measure of my days: / I would know how fleeting[c] my life is.
Note c: meaning of Hebrew uncertain.

Printed Version
As committee draft, except that note c is omitted.
[We rendered Ps. 89.48 אני מה חלד 'how short my life is' noting its uncertainty—is חלד transposed from our חדל? But we became convinced that our Heb., from a root meaning 'come to an end', has the semantic range of 'ephemeral'.]

39.6 הנה טפחות נתתה ימי\ וחלדי כאין נגדך \ אך כל־הבל כל־אדם נצב סלה

Sarna Draft
Lo, you have set [e]a strict measure[e] for my days; / My life span is as nothing in your sight / [d] Surely all upstanding men are utter futility[d].
Note e-e: lit. handbreaths; note d-d: meaning of Hebrew uncertain
Annotation: 'upstanding' = anthropos erectus!

Discussion
6a-b
Greenberg: We must get in the visual image of טפחות, 'handbreaths'; note the use of הנה to call attention to טפחות. I suggest 'you have made my life just handbreaths long; / Its span is as nothing in your sight.'

Committee Draft (= Printed Version)
You have made my life just handbreaths long; / Its span is as nothing in your sight;

6c
Greenberg: With Sa[c]adya who translated *qawām jami[c]an-nās kal-haba* I take this verse to mean 'no man lasts any longer than a breath'. נצב is to be taken verbally as 'endures' and כל as כְּל, 'comparable to, as'.
Greenfield: Can נצב mean 'set up', i.e. 'man is initially set up as הבל'?
Rozenberg: 'every man of station is as nothing' or, 'every man in existence is but nothing'.
Shapiro: This phrase does not refer to anthropos erectus. The fact that man is upstanding has no particular significance as far as the transitory character of his existence is concerned. Why not 'firmly planted' following the Aramaic use of נצב, with the accent on the ephemeral existence of the seemingly firmly planted.
[The committee decided to follow Sa[c]adya but to mark it as 'meaning of Hebrew uncertain'.]

Committee Draft (= Printed Version)
[c-]No man endures any longer than a breath.[-c]
Note c-c: meaning of Hebrew uncertain.

39.7 אך בצלם יתהלך־איש \ אך־הבל יהמיון \ יצבר ולא־ידע \ מי אספם

Sarna Draft
Surely, man goes his way in darkness[f]; / Surely, he bustles about in vain, / Heaping up (wealth), knowing not who will take it home.
Note f: or 'as a shadow'. Annotation to 'darkness'; 'as Rashi, Qimhi, Ibn Janah'.

Discussion
7a
Greenberg: צלם is to be taken as parallel with הבל which encases it, 'Mere, no more' renders repeated אך better than 'surely'. Proposal: 'As no more than a figment he walks about'.
Greenfield: What is a figment and how does it translate הבל? Man's walking in darkness is a thematic metaphor, and 'darkness' is from the etymological and contextual point of view the best translation.
Rozenberg: Change the order: 'man moves about as a mere shadow'.
Leeman: I'm a bit disturbed by three consecutive lines, all beginning with 'Surely'. Surely, we can find some way out.

Committee Draft
As a mere shadow he walks about;

Printed Version
Man walks about as a mere shadow;
[The committee finally preferred a more straightforward translation.]

7b
Greenberg: Mere futility is his hustle and bustle.
Rozenberg: His bustle sheer futility.

Committee Draft (= Printed Version)
Mere futility is his hustle and bustle.

7c
Greenberg: 'Amassing and not knowing who will take it away'.
Rozenberg: Two alternatives: 'He hoards and knows not who will reap the benefit' or, 'He heaps up and knows not who will gather it'.
Shapiro: The nuance in the third clause is 'who will possess it' rather than, 'Who will take it home'.
Leeman: 'Storing up, not knowing who will gather it in', I don't think the bracketed [wealth] is necessary.
Greenfield: The figure in v. 7c is that of heaping up grain and not knowing who will be gathering it in. Therefore, with Shapiro, 'Amassing and not knowing who will possess it'.

Committee Draft (= Printed Version)
Amassing and not knowing who will gather it in.

39.8 ועתה מה־קויתי אדני\תוחלתי לך היא

Sarna Draft
What, then, can I count on, O my Lord? / In you my hope lies.

Discussion
Rozenberg: There is a difference between dependence and hope. Rather, 'look to', especially in view of תוחלתי in v. 8b.

Committee Draft (= Printed Version)
What, then, can I count on, O Lord? / In you my hope lies.

39.9. מכל־פשעי הצלני\חרפת נבל אל תשימני

Sarna Draft
Deliver me from all my transgressions; / Make me not the butt of the benighted man.

Discussion
9a
Greenberg: 'Save me from the effects of all my misdeeds'. This will make the meaning clearer.
Leeman: פשעי equals 'my punishment', therefore, 'Spare me from my punishment'.

Rozenberg: הצילני, ‘spare’ (Leeman) and ‘save’ (Greenberg) are good since the verb conveys the idea of avoiding the temptation to sin altogether.

9b
Rozenberg: ‘Benighted’ is too long and too civilized, and lacks in contempt and derision. If we can’t settle on ‘rogue’ or similar adjectives then let’s use stronger adjectives.

Committee Draft (= Printed Version)
Deliver me from all my transgressions; / Make me not the butt of the benighted.

39.10 נאלמתי לא אפתח־פי\כי אתה עשית

Sarna Draft
I keep dumb, opening not my mouth, / [g-]For you will act[-g].
Note g-g: or ‘for it is your doing’

Discussion
10a-b
Greenberg: ‘I am dumb, I do not open my mouth, for it is your doing.’
Rozenberg: Prefer ‘for you do act’.
Leeman: Text of note much to be preferred.

Committee Draft
I am dumb, I do not open my mouth / For it is your doing

Printed Version
I am dumb, I do not speak up, / For it is your doing.
[Possibly reflects the desire to continue the directness of ‘I am dumb’; see above ‘3a, ‘I was dumb, silent’.]

39.11 הסר מעלי נגעך\מתגרת ידך אני כליתי

Sarna Draft
Avert your stroke from me: / I am exhausted from [d-]your blows[-d].
Note d-d: meaning of Hebrew uncertain.

Discussion
Greenberg: ‘Take away your plague from me; I perish etc.’
Leeman: ‘Exhausted’ is too mild; prefer ‘consumed, destroyed, etc.’

Committee Draft (=Printed Version)
Take away your plague from me; I perish from your blows.

39.12 בתוכחות על־עון יסרת איש\ ותמס כעש חמודו \ אך הבל כל אדם סלה

Sarna Draft
You chastise a man in punishment for his sin, / Dissolving what he treasures, like a moth. / Surely all men are futility.
Annotation: ‘treasures’—really quite uncertain as to reference. Job 20.20; Isa. 44.9 do not help a lot.

Discussion
12a
Rozenberg: Follow Hebrew word order: ‘With reproofs you correct man for his sin’.

12b
Leeman: Draft version, when read, would evoke the question, ‘What does a moth treasure?’ I suggest, ‘Consuming as a moth his treasures’.
Greenberg: With Leeman, ‘consuming’ is preferable.

12c
Greenberg: Render either, ‘All men are nothing but a breath’ or, ‘No man is more than a breath’.
Leeman: ‘A mere nothing’ instead of ‘all men are futility’.
Rozenberg: Agrees with Leeman.

Committee Draft (= Printed Version)
You chastise a man in punishment for his sin, / Consuming like a moth what he treasures. / No man is more than a breath.

39.13 שמעה תפלתי ה׳\ושועתי האזינה\אל־דמעתי אל־תחרש\כי גר אנכי
עמך\תושב ככל־אבותי

Sarna Draft
Hear my prayer, O Lord, / Give ear to my cry, / Disregard not my tears; / For like all my ancestors, / I am an alien resident with you.

Discussion
13c
Greenberg: 'Do not disregard'. [This order is closer to modern speech.]

13e-f
[The proposed 'alien resident' for גר ותושב aroused much discussion.]
Leeman: Neither 'alien resident' nor 'resident alien' of Gen. 23.4 seem to fit here as well as, 'For I am a sojourner with you / Like all my ancestors, only a temporary resident'.
Rozenberg: Keep גר ותושב split for better effect. OJPS not bad. [OJPS: 'I am a stranger with Thee, / A sojourner, as all my fathers were'.]
Shapiro: 'Alien resident' may be too technical. Perhaps 'a stranger dwelling with you', cf. comment of Leeman. [This problem was solved simply by placing a comma between alien and resident.]

Committee Draft
Hear my prayer, O Lord; / Give ear to my cry; / Do not disregard my tears; / For like all my ancestors, / I am an alien, resident with you.

Printed Version
Hear my prayer, O Lord, / Give ear to my cry, / Do not disregard my tears; / For like all my forbears / I am an alien, resident with you.
[The printed version substitutes 'forbears' for 'ancestors' since the reference is to recent ancestors rather than those in the distant past, and the word is less connotative of sentiment.]

39.14 השע ממני ואבליגה\בטרם אלך ואינני

Sarna Draft
Look away from me that [d]I might brighten up[d] / Ere I pass away and be no more.

Annotation: 'brighten up'—Arabic *balaja*. Tur-Sinai, HaLashon, p. 377, takes it as equal to הפליג דעתו, 'diverting attention'; 'pass away' i.e. 'die', as Gen. 15.2.

Discussion
14a
Leeman: ואבליגה, 'that I might know some cheer'.
Greenberg: 'Show a smile' (*BDB*) or Leeman's 'know some cheer' better than 'brighten'.
Greenfield: 'Look away' as translation of השע. Ibn Ezra and others equated it with הרפה on the basis of Job 14.6 etc. It is 'close your eyes' on the basis of Isa. 6.10, etc., a *hiphil* of שעע, the intent being 'do not examine me constantly'. Despite the Arabic cognate does ואבליגה means 'brighten, cheer up'. OJPS 'that I may take comfort' or the traditional 'that I may be strengthened' seems preferable.

14b
Rozenberg: Isn't 'ere' archaic?
Greenberg: Prefer 'am' to 'be'.

Committee Draft (= Printed Version)
Look away from me, that I may recover, / Before I pass away and am gone.
[The printed version adds 'meaning of Hebrew uncertain' for 'that I may recover'.]

Sarna Version, Psalm 39	*NJPS Printed Version, Psalm 39*
1. For the leader; For Jeduthun. A Psalm of David.	For the leader; for Jeduthun. A psalm of David.
2. I resolved, 'I will guard my ways, Lest I sin with my tongue; I will keep my mouth curbed, So long as the wicked man is present.'	2. I resolved I would watch my step lest I offend by my speech; I would keep my mouth muzzled while the wicked man was in my presence.

3. I was dumb, silence itself; I held back from pleasure, While my pain was troublesome.	3. I was dumb, silent; I was very[a] still while my pain was intense.
4. My blood[a] boiled inside me; At the thought of it [b]I was in a furor;[-b] I spoke aloud.[c]	4. My mind was in a rage, my thoughts were all aflame; I spoke out:
5. LORD, Let me know when my end will come, What be the measure of my days, That I might know how [d]fleeting is my life.[-d]	5. Tell me, O LORD, what my term is, what is the measure of my days; I would know how fleeting my life is.
6. Lo, You have set [e]a strict measure[-e] for my days; My life-span is as nothing in Your sight; [d]Surely, all upstanding men are utter futility.[-d]	6. You have made my life just handbreaths long; its span is as nothing in Your sight; [b-]no man endures any longer than a breath.[-b] *Selah.*
7. Surely, man goes his way in darkness;[f] surely, he bustles about in vain, Heaping up (wealth), knowing not who will take it home.	7. Man walks about as a mere shadow; mere futility is his hustle and bustle, amassing and not knowing who will gather in.
8. What, then, can I count on, O my Lord? In You my hope lies.	8. What, then, can I count on, O Lord? In You my hope lies.
9. Deliver me from all my transgressions; Make me not the butt of the benighted man.	9. Deliver me from all my transgressions; make me not the butt of the benighted.
10. I keep dumb, opening not my mouth, [g]For You will act.[-g]	10. I am dumb, I do not speak up, for it is Your doing.
11. Avert Your stroke from me; I am exhausted from [d]Your blows.[-d]	11. Take away Your plague from me; I perish from Your blows.

12. You chastise a man in punishment for sin, Dissolving what he treasures, like a moth. Surely all men are futility.	12. You chastise a man in punishment for his sin, consuming like a moth what he treasures. No man is more than a breath. *Selah*.
13. Hear my prayer, O LORD Give ear to my cry, Disregard not my tears; For like my ancestors, I am an alien resident with You.	13. Hear my prayer, O LORD; give ear to my cry; do not disregard my tears; for like all my forebears I am an alien, resident with You.
14. Look away from me that [d]I might brighten up[-d] Ere I pass away and be no more	14. Look away from me, [b-]that I may recover,[-b] before I pass away and am gone.
a. Lit. 'heart' b-b Lit. 'a fire blazed'. c. Lit. 'with my tongue'. d-d. Meaning of Hebrew uncertain. e-e. Lit. 'handbreadths'. f. Or 'as a shadow'. g-g. Or 'For it is Your doing'.	a. Cf. use of *ṭwb* in Hos. 10.1; Jon. 4.4. b-b Meaning of Hebrew uncertain

Epilogue

The procedure described above was followed throughout our work on the Psalms and then on the other books of Ketuvim which we translated (the first committee had already completed the Five Megillot). The traditional Hebrew text served as the base for our work and emendations were eschewed. All the available modern scholarly means were used in our work, and at the same time we took cognizance of the insights and interpretations offered by early rabbinic and medieval Jewish commentators. The translation of such basic words as לב, לשון and פה, all of which occur in Psalm 39, presented us with the interesting problem of literalness since לב can be translated 'heart' or 'mind', לשון 'tongue' or 'speech', and פה 'mouth' or 'speech'. Should these be taken simply as metaphors and translated abstractly, or should a more concrete version be chosen? Thus לא אפתח פי of v. 10 is concrete in Sarna's draft, 'opening not my mouth', and in the committee's draft, 'I do not open my mouth', but not in the printed version, 'I do not speak up'. In v. 2, however, פי is translated concretely, 'my mouth', in all of our versions as befits that verse. In this and in other matters disagreement was usually more about mode of expression and less about meaning.

As can be seen from the above distillation of our notes and comments there was a degree of unevenness in the number of comments on various verses. Much was left unwritten and was reserved by the participants for the oral discussion of the draft version. We cannot, however, hope to recapture that material. Indeed, in the course of time, as we became accustomed to the work and also attuned to each other the written notes became fewer. A consensus developed as to the proper way for us to approach a verse and also the mode of translation that we preferred. It was on the early draft translation provided by Nahum Sarna that our approach was initially tried. Nahum was in many ways one of the prime revisionists, approaching his draft with an open mind, defending its basic meaning but always willing to participate in the deconstruction of the draft and the forging of the new translation. All drafts were treated in the same manner, and received detailed, critical attention, and even at the last stage of our translation work there was a great deal of revision of the draft texts. In sum, about fifteen years were spent together in fellowship and scholarly cooperation. A strong bond developed among us and we think back warmly about this period.

Addendum

Saul Leeman

The reader may be puzzled as to why the committee, which quibbles as to whether לשון should be rendered 'tongue' or 'speech', accepts the rendering of נבל as 'benighted man' without any real discussion or dissension. The reason is that this battle was fought at the opening of Psalm 14 (the first occurrence of that word). There the committee faced the dilema as to whether it should interpret נבל as a person deficient in intelligence, i.e. 'a fool', or as one lacking in morality, i.e. 'a rogue' or 'a scoundrel'. After some discussion it was agreed that the word נבל combined *both* qualities. The committee then embarked on a search for the one word in English that would express both attributes and finally concluded that that word is 'benighted'.

How Modern are Modern Biblical Studies?

Frederick E. Greenspahn

Over the years, Nahum Sarna has played a signal role in the development of both biblical and Judaic studies. His scholarship has enriched our understanding of numerous issues, ranging from connections between the Bible and the cultures of the Near Eastern world in which it was born to the history of contemporary biblical scholarship. He has trained and nurtured a generation of students without creating clones and has worked tirelessly to disseminate Judaic learning in a world which often seems content to accept pale imitations of true scholarship, making his knowledge freely available to those who seek it.

Among Sarna's most important contributions has been his recognition of the place occupied by his own discipline within the larger context of Jewish cultural achievements—this despite the Protestant garb in which contemporary biblical studies is frequently clothed. In a series of important essays, he has traced contemporary methods of biblical scholarship back to the Middle Ages, when rigorous interest in the Bible as a entity in itself was beginning to unfold within the Jewish community.[1] Collectively, his research casts light on an unfortunately little-known chapter in the history of biblical studies

1. 'The Bible and Judaic Studies', in *The Teaching of Judaica in American Universities* (ed. L.A. Jick; New York: Ktav, 1970), pp. 35-40; 'The Modern Study of the Bible in the Framework of Jewish Studies', in *Proceedings of the Eighth World Congress of Jewish Studies* (Jerusalem, 1983), pp. 19-27; 'Hebrew and Bible Studies in Medieval Spain', in *The Sephardi Heritage* (ed. R.D. Barnett: New York: Ktav, 1971), pp. 323-66; '*Hebeṭim Lo' Meṣu'im shel Parshanut ha-Miqra' bi-Yemei ha-Beynayim*', in *Hagut u-Ma'aseh, Sefer Zikkaron le-Shim'on Rawidowicz* (Haifa: Tcherikover, 1983), pp. 35-42; 'The Authority and Interpretation of Scripture in Jewish Tradition', in *Understanding Scripture, Explorations of Jewish and Christian Traditions of Interpretation* (ed. C. Thoma and M. Wyschogrod: Mahwah, NJ: Paulist Press, 1987), pp. 9-20.

and suggests its largely untapped potential for contemporary scholars.

Although Sarna is not the first to have seen the connection between modern biblical studies and those of earlier periods,[1] his position has often been a lonely one. Not only do most Christians trace the discipline's history to the Enlightenment, but many Jews have also denied any linkage between modern scholarship and earlier forms of biblical interpretation.[2] Among the most recent to take this position has been Jon Levenson, who challenges contemporary scholarship's claim to religious neutrality by drawing attention to its historically Protestant character. In that context, he dismisses Sarna's view of contemporary methods as having been anticipated by pre-modern scholars as simply an effort on the part of 'some Jewish traditionalists, eager to show that modern biblical criticism is kosher'.[3]

Elsewhere, Levenson has acknowledged that Sarna's agenda is somewhat different from what this characterization might imply, observing that '*all* he has done is to show the narrowness of the fundamentalists' image of the tradition'.[4] Rather than legitimating biblical studies in the eyes of Jewish traditionalists, for whom so many of its conclusions are anathema, Sarna has challenged *their* legitimacy by

1. Cf. N. Krochmal, *Moreh Nevukhei ha-Zeman*, in *The Collected Works of Nachman Krochmal* (ed. S. Rawidowicz; Waltham, MA: Ararat, 2nd edn, 1961), pp. 114-15 and 142-43, and Menahem Soloweitschik and Salman Rubascheff, *Toledot Biqqoret ha-Miqra'* (Berlin: Dwir-Mikra, 1925).

2. E.g. M. Haran: 'The critical study of the Bible, as it emerged in the wake of the European Renaissance, is, then, a novel manifestation and it would be vain to look for its first sparks in the statements of Talmudic or medieval sages. In historical terms, it was in the nature of a sudden and steep departure' ('Midrashic and Literal Exegesis and the Critical Method in Biblical Research', in *Studies in Bible, 1986* [ed. S. Japhet; ScrHier, 31; Jerusalem: Magnes Press, 1986], p. 45). For examples of similar statements by Christian scholars, see F.E, Greenspahn, 'Biblical Scholars, Medieval and Modern', in *Judaic Perspectives on Ancient Israel* (ed. J. Neusner, B.A. Levine and E.S. Frerichs; Philadelphia: Fortress Press, 1987), p. 253 n. 1.

3. 'Theological Consensus or Historicist Evasion? Jews and Christians in Biblical Studies', in *Hebrew Bible or Old Testament? Studying the Bible in Judaism and Christianity* (ed. R. Brooks and J. Collins; Notre Dame, IN: University of Notre Dame, 1990), p. 119. Levenson's assessment of Sarna echoes that leveled at Nachman Krochmal by S.D. Luzzato (*Meḥqarei ha-Yahadut* [Warsaw: Ha-Tsefirah, 1913], p. 36).

4. 'The Eighth Principle of Judaism and the Literary Simultaneity of Scripture', *JR* 68 (1988), p. 212 (emphasis added).

demonstrating the diverse ways in which Jews have approached the Bible, oftentimes far less defensively than modern orthodoxy will allow.[1]

A common version of the traditionalist viewpoint is presented by Chaim Potok in his novel *In the Beginning*, in which Max Lurie opposes his yeshiva-student son's interest in university-based biblical studies, noting that 'Your teachers will be goyim. . . and. . . Jews who are like goyim. What do they know of the Torah.'[2] The fact that such feelings are widespread within the Jewish community does not make them historically reliable, nor does Potok allow them to stand unchallenged. Although the centrality of talmudic studies in yeshiva scholarship is a major factor in his book, Potok suggests that those who have mastered its intricacies are often deficient in their understanding of the Bible. For example, he contrasts the error-filled Bible reading in his protagonist's Orthodox synagogue with that in the liberal congregations also visited by his hero (pp. 378-79). In the same vein, the yeshiva's leading Talmud student turns out to be unfamiliar with traditional Jewish biblical exegesis, including even that of Maimonides, whom he characterizes as one of the 'apikorsishe grammarians' (pp. 338-39). Potok's position emerges most clearly in his portrayal of the talmudic scholar who stands at the pinnacle of the yeshiva community. Not only has he read non-Jewish theology, including modern biblical scholarship, but, in a climatic scene, he condemns his students for their inability to think critically, commenting, 'I could teach you nonsense and you would accept it as Torah' (pp. 410-20). Potok's view of what passes for Torah in Orthodox life could not be much clearer. As for contemporary biblical studies, that same rebbe hardly shares Max Lurie's fear of academe. He responds to the junior Lurie's plan to enter the university by observing, 'If the Torah cannot go out into your world of scholarship and return stronger, then we are all fools and charlatans. I have faith in the Torah. I am not afraid of truth' (p. 435).

1. The modern elements within Jewish orthodoxy are pointed out by J. Katz, 'Orthodoxy in Historical Perspective', *Studies in Contemporary Jewry* 2 (1986), pp. 3-17; a similar point underlies J.B. Rogers and D.K. McKim, *The Authority and Interpretation of the Bible: An Historical Approach* (San Francisco: Harper & Row, 1979).

2. New York: Alfred A. Knopf, 1975, p. 444, cited by Levenson, 'Theological Consensus or Historicist Evasion?', pp. 110-11.

Whatever the position of Chaim Potok, the Max Luries of this world are not the only ones who consider biblical studies to be quintessentially 'goyish'. Contemporary Jewish scholars themselves frequently overlook their discipline's Jewish roots, explaining it instead as a product of the Renaissance or Reformation.[1] Indeed, Max Lurie reflects a deeply rooted element in Jewish culture, which has long suspected biblical studies of Christian taint. The most notable expression of this sentiment came in Solomon Schechter's famous description of higher criticism as the higher anti-semitism.[2] However, the roots of this view can be traced in part to Jewish ambivalence about the Bible itself, growing out of the way in which this originally Jewish work was coopted by the Christian community which gave it what has come to be seen as a decidedly anti-Jewish interpretation.[3] The resulting alienation was compounded by Christian reliance on Jews (frequently apostates) for biblical training, and contributed to growing Jewish focus on the Talmud.[4]

Whatever transformations have taken place in the Bible's role within Christian and Jewish life, its Jewish origin and character are not easily ignored, nor should the reality of premodern Jewish influence on contemporary scholarship be denied. A particularly vivid example is provided by the field of Semitic studies, since it is well know that many of the so-called founders of Hebrew philology within Christendom relied on the intellectual heirs of the medieval Jewish tradition whose contribution Nahum Sarna has so effectively presented.[5] Less widely recognized is the fact that the medieval Jews who

1. E.g. M. Greenberg: 'Modern critical scholarship is a creation of Christian Europe; its Jewish embodiment is derivative' ('Can Modern Critical Bible Scholarship Have a Jewish Character', *Immanuel* 15 [1982–83], p. 7).

2. *Seminary Addresses and Other Papers* (New York: Arno Press, 1969), pp. 35-39.

3. Cf. *Midr. Tanḥuma Ki Tissa'* 34 (Vilna; reprinted Jerusalem: Levin-Epstein, n.d.), p. 127; *Midr. Tanḥuma* (Buber) *Va-Yera'* 6 (p. 44b); *Num. R.* 14.10; and *Pes. R.* 5.1.

4. F. Talmage, 'Keep Your Sons from Scripture: The Bible in Medieval Jewish Scholarship and Spirituality', in *Understanding Scripture, Explorations of Jewish and Christian Traditions of Interpretation* (ed. C. Thoma and M. Wyschogrod: Mahwah, NJ: Paulist Press, 1987), pp. 81-101.

5. Cf. J. Friedman, *The Most Ancient Testimony, Sixteenth Century Christian-Hebraica in the Age of Renaissance Nostalgia* (Athens, OH: Ohio University Press, 1983).

developed this approach with such sophistication could hardly have thought of themselves as innovators, since similar efforts had been accepted within Jewish tradition for centuries. Rabbinic sources are unhesitating in mining related languages as well as contemporary usage in order to explicate what were perceived as difficult biblical terms.[1] This approach was justified by the long-standing rabbinic view that obscure passages are best explained on the basis of clearer usage elsewhere (*yilmad satum mi-meforash*).[2] To be sure, modern methods are more sophisticated than the rabbis, and our knowledge of linguistic relationships has progressed far beyond their often naive conclusions. Nonetheless, their fundamental approach of looking for wider attestations in order to enhance our understanding of obscure biblical terms, reaching even beyond the Hebrew lexicon when necessary, is precisely that which is used to this day.

The rabbis' linguistic interests were not limited to lexicography. Among the grammatical phenomena they identified in the course of interpreting the Bible were number,[3] gender,[4] and various verbal forms,[5] as well as syntactic features such as the *heh locale*[6] and several

1. Popular usage is cited in *b. Roš. Haš.* 25a-26b and *b. Meg.* 18a; cf. *b. Ber.* 6b and *Lam. R.* 1.15 §44. Among the foreign languages invoked are Greek (*b. Sanh.* 76b; *b. Šab.* 31b; 63ab; *Gen. R.* 81.5; 99.7; *Exod. R.* 36.1; *Lev. R.* 16.1; *Esth. R.* 3.12; *Midr. Tanḥuma* [Buber] *Ṣav* 4, p. 8a; and *Midr. Pss.* 42.2; cf. *b. Sukk.* 35a and *Midr. Tanḥuma* [Buber] *Mishpaṭim*, p. 43a, n. 60; Latin (*j. Ber.* 19.1 13c); Arabic (*j. Ber.* 19.1 13c; *b. Roš. Haš.* 26a-b; *b. Meg.* 18a; *Gen. R.* 36.1, 79.7; *Exod. R.* 42.4; *Lev. R.* 1.3, 25.5; *Lam. R.* 1.15 §44, 2.13 §17; *Cant. R.* 4.1 §3; *Midr. Tanḥuma* [Buber] *Terumah* 7, p. 46b; *Tazri'a* 8, p. 18a; *Yalq. Shim.* §940, p. 489b and §924, p. 510b; Syriac (*b. Pes.* 61a and *Mechilta Bo'* 3.1 [ed. Horovitz, p. 12]; Canaanite (*Sifre* Deuteronomy §306 [ed. L. Finkelstein, p. 336]; Persian (*b. 'Avod. Zar.* 24b and *b. Pes.* 41a; African (*j. Ber.* 19.1 13c and *b. Roš. Haš* 26a); and Egyptian (*b. Men.* 34b; *b. Sanh.* 4b; *PRK* 12 §24 [ed. B. Mandelbaum, p. 223] and *Midr. 'Aseret ha-Dibberot* [in A. Jellinek, *Bet ha-Midrash* (Jerusalem: Wahrmann Books, 3rd edn, 1967) 1.63]). A similar etymological method is used within Hebrew at *Gen. R.* 42.4.

2. *B. Tem.* 16b, *b. Zeb.* 53a, *b. Yom.* 59a.

3. E.g. *Mechilta Beshallaḥ* 1 (ed. Horovitz, p. 116).

4. *Sifra Be-Ḥuqotay* 11 (Vienna: Schlossberg, reprinted New York: Om, 1946), p. 114b, and *b. Qid.* 2b; cf. *b. Tem.* 2b.

5. *Mechilta Beshallaḥ* 1 (ed. Horovitz, p. 116).

6. *B. Yeb.* 13b; *j. Yeb.* 1.6 3a.

uses of the particle *kî*.[1] In short, the study of the Hebrew language, which flowered so remarkably in the nurturing ambience of medieval Islam, owed much to interests and techniques which were presented during the earlier rabbinic period.

How this could have happened is not hard to understand. Although linguistic skills tend to be intuitive, even the simplest features become objects of concern once they cease to be natural forms of expression. By the Middle Ages, biblical Hebrew was no longer native for many Jews. The intrinsic importance of the Bible, coupled with the model of Islamic treatment of the Qur'an and the challenge of Karaism, thus provided fertile soil in which the study of this sacred text could flourish. Furthermore, the familiarity of Arabic provided not only a basis of comparison but also a mine of related parallels, easily recognized given its common Semitic heritage with Hebrew.

Similar conditions prevailed during Greco-Roman times. Then, too, Jews were sufficiently removed from the biblical milieu to find its language sometimes problematic, as acknowledged by talmudic citations of differences between biblical and rabbinic usage.[2] Living in a non-Hebrew environment may have made the rabbis more sensitive to various features of their language, while their familiarity with Aramaic provided the same kind of resources and perspective later broadened through contact with Arabic.[3]

Contributing to the rabbis' interest in the philological dimension of biblical interpretation was the Bible's own concern with matters of language. Besides the story of Babel and the shibboleth incident (Judg. 12.6), it contains several accounts in which the importance of Hebrew

1. *B. Giṭ.* 90a; *b. Roš. Haš.* 3a.

2. *B. 'Avod. Zar.* 58b; *b. Ḥul.* 137b; *b. Qid.* 2b; cf. *b. Šab.* 36a and *Pes. R.* 3.2. The significance of these observations is described by Y. Kutscher, '*Bitsu'a Tenu'ot I U be-Ta'atiqei ha-'Ivrit ha-Miqra'it be-'Aramit ha-Gelilit uve-leshon Ḥazal*', in *Benjamin de Vries Memorial Volume* (ed. E.Z. Melamed; Jerusalem: Tel Aviv University, 1968), p. 230. The incorporation of foreign words into Esth. 8.10 underlines *b. Meg.* 18a, as are what they regarded as Aramaisms in Ps. 139.17 in *b. Sanh.* 38b. *B. Giṭ.* 65b refers to dialectic differences between the Babylonian and Palestinian communities, and there are numerous allusions to the linguistic idiosyncrasies of Galilean Jews (e.g. *b. Erub.* 53a-b; *b. Ber.* 32a; cf. *b. Meg.* 24b).

3. On rabbinic references to Arabic, see A. Cohen, 'Arabisms in Rabbinic Literature', *JQR* ns 3 (1912–13), pp. 221-33. Evidence of multilinguality can be found in *b. Sanh.* 17b.

is apparent, including the Rab-Shakeh's insistence on using that language (2 Kgs 18.26-29) and Nehemiah's concern for people's linguistic facility (Neh. 13.24). Most directly germane to our focus, however, are the aetiologies which so permeate the book of Genesis and reflect a self-consciousness about language and an interest in accounting for the history of specific words, no matter how questionable their linguistic validity.[1] Such materials provide both an initial orientation towards and also legitimation for Judaism's continuing interest in approaching the Bible philologically. However much this method may have developed beyond what is found in Genesis, its roots lie within the biblical period itself.

Another aspect of modern biblical studies which can be traced back further than is usually allowed is what is commonly termed 'lower' or text criticism. Despite the high status historically granted to the so-called Masoretic Text, medieval scholars accepted the possibility of textual corruption, as Nahum Sarna has demonstrated.[2] However, this, too, was no innovation. Although the Mishnah cautions against making changes in the authoritative Torah scroll (*sefer ha-'azarah*),[3] the rabbis believed that the reason that three scrolls had been kept in the Jerusalem Temple was so that the 'correct' reading could be determined by a majority, since no one of them was perfect.[4] Elsewhere, they mention several specific scrolls which also deviated from the accepted norm, including one located in a Roman synagogue, another which belonged to Rabbi Meir, and a third which served as the *Vorlage* for the Septuagint.[5] In addition, they knew of people whose

1. Hartwig Hirschfield calls the biblical aetiologies 'rudimentary trials at linguistic explanation' (*Literary History of Hebrew Grammarians and Lexicographers* [London: Oxford University Press, 1926], p. 5).

2. 'The Modern Study of the Bible', pp. 24-26, and 'Hebrew and Bible Studies in Medieval Spain', pp. 344-49 and especially n. 135 on p. 365; cf. U. Simon, *'R'b'' ve-Rd"q—Shetei Gishot le-She'elat Meheimanut Nusaḥ ha-Miqra'i'*, *Bar-Ilan* 6 (1968), pp. 191-237, and M. Cohen, *'Ha-Idea be-Devar Qedushat ha-Nusaḥ le-'Otiotav u-Viqqoret ha-Text'*, in *Ha-Miqra' va-'Anaḥnu* (ed. U. Simon; Tel Aviv: Devir, 1979), pp. 42-69.'

3. *M. Mo'ed Qaṭ.* 3.4; cf. *j. Shek.* 4.3 48a; *j. Sanh.* 2.6 20c.

4. *Sof.* 6.4; cf. *j. Ta'an.* 4.2 68a; *ARN* B 46, p. 65a; and *Sifre* Deuteronomy §356 (ed. C. Finkelstein, p. 423).

5. *Midr. Gen. Rabbati* (ed. H. Albek; Jerusalem: Mekize Nirdamim, 2nd edn, 1940), pp. 209-12; *Gen. R.* 9.5; 20.12; 94.7; *j. Ta'an* 1.1 64a; cf. *Sof.* 1.7-8; *b. Meg.* 9a; *Mechilta Bo'* 14 (ed. Horovitz, pp. 50-51). Note also the various *'al tiqre'*

job it was to correct the biblical text,[1] which contained what *they* called scribal emendations (*tiqqunei soferim*).[2] To be sure, each of these traditions has its own history, and their reliability has been assessed in various ways. For our purposes, however, the antiquity or homiletical character of these accounts makes little difference. Even if such scrolls never existed and the emendations are pure fantasy, the traditions about them demonstrate that the rabbis accepted the possibility that their texts may not have been original or correct. It is thus clear that the principles of both comparative philology and textual criticism—methods widely associated with contemporary biblical studies—can be traced back at least as far as the rabbinic period and sometimes even further.[3]

For Levenson, however, it is not linguistic or textual matters which are crucial, but the historical-critical method itself, which he uses to support his contention that the Bible is studied differently today than it has been in the past. In order to demonstrate this, he draws on Peter Burke's identification of three attitudes as characteristic of post-medieval historical studies: (1) the sense of anachronism, (2) the awareness of evidence, and (3) the interest in causation.[4] It is these, Levenson claims, which are not to be found among medieval exegetes and thus make contemporary biblical studies unique.

The intuitive appeal of such statements does not exempt them from careful scrutiny. In fact, Burke never argues that this approach was a Renaissance novelty, but only that it marks the re-emergence of an impulse he traces back to classical antiquity, whatever one makes of

traditions and the ascription of the *ketiv/qere* phenomenon to Sinai (e.g. *b. Ned.* 37b-38a). Variations in word division and versification are mentioned in *b. Qid.* 30a; *b. Pes.* 117a; and *b. Ned.* 37b.

1. E.g. *t. Sanh.* 4.7; *b. Ket.* 106a; cf. *b. Pes.* 112a.

2. *Mechilta Beshallaḥ Shirata'* 6 (ed. Horovitz, p. 135); *Sifre* Numbers 84 (ed. M. Friedman; Vilna, 1864; reprinted New York: Om, 1948), p. 22b; *Midr. Tanḥuma Beshallaḥ* 16, pp. 89a-b; *Gen. R.* 18.22; *Lev. R.* 11.5; cf. *Exod. R.* 13.1; 41.4; *Midr. Pss.* 18.22, 29. Masoretic lists also refer to *sevirin*.

3. Classical influence, particularly as it emanated out of Alexandria, no doubt also played a major role in the development of 'lower' criticism; cf. M. Stern, '*Ḥivi ha-Balkhi—Marcion ha-Yehudi*,' in *Sefer Klausner* (ed. N.H. Torczyner *et al.*; Tel Aviv: Hotsa'at ha-Yovel, 1937–38), p. 210.

4. P. Burke, *The Renaissance Sense of the Past* (New York: St Martin's Press, 1969), p. 1.

his distinction between Jerusalem and Rome.[1] However, a closer study of his three criteria will amply demonstrate their inadequacy vis-à-vis Judaism for both the medieval period and before.

This point can be illustrated with the last of Burke's categories, the interest in causation. For this the Bible proves uniquely useful, since causation plays so central a role in its view of history. Its theological approach is, of course, far removed from that of contemporary historiography, but it is a theory of causation, no more or less abstract than our own understanding of social and economic forces and often allowing for the possibility of various views. To take only the most blatant example, the book of Kings ascribes the Babylonian exile to a very different cause than does the Chronicler, and such prophets as Jeremiah and Ezekiel would probably have offered explanations of their own.[2] All of these would have agreed that the exile was a punishment from God, but they attributed it to very different actions on the part of Israel. Moreover, all are causal views of history, however much their approaches may differ from our own, and their juxtaposition even allows for discussion of their relative merits.

Burke's second criterion has to do with evidence. Although this is difficult to find within the Bible, it is frequently present in rabbinic exegesis. For example, one rabbi defended his view that the Bible was originally written in the same script as that current in his day by pointing to its use of the Hebrew word *vav*, which is also the name of the alphabet's sixth letter, to describe a hook in the desert tabernacle, a meaning dependent on that letter's shape in the existing block script.[3]

Burke himself suggests that this criterion sets medieval approaches to biblical study apart from modern methods in his observation that among medievals 'the Bible. . . was taken as given. Since it was the work of God, who was eternal, there was no point in asking when the different parts of it were written down. It was not taken as a historical document, but as an oracle.'[4] Were it true, this would be an important point for the history of biblical studies, given the prominent role that

1. Burke, *Sense of the Past*, p. 141.
2. 2 Kgs 21.10-15 and 2 Chron. 36.11-21; cf. Jer. 3.6-13 and Ezek. 23.
3. *B. Sanh.* 22a and *j. Meg.* 1.11 71c.
4. Burke, *Sense of the Past*, p. 3. Contrast Josephus's effort to date the exodus, which is in no way qualitatively different from modern parallels (*Apion* 2.15-19).

questions of dating and authorship have played in modern scholarship.[1] However, such statements, which may be accurate portrayals of medieval Christian interpretation, simply do not withstand comparison to much of Jewish exegesis during that same time. It is true that all Jewish interpreters, with the possible exception of heretics, would have accepted the Bible's divine origin. However, the Jewish 'dogma' of *torah min ha-shamayim* did not relegate questions of authorship to irrelevance, but instead freed Jewish exegetes from a fear of heresy, since it entailed no commitment to the date or the human intermediary through whom the biblical writings had been given.[2] It is this which accounts for the profound interest in questions of both date and authorship among the medievals, particularly where the Bible itself left such matters open, and sometimes even where it did not. The Tosafot, for example, reject the Gemara's assertion that Hezekiah had written the book of Isaiah by calculating that he had died before the time of Isaiah.[3] In response to the same talmudic passage, Rashi observes that the prophets were responsible for only the initial stage of the books which bear their names. In a similar vein, the tenth-

1. J. Levenson, 'Theological Consensus or Historicist Evasion?', p. 119 and 'Eighth Principle', p. 210. This subject should be treated cautiously, given the tendency of several contemporary scholars to deride this approach as unfortunate (e.g. R. Alter, *The Art of Biblical Narrative* [New York: Basic Books, 1981], pp. 13-14).

2. See J. Petuchowski, 'The Supposed Dogma of the Mosaic Authorship of the Pentateuch', *Hibbert Journal* 57 (1958–59), pp. 356-60. Thus Joseph (ben Eliezer Tob Elem) Bonfils' comment, 'What difference does it make to me whether Moses or some other prophet wrote [the Torah], since all of their words are true and inspired?' (*Tsafenat Pa'aneaḥ* [ed. D. Herzog; Cracow; Joseph Fischer, 1911; reprinted University of Haifa, 1967] I, p. 92, cited by N.M. Sarna ['The Modern Study of the Bible', pp. 22-23], M. Greenberg [*'Al ha-Miqra' ve-'al ha-Yahadut, Qoveṣ Ketavim* (ed. A. Shapira; Tel Aviv: Am Oved, 1984), p. 276, from an interview with Noam Zohar originally published in *Gesher* 33 (1976)], and J.D. Levenson ['Theological Consensus or Historicist Evasion?', p. 119 and 'The Eighth Principle of Judaism', p. 210]) is offered only *after* his agreement with Ibn Ezra's comment that Moses could not have written Gen. 12.6, much as Solomon could not have written the book of Proverbs (cf. also his comments in vol. I, p. 112 and vol. II, p. 65 regarding Gen. 22.14, Deut. 1.2 and 31.9, as well as Abravanel's denial that Joshua and Samuel had written the books bearing their names on the basis of content clearly written after their deaths [*Peirush 'al Nevi'im Ri'shonim* (Jerusalem: Hotsa'at Sefarim Torah ve-Daat, 1955), pp. 71-b]).

3. At *b. B. Bat.* 15a.

century Karaite exegete Yefet ben-Ali proposed that the books of Micah and Hosea are abridgments (*mukhtaṣira*) containing only those sections of the prophets' writings which the 'men of the exile' (*'ahl 'al-galut*) found relevant.[1] Even more pertinent is the approach to the book of Psalms. Although that collection is 'traditionally' ascribed to David, various medieval scholars dated its various poems to the pre- or postexilic period, depending on their content, much as is commonly done today. So powerful was the drive to determine the origin of each psalm on this basis that the superscription *le-David*, which is conventionally taken as indicating Davidic authorship, was given a variety of interpretations by medieval scholars, who included the possibilities that it reflects a work's content or style as well as its date.[2]

In this the medievals were hardly innovative, for the earlier rabbis had already recognized the Psalter's diverse authorship.[3] Moreover, similar conclusions had been drawn for other, less obviously heterogenous works, such as the books of Isaiah, Jeremiah and Nahum.[4] Even sections of the Pentateuch were recognized as unlikely to be Mosaic, not just by Spinoza or his acknowledged source, Ibn Ezra, but by the Talmud, which points out that Moses could not have written Deuteronomy's description of his own death, nor Joshua or Samuel about their deaths, despite their inclusion in books traditionally ascribed to them.[5]

1. P. Birnbaum, *The Arabic Commentary of Yefet ben 'Ali the Karaite on the Book of Hosea* (Philadelphia: Dropsie College, 1942), p. 7. In this, Yefet's view parallels that expressed in *b. Meg.* 14a that prophetic books contain only those teachings which were judged useful for later generations. It is a pleasure to acknowledge Seth Ward's assistance with this passage.

2. U. Simon, *Four Approaches to the Book of Psalms, From Saadiah Gaon to Abraham ibn Ezra* (Albany, NY: State University of New York Press, 1991), pp. 121 and 178; several different medieval views as to the book's origin are conveniently summarized on pp. 13, 76-78, 120-32, 198-99. Similar claims were made regarding Proverbs (Simon, *Four Approaches*, p. 38).

3. *Qoh. R.* 7.19 §4; *b. B. Bat.* 14b; *Cant. R.* 4.4 §1; *Midr. Pss.* 1.6; *t. Soṭ.* 9.8; cf. the debate in *b. Pes.* 117a as to whether the Hallel (Psalms 113-18) had originated in the time of Moses or of David and the effort to distinguish between individual and communal Psalms.

4. *Lev. R.* 6.6; *Lam. R.* proem 34; *Sifre Deuteronomy* 1 (ed. L. Finkelstein, p. 2) and *t. Soṭ.* 9.6-7; cf. *b. Šab.* 30b regarding contradictions in Proverbs and Qohelet.

5. *B. B. Bat.* 14b-15a; *b. Men.* 30a; *b. Mak.* 11a. *B. Šab.* 115b-116a considers

Even Scripture's divine inspiration, which is usually considered to have been a given in pre-modern times, was not an entirely closed subject for the rabbis. Their condemnation of those who deny the divine origin of biblical writings[1] was clearly not universal, at least not with regard to certain books, such as Proverbs and Ecclesiastes which were said to contain Solomon's own thoughts rather than those of God.[2] Nor are such statements possible only for those who rejected the canonicity of such texts. The classic *baraitha* on this subject includes statements of authorship in its enumeration of the biblical books.[3] Elsewhere, the Talmud comments on the stylistic idiosyncrasies of the individual prophets, despite the common origin of their prophecies.[4] Moreover, the naivete of the rabbis' conclusions does not change the fact that their method of ascribing authorship to known figures from the period with which a book is concerned is a staple of modern scholarship.[5]

Num. 10.35-36 to be either a separate book or, at least, out of place in its present location.

1. *B. Sanh.* 99a includes 'even one who says that all of the entire Torah is from *shamayim* except for one verse. . .' ; cf. *Sifre* Numbers §112 (Vienna, 1864, p. 339).

2. *B. Ber.* 4a; *b. Soṭ.* 44a; *b. Meg.* 7a; *b. Šab.* 151b, 153a; cf. *t. Yad.* 2.14; cf. *b. Meg.* 31b, which explains the differences between the curses in Deuteronomy and those in Leviticus as due to the fact that the latter had been said in Moses' own name. The rabbis despaired of explaining the contradictions between the Pentateuch and Ezekiel (*b. Men.* 45a).

3. *B. B. Bat.* 14b-15a.

4. *B. Sanh.* 89a; cf. *b. Ḥag.* 13b.

5. For example, R.E. Friedman infers that Jeremiah may have written the Deuteronomistic history since he 'was alive and writing in precisely the years. . . [and] possessed the literary skill' (*Who Wrote the Bible*? [New York: Summit Books, 1987], p. 146). The same goes for connections of various sorts, including Chileab with Daniel (*b. Ber.* 4a), Amraphael with Nimrod (*b. Erub.* 53a), and Malachi with Ezra (*b. Meg.* 15a and *Targ. Mal.* 1.1) or Mordecai (*b. Meg.* 14a). Similarly, the Obadiah mentioned in 1 Kgs 18.4 is considered the author of the book of Obadiah (*b. Sanh.* 39b), the Jonah mentioned in 2 Kgs 14.25 the author of the book of Jonah (*b. Yeb.* 98b), and the Zechariah mentioned in Isa. 8.2 the author of the book of Zechariah (*b. Makk.* 24b). Biblical antecedents of this process might include the identification of Jerusalem with Salem (Ps. 76.3) and Mount Moriah (2 Chron. 3.1) and the implied identification of Micaiah (1 Kgs 22.28) with Micah (1.2); cf. 1 Chron. 16.8-36, which is composed of sections from various psalms, including 96.1-13, 105.1-15, and 106.47-48.

Dating biblical works was both an accepted and, apparently, an important topic of discussion, at least when it was not 'obvious' from the text, as in the case of Job for which a wide range of possible dates, extending from the patriarchal to the postexilic periods, was proposed.[1] Again, the fact that we do not find the supporting evidence convincing is not the point. The subject was debated and evidence provided, using contemporary methods even if not contemporary standards.

There is no indication that rabbinic interest in these matters was considered unusual or controversial. Nor is there any reason it should have been, since similar issues had been discussed for quite some time. The Septuagint's attribution of the book of Lamentations to Jeremiah, which accords with that given in the Talmud, was not dogmatically based, but derived from available evidence that Jeremiah had lived at the appropriate time and composed poetry,[2] leaving him a reasonable candidate to have authored such a book. More striking are the historical superscriptions which have been added to various psalms.[3] Although tradition may have held that these poems originated during the lifetime of David, their correlation with specific events in his career is nothing less than an early attempt to find a suitable *Sitz im Leben*, using exactly the tools of modern form critics.[4]

This interest in historical circumstance is crucial for the sense of anachronism, which is the last of Burke's characteristics of modern historical method, although it should by now be clear that this awareness can be found long before modernity. It is the sensitivity to anachronism which permits the recognition of distinctions between discrete historical periods.[5] For Ibn Ezra, that meant being conscious of where the Israelites were at the time to which a certain passage

1. *B. B. Bat.* 15a-b.
2. Cf. 2 Chron. 35.25.
3. Psalms 3, 18, 30, 34, 51, 52, 54, 56, 57, 59, 60, 63, 142; cf. LXX Psalm 96.
4. F.F. Bruce, 'The Earliest Old Testament Interpretation', *OTS* 17 (1972), pp. 37-52; cf. A. Shinan and Y. Zakovitch, 'Midrash on Scripture and Midrash within Scripture', in *Studies in Bible, 1986* (ed. S. Japhet; ScrHier 31; Jerusalem, 1986), p. 276.
5. According to Burke, 'Medieval men lacked a sense of the "differentness" of the past' (*Sense of the Past*, p. 6).

refers.[1] But the rabbis were fully capable of such observations. Their distinction between biblical language and their own is only one of several ways in which they acknowledged that their period was different from that of the Bible.[2] They also enumerated a variety of phenomena which had been present during the First Temple period but not that of the Second.[3]

This awareness, too, has biblical precedent in various passages which correlate specific phenomena, such as the Urim and Thummim, with identifiable historical periods.[4] It is also at the root of the Bible's anticipation of a future time, radically different from the present, as well as its recollection of a past which was fundamentally distinct from the epoch we inhabit.

1. Thus his challenge to the Mosaic authorship on the basis of its reference to Trans-Jordan as being on 'the *other* side of the Jordan', a statement which could only have been made by someone in Cis-Jordan, and hence not Moses (cf. his comment on Deut. 1.2).

2. See p. 169 n. 2 above. Contrast Burke's description of the awareness that language changed over time as a 'Renaissance discovery' (p. 142). Other examples of the rabbis' ability to periodize can be found in *b. Šab.* 112b; *b. Yom.* 9b, and the notion that one could not (any longer) construct a *gezerah shavah* on his own (*b. Pes.* 66a; *b. Nid.* 19b; cf. *b. Erub.* 53a and A. Qariv, *Shiv'at 'Amudei ha-Tanakh, 'Ishim ve-'Ide'ot be-Sefer ha-Sefarim* [Tel Aviv: Am Oved, 1968], pp. 232-35).

3. E.g. *j. Ta'an.* 65a; *b. Yom.* 21b; *Num. R.* 15.10; *Cant. R.* 8.9 3; cf. *m. Soṭ.* 9.12; *t. Soṭ.* 13.2; *b. B. Bat.* 12a; *Num. R.* 18.21; and *Pes. R.* 35.1. A similar awareness can be detected in *j. Soṭ.* 24b, *b. Soṭ.* 48b, *b. Yom.* 9b, and *b. B. Bat.* 11a which draw the line 'with the death of Haggai, Zechariah, and Malachi' and *Seder 'Olam Rab.* 70b §30 (ed. B. Ratner [Vilna: Romm, 1897], p. 140), which alludes to the time after Alexander the Great. See F.E. Greenspahn, 'Why Prophecy Ceased', *JBL* 108 (1989), p. 6. Related to this conception are the references to events which did (or did not) take place *mikka'n we'elak* (e.g. *t. Yad.* 2.13; cf. *j. Sanh.* 27c-28a; cf. *Midr. Pss.* 22.10).

4. Gen. 36.31; Exod. 6.3; Josh. 5.5, 12; Judg. 17.6; 18.1; 19.1; 21.25; 1 Sam. 9.9; Ezek. 18.1-4; Ruth 4.7; Ezra 2.63; cf. Jer. 34.6-15; Zech. 7.1-6; 8.19; 1 Macc. 9.27; *Apion* 1.8 §40-41. Further evidence that biblical authors also had a sense of periodization may be discerned in the idiosyncratic selection of names during the patriarchal period (see N.M. Sarna, *Genesis* [Philadelphia: Jewish Publication Society, 1989], p. xvi) and its restriction of idolatry to two periods (Y. Kaufmann, *Toledot ha-Emunah ha-Yisra'elit* [Jerusalem: Mosad Bialik; Tel Aviv: Devir] II.1 p. 113). Contrast Burke's statement that Herodotus's awareness 'that religion had a history. . . was unusual in his time' (p. 139).

In sum, traces of all three of Burke's hallmarks of modern historical consciousness—sensitivity to anachronism, evidence and causation—have existed since antiquity, and sometimes within the Bible itself. Not only are these criteria, therefore, incapable of setting our age apart from those which preceded, but, within the context of biblical studies, they demonstrate methodological continuity going back to the rabbis and even the Bible.

These observations should not be construed as overlooking the very real differences between our work and that of earlier ages; no one familiar with the Talmud or the midrashim could possibly confuse them with modern scholarship. The rabbis were not modern, much less the earlier biblical authors. But that fact is true by definition, and, like most tautological propositions, fundamentally unimportant. What must be borne in mind is that, despite our natural predilection for identifying a specific moment as the point of origin of new developments and ideas, most cultural change is slow and evolutionary.[1] In this, biblical studies is no exception. Whatever the achievements of modern scholarship, its uniqueness and novelty should not be exaggerated at the expense of the fundamental continuities, which have received far less attention than they are due. As the preceding discussion has attempted to show, each of the features which Burke associates with modern historical attitudes can, in fact, be found within medieval Jewish scholarship and, often, in rabbinic and even biblical texts.

Biblical studies is not a product of the Renaissance or Reformation, although its self-understanding may well be. It is, in fact, a very ancient endeavor, born out of the cultural distance between the Bible and those who are committed to its value. Without denying that our ability to understand the Bible has improved, the extent of that improvement should not be exaggerated nor its causes misunderstood. Whatever truth our conclusions may contain owes less to the development of new methods than to the dramatically increased resources made available over the past century. Nor should modern scholarly rhetoric be taken more seriously than it deserves. Such assertions often overstate both sides of the historical divide—our own and that of ages past—slipping into caricatures of the extent to which earlier

1. See S.J. Gould, 'The Creation Myths of Cooperstown', in *Bully for Brontosaurus: Reflections on Natural History* (New York: Norton, 1991), p. 57.

generations were restrained by the blinders of theological orthodoxy even as they ignore our own subjectivity.

More than the methods we use or the issues we address, what really sets modern scholarship apart from its antecedents is its claim to be radically different from the past, which may owe less to the reality of contemporary biblical studies than to that most modern of conceits, the denial of its roots. Like the corollary placement of its origins sometime in the last few centuries, this rejection of any connection, either methodological or genetic, between contemporary scholarship and its forebears should be approached with caution. Our claims of objectivity, as appealing as they may feel, can be easily contradicted by anyone who has read much of contemporary biblical scholarship.

These assertions do not exist in a vacuum. Many modern biblical scholars find themselves ensconced in secular universities, where religious studies of all sorts are suspect and 'scientific rigor' the norm for measuring academic respectability. Even ostensibly religious institutions share these aspirations. Claims of objectivity and religious neutrality are the hallmarks of status and success in the academic world, legitimizing this potentially suspect field and allowing its practitioners to function in an environment where the products of their research must be credible even to those from other religious communities or, for that matter, from none at all. For Jews, objectivity has a special appeal, as they seek acceptance in a field where Christians enjoy both historical advantage and overwhelming numerical superiority.[1] The university thus provides the *Sitz im Leben* for contemporary claims about biblical studies.

This approach has been reinforced by the privatization of religion in our society, even as it tolerates other ideological stances, such as Freudianism, Marxism, and the like. But only the naive accept such statements as accurate descriptions of academic reality. Rather than having eliminated the religious influence on biblical interpretation, modernity has simply driven it underground, providing a blanket of secularism which permits scholars from diverse backgrounds to use common methods and a common language to communicate with each other in a world where Jewish and Christian exegetes often find their work evaluated by individuals with different beliefs.

1. Jewish appeals to first-amendment religious neutrality as a way of protecting their interests as a minority are fundamentally analogous.

The persistence of religious motivation can be illustrated in the career of Julius Wellhausen, that paragon of modern scholarship, whose recognition of the gap between his approach and the needs of the theological faculty at Griefswald to which he was appointed led him to resign in 1882 lest 'despite all caution on my own part I make my hearers unfit for their office'.[1] Despite his own sense of having moved beyond the realm of institutional Christianity, Wellhausen later wrote that 'the Gospel. . . preaches the most noble individualism, the freedom of the children of God' (*Das Evangelium ist nur das Salz der Erde; wo est mehr sein will, ist est weniger. Est predigt den edelsten Individualismus, die Freiheit der Kinder Gottes*).[2]

The Jewish scholars attacked by Max Lurie are no more immune from religious motivations than their non-Jewish colleagues. Lurie's own son sought to enter biblical scholarship in order to defend Judaism against the slander of its Christian practitioners, a goal shared with Solomon Schechter, who closed his condemnation of biblical criticism with the hope that a cadre of Jewish biblical scholars would be able to rid that discipline of its historic taint.[3] Nor can those who have taken up this challenge legitimately be called 'goyish', except perhaps by the most narrow of definitions. Modern Judaism is simply too diverse to fit comfortably under such rubrics. As Nahum Sarna reminds us, it has never been as rigid as its modern-day 'defenders' contend. Whether or not contemporary Jewish scholars accept the authority of halacha (and a significant number of them are more observant than their detractors allow), only the most limited view

1. Quoted by R. Smend, 'Julius Wellhausen and His *Prolegomena to the History of Israel*', *Sem* 25 (1983), p. 6.

2. *Israelitische und Jüdische Geschichte* (Berlin: de Gruyter, 7th edn, 1958), p. 371; the translation is from J.D. Levenson, 'The Hebrew Bible, the Old Testament, and Historical Criticism', in *The Future of Biblical Studies, The Hebrew Scriptures* (ed. R.E. Friedman and H.G.M. Williamson; Atlanta: Scholars Press, 1987), p. 31. Significantly, the words *den edelsten* ('most noble') are not in the first edition (Berlin: Georg Reimer, 1894, p. 321), which was itself published twelve years after Wellhausen resigned from Griefswald.

3. *Seminary Addresses and Other Papers*, p. 38 and *In the Beginning*, p. 392; cf. Potok's comment that 'some of my friends. . . entered Bible scholarship in order to change the attitude of the discipline towards Jews—and they have succeeded' ('Judaism Under the Secular Umbrella', Cheryl Forbes, *Christianity Today*, 22.21 [September 8, 1978], p. 20).

could fail to recognize the inherent Jewishness of much that they do, whatever the source of their methods.[1] Yigael Yadin, Yehezkel Kaufmann and Sheldon Blank all represent decidedly Jewish approaches to the Bible, however much they may differ from an Orthodox view.

Modern biblical studies did not emerge *ex nihilo*—any more than any aspect of human culture is the result of spontaneous generation. No matter what its myth of origins, contemporary biblical studies, like all scholarship, is a cumulative process, in which each generation, including those of Gesenius, Wellhausen and even Spinoza, extend what they have inherited on the basis of their own experience. Only a secularized version of the chosen people concept, coupled with early Protestantism's belief in its own ability to read the biblical authors without mediation, can account for modern scholars' conceit in disconnecting themselves from the long tradition of those who have also studied this most influential of texts. As modern and objective as our methods may (or should) be, they are but the criteria of our culture, without which no interpretation could be accepted. In that regard, too, the enterprise of modern biblical scholarship functions much like its forbears, which also sought to explain the Bible according to the canons of their time, even granting that the expectations of today's world are inevitably different from those of previous centuries.[2] Our understanding of history, our commitment to objectivity and scientific methods may render the conclusions of the past untenable, but it is the criteria of acceptability which have changed, not the methods nor even the underlying goal.

No one has demonstrated these continuities more effectively than Nahum Sarna, who has recognized modern Jewish biblical studies as 'another link in an unbroken chain of Jewish exegesis'.[3] His technical

1. The classic rabbinic methods of exegesis were themselves influenced by, if not borrowed from, outside sources; see D. Daube, 'Rabbinic Methods of Interpretation and Hellenistic Rhetoric', *HUCA* 22 (1949), pp. 239-64, although S. Lieberman offers an important caution (*Hellenism in Jewish Palestine* [New York: Jewish Theological Seminary of America, 1952], pp. 53-68).

2. Levenson observes how the careers of many practitioners of this trade began with some sort of religious training ('Theological Consensus or Historicist Evasion', p. 133), although this should be considered within the larger context of 'research' careers, which often develop out of an initially practical orientation.

3. 'The Modern Study of the Bible', p. 20.

skills and his willingness to share the product of their application with a broader audience in a way that is respectful of their interests place his well within the mainstream of a long and rich tradition.[1]

1. My thinking about the issues treated in this paper has benefited greatly from extensive discussions with John Livingston.

Disturbing the Dead*

William W. Hallo

Disturbing the dead was fraught with danger not only in the biblical view but across the whole ancient Near East, from Mesopotamia to Phoenicia. In what follows, old and new documentation will be offered to this effect, and some recent discussions of the theme will be considered.

In 'Death and the Netherworld according to the Sumerian Literary Texts', S.N. Kramer decried the fact that 'the Sumerian ideas relating to death and the netherworld... were neither clear, precise or consistent'.[1] Much the same could probably be said of most cultures. But in fact the consistency and continuity of the Sumerian view, and its survival in Akkadian texts, is quite impressive. Nowhere is this better exemplified than in the tale to which Kramer himself gave the title 'Gilgamesh, Enkidu and the Netherworld'.[2] The first half of this tale was edited by Kramer under the title 'Gilgamesh and the Huluppu-Tree' at the start of his long career of editing Sumerian literary texts.[3] Its second half, translated verbatim into Akkadian, became the last (12th) tablet of the latest recension of the Akkadian *Epic of Gilgamesh*[4]—itself a literary phenomenon almost without parallel in the history of cuneiform literature.[5]

* Paper submitted to the 24th Annual Conference of the Association for Jewish Studies, Boston, December 13-15 1992, and here offered in warm tribute to Nahum Sarna.

1. *Iraq* 22 (1960), pp. 59-68, esp. p. 65.

2. *PAPhS* 85 (1942), p. 321; *JAOS* 64 (1944), pp. 7-23, esp. pp. 19-22.

3. *Gilgamesh and the Huluppu-Tree* (*AS* 10 [1938]); preceded by 'Gilgamesh and the Willow Tree', *The Open Court* 50 (1936), pp. 18-33.

4. A. Shaffer, *Sumerian Sources of Tablet XII of the Epic of Gilgameš* (Ann Arbor, MI: University Microfilms, 1963).

5. W.W. Hallo, 'Problems in Sumerian Hermeneutics', *Perspectives in Jewish*

According to this account, when Enkidu descended to the netherworld to recover the hoop and driving stick[1] of Gilgamesh, or his drum and drumstick[2] if a 'shamanistic' reading is preferred,[3] the latter counseled him not to offend or disturb the dead.[4] In particular, he warned, 'Do not take a staff in your hands [or] the spirits will panic before you'.[5] Enkidu, however, ignored the warning, and a few lines later on we read that 'he took a staff in his hands and the spirits panicked [because of him]'.[6] In a recent study of the passage, Aase Koefoed interprets the warning as 'taboo rules' which 'seem to correspond to the actual rules for conduct during a mourning ceremony'[7] and their violation by Enkidu as the reason for his untimely death.[8] She compares the staff of cornel-wood[9] to the '*rhabdos* in Greek religion, where it is the stick or magic wand used by Hermes to invoke and drive the ghosts'.[10]

These ghosts (g i d i m = *eṭemmu*) could easily turn into demons (GIDIM₄ = u d u g = *utukku*) which, if improperly buried or

Learning 5 (1973), pp. 1-12, esp. p. 7; 'Toward a History of Sumerian Literature', in S.J. Lieberman (ed.), *Sumerological Studies in Honor of Thorkild Jacobsen* (AS, 20; 1976), pp. 181-203, esp. pp. 189-90 and n. 57; review of B. Alster, *The Instructions of Suruppak*, *JNES* 37 (1978), pp. 269-73, esp. p. 272 (D).

1. Sumerian g i š – e l l a g and g i š – E.KÌD – m a, Akkadian *pukku* and *mekkû*; cf. *CAD* M/2 *s.v. mekku* A, based on B. Landsberger, *WZKM* 56 (1960), pp. 124-26; 57 (1961), p. 23.

2. This is Landsberger's earlier translation, and survives in *ANET* (3rd edn, 1969), p. 507.

3. 'I judge that the readings "drum" and "drumstick" are clinched by the widespread Siberian tradition that the frames of shaman-drums come from wood of the World Tree'; A.T. Hatto, *Shamanism and Epic Poetry in Northern Asia* (London: SOAS, 1970), p. 4. But cf. C.R. Bawden, *BASOS* 35 (1972), p. 394.

4. 'Gilgamesh, Enkidu and the Netherworld', ll. 185-99; see Shaffer, *Sumerian Sources*, pp. 74-76, 108-109.

5. 'Gilgamesh, Enkidu and the Netherworld', ll. 191-92; cf. *CAD* A/2, pp. 236-37; *s.v. araru* B; *CAD* S/10, *s.v. šabbiṭu*.

6. 'Gilgamesh, Enkidu and the Netherworld', ll. 213-14.

7. See pp. 190-91 for possible elements of such ceremonies.

8. A. Koefoed, 'Gilgamesh, Enkidu and the Netherworld', *ASJ* 5 (1983), pp. 17-23, esp. p. 20.

9. g i š – m a – n u, ordinarily translated by Akkadian *e'ru*, which 'is well-known as the magical wand used in incantations against demons'; cf. Koefoed, 'Gilgameš', p. 23 n. 13.

10. Koefoed, 'Gilgameš', p. 20.

disturbed, could return to haunt and terrify the living.[1] The Sumerian incantations known as 'Evil Spirits' (u d u g – h u l)[2] and the bilingual series into which they evolved (*utukkū lemnūtu*)[3] were designed to ward off that possibility. This is illustrated by such lines as '[these demons] agitated the distraught man'[4] and '[the demons] caused panic in the land'.[5] The former passage recurs in a bilingual exercise text where the Akkadian verb used is the same as in *Gilgamesh* XII (exceptionally in transitive usage).[6]

Violation of a grave was therefore considered a particularly severe form of punishment, as for example when Assurbanipal of Assyria (668–627 BC) destroyed the tombs of the Elamite kings during his sack of the Elamite capital at Susa,[7] carrying their bones to Assur, condemning their spirits to restlessness, and depriving them of funerary repasts[8] and water libations (*eṭemmešunu la ṣalālu ēmid kispī nāq mê uzammēšunūti*).[9] Perhaps this was a specific revenge for their having been 'the disturbers (*munarriṭū*)[10] of the kings my ancestors', that is, of the graves of the departed royalty. But more likely the reference here was simply to the harassment and terrorism to which the royal Assyrian ancestors had been subjected during their reigns.[11]

1. W.W. Hallo, 'Royal Ancestor Worship in the Biblical World', in *Sha'arei Talmon: Studies. . . presented to Shemaryahu Talmon* (Winona Lake, IN: Eisenbrauns, 1992), pp. 381-401, esp. p. 389 and nn. 56-59.

2. M.J. Geller, *Forerunners to Udug-hul: Sumerian Exorcistic Incantations* (Freiburger Altorientalische Studien, 12; 1985).

3. R.C. Thompson, *The Devils and Evil Spirits of Babylonia*, I (London: Luzac, 1903).

4. Thompson, *Devils*, pp. 20-21, l. 2.

5. Thompson, *Devils*, pp. 34-35, l. 255, with note *ad loc.* (p. 99).

6. UET 6.392, cited *CAD* A/2, pp. 236-37; *s.v. arāru* B. 22.

7. For this event and its aftermath cf. W.W. Hallo, 'An Assurbanipal Text Recovered', *The Israel Museum Journal* 6 (1987), pp. 33-37; P.D. Gerardi, *Assurbanipal's Elamite Campaigns: A Literary and Political Study* (Ann Arbor, MI: 1987), esp. pp. 195-213; E. Carter and M.W. Stolper, *Elam* (Near Eastern Studies, 25; University of California Publications, 1984), p. 52.

8. For these see below, pp. 191-92.

9. *CAD* E, 399a; Z, 156d.

10. *CAD* N/1, 349a; cited Hallo, *loc. cit.* (see next note), but correct citation accordingly.

11. A. Tsukimoto, *Untersuchungen zur Totenpflege (*kispum*) im alten Mesopotamien* (AOAT, 216; Neukirchen–Vluyn: Neukirchener Verlag, 1985),

The prevention of such desecration thus became the particular objective of another genre of texts, that of the funerary inscription. This genre is relatively less well attested in cuneiform than in some other ancient Near Eastern corpora of inscriptions. Such evidence as was by then available, was assembled and discussed by Jean Bottero in 1981.[1] A good illustration of the genre is the mortuary inscription of Shamash-ibni,[2] the Chaldean of Bit-Dakkuri who died in Assyria and whose 'body was returned to his native land for burial only in the time of Ashur-etel-ilani, about half a century later',[3] that is, under one of the last kings of Assyria (626–624 BC). The most famous example may well be the *Autobiography of Adadguppi*, which can be dated to the ninth year of Nabonidus, last king of Babylon (547 BC).[4]

But recent discoveries have added significantly to the corpus. The graves of three neo-Assyrian queens recovered together with their spectacular contents at Nimrud in 1989 have yielded as many funerary inscriptions, two of them published by A. Fadhil the following year.[5] These include explicit injunctions against disturbing the entombed bodies, using the verb *dēkû*, 'to arouse (from sleep or rest)',[6] but here

pp. 114-15; cited in W.W. Hallo, 'The Death of Kings: Traditional Historiography in Contextual Perspective', in M. Cogan and I. Eph'al (eds.), *Ah, Assyria. . . : Studies. . . presented to Hayim Tadmor* (ScrHier, 33; 1991), pp. 148-65, esp. p. 162 n. 126.

1. J. Bottéro, 'Les inscriptions cunéiformes funéraires', in G. Gnoli and J.-P. Vernant, (eds.), *La mort, les morts dans les Sociétés Anciennes* (Cambridge: Cambridge University Press, 1982), pp. 373-406.

2. Bottéro, 'Les inscriptions', pp. 384-85, based on YOS 1.43; 9.81-82.

3. J.A. Brinkman, *Prelude to Empire: Babylonian Society and Politics, 747–626 BC* (Occasional Publications of the Babylonian Fund, 7; 1984), p. 80 and n. 388, based on YOS 1.43 and YOS 9.81-82.

4. *ANET* (3rd edn, 1969), pp. 560-62; latest translation by T. Longman, *Fictional Akkadian Autobiography: A Generic and Comparative Study* (Winona Lake, IN: Eisenbrauns, 1991), pp. 225-28; cf. pp. 97-103, and P.-A. Beaulieu, *The Reign of Nabonidus, King of Babylon 556–539 BC* (YNER, 10; 1989), pp. 78-79 and *passim.*

5. A. Fadhil, 'Die in Nimrud/Kalhu aufgefundene Grabinschrift der Jabâ', *BaM* 21 (1990), pp. 461-70; 'Die Grabinschrift der Mullissu-mukannišat-Ninua aus Nimrud/Kalhu', *BaM* 21 (1990), pp. 471-82 and pls. 39-45.

6. *CAD* 123d and 125bc.

in the sense of 'to disturb the dead', as seen by A. Livingstone.[1] He compares the language of neo-Assyrian royal land grants where the same verb is used in the same sense in connection with the verb *ṣalālu*, 'to lie down, to sleep',[2] concluding 'that "to wake the sleeper" was a euphemistic expression for "to disturb the dead"'.

The same idiom already occurs in Sumerian literary texts, where l ú – n á – a z i – z i means 'to wake the sleeper' as in a 'tambourine-lament' (é r – š è m – m a) of Inanna and Dumuzi where a demon (g a l a) 'wakes Dumuzi, who is sleeping, from [his] sleep. . . wakes the spouse of holy Inanna, who is sleeping, from [his] sleep'.[3] That 'the phrase is also employed, however, as a euphemism for those who sleep the "treacherous" sleep (ù – l u l – l a) of death' was recognized long ago by T. Jacobsen,[4] although it must be admitted that the sleep in question can also be a 'feigned sleep', for example when it is attributed to Enlil in one of that deity's standard 'heroic' epithets' as seen by R. Kutscher.[5] Sleep as a premonition of death is familiar from the eleventh tablet of the *Gilgamesh Epic*, when the hero complains to Utnapishtim, 'Scarcely had sleep surged over me, when straightway thou dost touch and rouse me (*taddekkanni*)!'—when in fact he had already slept for seven days.[6]

The common use of 'sleep' as a metaphor or euphemism for death also explains the use of 'place of silence' as a circumlocution or epithet for 'grave' in an inscription of Shamshi-Adad I of Assyria

1. A. Livingstone, 'To Disturb the Dead: Taboo to Enmesarra?', *NABU* 1.1 (1991).

2. Livingstone, 'To Disturb the Dead', citing J.N. Postgate, *Neo-Assyrian Grants and Decrees* (Studia Pohl Series Maior, 1; 1969), no. 9 (p. 29), ll. 55-57, 60; cf. also nos. 10-12.

3. M.E. Cohen, *Sumerian Hymnology: The Eršemma* (HUCA Supplements, 2; 1981), pp. 76 and 81, ll. 48-49. The same lines were dealt with earlier by T. Jacobsen, 'The Myth of Inanna and Bilulu', *JNES* 12 (1953), pp. 160-87, esp. pp. 182-83 n. 50; repr. in *Toward the Image of Tammuz and other Essays on Mesopotamian History and Culture* (ed. W.L. Moran; HSS, 21; Cambridge, MA: Harvard University Press, 1970), p. 346 n. 50.

4. Jacobsen, 'The Myth of Inanna and Bilulu', pp. 182-83 n. 50; *Toward the Image*, p. 346 n. 50.

5. R. Kutscher, *Oh Angry Sea* (a - a b - b a h u - l u h - h a): *The History of a Sumerian Congregational Lament* (YNER, 6; 1975), p. 49.

6. *ANET* (3rd edn, 1969), p. 96, ll. 220-21.

(c. 1813–1781 BC),[1] and more particularly of 'rest house' as a poetic designation for the grave. This is clearest on bricks from the royal sepulcher at Assur, which describe the grave of Sennaherib (704–681 BC) as 'a palace of sleeping, a grave of rest, a habitation of eternity' (*ekal ṣalāli kimah tapšuhti šubat dārâti*), or as a 'palace of rest, habitation of eternity' (*ekal tapšuhti šubat dārâti*).[2]

While the concept of 'eternal habitation' can be paralleled in West Semitic usage, both biblical (Eccl. 12.5) and epigraphic,[3] that of 'place' or 'house of rest' can be traced back to Sumerian usage. The Sumerian equivalent to 'house of rest' (*bit tapšuhti*) is é – n í – d ú b – b u (- d a).[4] It occurs in a unilingual lexical list[5] and as an epithet of temples and storage houses built by the kings of Isin and Larsa.[6] The Sumerian equivalent to 'resting-place' (*ašar tapšuhti*) is k i – n í – d ú b – b u – d a; it occurs in an inscription of Warad-Sin of Larsa (c. 1834–1823 BC) as an epithet of the temple of Nin-Isina called E-unamtila, literally 'house [of] the plant of life'.[7]

To return to the idiom of 'waking the sleeper', Livingstone has also discovered it in a late Akkadian literary text[8] which he treated under the heading of 'works. . . explaining state rituals in terms of myths' in 1986[9] and as 'mystical miscellanea' in 1989.[10] Here Jacobsen had

1. É. KI.SI.GA É *qú-ul-ti-šu*; A.K. Grayson, *Assyrian Rulers of the Third and Second Millennium BC (to 1115 BC)* (RIMA 1; Toronto: University of Toronto Press, 1987), pp. 59-60, no. 8; cf. Bottéro, 'Les inscriptions', p. 403 n. 18, who, however, seems to take É KI.SI.GA as a phonetic (?) spelling for É KI.SÌ.GA, hence rendering it '*Salle-au-kispu*'. Differently *CAD* Q 302d.

2. OIP 2.151.14.3 and 13.2 respectively; cf. Bottéro, 'Les inscriptions', p. 382.

3. See in general H. Tawil, 'A Note on the Ahiram Inscription', *JANESCU* 3 (1970–71), pp. 32-36, esp. p. 36; A. Negev, 'A Nabataean Epitaph from Trans-Jordan', *IEJ* 21 (1971), pp. 50-53, esp. pp. 50-51, with nn. 4-9.

4. W.W. Hallo, 'Oriental Institute Museum Notes No. 10: The Last Years of the Kings of Isin', *JNES* 18 (1959), pp. 54-72, esp. p. 54 and n. 2, based on A. Deimel, *Šumerisches Lexikon*, III.2 (Rome: Pontifical Biblical Institute, 1932), no. 399, 177 based in turn on K.D. Macmillan, 'Some Cuneiform Tablets. . . ', *BA* 5 (1906), p. 634 l. 13; cf. p. 573, ll. 13-14 and p. 588 l. 11.

5. MSL 13.69.108.

6. Hallo, 'The Last Years', p. 54 and nn. 5-6.

7. D.R. Frayne, *Old Babylonian Period (2003–1595 BC)* (RIME, 4; Toronto: University of Toronto Press, 1990), pp. 244-45, no. 22 (l. 14).

8. KAR 307.28-29.

9. A. Livingstone, *Mystical and Mythological Explanatory Works of Assyrian and*

read 'The sill of the temple of Enmesharra: he hitched up at the wall, / the tallow of fleece (I.UDU *it-qi*) is taboo for Enmesharra'.[1] Livingstone, however, reads, 'He hung the ladders of the house of Enmesarra on the wall and woke up the sleepers (*ṣal-lu id-ki*). Taboo of Enmesarra',[2] and adds, 'it would not be difficult to suppose that disturbing the dead was anathema to the underworld deity Enmesarra'.[3]

The concept of a divine taboo or anathema has been the subject of two recent studies. In 1985 I selected some fourteen examples of the theme from Sumerian and Akkadian literature, and compared them with the biblical concept of divine abominations.[4] Klein and Sefati covered much the same ground in 1988, in another volume dedicated to the memory of Moshe Held.[5] I concluded that, between the early second millennium and the early first millennium, 'the emphasis of the taboos... shifted from a principal preoccupation with morals and manners to an at least equal concern with cultic matters',[6] and eventually 'to normally legitimate activities which happen to be conducted on an unacceptable day'.[7] The 'taboo of Enmesarra' fits well into this scheme, as it appears to represent a cultic infraction whether on Jacobsen's reading or Livingstone's.

A third meaning was suggested as the common denominator of the biblical abominations: they are primarily 'acts enjoined by alien cults but anathema to God'.[8] At first blush the biblical evidence does not seem to bear on our theme. Disturbing the dead is not a cultic

Babylonian Scholars (Oxford: Clarendon Press, 1986), ch. 4, esp. pp. 124-25.

10. A. Livingstone, *Court Poetry and Literary Miscellanea* (SAA, 3; Helsinki: Helsinki University Press, 1989), pp. 99-102.

1. T. Jacobsen, 'Religious Drama in Ancient Mesopotamia', in H. Goedicke and J.J.M. Roberts (eds.), *Unity and Diversity* (Johns Hopkins Near Eastern Studies, [7]; Baltimore: Johns Hopkins University Press, 1975), pp. 63-97, esp. p. 95 n. 58.

2. Livingstone, *Court Poetry*, p. 100.

3. *NABU* 1991.1.

4. W.W. Hallo, 'Biblical Abominations and Sumerian Taboos', *JQR* 76 (1985), pp. 21-40.

5. J. Klein and Y. Sefati, 'The Concept of "Abomination" in Mesopotamian Literature and the Bible', *Beer-Sheva* 3 (1988), pp. 131-48 (in Hebrew; English summary pp. 12*ff.).

6. Hallo, 'Biblical Abominations', p. 29.

7. Hallo, 'Biblical Abominations', p. 33.

8. Hallo, 'Biblical Abominations', p. 38.

requirement in paganism—on the contrary it is a taboo already there. It is not implied in the idiom for waking the sleeper; when used in a literal sense, that idiom refers rather to the impossibility of waking the dead;[1] when used in other than a literal sense, it alludes to *resurrecting* the dead.[2] It may be noted in the latter connection that the modern renaissance of Jewish culture was promoted by a society for the publication of medieval Hebrew literature founded in 1862 under the name of *Mekize Nirdamim*, 'rousers of those who slumber'.[3]

But in fact biblical Hebrew *does* feature a functional equivalent of the Sumero–Akkadian idiom. It employs not the root 'to awake' (*qyṣ*, *yqṣ*) but the root 'quiver, agitate' (*rgz*), and occurs in two telling contexts. The first concerns Saul who persuaded the witch of En-Dor to 'bring up' the deceased Samuel, who thereupon complained, 'Why have you disturbed me (*hirgaztāni*) and brought me up?' (1 Sam. 28.15) and presumably cursed Saul and his progeny with imminent death (1 Sam. 28.19).[4] The second involves Sargon II of Assyria whose death in battle in 705 BC—a royal fate almost without precedent in Mesopotamian history—was, in the biblical view, at least partially the punishment for his rousing the dead kings from their rest. In the words of Isaiah (Isa. 14.9), 'Sheol below was astir (*ragzāh*) to greet your coming—rousing for you the shades (*rep̄ā'îm*)[5] of all earth's chieftains, raising from their thrones all the kings of the nations'.[6] For good measure it maybe pointed out again that the same root (*rgz*) is employed in Phoenician funerary inscriptions,[7] notably

1. Cf. 2 Kgs 4.31; Jer. 51.39, 57; Job. 14.12.
2. Isa. 26.19; Dan. 12.2.
3. *EncJud*, XI, pp. 1270ff.; *s.v.* Mekiẓe Nirdamiṃ.
4. J.C. Greenfield, 'Scripture and Inscription: The Literary and Rhetorical Element in some Early Phoenician Inscriptions', in H. Goedicke (ed.), *Near Eastern Studies in Honor of William Foxwell Albright* (Baltimore: Johns Hopkins University Press, 1971), pp. 253-68, esp. pp. 258ff.; Hallo, 'The Death of Kings', pp. 151, 162.
5. On the *rep̄ā'îm* see most recently Hallo, 'Royal Ancestor Worship', esp. pp. 382-86.
6. See previous note and cf. H.L. Ginsberg, 'Reflexes of Sargon in Isaiah after 715 BCE', in W.W. Hallo (ed.), *Essays in Memory of E.A. Speiser* (AOS, 53; New Haven: American Oriental Society), repr. from *JAOS* 88 (1968), pp. 47-53.
7. On their typology see H.-P. Müller, 'Die Phönizische Grabinschrift aus dem Zypern-Museum KAI 30 und die Formgeschichte des Nordwestsemitischen Epitaphs', *ZA* 65 (1975), pp. 104-32, esp. pp. 109-10, 118-19. Cf. also

those of Tabnit of Sidon[1] and of the son of Shipit-Baal of Byblos.[2]

By contrast to such practices, subject to dreadful curses and dire punishments, the proper respect for the departed required, in the first place, the recitation of appropriate lamentations, presumably at the time of interment. That appears to be the sense of the Sumerian notation 'when he entered ['turned into' is a possible translation but unlikely here] the office of lamentation-priests' (u n a m – g a l a – š è i n – k u$_4$ - r a) which is frequently encountered in neo-Sumerian accounts justifying the expenditure of modest numbers of sacrificial animals[3] by the next of kin (?), whose ranks include two cooks, a courier, a bowman, a foot-soldier—all lay professions—and three Amorites.[4] Given the diversity of these origins, it seems unlikely that we should translate here, 'when they entered the office of lamentation-priest',[5] the more so since a single name at most recurs among the numerous named lamentation-priests on neo-Sumerian documents.[6]

Once buried, the dead required above all a 'commemorative funerary meal', called *kispu* in Akkadian and k i – s ì – g a in Sumerian.[7] Because the Sumerian term, in the form 'house (é) of the k i – s ì - g a', is otherwise equated with Akkadian words for grave (*kimāhu*, *qubūru*),[8] the existence of a true Sumerian equivalent has hitherto

K. Galling, 'Die Grabinschrift Hiobs', *Welt des Orients* 2 (1954), pp. 3-6 *ad* Job 19.23-27.

1. *ANET* (3rd edn, 1969), p. 662. Cf. above p. 190 n. 4, but correct the reference in 'The Death of Kings' (n. 125) accordingly.

2. H. Donner and W. Röllig, *KAI*, II (Wiesbaden: Otto Harrassowitz, 1973), pp. 10-11.

3. Typically five sheep and/or goats; once two grain-fattened sheep and once three adult goats.

4. T. Fish, '*Gala* on Ur III Tablets', *MCS* 7 (1957), pp. 25-27; M. Sigrist, *AUCT* 3 (1988), no. 42; *idem*, *Tablettes du Princeton Theological Seminary: Epoque d'Ur III* (Occasional Publications of the Samuel Noah Kramer Fund, 10; 1990), no. 90; see below n. 6.

5. As implied by H. Hartmann, *Die Musik in der Sumerischen Kultur* (Frankfurt 1960), pp. 141-42.

6. Hartmann, *Die Musik*, pp. 166-79, 356-61. The possible exception, as noted by Hartmann (p. 173 n. 4), is N. Schneider, 'Keilschrifturkunden aus Drehem und Djoha', *Or* o.s. 18 (1925), no. 17, pp. 17-19; the profession of ù – k u l registered there is otherwise unknown to me.

7. See Hallo, 'Royal Ancestor Worship', p. 394 and cf. above p. 188 n. 1.

8. Hallo, 'Royal Ancestor Worship', p. 392 and n. 69.

been overlooked. I propose as such an equivalent g i z b u n, a Sumerian word generally translated by '(festive) meal, banquet', based in part on its logographic writing with the signs for 'place where beer is put' (KI.KAS.GAR).[1] Later the Sumerian term was equated with Akkadian *takultu*, 'divine repast',[2] illustrating once again the tendency of cultic terms to evolve out of everyday language.[3] The fact that the 'logogram' was at times still pronounced as written (k i – k a š – g a r – r a)[4] strongly suggests that g i z b u n is an alternate reading of the signs, and hence a loan-word from Akkadian, rather than vice versa.[5]

Since the cultic meal in question is most at home in Mari, at or near the border between the Mesopotamian and the biblical worlds, its evidence may be added to that of the other common features of funerary practices and beliefs as yet further testimony to the interconnectedness of the entire ancient Near East.

1. Cf. e.g. Lugalbanda I ll. 365 and 367 for which see W.W. Hallo, 'Lugalbanda Excavated', in J.M. Sasson (ed.), *Studies. . . Dedicated to Samuel Noah Kramer* (AOS, 65; New Haven: American Oriental Society, 1984), repr. from *JAOS* 103 (1983), pp. 165-80, esp. pp. 174 and 178-79.

2. Cf. Hallo, 'Lugalbanda Excavated', and *idem*, 'The Origins of the Sacrificial Cult: New Evidence from Mesopotamia and Israel', in P.D. Miller *et al.* (eds.), *Ancient Israelite Religion: Essays in Honor of Frank Moore Cross* (Philadelphia: Fortress Press, 1987), pp. 3-13, esp. p. 9, for the significance of the equation for the given context.

3. Cf. B.A. Levine, *In the Presence of the Lord: A Study of Cult and some Cultic Terms in Ancient Israel* (SJLA, 5; 1974), esp. pp. 8-20.

4. Cf. M. Civil, 'The Anzu-Bird and Scribal Whimsies', *JAOS* 92 (1972), p. 271.

5. For the Semitic etymologies proposed for *kispum*, see Tsukimoto, *Untersuchungen*, pp. 23-26.

11QPs[a] AND THE CANONICAL BOOK OF PSALMS

Menahem Haran

I

From the moment psalm scrolls began to be discovered at Qumran, scholars have become more and more aware that all these scrolls are dependent on the canonical book of Psalms. Some 40 psalm manuscripts have turned up in the Judean desert, all of them partial, and most of them extremely fragmentary.[1] Yet, in spite of the many deficiencies, it is clear that those manuscripts which do contain a number of chapters are arranged according to the order of the Masoretic Text and LXX. Thus, as far as the book of Psalms' internal order is concerned, the manuscripts may be taken as testifying to a basically agreed-upon convention.

A number of additional considerations also lend probability to the antiquity of the book's composition in relation to the Qumran period. First, the existence of Qumran commentaries, *pesharîm*, on the book of Psalms proves that the latter was composed in an earlier period and that the people of Qumran held it to be canonical. Secondly, the writing of original lyrical-religious poetry did not stop in the Qumran period. Examples of it appear in the Thanksgiving Scroll (1QH), but these are already influenced by the biblical psalms as well as by other parts of the Bible. It follows that the biblical psalmodic poetry represents a more ancient form, which gradually disappeared by the end of the Persian period—although, because of its tremendous vitality, this

1. See J.A. Sanders' list ('Pre-Masoretic Psalter Texts', *CBQ* 27 [1965], pp. 114-23). Sanders lists fragments from 37 scrolls (of which the longest is 11QPs[a]), including three extremely small fragments (which are entered under '21a' and therefore do not influence his count), four *pesharîm*, one text from Naḥal Ḥever and two from Massada. From Qumran Cave 4 alone, fragments of 16 scrolls have been identified, to which the three very small fragments should be added.

poetry continued to radiate a certain influence in later times and its glimmerings were still discernible in the beginning of the Hellenistic period.[1] We may add a third consideration, that, despite the slight differences between the Masoretic Text and LXX when it comes to the conjunction of chapters, the two versions are essentially the same in their arrangement of the actual material. This indicates that the canonical book must have achieved its form before it was translated into Greek—which was no later than the first half of the second century BCE.[2] Thus, we cannot escape the conclusion that the complete book of Psalms already existed by the time of Qumran.

There are few exceptions to the above-mentioned rule that, in the Qumran scrolls, the chapters of Psalms generally follow the order of the Masoretic Text and LXX. Although these exceptions may at times surprise us, they cannot obscure the basic agreement between the versions. We are frequently confronted by large gaps between chapters, such as the gaps in 1QPs[a] between Pss. 96–119, 4QPs[a] between Pss. 6–21, 4QPs[f] between Pss. 22–107, and 4QPs[k] between Pss. 30–135. Needless to say, in such cases no inference should be drawn from what is lacking. However, in 4QPs[a] and 4QPs[q], it is obvious that ch. 32 is missing from its position between 31 and 33, and 4QPs[b] omits

1. Cf. J.P. Hyatt, 'The Dead Sea Discoveries: Retrospect and Challenge', *JBL* 76 (1957), p. 5: M. Burrows, *More Light on the Dead Sea Scrolls* (New York: Viking Press, 1958), pp. 169-71; F.M. Cross, *The Ancient Library of Qumran* (Garden City, NY: Doubleday 1961), pp. 165-66; *idem*, 'The History of the Biblical Text in the Light of Discoveries in the Judean Desert', *HTR* 57 (1964), pp. 286, 295-99. The above formulation is mine. Examples of Hellenistic glimmerings of psalmodic poetry include: Psalm 151, of which a Greek version appears in the LXX and an extended version is found in 11QPs[a] (on which, see my article, 'The Two Text-Forms of Psalm 151', *JJS* 39 [1988], pp. 171-82); Psalms 154–155, found in the Syriac and in Hebrew form in 11QPs[a]; Psalms 152–153, which were translated from Hebrew into Syriac, but have not been preserved in Hebrew; the psalm of thanksgiving that appears at the end of Sirach (Sir. 51.1-8, according to M.H. Segal's division) and a psalm of praise which imitates Psalm 136 and is found in the same chapter (Sir. 51.21-35), but is omitted from the Greek and Syriac versions.

2. Greek translations of Chronicles and Esther appeared already in the second century BCE, and it cannot be supposed that the Greek translation of Psalms came after these. The preface written by Ben Sira's grandson to the Greek version of his grandfather's book indicates clearly that a Greek translation of the entire Bible existed, divided into Torah, Prophets, and 'other books'. This third grouping is unimaginable without the book of Psalms.

everything from chs. 104 to 111.[1] In a few scrolls, the standard chapter order has been disturbed. For example, in 4QPs[a]. ch. 71 immediately follows ch. 38.[2] In 4QPs[d] (which is in reality two clusters of tiny fragments), ch. 147 is positioned before ch. 104. Nevertheless, these exceptions do not negate the basic agreement in psalm order that exists between the Qumran scrolls and our versions. Let us not forget that *homoioteleuton* and *homoioarchton* also resulted in the omission of psalms from medieval manuscripts, sometimes even from the latest of them.[3] How much more likely it is that, in Second Temple times, flawed manuscripts should have existed. It may also be that some manuscripts were not intended to contain the whole of the book of Psalms, but rather represented abridged editions in which some sections were omitted. The reason for this might have been purely practical, such as the high price of parchment or the copyist's preference to fit everything onto the scroll he had at his disposal, thereby avoiding the necessity of attaching additional sheets. Other scrolls might have been mere collections of psalms, with no intention to reproduce the canonical book in its entirety, as we shall see shortly.

II

The publication of the long 11QPs[a] ostensibly represented a turning-point in the appraisal of the Qumran psalters, when certain supposedly new claims concerning the composition of Psalms were in fact revived. Any attempt to explain the book's composition raises a

1. On this omission, see P.W. Skehan. 'The Qumran Manuscripts and Textual Criticism', in *Volume du Congres Strasbourg 1956* (VTSup, 4; Leiden: Brill, 1957), pp. 153-54. Skehan pointed out that, considering the scroll's narrow columns and the wide spaces between them, it is difficult to imagine that 4QPs[b] ever contained all of Psalms. On the omission of Psalm 32 from 4QPs[a], cf. 'The Qumran Manuscripts', p. 154 (where Skehan writes that the second scroll in which Psalm 32 was omitted is 'not from cave 4 at Qumran'; Sanders, however identifies this scroll as 4QPs[q]).

2. Skehan suggests that, in this scroll, the drift into 71 resulted from the similarity between the ending of ch. 38 and that of ch. 70, which led the scribe straight into 71 from 38.

3. An example is provided by British Library MS 9399 from the 13th century, in which the copyist skipped over Psalm 47 because its opening resembles that of Psalm 48; this is surely not the only example of its kind.

number of questions, most of them interdependent and therefore the source of added complications. A basic issue is whether the book was produced in stages, the result of cumulative growth from the earliest groupings of psalms until its final expansions, or whether it was put together on one specific occasion from collections of psalms, both ancient and relatively late. Additionally, is there a connection between the four doxologies woven into our book of Psalms (Pss. 41.14; 72.18-19; 89.53; 106.47-48) and the proposed stages of the book's growth, or were the doxologies inserted after the book of Psalms had attained its final dimensions? Still another question is, should a distinction be made between the first three doxologies (which are placed at points of division between distinct collections of psalms) and the fourth (which was inserted in the middle of a group of psalms and may therefore have served a purely liturgical purpose), or do all the doxologies fall into the same category? Examination of these questions, and others like them, must be reserved for another occasion.

At this juncture, let us limit our discussion to the following question: does the evidence of 11QPs[a] contradict the contention that the book of Psalms already existed in its present form by the time of Qumran? In other words, does this manuscript prove that the book of Psalms was produced through a gradual process of composition which continued to the end of the Second Temple period and was still under way in the days of the Qumran community?

11QPs[a] is made up of some 40 psalms from chs. 93–140 of the book of Psalms. Unlike the other scrolls mentioned above, it has not only omissions or transpositions of a certain chapter or chapters, but is a hotch-potch of psalms, with no indication that any particular method of organization prevails, with constant skippings forwards and backwards. Its psalms are arranged in the following order: (101–103, 109, 118 [vv. 25-29], 104, 147, 105 [until v. 12]), 105 (vv. 25ff.), 146, 148, 121–132, 119, 135–136, 118 (vv. 15-16, 8-9, 29?), 145, 139, 137–138, 93, 141, 133, 144, 142–143, 149–150, 140, 134.[1] In

1. The first eight chapters, which have been placed in parentheses, appear in five fragments, A to E, torn from the beginning of the scroll. The first publication essentially covered the scroll, together with fragments A to D. Fragment E was later published by Yadin. See J.A. Sanders, *The Psalms Scroll of Qumran Cave II* (DJD, 4; Oxford: Clarendon Press, 1965), pp. 3-49: Y. Yadin, 'Another Fragment of the Psalms Scroll from Qumran Cave 11', *Textus* 5 (1966), pp. 1-10. The scroll's bottom margin is worn throughout, but in general it does not appear that the margin

addition to this muddle, the scroll contains eight short pieces, most of which are not part of the canonical book in either the Masoretic Text or LXX, and some of which were probably composed by the Qumran scribes themselves. These pieces are inserted intermittently among the scroll's biblical psalms and they all appear in its second half, between Psalm 145 and the end of the scroll. Since there seems to be neither rhyme nor reason to their arrangement, I shall not list them according to their order in the scroll. The eight pieces are: (1) Psalm 151, known to us in Greek from the LXX and, of all these eight works, the only one connected there to the book of Psalms; (2–3) Psalms 154–155, found in a Syriac translation; (4) the acrostic poem in praise of wisdom, designated as 11QPs^a Sirach and known from the end of the book of Sirach: (5) a Plea for Deliverance, 11QPs^a Plea; (6) Apostrophe to Zion, 11QPs^a Zion; (7) a Hymn to the Creator, 11QPs^a Creat.; (8) a prose paragraph which describes David's compositions, has no literary pretensions, designated as 11QPs^a DavComp and may well have been written by the scribe who compiled the scroll.[1]

J.A. Sanders, who published the scroll, assumed that it contains the 'canonical' book of Psalms and thus entitled the discovery, *The Psalms Scroll*, implying 'the scroll of (the book of) Psalms', and not 'the scroll of psalms'. This assumption led him into something of a trap, since he then had to find the connection between the scroll and our book of Psalms. He was forced into the claim that the scroll represents a certain stage of the long, complex process by which the Psalter was canonized, a stage that precedes the final form adopted by the rabbis' decision at Yavneh. However, since the scroll is much shorter than the canonical book, he argued that it represents a stage in the formation of

was sufficiently wide to permit the inclusion of an additional chapter.

1. The second part of Sanders's *The Psalms Scroll* (pp. 53-93) contains a translation of and commentary on all eight works. 11QPs^a Plea appears in an additional scroll from the same cave (11QPs^b), of which six fragments remain. These two scrolls also resemble each other in that Psalms 141, 133 and 144 appear in the same order and the combination of verses from Psalm 118 seems to be identical in both. See J. van der Ploeg, 'Fragments d'un manuscrit de Psaumes de Qumrân (11QPs^b)', *RB* 74 (1967), pp. 408-12; J.A. Sanders, *McCormick Quarterly* 21 (1968), pp. 286-88. It may therefore be that the two scrolls represent similar collections or copies of the same collection. It may also be possible to discern traces of 11QPs^a Zion in 11QPs^f, which contains two more non-biblical hymns (Sanders, *McCormick Quarterly*, pp. 297-98).

the last two 'books' of Psalms—chs. 90–106 and 107–150, separated by the fourth doxology (Ps. 106.47-48).[1] This argument assumes that there is something which might explain the transition from the 40 psalms in the Qumran scroll to the sequence of 61 psalms in that part of the book of Psalms (supposing, for the sake of argument, that the book of Psalms was actually produced by a slow process of stages). Moreover, according to this argument one must imagine that the people of Qumran hastened to write *pesharîm* on the biblical Psalter even before the book had taken shape, while it was still unclear which psalms would be included and what their arrangement would be. On this point, I am prepared to take the part of those who have argued that the Qumran scroll was not intended to represent the book of Psalms or any section of it. It is simply a liturgical collection containing psalms *from* the biblical Psalter, as well as a few quasi-biblical or extra-biblical works.[2]

III

Once Sanders assumed that 11QPs^a was intended to represent the book of Psalms (or rather, its last two sections) at a certain stage of the book's formation, he was drawn into two further claims, neither of which will stand up to critical examination. First, he had to argue that, to the people of Qumran, the scroll's eight non-biblical works, men-

1. See J.A. Sanders, '*Variorum* in the Psalms Scroll (11QPs^a)', *HTR* 59 (1968), pp. 88-94, where (pp. 88, 90) he speaks of the separate crystallization of the Psalter's five books and sees 11QPs^a as evidence of the weak, unformed state of the two final books at that time. Cf. also his article in *McCormick Quarterly*, pp. 291-97. A detailed discussion of Sanders's views and those of his opponents in this matter appears in R.G. Wilson, *The Editing of the Hebrew Psalter* (Chico, CA: Scholars Press, 1985), pp. 63-81.

2. Thus Goshen-Gottstein, Skehan and Talmon, each with his own line of argumentation. See M.H. Goshen-Gottstein, 'The Psalms Scroll (11QPs^a)', *Textus* 5 (1966), pp. 22-33; P.W. Skehan, 'Qumran and the OT Criticism', in M. Delcor (ed.), *Qumran: Sa piété, sa théologie et son milieu* (Paris-Gembloux: Duculot, 1978), pp. 163-82; S. Talmon, 'Hebrew Apocryphal Psalms from Qumran', *Tarbiẓ* 35 (1966), pp. 215-16 (in Hebrew); *idem*, 'The Psalms Scroll of Qumran', *Tarbiẓ* 37 (1968), pp. 100-101 (in Hebrew). Only Skehan stresses the dependence of 11QPs^a on a canonical Psalter that had assumed its present form before Qumran. Wilson's claims (see above n. 1), which tend to support Sanders's position, appear rather shaky to me.

tioned above, were ordinary parts of a canonical collection. After all, anyone who assumes, as Sanders did, that the Qumran community viewed the scroll *bona fide* in good faith, as a normative Psalter cannot possibly avoid claiming that there is no difference between these eight works and the biblical psalms among which they are inserted.[1] Such a claim may be countered, for instance, by asking why, if the eight aforementioned works were equal in sanctity to other psalms at this stage, they have dropped out of the book of Psalms. In fact, however, the claim that they were at the time considered ordinary psalms is itself only an assumption which needs proof. For this assumption is precisely the point which is under examination: does the scroll really represent a stage in the formation of the biblical Psalter, or does it make up a collection of biblical psalms *with* a number of non-biblical works?

Furthermore, the eight non-biblical works themselves are not all of the same quality. Four of them, items 1–4 as listed above, probably came to the Qumran copyists ready-made and verge upon biblical literature, although their language has been somewhat blunted by the scribes' quill.[2] The other four, 5–8, are apparently the personal creations of scribes—or one scribe—at Qumran; in this respect, they parallel the lyrical prayers of the Thanksgiving Scroll, which are also Qumran creations. Yet in spite of the efforts to emulate the style of biblical poetry (except in the case of the prose text, no. 8), the scribes, or the scribe, failed to keep the language of these works from sounding secondary and imitative. The non-biblical basis of these works did not prevent them from acquiring some measure of sanctity. In the same way, the poetic prayers of 1QH must have been considered holy, to a certain extent, by the Qumran community. However, the fact that all these eight works are non-biblical and apparently represented a lower degree of sanctity could not rule out the possibility of their being included in a scroll alongside biblical psalms. Let us not forget

1. Sanders, '*Variorum* in the Psalms Scroll', pp. 84-86.

2. On the antiquity of Psalm 151 and items 2-4 in relation to Qumran, see my article 'The Two Text-Forms of Psalm 151', pp. 172-74, 178. That Psalm 155 (item 3) preceded Qumran may be seen from the fact that its alphabetic acrostic has already been spoiled and abridged in 11QPs^a, whereas the Apostrophe to Zion (item 6), for example, presents its acrostic intact. The poem in praise of wisdom that closes Sirach (item 4) must, like the entire book of Sirach, be anterior to the Hasmonean period. Cf. above p. 194 n. 1.

that the later prayer book also places biblical psalms side by side with blessings and liturgical pieces, both old and new.

IV

The second claim made by Sanders in support of his view that 11QPs^a represents a certain stage in the formation of the biblical Psalter is that all the scroll's works, biblical and non-biblical alike, were attributed to King David.[1] In order to strengthen this second claim, which looks even more peculiar than the first, he adduced some evidences that can be easily refuted. I shall only mention briefly the most important of these.

According to Sanders, the tendency to attribute the biblical Psalter to David, which he believes is evident in the New Testament and the rabbinic literature, achieves its full expression in 11QPs^a. Now, the rabbis had the entire book of Psalms in front of them, just as the authors of the New Testament relied on the Greek translation of the Bible. Nevertheless, there is no real indication that either the Masoretic Text or the LXX tend to attribute the whole Psalter to David; more than half of the psalms are not attributed to him or refer expressly to other personalities. The statement Sanders cited in the name of the rabbis, that 'David wrote the book of Psalms', must be quoted to its end: 'by [means of] ten elders', from Adam to the sons of Korah (*b. Meṣ.* 14b). A midrashic saying such as 'David gave them [Israel] the book of Psalms' (*Midr.Šoḥer Ṭob.* I) proves nothing here, as it is expressed in brief, whereas we are not interested in midrashic formulations but, rather, in specifying the author assumed by the people of Qumran to have been behind each psalm. In addition, the prose passage 11QPs^a DavComp states that David wrote 4050 'psalms' and songs, and Sanders opines that the scroll's eight non-biblical works are meant to be included in that number. However, the passage is a mere item of information, or tale, that does not indicate the hiding-place of those thousands of songs, or even whether or not they still exist. In just the same way, 1 Kgs 5.12-13 does not tell us where to find Solomon's three thousand proverbs and one thousand and five songs about plants and animals. Clearly, the passage does not refer to the didactic proverbs attributed to Solomon in the canonical book,

1. See Sanders, *The Psalms Scroll*, pp. 58, 63-76, 92, and so on; also his article '*Variorum* in the Psalms Scroll', pp. 84-88.

since these do not speak of flora and fauna.

Sanders also believes that the scroll's last columns 'establish quite clearly that the Qumran psalter as a whole was attributed to David'[1] just because these columns contain works that are explicitly ascribed to David and therefore supposedly refer to the scroll as a whole. He ignores the fact that Psalm 134, which is not attributed to David in the Masoretic Text or in the LXX, appears in these columns.[2] In any case, the texts that appear there can have no application to the rest of the scroll. It is true that Psalm 151, which closes both 11QPs^a and the LXX version, is attributed to David. However, this in no way changes the fact that in LXX the Psalms are attributed to a great variety of writers, no less—perhaps even more—than in the Masoretic Text.[3] Suffice it to say that the scroll also contains the poem in praise of wisdom that ends the book of Sirach. Even if Ben Sira was not its author, it is an obviously late product of Wisdom literature and could not have preceded Ben Sira by a long time. Yet Sanders is forced to claim that, at Qumran, this poem was ascribed to David. Moreover, he himself is compelled to admit that the poem is more appropriate to Ben Sira than to 'a Davidic psalter'. Yet he insists that in Qumran it was ascribed to David.[4] This insistence does not seem to speak well for his propositions.

1. Sanders, *The Psalms Scroll*, pp. 76, 92.
2. In 11QPs^a the line containing the psalm's opening is missing: however, given the width of the column, there is no room for a change from the known version.
3. I wonder at Goshen-Gottstein's readiness to accept Sanders's view that all the works refer to David ('The Psalms Scroll', pp. 27-28).
4. Sanders, *The Psalms Scroll*, pp. 83, 85.

An Essay on Prophetic Attitudes Toward Temple and Cult in Biblical Israel

Baruch A. Levine

The ethical message of the biblical prophets may be formulated simply: in the eyes of the God of Israel, it is more important that Israelites follow the dictates of morality and justice, commanded by him, than that they offer sacrifices to him and celebrate sacred festivals. Furthermore, no amount of ritual purification will expiate wrongdoing between one human being and another, or atone for an unjust and corrupt society.

Nevertheless, different prophetic statements of this essential doctrine differ in their emphasis and perspective, and are set in different historical situations. They often leave us unclear as to the proper role of temple, cult and worship in the ideal Israelite society, in which justice would prevail.

Here I will examine this prophetic message in three principal dimensions. I begin with Jeremiah 7, a relatively late, but powerful, statement of the view that the presence of the temple and the performance of the cult do not guarantee divine favor or ensure national security. I will then take up Micah 6 and Isaiah 1, earlier prophetic statements on the same theme, with primary attention being given to Isaiah 1. This opening chapter of the book of Isaiah is informed by deep perceptions of Israel's culpability, and it presents a universal vision of Jerusalem's role as a reconstituted temple city. I will conclude with a discussion of the tension between prophetic and other biblical views on cultic efficacy, and the extent of their integration within the Israelite ethos.

In a volume of studies honoring our colleague and teacher Nahum Sarna, a discussion of biblical religion is certainly appropriate. The present discussion will be presented in the form of an essay, with a minimum of annotation.

1. *The Prophetic Definition of Obedience*

No prophet of the classical period, from First Hosea of the ninth century BCE to Jeremiah of the late seventh century BCE, ever explicitly advocated suspension of the formal, sacred worship of the God of Israel.[1] The classical prophets acknowledged an ongoing cult, or cults at various temples, and surely appreciated the meaning of worship and celebration. First Hosea prophesied the suspension of Israel's joyous pilgrimage festivals, new moons and Sabbaths as God's punishment of his people (Hos. 2.13). He describes Israel rejected as a society devoid of a proper cult and undermined by political anarchy both as consequences of divine abandonment (Hos. 3.4).

It is relevant to observe, nevertheless, that prior to the advocacy of Sabbath observance in Jer. 17.19-27, we do not find a single explicit prophetic exhortation to the Israelites to be more pious or ritually observant, in the usual sense.[2] Prophetic statements on the subject of cult and ritual in the classical period show concern for maintaining strict monotheism in worship, condemning all forms of paganism. While criticizing the pollution of contemporary religiosity through idolatrous practices, and insisting on ethical behavior as a precondition of divine favor, the prophets did not at the same time urge the people to be present at temples more often, or to increase their dedications and offerings, for example.

Indeed, only when the prospect of national destruction and exile was imminent do we find prophets stressing the importance of the Sabbath (Jer. 17.19-27), or deploring cultic impurity in the selection of sacrificial materials (Ezek. 4.13-14). This emphasis was to endure throughout the exile and the period of the return, and may reflect a sense of collective guilt, what we would call an identity crisis. Later prophetic endorsements of cultic correctness require a separate study, and were not representative of the prophetic agenda for almost the

1. The view that there are two Hoseas, First Hosea of the ninth century BCE (Hosea 1–3) and Second Hosea of the eighth century, was most convincingly advanced by H.L. Ginsberg ('Studies in Hosea', in M. Haran (ed.) *Yehezkel Kaufmann Jubilee Volume* [Jerusalem: Magnes Press, 1960], pp. 50-69).

2. For an awareness of the problem, see H.L. Ginsberg, *The Israelian Heritage of Judaism* (New York: Jewish Theological Seminary, 1982), p. 7 n. 8. As noted by Ginsberg, Jer. 17.19-27 sound very much like Neh. 13.19-21.

entire pre-exilic period. Prior to the deportations preceding the final destruction of Jerusalem and Judah in 586 BCE, Jeremiah was still echoing the thoughts of earlier prophets:

> Thus says YHWH, God of the heavenly hosts, the God of Israel: Add your burnt offerings to your other sacrifices and eat meat. Verily, I did not speak with your ancestors nor did I command them, at the time I brought them out of the land of Egypt, on matters of burnt offerings and sacred feasts. Rather, it is this oracle that I commanded them, saying: Heed my voice; then I will be your God and you shall be my people. You must traverse the entire path that I direct you in order that things will be well with you (Jer. 7.21-23).

It is this message of obedience and loyalty that the people had failed to comprehend, pursuant to repeated and reinforced prophetic admonitions, not the essential obligation to offer sacrifice as participants in the cult of the Jerusalem temple. The message of Jeremiah is that obedience to the God of Israel and the pursuit of his path require both a just society and strict monotheism in the cult. In the negative dimension, social sins balance with pagan worship as abomination (*tô'ēbāh*), and provoke God's wrath. One seeking to make sense out of impending disaster must understand this dynamic, so Jeremiah would insist.

Nevertheless, Jeremiah's characterization of what God had and had not commanded Israel at the exodus is somewhat puzzling. It is part of a larger prophecy, declaimed at the gate of the Jerusalem temple, in which the sanction of the temple is declared to be conditional and revocable, not eternal. God had brought about the earlier destruction of Shiloh and the northern Israelite kingdom, and he would do the same with respect to the temple of Jerusalem and the kingdom of Judah. Those who proclaimed, 'The temple of YHWH! The temple of YHWH! The temple of YHWH' (Jer. 7.4) would be severely disappointed. Jeremiah goes on to describe the horrific situation that obtained in Jerusalem and its environs, with the deadly Tophet and the improper *bāmôt*, and he reiterates God's firm intention to abandon 'the generation of his wrath', who had defiled the temple.

How can the prophet maintain, however, that the God of Israel had not commanded the Israelites of the exodus to worship him through sacrifice? Which sources, records or policies could Jeremiah have had in mind when he made this assertion? Was he merely indulging in hyperbole (an unlikely conclusion), or was he, perhaps, recasting the traditions of the exodus and Sinai? Surely, he was not conforming to the priestly traditions of Exod. 24.15–31.18 and chs. 35–40, which effectively join the Tabernacle cult, with all of its specifications, to the Sinaitic revelation of laws and commandments. Nor, as a matter of fact, could he have been thinking of early laws preserved in the Book of the Covenant, for these also enjoin sacrifices, though with less specification. Even the primary statement of the Passover law in Exodus 12–13 calls for a *ḥag*, 'pilgrimage festival', to celebrate the exodus; and the Decalogue, for its part, enjoins the observance of the Sabbath.

To satisfy our curiosity we must, first of all, elucidate Jeremiah's own viewpoint on the issue of obedience to God. By further tracing the diction of Jeremiah's statement we may then be able to align his views with other biblical traditions on this question. The main components of Jeremiah's statement are his emphasis on heeding God's voice, expressed by the idiom *šāma^{c} beqôl*, coupled with the notion of a path, *derek*, commanded by God and to be walked or traversed, an action expressed by the verb *hālak*. There is also the theme of Israel's becoming YHWH's own people, expressed by the idiom *hāyāh le'ām*.

We should note that Jeremiah himself uses similar diction elsewhere. Most enlightening for the present discussion are the prophet's statements in Jer. 11.3-7, also referring to what God had commanded the Israelites at the exodus. Thus:

> Say to them: Thus says YHWH, God of Israel: Cursed by the person who will not heed the terms of this covenant, which I commanded your ancestors on the day I brought them out of the Land of Egypt, from the iron crucible, as follows: Heed my voice, and observe them, in accordance with all I have commanded you, that you may become my people and I may be your God (Jer. 11.3-4).

Here we find expressed two of the three themes contained in Jeremiah's temple prophecy: the command to heed God and God's election of Israel.[1] With respect to the notion of the 'path' to be followed or traversed, we find in Jeremiah only a few occurrences of the precise idiom *hālak bederek* (Jer. 6.16, 42.3, occurring not long before Jer. 42.13, the reference noted above to heeding God's voice). More dominant in Jeremiah's thinking is the general theme of a proper path, YHWH's path. The prophet searches the markets of

1. Cf. Jer. 3.13, 25; 18.10; 22.21; 42.13; 13.11; 24.7; 30.22; 31.1

Jerusalem in vain for any of the common folk who know this path (Jer. 5.1-4), and then in disappointment rationalizes that the wealthy might understand what the poor did not: 'So I will go to the wealthy and speak with them, for they surely know (*yāde'û*) the path of YHWH (*derek YHWH*)—but they as well had broken the yoke, had snapped the bonds' (Jer. 5.5).

As Jeremiah sees the world, every nation follows its *derek*, adhering to a particular pattern of belief and behavior (Jer. 10.2), but Israel is admonished against following the 'way' of other nations. The wicked among Israel likewise pursue an evil *derek* (Jer. 2.33, 36; 3.21; 12.1; 22.21; 31.20), whereas there is a proper path, the path of life (Jer. 21.6), the just path of obedience to YHWH (Jer. 32.39). It seems, however, that only in Jer. 7.23 does the prophet combine all three components—the themes of heeding God's voice, God's election of Israel and the ordained, right path—in a single statement.

When we look beyond the book of Jeremiah in our effort to identify and align Jeremiah's views we are led first to the Deuteronomist's recounting of the exodus, in which the themes of 'heeding', conveyed by the verb *šāma*^{c}, and of 'the way', as well as of Israel's becoming YHWH's people, figure prominently.

The Deuteronomist repeatedly calls upon the Israelites to listen, heed, and perhaps also learn, what YHWH speaks and commands, a complex of ideas expressed by the verb *šāma*^{c} (Deut. 5.1; 6.3-4; 7.12; 11.13). As if to verify that God is the source of the commandments attributed to him, the Israelites are reminded that they have actually heard God's voice (Deut. 4.12, 33; 5.19-20, 22-23). The precise idiom *šāma*^{c} *beqôl* characterizes the diction of the Deuteronomist.[1] On the theme of the path to be traversed, we find in Deut. 5.30 a partial paraphrase of Jer. 7.23: 'You must traverse the entire path which YHWH, your God, has commanded you so that you may live, and that it go well for you, and you long endure in the land which you shall possess'.

Just as Israel has literally heard God's voice and is now commanded

1. Deut. 3.20, 28.1. 15, 45, 62; 30.8, and cf. Kgs 20.36, 2 Kgs 18.12. It is probable that most of the occurrences of the idiom *šāma*^{c} *beqôl* in Deuteronomy are, in fact, attributable to the work of the Deuteronomist, not to the core of Deuteronomy. This is especially likely in those statements which speak of YHWH's commandments (*miṣwôt*), such as Deut. 13.5, 15.5.

to heed it, so Israel has been led by God on a path to its promised land (Deut. 1.22, 31, 33; 8.2) and is now commanded to follow God's path, and is admonished against departing from it (cf. Deut. 9.12, 16; 11.28; 31.29; 2 Kgs 21.22). Actually, the notion of following a path, in the sense of persisting in the behavior of a predecessor, typifies the diction of the books of Kings in their condemnation of wicked rulers (cf. 1 Kgs 15.26, 34; 22.43, 53; 2 Kgs 8.18; 16.3; 22.2).

The theme of becoming YHWH's people also links Jeremiah to the Deuteronomic school. The idiom *hāyāh le'ām* is frequent in the writings of the Deuteronomist (Deut. 4.20; 7.6; 26.18; 27.9; 28.9; 29.12), and is echoed in 2 Kgs 11.17. These correlations should hardly surprise us, since they merely confirm the close association of Jeremiah with the so-called Deuteronomic school active at the end of the seventh century BCE and at the beginning of the sixth century.

It would be inaccurate, however, to view Jeremiah's themes as being primarily of contemporary origin. The notion of obedience expressed as *šāma^{c} beqôl*, 'to heed the voice', harks back to both the Yahwist and the Elohist in Torah tradition, and to narratives preserved in Judges and Samuel.

The general principle to be applied to the dictional analysis of biblical Hebrew idioms for 'heeding' is that sources which normally use the idiom *šāma^{c} beqôl* will more specifically express obedience to God in this way. Although such diction is not specific to northern Israelite literature, it seems to be prominent there. This emerges most clearly from the cycle of Samuel narratives, which are largely of northern Israelite provenance. Samuel is instructed by God to heed the people in their demand for a king (2 Sam. 8.7; 9.22), while the people refuse to heed Samuel in doing without a king (1 Sam. 8.19), both actions being conveyed by the use of the idiom *šāma^{c} beqôl*. Similarly, Samuel admonishes the people to heed God's voice, warning them of the consequences of refusing to heed (1 Sam. 12.14-15). Most enlightening is the sequence of statements centering on the notion of obedience in 1 Sam. 15.17-23.

We first hear Samuel castigating Saul for not heeding YHWH's voice in failing to proscribe the spoils of the Amalekite war. Then, we hear Saul protesting that he had, by his understanding, heeded YHWH's voice, and had even 'walked in the path in which YHWH sent me', echoing another of the three themes under discussion. Finally we have

Samuel's classic statement of the prophetic view on the subject of obedience to God, weighed against cultic devotion:

> Does YHWH have desire of burnt offerings and sacred feasts as much as heeding the voice of YHWH (*kišmô*^{c}*a beqôl YHWH*)? Surely, heeding (*šemô'a*) is preferable to sacred feasts; to obey—more than the fat of rams. For recalcitrance amounts to the sin of divination; obstinacy—to inquitous teraphim (1 Sam. 15.22-23a).

Obedience expressed as *šāma*^{c} *beqôl* figures in the narrative of Judges 13 recounting episodes in the southern Shephelah. We first read that the angel heeded Manoah's voice (Judg. 13.9), and later that God had allowed Manoah and his wife to 'hear' great tidings (Judg. 13.23). In the northern narrative of Judges 20 we read that the Benjamites refused to heed the charge of their kinsmen from the other Israelite tribes (Judg. 20.13). The same theme informs the ideological review of Israelite history in Judges 2, which, however, actually sounds like the work of a student of the Deuteronomist!

The Elohist in Genesis likes to speak of heeding God's voice. Abraham will be blessed by all the nations of the earth because he has heeded God's voice (Gen. 22.18), while Rachel is grateful that God has heeded her request for a child (Gen. 30.6). Note, however, that the Yahwist in Gen. 26.5 matches the Elohist of Gen. 22.18 in crediting Abraham's obedience to YHWH as the basis for the blessing of his seed. The Yahwist also employs the idiom *šāma*^{c} *beqôl* freely in Gen. 27.8, 13, 43 in human contexts, as he does with respect to obedience to the divine will in Exod. 4.1 and Num. 14.22.

Of particular interest is the theme of obedience in Exodus 18–19, the former being primarily the work of the Elohist and the latter primarily that of the Yahwist. Both compositions are set in the time-frame immediately following the exodus from Egypt, and their relevance to Jeremiah's utterances is, therefore, direct and significant.

In Exodus 18 the Elohist presents us with a complex of transactions on the theme of hearing, expressed by the verb *šāma'*. Jethro 'hears' of God's great acts of providence (18.1), and, upon observing the extent of Moses' burden as arbiter of the people's grievances, urges him to heed his advice (18.19), using the idiom, *šāma' beqôl*. Thereupon Moses in fact heeds his father-in-law's counsel (18.24), appointing subordinates to assist him. Along the way, Jethro opines that a better system of leadership would enable Moses to show the people the path in which they were to walk (18.20), thereby giving expression to another of the three themes of Jeremiah.

In Exodus 19, the Yahwist similarly emphasizes the importance of heeding YHWH's voice, using the idiom *šāma^{c} beqôl*. Most dramatic are the words of Exod. 19.5-6a: 'And now, if you will heed my voice and observe my covenant, you shall be my possession from among all the peoples, for all the earth is mine. You shall be my kingdom of priests and holy nation.'

This theme is resumed by the Elohist in Exod. 20.19 after the presentation of the Decalogue, when the people say to Moses, 'You speak with us and we will heed (*wenišmā^{c}āh*), but let not God speak with us lest we die!' Even further, the theme of obedience is dramatized in Exod. 23.20-27, a passage of probable northern Israelite derivation, in which Israel is admonished against disobeying the angel whom God will dispatch to lead the people to its land, and to accomplish the defeat of the Canaanite peoples.

If we apply the same method to tracing the theme of the path (*derek*), we immediately perceive that this is a major motif of biblical Wisdom literature, just as we would expect. It also informs early narrative and classical prophecy, even though it hardly predominates in those contexts. It would be reasonable to assume that prophets and other biblical writers knew Wisdom, and often formulated their teachings and writings didactically. When doing so, they would employ Wisdom categories and the notion of the right path was one of them. This motif could be explored further, and with great profit, but to do so here would carry us far afield.

The theme of the divine election of Israel, expressed by the idiom *hāyāh (lî/lô) le^{c}ām*, and variations of the same, clearly harks back further than the Deuteronomist.[1] The Yahwist of Exod. 6.2-9 features this motif, expressed quite similarly: 'I will acquire (*welāqaḥtî*) you for myself as a people, and I will become your God' (Exod. 6.7a; cf. Exod. 19.5-6).

It should not surprise us that Samuel, in his parting words, reassures the Israelite people as follows: 'For YHWH will not abandon his people (*^{c}ammô*) on account of his great name, for YHWH has agree to

1. See S.-T. Sohn, *The Divine Election of Israel* (Grand Rapids, MI: Eerdmans, 1991), pp. 123-82), for a discussion of how the idea of Israel's election developed.

make you his people (*la*ᶜ*ásôt 'etkem lô le'ām*)' (1 Sam. 12.22, and cf. 2 Sam. 7.23-24).

What was the context of Jeremiah's writing? Jeremiah studied Torah literature, particularly the works of the Elohist and Yahwist in their respective presentations of the exodus saga, where the commandment of obedience figures prominently. This very idea informs the narratives in 1 Samuel 8.12 and 15, especially the prophetic interpretation of the Amalekite war in 1 Samuel 15. That account provides a twofold etiology: it explains the rejection of Saul's dynasty, albeit in a less than fully credible way, and it makes a prophetic pronouncement on the priority of obedience to God over cultic devotion.

The ironic position of an Israelite king claiming, sincerely or hypocritically (one can hardly tell), that he had sought to please God precisely in a manner involving disobedience to God's command makes the statement that the God of Israel will reject the sacrifices of those who disobey him. The dictional links between Jeremiah's pronouncements and the Samuel narratives are what suggest the interpretation, epitomized both in the narratives of the exodus and in those of the conquest of Canaan, that the first duty of the Israelites and their leaders is to obey God, not simply to worship him in accepted or expected ways. According to Jeremiah, this is what the Judeans and Jerusalemites of his day had failed to understand. The presence of the temple of Jerusalem was not unconditional evidence of divine favor, nor was performance of the cult a guarantee of security.

2. *The City of God*

One of the earliest statements of prophetic doctrine on the primacy of ethical behavior appears in Mic. 6.6-8, a passage of Israelian, or north-Israelite provenance. H.L. Ginsberg has dated Micah 6–7 to the early part of the reign of Jeroboam II, during the third quarter of the eighth century BCE.[1] The relevant passage appears in a group of oracles in which denunciation is followed by a vision of Israel's restoration. The prophet refers to a law-suit between YHWH and his people, in which the God of Israel acts both as prosecutor and judge:

> For YHWH has a case (*rîb*) against his people,
> He is pressing a verdict (*yitwakkāḥ*) against Israel (Mic. 6.2b)

1. See Ginsberg, *The Israelian Heritage*, pp. 25-27.

After recounting how God had liberated Israel from Egyptian bondage, had sent Moses, Aaron and Miriam to lead his people and had accomplished triumphs on behalf of his people, the prophet poses the quintessential question of biblical religion:

> With what shall I come into the presence of YHWH,
> Do homage to the celestial God?
> Shall I come into his presence with burnt offerings,
> With yearling calves?
> Would YHWH be pleased by thousands of rams,
> By myriad streams of oil?
> Should I offer my firstborn for my sin,
> The fruit of my loins for my own transgression?
> It has been told to you, O man, what is proper;
> What YHWH requires of you:
> Only to administer justice,
> To love kindness,
> To deport yourself modestly when close to your God.
> Then will your name experience wisdom.[1]

The comparison of cultic and ethical behavior is somewhat overdrawn, to be sure, but that seems to be the point. The dictum *haṣnēᶜa leket 'im 'elôhêkā* is translated in a different way from its usual rendering, because it is our sense that the issue being addressed is, precisely, the profusion of cultic activity in northern Israel. Hence, *'im 'elôhêkā* should refer to what is performed in sacred space, in the presence of the LORD. The prophet is decrying the elaborate cult of Samaria, operating in an unjust society. He foresees what was to be the Assyrian conquest of northern Israel, and his references and allusions resemble what we read in Hosea, another northern prophet of the period.[2]

As we shall observe, several of Micah's themes also inform the opening prophecy of Isaiah, a dramatic statement on the primacy of

1. See *Tanakh* (Philadelphia: JPS, 1985), p. 1051, s.v. Mic. 6.8-9. The suggested translation excerpts from v. 9 the words *wetûšîyyāh yir'eh šemekâ*, which seem to be out of place, and inserts them at the end of v. 8, so that the anticipated result of deporting oneself properly is the acquisition of wisdom.

2. See B.A. Levine's review of Ginsberg, *The Israelian Heritage*, in *AJS Review* 12 (1987), pp. 43-157. There, Hosea's objection to the proliferation of altars and to the elaborate royally sponsored cult of the northern Israelite kingdom in the period before the Assyrian onslaught is discussed.

ethical behavior. One is hardly surprised to find Isaiah and Micah employing the same diction and expressing the same themes. Isaiah 1 is set in the period when Jerusalem and Judah, rather than the northern kingdom, were threatened by neo-Assyrian power. There has always been a question, however, as to the position of Isaiah 1 in the chronological sequence of the prophet's speeches, since the prophet's initiation does not come until Isaiah 6. It is not certain, therefore, that Isaiah 1 marks the beginning of Isaiah's ministry, and it is entirely possible that Isaiah 1–5, in part or in whole, are out of sequence and originate from later phases of the prophet's career.

Isaiah 1 might well refer to the situation during the third campaign of Sennacherib to Judah in 701 BCE. The prophet describes Jerusalem as a besieged city, and speaks of few survivors in Judah. The towns of Judah are laid waste, with foreigners consuming the produce of the land; many are wounded. The prophet wonders why the people persist in offending their God since such behavior would only invite further suffering (Isa. 1.5-9). What is more, Isaiah predicts a restoration, which makes sense because, in fact Jerusalem was spared destruction in 701 BCE and the Assyrian siege was withdrawn.

In any event, the argument advanced in Isaiah 1, like those informing Micah 6–7 and Jeremiah 7, is only understandable in the context of a national disaster, imminent or already in progress. The prophet offers his interpretation of 'knowing' (the verb *yāda*ᶜ) as he denounces a sinful Israel, whose failure to acknowledge God's role in history accounts for its continuing disobedience. If Israel possessed knowledge it would understand the causes of its adversity, depicted by Isaiah in considerable detail. But Israel persists in offending God because it lacks such knowledge:

> An ox knows its owner,
> An ass its owner's crib;
> *Yísrā'ēl lô' yāda*ᶜ
> Israel does not acknowledge,
> My people does not realize (*lô' hitbônān*) (Isa. 1.3).

What Israel fails to realize is that God is enraged by the injustice and corruption of Jerusalem and Judah, and will not be appeased by the glorification of his name in the cult of Jerusalem's temple. Jeremiah had spoken of 'the generation of my wrath', whereas Isaiah gives verbal definition to divine wrath, having God speak in the first person.

But in Isa. 1.10-23, the most dramatic of all prophetic critiques of cultic correctness, there is no mention of paganism, as was true in Jeremiah 7, only of societal evil. In all of Isaiah 1 the only reference to paganism comes in v. 29, where the prophet predicts that when Jerusalem recovers from its wickedness, the sinful of Israel will abandon in disgrace the groves and gardens where they had engaged in idolatrous practices. For the rest, Isaiah seems to be concerned exclusively with the people's reliance on the temple cult at the same time that their hands are filled with blood:

> Hear the word of YHWH
> You chieftains of Sodom;
> Give ear to the teaching of our God,
> People of Gomorrah!
> What need have I of all your sacrifices?
> —says YHWH.
> I am sated with burnt offerings of rams,
> And suet of fatlings,
> And blood of bulls;
> I take no delight
> in lambs and he-goats.
> When you make an appearance before me—
> Who asked such from your hand?
> Trample my courts no more!
> Bringing grain offerings is futile;
> Incense is an abomination to me!
> New Moon and Sabbath,
> The proclamation of a convocation,
> Fast day and assembly—
> I cannot abide
> Your New Moons and annual feasts
> My feelings despise;
> They have become burdensome to me,
> I cannot bear them.
> When you raise your palms,
> I will turn my eyes away from you.
> Though you pray at length,
> I am not listening.
> Your hands are filled with blood! (Isa. 1.10-15)

The God of Israel is annoyed with the cult of the Jerusalem temple, though it was undoubtedly being performed properly. Its continuance, under existing conditions of societal evil, is the brunt of prophetic ridicule. The chieftains and people of Jerusalem were presiding over, and living in a wicked and perverse city, being compared to Sodom and Gomorrah, and to be spared the fate of those towns only through God's mercy (v. 9). In such circumstances, not only are sacrifices futile, even loathsome, and Sabbaths and festivals unbearable to God, but prayer is not efficacious either. The reason is simple: 'Your hands are filled with blood (*yedêkem dāmîm mālē'û*)'.

The nuances of the Hebrew term *dāmîm*, 'blood', have led some to translate it as 'crime', because in legal contexts *dāmîm* connotes capital crime. In an example of inner-biblical exegesis, Ezek. 7.23 understands the passage in this way: 'For the land is filled with bloody crimes (*mišpaṭ dāmîm*), and the city is full of lawlessness'. This sense is expressed in the characterization *'îr haddāmîm*, 'the city of murder', used elsewhere by Ezekiel in speaking of Jerusalem (Ezek. 22.2; 24.6, 9).

And yet, one senses a cultic, along with a legal, nuance in the reference to bloodied hands in Isa. 1.15. In the continuation of Isaiah's oracle we read that the blood of guilt must be washed away, and v. 18 speaks of sins red as crimson, another allusion to blood. One is immediately reminded of the ritual of the heifer prescribed in Deuteronomy 21. That unusual ceremony, which combines ritual, magical, and legal acts, also has as its referent the responsibilities of a city. In Deuteronomy, we encounter a town seeking to acquit itself of guilt for an unsolved murder that has occurred near its municipal limits.

The town's elders wash their hands over a heifer whose neck has been severed, as its blood runs into the stream, and they declare, 'Our hands did not spill this blood nor did our eyes see. Grant expiation to your people, Israel, whom you redeemed (*'ašer pādîtā*) YHWH' (Deut. 21.7-8). The prayer goes on to express the hope that guilt for the blood of the innocent will be removed from among the people of Israel. Isaiah also urges cleansing:

> Wash yourselves, be purified (*hizzakkû*).
> Remove your evil deeds from my purview.
> Cease to do evil; learn to do good.
> Promote justice,
> Support the oppressed,
> Take up the case of the orphan,
> Plead the cause of the widow (Isa. 1.16-17).

The Hebrew form *hizzakkû* has been variously analyzed, some deriving it from *zkh*, 'to merit acquittal, clearance' as a byform of the *hithpael hitzakkū*, and others from *zkk*, 'to be pure', as a *niphal* imperative.[1] Actually, *zkh* is probably just another realization of geminate *zkk*, whose specialized meaning is more appropriate here. Initially, one is cleansed or purified by washing, and only exonerated as a result of this. We know, of course, of the transactions attendant upon terms for cleansing and purification, whereby they signify legal clearance, acquittal and innocence, and such a transaction is certainly at work in Isa. 1.16. The implication is that a pure or proper temple cult will not save Jerusalem, only the re-establishment of justice within the city's jurisdiction. The purification required of the people is not ritual but rather ethical, legal and social. The two images which express the required transformation are the washing away of blood and the purging of alloys to produce pure metals, the well-known image of the crucible. Of the two, the image of blood as guilt and of its cleansing with water is closer to cultic phenomena and yet does not reflect a standard means of ritual purification.

The responsibility of a good city to prosecute justice informs Isaiah's prophecy, as it does the law of Deuteronomy 21. This is borne out by Isa. 1.21:

> Alas, she has become a harlot,
> The faithful city
> That was filled with justice.
> Where righteousness dwelt—
> But now murderers!

Unlike the good judges, elders, and Levitical priests of the Deuteronomic city, who are concerned with murders committed even outside their city limits, the Jerusalemites have forsaken the pursuit of justice within their city proper. The verb *pādāh*, 'to redeem', used in the Deuteronomic prayer cited above (Deut. 21.7-8) further links Isaiah 1 to Deuteronomy, for in Isa. 1.27 we read,

> Zion shall be redeemed (*tippādeh*) through justice,
> And her restored people (*wešābêhā*) through righteousness.

Of course, others have translated this verse differently, interpreting it to mean that in the judgment to come, Zion will be redeemed, and

1. Cf. the *niphal* imperfect *yissabbû*, 'they rotate', from *sbb* in Ezek. 1.9.

her 'penitents' will be redeemed with her.[1] It is argued that Isaiah 1 nowhere projects Jerusalem's destruction and the exile of its populace, so that it would be imprecise to understand *šābêhā* in the sense of 'her returnees'. And yet, Isaiah is actually envisioning a rebirth of the city and its citizenry. Though Jerusalem will not 'fall' in the usual way of being conquered and razed, it will be struck down in the way that a revolution brings about the fall of an entrenched government. This revolution will be mounted by God himself, who regards the rulers, judges and the corrupt of the citizenry as his foes:

> Ah, I will get satisfaction from my foes,
> I will wreak vengeance on my enemies (Isa. 1.24b).

One should definitely allow for the likelihood of *double entendre* in the usage of the Hebrew form *'mišpāṭ*, 'justice/judgment' and participial *šābêhā*, 'those restored to her/her penitents'. And yet, the primary image seems to be that of the restoration of a city through the re-establishment of justice and righteousness within its limits. This is at least a logical way of understanding the sequence of (1) Zion's lapse from justice, described dramatically in Isa. 1.21-23, followed by (2) Zion's purging and reconstitution as a just municipality in vv. 24-27. As *double entendre*, participial *šābêhā* may connote the 'return' or the penitence of the sinful, but the diction of the preceding verses more clearly suggests the dynamics of restoration:

> 25 I will bring down my arm (*we'āšîbāh yādî*) upon you.
> 26 I will restore (*we'āšîbāh*) your judges as formerly.

The author is playing on the nuances of the verb *šûb*, 'to return', *hiphil hēšîb*, 'to restore, bring down (the arm)'. Idiomatic *hēšîb* + *yād* + *'al* means 'to strike down', by an action of lowering one's arm with force (Ezek. 38.12; Amos 1.8; Ps. 81.15). First, the God of Israel will strike down the corrupt of Jerusalem, the dregs and dross, and eventually they will perish like tow hit by a spark (Isa. 1.28-31). God will then restore Jerusalem's proper judges, and following that Jerusalem itself will be redeemed and acquitted of its guilt, and its populace reconstituted within a righteous city. When all of this has

1. Thus the NJPSV, but see S.D. Luzzatto, *Il Profeta Isaia* (Padova, 1867; repr. Jerusalem: Akademon, AM 5727), Isa. 1.27, and Luzzatto's Hebrew commentary, pp. 42-43. Luzzatto strongly objects to the sense of 'penitents' for Hebrew *šābêhā*, an interpretation actually endorsed by Rashi and Ibn Ezra.

happened, a new role will begin for Jerusalem and its temple, as predicted in Isa. 2.1-4.

Before leaving Isaiah 1 to take up the vision of Isa. 2.2-4 which follows, we should comment on Isa. 1.18-20, which speaks of the law-suit brought against Jerusalem by the God of Israel. In legal language, one could say that Jerusalem is found guilty, but will be spared destruction and be placed on probation:

> Come, now, let us reach a verdict (*weniwwākeḥāh*),
> Says YHWH.
> Be your sins like crimson,
> They can turn snow-white;
> They can become like fleece.
> If you consent and pay heed,
> You will eat the bounty of the land.
> But if you refuse and disobey,
> You will be devoured by the sword,
> For it was YHWH who spoke (Isa. 1.18-20).

The student of the Bible is aware of the ambiguity of this passage. The suggested translation, 'reach a verdict', represents an attempt to make sense out of the *niphal* form *niwwākeḥāh*. Etymologically, the English word 'verdict' harks back to the Latin *vere dictum*, words 'truly said', thereby conveying the sense of 'proof, demonstration' associated with the Hebrew verb *w-k-ḥ*. The English 'verdict' also conveys the nuance in the closure of this passage: 'For it was YHWH who spoke', that is, it was YHWH who issued the verdict. What is more, Isa. 2.4 states that in the restored Jerusalem the God of Israel 'will arbitrate, render verdicts' (Hebrew *wehôkîaḥ*) between disputing nations, further echoing *weniwwākeḥāh* in Isa. 1.18. Earlier I noted that Mic. 6.2b uses the *hithpael* form *yitwakkāḥ* ('He [= God] is pressing a verdict') against Israel in a law-suit. We are not far from the mark in proposing that Isaiah 1 be understood as a law-suit brought by the God of Israel against his people.

The theme of obedience, so prominent in Jeremiah's prophecy, is delivered by Isaiah in a binary statement. The entire future of Jerusalem is made contingent on Israel's obedience, and Isaiah has defined obedience primarily in judicial and ethical terms.

Now it becomes possible to comprehend Isaiah's vision of days to come, of a restored Jerusalem, that is projected in Isa. 2.4. A temple will stand on Mount Zion, to be sure, but it will be more than a house of worship. It will serve as an international court of justice, where disputes among nations will be settled through verdicts issued oracularly by the God of Israel himself.

In the days to come,
YHWH's temple mount
Shall stand firm above the mountains,
And be raised higher than the hills.
All the nations shall look brightly upon it.
Many peoples shall set out [for it], saying:
Come, let us ascend the mountain of YHWH,
To the temple of the God of Jacob;
That he may instruct us of his ways,
So that we will walk in his paths.
For rulings are issued from Zion,
YHWH's oracle from Jerusalem.
Thus he shall adjudicate between the nations,
And render verdicts to many peoples.
They shall beat their swords into plowshares,
Their spears into pruning hooks.
One nation shall not raise the sword
    against another nation,
They shall never again train for war.

This passage can be interpreted from many different perspectives. Here we are concerned with Isaiah's attitude toward the temple of Jerusalem and its cult, and my comments will consequently focus on this aspect. Several relevant themes inform the prophecy. We should note, first of all, the figure of firmness associated with the temple: it will be *nākôn*, 'standing firm', unshakeable. We will have occasion further on to discuss the typology of temples in ancient Near Eastern literature. By saying that the temple of Jerusalem will stand firm Isaiah means to say that it is a temple of righteousness, for a temple of wickedness would not endure.

Several terms of reference also require comment. God's verdicts are to be rendered as *dābār* and *tôrāh*. In the present context, *dābār* is best translated 'oracle', and *tôrāh*, 'ruling'. The Hebrew term *tôrāh* is actually of priestly provenance, referring primarily to the rulings issued by priests on questions of law in their role as judges. This priestly function is most specifically expressed in Deuteronomy 17 which sounds as though it is related to Isaiah's prophecy:

> If a case is too deep for you to adjudicate, be it a dispute over homicide, civil damages, or assault, matters of dispute in your gates, you must promptly ascend to the cult-site (*māqôm*) which YHWH your God will have selected. You must approach the Levitical priests and the judge (*šôpēṭ*) presiding at that time, and request a decision. They will announce to you the verdict/oracle in the case (*debar hammišpāṭ*), and you must act in accordance with the verdict/oracle (*haddābār*) they announce to you at that cult-site which YHWH will have selected. You must carefully carry out all that they instruct you. In accordance with the ruling (*tôrāh*) they instruct you and in accordance with the judgment they inform you you must act (Deut. 17.8-11a).

Here we have all of the terms of reference featured in Isaiah's prophecy, and it is a moot point whether to translate *dābār* in Deuteronomy 17 as 'verdict' or 'oracle'.

The use of *dābār* in Isaiah's prophecy clearly expresses the function of the Jerusalem temple as an *oraculum*, a function epitomized in early traditions by the Tent of Meeting mentioned by the Elohist in Exod. 33.7-11; 34.34-35. One knowing *tôrāh* and in receipt of *dābār* would find YHWH's 'path', *derek* (and *'ôraḥ*), a theme already discussed in the treatment of Jeremiah 7.

It is improbable that Isaiah envisioned a temple in Jerusalem that would no longer serve as a house of worship of the God of Israel. What he seems to be saying is that Jerusalem has a role as the seat of justice and, conforming to the pervasive ancient Near Eastern pattern, the court would be located adjacent to the temple in an acropolis complex.

The court on Mount Zion, standing near the temple, would settle the wars of Assyrian conquest and domination through the rule of divinely revealed law. This process would end the direct threat to Jerusalem and Judah, and bring peace to other nations as well. But before Judah and Jerusalem could assume a role in international affairs, and before the God of Israel could enlighten the nations by revealing just settlements of international conflicts, the existing Jerusalem, with its injustice and corruption, must be reconstituted into a Jerusalem of righteousness.

In Isaiah's eyes, the persistence of a wicked society in Jerusalem, capital of Judah, was in reality preventing the fulfillment of YHWH's plan for his people and for the world. Could this be the reason for divine wrath over the profusion of cultic activity in the temple of a corrupt Jerusalem? What an irony! The Judeans delude themselves that they are glorifying YHWH in the temple, whereas in truth they are delaying YHWH's exaltation as God of all nations!

3. *The Offerings of the Wicked*

The reference to Shiloh in Jeremiah 7 is linked by diction and theme to the oracle of Ahijah the Shilonite in 1 Kings 14. There, as in Jeremiah 7, we read of doing evil. Thus in 1 Kgs 14.9 the verb *wattāra*[c] 'You' (= Jeroboam) have done evil' recalls Jer. 7.12, where we read that YHWH destroyed Shiloh 'because of the evil of my people Israel (*mippenê rā'at 'ammî Yiśra'ēl*). The Israelites 'anger' YHWH (the verb *hik'îs*) in 1 Kgs 14.9, as in Jer. 7.18-19. The result is that the God of Israel will 'cast off' his people (the verb *hišlîk*) from his presence, namely from the land (Jer. 7.5), just as in 1 Kgs 14.9 Jeroboam had cast YHWH off, discarded him over his shoulder!

Jeremiah's reference to Shilo as a symbol of the northern Israelite kingdom recalls Psalm 78, a Zion psalm that epitomizes the selection of Jerusalem and the rejection of Shiloh, God's abandonment of the northern Israelite kingdom and his election of the Davidic dynasty. There is, however, a salient difference in viewpoint between Jeremiah 7 and Psalm 78. In his lengthy review of Israelite history, the Psalmist endorses the essentials of the prophetic outlook, but when he speaks of the more recently chosen temple of Jerusalem (Ps. 78.60-72), his tone changes: 'He built his sanctuary like the heavens; like the earth that he established forever' (Ps. 78.69).

For the Psalmist, the dynastic covenant with David and the divine selection of Mount Zion as the site of the temple are eternal. These critical acts on the part of the God of Israel mark a break with the prior dynamic of Israelite history, and with the chronic shifts from divine favor to punishment that had characterized Israel's experience since Egypt. What had happened to Shiloh and northern Israel would not recur with respect to Jerusalem and Judah. Although the Psalmist hardly disputes the doctrine that Israel's historic misfortunes, most notably the loss of the northern kingdom, were the consequences of its persistent sinfulness, he voices the doctrine basic to cultic religion that the presence of the deity in the Jerusalem temple guarantees the security of city and kingdom. In this respect he belongs with the authors of other psalms who give expression to the same doctrine. Thus Psalm 46:

God is our refuge and stronghold,
A help in trouble; very near.
Therefore, we are not afraid
Though the earth reels,
Though mountains topple into the sea. . .
There is a river whose streams gladden God's city,
The dwelling place of the Most High.
God is in its midst, it will not be toppled;
By daybreak God will come to its aid.
Nations rage, kingdoms topple;
At the sound of his thunder the earth dissolves.
YHWH of Hosts is with us;
The God of Jacob is our haven.

Similarly, Ps. 48.9 states that the city of God will remain firm forever, just as in his prayer Solomon refers to the eternity of the temple of Jerusalem as God's seat (1 Kgs 8.13). This concept is common to the literature of the ancient Near East. Best known, perhaps, is the epilogue to the Code of Hammurabi, where it is stated that the king has erected a stela bearing his laws in the temple. He refers to Babylon and to Esagila, its main temple, as follows;

In Babylon, the city whose head Anum and Enlil raised aloft,
In Esagila, the temple whose foundations stand firm like heaven and earth
I wrote my precious words on my stela.[1]

Such expressions are of course hopeful, even wishful, but they represent the essential belief of the cultic establishment which the priesthood undoubtedly encouraged the people to accept. Ironically, this is the very notion denounced by Jeremiah as a falsehood (Jer. 7.4, 8), because it affords the unwarranted sense of security that the Israelite people attribute to the presence of God in his holy temple in Jerusalem.

Just as the author of Psalm 78 was familiar with prophetic teaching, so Jeremiah was familiar with the promise of an everlasting temple and kingdom. Only if the people fulfill the requirements of strict monotheism and uphold the moral code will YHWH 'allow you to dwell in this place, in the land that I gave to your fathers for all time' (Jer. 7.7). Otherwise 'I will do to the House which bears my name, on

1. See *ANET*, p. 178, ll. 63-67, in the Epilogue to the Code of Hammurabi (trans. by T. Meek).

which you rely, and to the cult-place which I gave you and your fathers, just what I did to Shiloh' (Jer. 7.14).

We should not, therefore, take the view that the policy of priests, kings and Psalmists was diametrically opposed to that of the prophets. Legitimate Israelite priests did not teach that moral behavior had no bearing on the efficacy of the cult nor that the offerings of the wicked were acceptable. We are dealing with differences in emphasis and values not with mutually exclusive doctrines. Furthermore, we are dealing with aspects of religion and culture that derive from different sources. The cultic view of the human–divine relationship was rooted in very ancient cosmic and mythological notions about temples and sacred space, about theophanies and sanctifications, whereas the moral view came from other sources—from Wisdom literature, from oracles and prophecy, and from law and political doctrine. The question that should occupy us is the extent to which these two outlooks were compatible with each other in biblical culture, as opposed to the extent to which there was tension and conflict between them.

For insight, we turn to Jeremiah 5 where, as in Isaiah 1, it is the verb *yādaᶜ*, with all of its subtleties and nuances, that informs the prophet's evaluation of the Israelite people of his day. Jeremiah suggests that there is a message or teaching which the Israelites fail to acknowledge, a notion of a moral order which they persist in doubting, notwithstanding the lessons of their past history and the danger of their current predicament. Their mind-set vis-à-vis the conditionality of cultic efficacy and its dependence on upholding the divinely ordained moral order parallels their thinking on the question of paganism in the cult. They do not accept the idea that compromising strict monotheism in worship invalidates the efficacy of the cult, just as they fail to face up to the fact that God will reject the offerings of the wicked.

There seems to be an ironic difference, however, between the two failures of the Israelite people. Although historically the prophetic insistence on strict monotheistic worship represents an innovation, and hardly reflects a consensus in the Israelite societies of pre-exilic times, the very notion of the indispensability of correct cultic procedures was hardly novel in ancient Near Eastern religions. The gods had ordained fixed and regular codes of cultic procedure, a notion expressed in Akkadian by the term *parṣu*. When the people reject the prophetic definition of the proper *parṣu*, so to speak, they act in disobedience of a code with which they may disagree in substance but whose attribution to divine will they understand. In other words the people believe that God, or the gods, eternally command the order of the cult and its specific components. One might say that the priestly traditions of the Hebrew Bible, especially those preserved in Torah literature, corresponded more closely to what the people understood religion to be about. The problem lay in the exclusivist character of Israelite monotheism, as defined by the prophets. Was this the true *parṣu*?

A different dynamic is at work in the prophetic insistence on obedience to the moral code as a condition of cultic efficacy. Culturally there is nothing new in the notion that moral behavior is requisite for divine approval. The ancient Egyptians, in protesting their guiltlessness at the time of death, insisted along with their declarations of piety that they had lived their lives in a moral and compassionate manner. In effect, they insisted that they had followed the wise teachings of the sages. A perusal of the list of these declarations reveals a certain quantitative balance between ethical and ritual attainments, and even shows a pattern of regularity in the alternation of the two categories in their sequence.[1] In ancient Near Eastern royal inscriptions kings and leaders declare that they have established justice in their realms, and boast that the gods regularly accept their sacrifices because they are pleased with their social and ethical behavior as well as with their devotion to and respect for the cult. The pantheons of the major ancient Near Eastern societies all include divine judges, who weigh the hearts of men according to standards of justice and goodness.

Internal Israelite sources yield the same information, namely that the God of Israel demands justice and kindness. This idea is basic to early formulations of the covenant between Israel and YHWH, and is implicit in the notion that the legal norms by which Israel was to be governed were revealed by YHWH and bore the sanction of divine commands. Unless one maintains that literary prophecy antedated the earliest statements of law as revelation in biblical Israel, hardly a tenable hypothesis, one is led to the conclusion that the Israelites of the ninth to the seventh century should have had no illusions on the subject of morality as a precondition of divine approval.

1. See *ANET*, pp. 34-36, 'The Protestation of Guiltlessness' (trans. J.A. Wilson).

It would be inaccurate to conclude, therefore, that the classical prophets of Israel first introduced into Israelite religion the notion that the efficacy of the cult was conditional upon upholding the moral order. What does it mean, then, to say that Israel does not 'know'? Perhaps it means that the notion of cultic indispensability was objectionable not for itself, but because its monotheistic restriction had not been acknowledged by king and people. For its part, the notion that the cult is conditional on obedience to the moral order was resisted because Israelites, like other human beings, often lacked moral fiber and were deluded into believing that they could deceive God.

It is probable nonetheless that in Israelite culture the integration of the moral and the cultic agenda had gone beyond what was typical of contemporary polytheistic cultures. This is evident from the biblical Wisdom tradition. If we compare the lament of the so-called 'Babylonian Job' in the composition entitled *Ludlul Bēl Nēmeqi* ('I will Praise the Lord of Wisdom') with the protestations of the biblical Job, such a difference in ethos is clarified. The similarities between the two compositions are compelling on many levels, as is their relative contemporaneity and their common attribution to the Wisdom tradition. Most striking is the similarity between the unfortunate conditions which each lamenter describes, and the sense of disappointment each experiences. There is also common ground in the sense expressed by both of being confounded by the seemingly irrational actions of the gods, or of God in the case of Job. It is significant, therefore, that in his complaint over his misfortune, the Babylonian appeals entirely to his piety and cultic devotion. He claims that he is being treated as one who has not performed all of the rites that he insists he has performed dutifully; that he has been treated by gods of various ranks as though he were a callously irreverent person:

> Like one who has not made libations to his god,
> Nor invoked the goddess when he ate,
> Does not make prostrations nor recognize [the necessity of] bowing
> down . . .
> Who has even neglected holy days, and ignored festivals,
> Who was negligent and did not observe the gods' rites,

Did not teach his people reverence and worship. . .
[Like such a one] do I appear.[1]

We observe a citizen or leader of some stature, not unlike the biblical Job, who characterizes himself as a dutifully religious man. One searches in vain for a similar emphasis on cultic devotion in biblical Wisdom, more particularly in the book of Job. In fact the biblical Job never appeals to his cultic correctness in pressing his case before God, whom he holds responsible for his suffering and for the loss of his former status and well-being. What he consistently cites as deserving of divine favor is his social responsibility, his probity and integrity, his compassion for the unfortunate and his civic leadership.

Those who would dispute the above conclusion by citing the piety ascribed to Job in the Prologue (Job 1–2) are on weak ground. The Prologue and Epilogue, where Job is indeed portrayed as a reverent man, are not made of the same cloth as the dialogues and speeches of the book of Job proper. These compositions not only differ in diction and literary character, but also serve to define the problem of Job within the context of traditional Jewish religion and culture by rationalizing Job's predicament as a divine test of faith. The dialogues proper never advance such a resolution. In fact the Prologue and Epilogue correlate more closely with the Babylonian Job's perspective on his suffering and eventual recovery. It appears, therefore, that in the Israelite Wisdom tradition cultic correctness counted for much less in the human–divine equation than it did in Babylonian Wisdom. Proverbs has the following to say on the subject:

Honor YHWH from your wealth,
and from the first of all your crop.
And your barns will will be filled with grain,
Your vats will burst with new wine (Prov. 3.9-10).

Indeed, God will bless those who make offerings to him. Be it known, however, that God's favor is conditional:

The sacrifice of the wicked is an abomination to YHWH,
But the prayer of the upright secures his favor
(Prov. 15.8; cf. Prov. 21.27).

1. See *ANET*, p. 597, 'I will Praise the Lord of Wisdom', ll. 13-23 (trans. R.D. Biggs).

TRANSLATION AS POLEMIC: THE CASE OF *TOLEDOT YESHU**

Martin I. Lockshin

The primary purpose of translation is the expansion of the boundaries of knowledge. The translator attempts to increase the circulation and dissemination of ideas and literary works to wider audiences. Generally the translator (or the person who commissions the translation) feels that the work is a valued one, that scholars who do not know the original language ought to have access to the work, or perhaps that the world would be a better place if more people were able to read that book.

Much less frequently a decision is made to translate a book that the translator feels is unremarkable or of little value. Paradoxically, if a book is deemed to be not just worthless but actually detrimental to the greater good of society, a translator might then be more motivated to dedicate the considerable effort required for translation in order to expose evil and/or encourage people to beware of hidden dangers.

Every translator knows well the temptation to 'improve' and amend the work being translated. When the work is one which the translator respects (or even venerates) that urge can generally be kept in check. When the translator is attempting to expose the evil involved in some despised work, the temptation to exaggerate and to vilify may be hard to resist.

In this paper I will examine a number of examples of Christian

* This article is written in honor of my teacher, Professor Nahum M. Sarna, who taught me many important things in numerous fields, including the art of translation.

I would like to express my indebtedness to my colleagues at York University, Professors Sydney Eisen, Steve Mason, Judith Rosner-Siegel and Paul Swarney with whom I have consulted about a number of different questions related to this article. I would also like to thank the students of my 1980–81 Humanities 4820 seminar at York University who first drew my attention to some strange passages in an English translation of *Toledot Yeshu* and thus piqued my interest in this topic.

translations[1] of a Jewish anti-Christian polemical work, *Toledot Yeshu*. While the paper will not touch on all the extant translations of that work, it will look at a representative sample. I hope to show the ways in which the translation of a polemical work can itself become a polemical act.

Toledot Yeshu, generically speaking, is a name that can be applied not just to one book but to a number of insulting Jewish 'biographies' of Jesus of Nazareth. It is not clear just how old the various Jewish legends about Jesus are. They were clearly well known during the Middle Ages and their roots lie in Talmudic times.[2] While it is hard to give any credence to Voltaire's assessment that *Toledot Yeshu* is older than the Gospels' accounts of the life of Jesus,[3] nevertheless the legends contained in such literature may be very old indeed. Still *Toledot Yeshu* ultimately tells us very little or nothing about Jesus and the roots of Christianity but a fair amount about the Jews who wrote such polemical literature.[4]

This paper will concentrate on translations of only one of the numerous versions of *Toledot Yeshu*,[5] the one commonly known as the Wagenseil version.[6] The choice of this version is not because it is to be seen as more original or more reliable than any other version.[7]

1. On changes introduced by a Jewish translator of a Jewish anti-Christian polemic, see D.J. Lasker, 'The Jewish Critique of Christianity under Islam', *PAAJR* 57 (1991), p. 132.

2. On *Toledot Yeshu* in general, see S. Krauss, *Das Leben Jesu nach jüdischen Quellen* (Hildesheim: G. Olms Verlag, repr., 1977). See further bibliography cited by D. Berger in *The Jewish-Christian Debate in the High Middle Ages* (Philadelphia: Jewish Publication Society, 1979), p. 253 n. 1, and also J.-P. Osier, *L'évangile du ghetto* (Paris: Berg, 1984).

3. See *Lettres sur les Juifs* in *Mélanges* (Paris: Pléiade, 1965), p. 1212, cited by Osier, *L'évangile*, p. 11 n. 11.

4. See J. Klausner, *Jesus of Nazareth* (trans. H. Danby; New York: Macmillan, 1925), pp. 51-53, and Krauss, *Leben*, p. 239.

5. See Krauss's exhaustive study of the various extant versions. Most of the versions of *Toledot Yeshu* can be found in Krauss's work both in Hebrew and in reliable German translations. Most of the versions can also be found in reliable French translations in Osier's work.

6. Published by J.C. Wagenseil in his *Tela ignea Satanae* (Altdorf, 1681).

7. In fact, Krauss himself does not even present the Wagenseil text in his book, as he sees it as derivative of other manuscripts and versions that he found. See Krauss, *Leben*, *passim*, and especially the section, 'Klassifieirung der Texte', written by

It is rather because the Wagenseil text became the version most often translated into other languages.

J.C. Wagenseil (1633–1705), a Christian Hebraist and a professor at the University of Altdorf, published a version of *Toledot Yeshu* in 1681 as part of a book which he called *Tela ignea Satanae*, as it purported to contain the 'fiery arrows' which 'Satan' (i.e. the Jews) shoots at Christianity. The volume contains the Hebrew originals of a number of Jewish anti-Christian polemical works, Wagenseil's column-by-column translation of those works into Latin and his refutations of them. Wagenseil's volume considerably increased the circulation of these texts and made them available to anyone who read Latin. He also made available to later generations of scholars many valuable recensions of Hebrew texts that might otherwise have been lost. The version that he chose to publish of *Toledot Yeshu* became the best known in most Christian circles. Quite often later Christian translations of *Toledot Yeshu* into other Western languages were not made from the Hebrew text but rather from Wagenseil's Latin translation.

Aside from analysing Wagenseil's Latin translation, I will be considering two English translations of *Toledot Yeshu*, both produced in London in 1885. *The Hebrew Account of our Lord* claims to be 'The sole English Edition, omitting nothing after the First Page.[1] Latinized by J.C. Wagenseil, 1681; Englished by E.L.G., 1885.' I have not been able to identify who E.L.G. in fact was. It appears clear to me, however, that he was a Christian who did not appreciate the way in which *Toledot Yeshu* parodied the life of Jesus.[2]

The other translation was published by two British freethinkers, G.W. Foote and J.M. Wheeler.[3] In the preface to their work, the editors acknowledged using and reworking an earlier translation which they think was translated from the Hebrew by some anonymous Jew. To me the claim that the book was 'translated from the Hebrew'

E. Bischoff and found in Krauss's book, pp. 27-31.

1. This wording was carefully chosen by the author for he did leave out quite a bit on the first page itself, as I shall point out below.

2. The book was published by James Burns, Spiritualistic, Occult and General Bookseller.

3. '*The Jewish Life of Christ* being the Sepher Toldoth Jeshu or Book of the Generation of Jesus. Translated from the Hebrew' (London: The Pioneer Press [G.W. Foote & Co. Ltd]).

is clearly mistaken; many passages show a total dependence on Wagenseil's Latin. These two editors, whose disdain for Christianity is obvious on almost every page of their book,[1] choose to present *Toledot Yeshu* to their readers as a version of the story of Jesus' birth and life that is more credible than the Gospel accounts.[2] So while E.L.G.'s translation, like Wagenseil's, may be seen as a polemic against Judaism, Foote and Wheeler published that same year in the same city a translation of *Toledot Yeshu* whose purpose it was to polemicize against Christianity.

The Plot of Wagenseil's Toledot Yeshu

A short summary of the plot-line of Wagenseil's version of *Toledot Yeshu* might be appropriate at this point. Jesus' mother Miriam had been affianced to a fine young man, a student of R. Shimon ben Shetah named Yohanan. A worthless rake named Joseph Pandera developed a great lust for that Miriam and, at the suggestion of his mother, went and lay in wait for her and had intercourse with her by force one Saturday night. She was at the time menstrually impure. She was also under the mistaken impression that it was her fiancé who was sleeping with her.

Miriam became pregnant and her fiancé, after pouring out his heart and telling the story to his teachers, left her and moved to Babylonia. A son was born who was named Joshua. Although he was bright he demonstrated impudent behavior towards the Sages and they in turn concluded that this child must be the illegitimate son (ממזר ובן הנידה) of said Miriam and Joseph Pandera. He was then renamed Yeshu[3] and a proclamation was made declaring him illegitimate and forbidding him from marrying any Jew.

Yeshu then connived to sneak into the Holy of Holies in the Temple in Jerusalem and learn the proper pronunciation of the Tetragrammaton. The rabbis had taken precautions to prevent that occurrence by placing two bronze lions at the entrance to the Holy of

1. See, e.g. the claim that the 'Gospel writers could misquote the Old Testament and blaspheme at the same time' (p. 22 n. 2), or the claim that the story in Mt. 28.11-15 is 'incredibly stupid' (p. 33 n. 6).

2. See the preface, esp. pp. iii and xii.

3. The author sees the Hebrew name ישו as an insult, based on the folk etymology that it is an acronym for ימח שמו וזכרו ('may his name and memory be erased').

Holies. Those lions roared at all who left and made them forget anything that they had learned. Yeshu however circumvented that problem by writing down God's name on a piece of paper while still in the Holy of Holies and hiding that piece of paper in an incision he made in his own body for that purpose. When he left the Holy of Holies the lions did make him forget but when he retrieved the piece of paper from his body he knew God's name and began to perform amazing miracles with that knowledge.

With the help of those miracles he was able to mislead many people into believing in his divinity, including Queen Helena,[1] who came to his rescue to save him from the Sages. The Sages, however, worked out how he had been able to perform those miracles and they sent one of their own ranks, a Rabbi Judah, into the Holy of Holies for him to learn God's name in the same manner that Yeshu had. Rabbi Judah eventually brought Yeshu to justice. Yeshu was stoned by a rabbinical court and then hanged on the stalk of a cabbage plant.

After his death his body disappeared for a while, causing many people, including Queen Helena, to assert his divinity. Eventually though his body was found and his followers were discredited.

Still the new movement made serious inroads among Jews. The Sages felt that it was necessary to separate this new movement from Judaism and they sent a Rabbi Shimon Keipha to infiltrate the movement and to convince them that they should not see themselves as Jews. This Shimon misled the Christians into thinking that he was one of them. He lived out his life among them, eating nothing but bread and water and living at the top of a tower. A building named Peter was built in Rome to honor this Shimon after his death.[2]

Shortly thereafter another teacher named Elijah[3] came to teach the

1. Queen Helena is identified in the Hebrew text (pp. 9-10) as הילנה המלכה אשת ינאי המלך הנזכר והיא מלכה אחרי מות אישה והיא נקראת גם כן אוליינא ובנה היה מונבז המלך הנקרא הורקנוס שהרגו הורקנוס עבדו. This confused description has elements both of the historical Queen Helena, a contemporary of Jesus of Nazareth, and elements of Queen Salome Alexandra, the sister of the above-mentioned Rabbi Shimon ben Shetah. Numerous Jewish stories about Yeshu place him in the days of Shimon ben Shetah and Queen Salome Alexandra. See, e.g., uncensored editions of *b. Sanh.* 107b.

2. The author is obviously conflating the story of Simon Peter and the story of Simon Stylites.

3. Loosely modeled on the story of Paul.

Christians that circumcision is of no value, that the Sabbath should be moved to Sunday and many other new laws. While Elijah was speaking a stone fell out of the church building in which he spoke, crushing his head and killing him. The author concludes the work with the fervent hope that all God's enemies will suffer similar fates.

The Quality of Wagenseil's Work

In general, the Hebrew text which Wagenseil published in his *Tela* is readable and understandable. There are a few examples of minor inaccuracies and misprints. For example, the phrase וישתחוו לא appears (p. 8), when לו is clearly meant. The phrase מזויינים וחומשים (p. 16) naturally should read וחמושים. Neither of these two errors leads to a mistranslation by Wagenseil (nor of course by the two English translators who translated from Wagenseil's Latin).

There are two more significant errors that appear right at the end of the Hebrew text. The 'Elijah' who appeared to the new Christian community and instructed them to adopt new laws that differed significantly from Jewish law taught them (pp. 23-24):

> מי שירצה לימל ימול וכל מי שאינו רוצה לימול יטבול במים סרוחים ואם לא טבל לא יהיה לו סכנה בעולם

The Hebrew text as it stands is very difficult. The translation offered by Wagenseil (and followed by the two English translators) is not helpful.[1] A minor correction of the Hebrew word סכנה to תקנה makes the text perfectly understandable. 'Elijah' then taught the new Christians that circumcision is optional but that being immersed in baptismal waters (מים סרוחים) [2] is obligatory. He who is not baptized cannot be saved (לא יהיה לו תקנה בעולם).[3]

The end of 'Elijah's' life is described as follows (p. 24) in Wagenseil's Hebrew:

> עוד הדבר בפיו ויפל אבן אחד גדול מהתו עבה ורצץ את גלגלתו.

1. E.L.G.'s translation, a faithful rendition of Wagenseils's Latin here, is not meaningful. It reads: 'Whoever will be circumcised do thou receive, but he that will not shall be plunged in filthy water (threatening however no greater punishment)'.

2. On the phrase מים מסורחים as a Jewish insult for baptism, see Krauss, *Leben*, p. 221.

3. Even Osier's fine French translation follows the incomprehensible Hebrew text presented by Wagenseil here.

The words מהתו עבה are not comprehensible and, while the word עבה makes some sense in the context, it is not easy to see how Wagenseil arrived at *& cecidit lapis ingentis vastaeque molis* (= E.L.G. [p. 19] 'a great stone fell upon him').[1] A simple combining of the two Hebrew words מהתו עבה into the one word מהתועבה makes the text easy to read. 'Elijah' died when a stone fell out of the תועבה, the previously mentioned tower or structure in Rome, where he was teaching.[2] While Wagenseil certainly considered himself an expert in Jewish insults about Christianity, it is possible that he was misled in the above two cases not only by a faulty Hebrew text but also by the fact that he was not expecting such nasty words as תועבה or מים סרוחים to be applied to hallowed Christian symbols and sacraments.

Generally Wagenseil is a competent translator. He is usually loyal to his text and knows when to rise above literalism, as can be seen when he deals with an idiom like לעלות לרגל (p. 19[2])[3] in a useful paraphrastic manner (*in majoribus festivatibus adire Hierosylmas*; so also E.L.G. [p. 16], 'to go up to Jerusalem at the greater feasts'). Some Hebrew phrases do give him a little trouble. The word נעשה in the phrase (p. 16) הגד נא לנו את כל אשר נעשה can, theoretically, be seen as either a past tense or a future tense verb. To my mind the context demands the former explanation.[4] Wagenseil opts for the latter option, *quid faciendum restet*. It would appear that the (not so unusual) syntactical construction זקן אחד מן הזקנים ('one of the elders'; p. 20[2]) confuses Wagenseil and leads to the rendering *vir quidam aetate gravis ex Senioribus*, in which the two appearances of the word זקן are seen as having two different meanings.[5] It would also appear that Wagenseil does not understand the Hebrew interjection להבדיל and translates the phrase (p. 19[2]) ויגדל מריבה בין הנוצרים ובין [ה]יהודים

1. Again here both Foote and Wheeler's English and Osier's French translate in the same manner as Wagenseil.

2. Or perhaps out of a stone crucifix under which he was teaching. On תועבה as an insulting name for a non-Jewish house of worship or for a cross, see E. Ben Yehuda, *Thesaurus Totius Hebraitatis*, XVI (New York: Yoseloff, 1959), p. 7694.

3. There is a problem in the pagination of *Toledot Yeshu* in Wagenseil's *Tela*. The page numbers proceed:. . . 18, 19, 20, 19, 20, 21, 22. . . I shall refer to the pages as:. . . 18, 19, 20, 19[2], 20[2], 21, 22. . .

4. So also Osier (*L'évangile*, p. 96), 'tout ce qui c'est passé'.

5. So also E.L.G. (p. 17), 'one of the Elders, a man of grave age'. Cf. Osier's simple French rendering, 'un ancien' (*L'évangile*, p. 100).

להבדיל as *inter Nazarenos & Judaeos contentio invaluit, ut a se invicem separationem facerent.*[1]

The Quality of the English Translations

The two English translations that I am examining are not of such high quality as the Latin of Wagenseil. It is doubtful that either translator was much of an expert in Latin. Some of the errors that creep into the English versions are understandable as being due to the 'broken telephone' nature of translating a Hebrew text into Latin and then translating that Latin text into English. When Yeshu's mother hired (שכרה) a teacher for him, Wagenseil uses the verb *conducit* (p. 5); both English translators decide that the verb meant 'to bring'. When Yeshu boasted (p. 7) that his mother had been impregnated through her head (דרך קדקדה)[2] Wagenseil renders that text as *per summum verticum*. E.L.G. in turn (pp. 5-6) translates that Latin phrase as 'from heaven', a possible translation of the Latin but presumably not the one intended by Wagenseil.[3] When the Sages (p. 10) summoned Yeshu (וישלחו אחר ישו) to appear before Queen Helena, Wagenseil writes reasonably *misere igitur accersitum Jesum*. E.L.G. (p. 8) fails to recognize the word *misere* as an apocopated form of the verb *miserunt* and, understandably enough, renders the text 'sadly therefore they summoned Jeshua'.[4] When Yeshu (p. 15) invited his disciples to accompany him to Jerusalem (לבא עמי לירושלים), Wagenseil's accurate Latin, *ut mecum contendatis Hierosolymas*, leads to Foote and Wheeler's mistranslation, 'As you go to fight for me at Jerusalem',[5] presumably because of the similarity of the Latin

1. E.L.G.'s English similarly reads (p. 16): '[There] arose the great contention between the Nazarenes and the Jews and so grew that they had to make a complete separation'. Cf. Osier's accurate French rendering (*L'évangile*, p. 99): 'la dissension entre Nazaréens et juifs (la comparaison entre eux n'est pas décente!) grandit'.

Naturally in all of the last three cases where Wagenseil errs and Osier does not, both English translations err, as they are dependent on Wagenseil's Latin.

2. On Mary being impregnated through her head (or through her ear), see Berger, *Debate*, p. 303, and the sources cited there, and see also Foote and Wheeler's note here, p. 19.

3. Foote and Wheeler understand the Latin text here correctly.

4. Again Foot and Wheeler's translation is more accurate than E.L.G.'s.

5. Here E.L.G.'s translation is the more accurate one.

contendatis to its English cognate ‘contend’. When Joseph Pandera (p. 3) received advice from his own mother (אמו) about how he should deal with his lust for Miriam, Wagenseil renders the text, *ait illi mater*, arguably leaving the question open whose mother it was who spoke to him. E.L.G. wrongly translates it as ‘her mother’. Foote and Wheeler’s translation (p. 14) decides not to take a stand and tells the entire first part of the story in rather cumbersome and clumsy English: ‘At length the mother said to him’, and ‘then said the mother’.

While it is not difficult to understand how the previously listed errors (and many others like them) occurred, there are a number of other English errors that are much harder to justify. Yeshu’s (p. 5) impudent behavior (עזות מצח; Wagenseil: *fronte perfricta*) becomes in Foote and Wheeler’s translation (p. 16) ‘touching his forehead’. When Yeshu (pp. 6-7) left upper Galilee and came secretly to Jerusalem (יצא מגליל העליון ובא בהחבא לירושלים; Wagenseil: *deserta Galiliæa superiore venit clanculum Hierosolymas*), E.L.G.’s English translation (p. 5) has Yeshu coming ‘secretly from the desert (!) of Upper Galilee to Jerusalem’.[1] E.L.G.’s translation in particular seems riddled with errors, ranging from the omission of crucial phrases,[2] to the confusion of similar Latin verbs,[3] to difficulties in understanding Latin syntax.[4]

The Embarrassment Factor

Changes that creep into translations because of the translators’ lack of linguistic proficiency are ultimately not of the greatest significance. The more interesting changes are the ones that occur when a

1. E.L.G. (p. 15) makes the same mistake again with Wagenseil’s ablative construction (p. 20) *multi desertis Hierosolymis. . . effugere* (translating the Hebrew יצאו רבים מירושלים לברוח) and translates it as ‘fled from Jerusalem into the deserts’.

2. For example (p. 4) the crucial words חה הוא הילד ההוא (Wagenseil: *atque hinc prodiit ille puer*)—when Yeshu was discovered to be the product of the illicit union of Joseph Pandera and Miriam—are entirely missing.

3. He confuses the verb *occurso* (to meet) with the verb *occurro* (to run) in his translation of the phrase (p. 9) *omnis civitas ei in occursum erumpit* (Hebrew: ותהם כל העיר לקראתו).

4. See the difficulty that he had with the phrase (p. 20[2]), *qui duodecim pervagantes regna* (Hebrew: ויתהלכו בשנים עשר מלכיות).

translator understands the text but comes to a conscious or subconscious decision to make a change in it.

The translators of *Toledot Yeshu* clearly find many aspects of the story embarrassing. None of the translators I am examining feels comfortable recording the fact that Miriam was menstrually impure when she was raped by Joseph Pandera and that Yeshu was hence branded a ממזר ובן הנידה. Wagenseil does not render that phrase into Latin but rather into the Greek μοιχίδιος καὶ ἀποκαθημένης[1] υἱὸς. (The phrase is repeated so often that eventually it becomes abbreviated [p. 14f.] to μ. κ. α. υι.) Wagenseil only hides a few phrases from his Latin readers by translating them into the less well-known Greek. Foote and Wheeler throw a blanket over the entire story of Miriam's seduction by leaving that story in Wagenseil's Latin (translating the Greek phrases into Latin or simply omitting them) and inserting it in the appropriate place in their English text. E.L.G. decides that the entire story is too prurient for readers of any language and leaves it out entirely, telling his readers only that 'Joseph, however,... [deceived, and by her mother's connivance, seduced her. The details of this being indecent and quite redundant, we omit.]'[2] The suggestion to Joseph Pandera (p. 3) that he force Miriam—ראה והחזיק בה (Wagenseil: *vide ut ea potians*)—is toned down by Foote and Wheeler (p. 16): 'See if she is willing'. A further story of how Rabbi Judah counteracted Yeshu's powers by rendering him ritually unclean by urinating on him (p. 13) is also censored and/or omitted by our nineteenth-century English translators. It is noteworthy but not too surprising that these two Victorian translations are considerably more prudish than Wagenseil's seventeenth-century work.

It is not only the sexually prurient passages that Wagenseil feels a need to tone down. On a number of occasions the insults about Yeshu or his disciples are presumably too much for Wagenseil to stomach and he refuses to write them out in Latin. For example, when Rabbi Judah grabbed Yeshu (p. 13), Wagenseil feels obliged to write Yeshu's name in Greek,[3] despite the fact that throughout the story

1. Using the common phrase for a menstruating woman found in the Septuagint, e.g. *ad* Isa. 30.22.

2. Page 3. Hence E.L.G.'s claim on his title page, 'omitting nothing after the First Page'.

3. τὸν Ἰεσχοῦω *invadit.*

Wagenseil writes Yeshu's name in Latin characters, *Jeschu*. Similarly when the Hebrew (p. 19[2]) refers to Yeshu's disciples as שנים עשר רשעים בני פריצים, Wagenseil feels the need to write that insult in Greek, too.

Censorship is not the reason involved each and every time that Wagenseil resorts to Greek. The recurring dramatic claim that Yeshu is in fact the (or, perhaps, a) son of God (שבן אלקים אתה; e.g. on p. 9) is usually, but not always, translated into the Greek. References to the Tetragrammaton are generally translated as '*nomen* ἀνεκφώνητον'[1] although on occasion it appears that Wagenseil forgets and writes *nomen ineffabile*.[2] Many other terms used when describing Yeshu's powers to perform miracles through the use of God's name (e.g. ושכח את השם, האותיות הקדושים, or even such a phrase as אבן [ה]שתייה) are usually rendered by Wagenseil into Greek, not Latin. Perhaps a Christian Hebraist like Wagenseil takes Kabbalistic claims about the power of God's name seriously enough that he hesitates to write out these stories in such an easily accessible language as Latin.

References to Magic

At times each of our translators seems to increase the number of references to magic that one can find in the text. Both a reference to the Sages doing something בשמות (p. 6) and a reference to Yeshu accomplishing something על ידי . . . שם טומאה are translated by Wagenseil as *incantaminibus* or *vi incantaminum*. In both English translations these phrases and many others simply become 'by magic'. The claim that Yeshu had to be hanged on a cabbage plant because he had in his lifetime made all the trees swear (השביע את כל העצים [p. 18]) that they would not suspend him, becomes 'enchanted all the trees' in both of our English versions. A simple reference (p. 15) to God's name (השם; Wagenseil: *Nominis*) becomes in E.L.G.'s text 'the magical name'. Perhaps the translators are trying to make the text look even more superstitious than it is.

Conversely, on a number of occasions the precisely opposite phenomenon may be observed. The translators sometimes are taken aback at the prospect of describing Yeshu himself as a magician.

1. E.g. p. 7.
2. E.g. p. 6.

Hence a number of direct references to Yeshu's performance of magic in the Hebrew (and the Latin) are removed from the text by E.L.G. More than once in *Toledot Yeshu*, Yeshu's contemporaries accuse him of being a sorcerer. The claim (p. 10) that Yeshu מכשיל ומטעה את הבריות בכישוף becomes in E.L.G.'s English 'he leads all men into error through his venomous deceits'.[1] When the Queen refused to believe that Yeshu was a מכשף (p. 8), again the term is translated by E.L.G. as 'deceiver'.[2] Considering the long and persistent history of the Jewish accusation that Jesus was a sorcerer,[3] it is possible that a believing Christian like E.L.G. is tempted to refrain from writing out that accusation whenever he can. Then when the opposite tendency—to increase the number of references to magic in the work—is taken into account, one can understand how an inconsistent translation results.

Harmonizing with Christian Texts

Christians like Wagenseil and E.L.G. presumably feel that *Toledot Yeshu* is a scandalous work that one should hardly mention in the same breath as the holy Gospel accounts of the life of Jesus. Yet one can uncover a curious tendency in their translations, conscious or subconscious, to attempt to harmonize *Toledot Yeshu* with traditional Christian texts.

The Hebrew text of *Toledot Yeshu* (pp. 19[2]-20[2]) suggests that immediately after the death of Yeshu, the twelve Nazarene disciples directed all their efforts to attract new followers to their movement *within* the confines of Judaism. It also suggests that such efforts were very successful (ויתנבאו בתוך המחנה נביאות שקר ויטעו ישראל אחריהם . . . ויתלקטו אחריהם עם רב מבני ישראל). Wagenseil's Latin translation sees the missionizing efforts as directed towards the world at large.[4] Perhaps Wagenseil's mistranslation is based on some strange understanding of the Hebrew word מחנה. It seems more likely to me,

1. In Wagenseil and in Foote and Wheeler the references to magic are fairly clear.

2. Later on that page Yeshu is again referred to by the rabbis as a מכשף and this time E.L.G. does translate the word as 'sorcerer'.

3. For sources, see Berger, *Debate*, p. 253.

4. *Inter coetus mortalium falsa spargebant vaticinia. Eos aliqui Israëlitarum sequuri sunt.* So also E.L.G. (p. 16): '. . . dispersed false prophecies among the whole swarm of mortals. Them also did many of the Israelites follow.'

though, that on some level he is attempting to make the story of Yeshu conform to what he believes about the story of the spread of the Jesus movement, based on the Great Commission text in Matthew (28.16-20).

Yeshu in *Toledot Yeshu* (p. 14) is reputed to have taken two mill-stones, seated himself upon them (וישב עליהם), and gone floating on the water. Wagenseil's translation of that text is unremarkable (*super quibus considens*). Suddenly in E.L.G.'s translation (p. 11) it is no longer so clear that Yeshu was sitting ('. . . upon which walking or seated. . . '). It seems clear that E.L.G. is emphasizing the parallel between this story of Yeshu and the story of Jesus *walking* on water.[1]

A Christian who sees the character Yeshu as not representing the real Jesus, but merely as a blasphemous caricature, presumably would find no reason to attempt to increase the reader's sympathy for Yeshu. Yet that seems to be what the Christian translators of *Toledot Yeshu* occasionally do. For example, when Yeshu was about to be killed, the Hebrew text (p. 17) notes simply that he was thirsty (ויצמא). Wagenseil's Latin is slightly more descriptive: *siti compulsus*. E.L.G.'s English (p. 13), 'tortured by thirst', is an obvious attempt, conscious or otherwise, to increase the drama of the scene and to make the reader feel the pain of Yeshu.

It is possible to argue that one can find in Foote and Wheeler's translation precisely the opposite phenomenon—i.e. the attempt to diminish the number of parallels between *Toledot Yeshu* and the New Testament. At one point in the Hebrew text (p. 7) Yeshu is reported to have gone to his birthplace, Bethlehem (והלך לבית לחם יהודא מקום לידתו). Wagenseil's Latin and E.L.G.'s English are unremarkable. Yet in Foote and Wheeler (p. 19) the text is curiously shortened, 'he went to the place of his nativity'. There is no mention of Bethlehem. Perhaps the cause of that omission is mere sloppiness. Yet it is also possible that Foote and Wheeler, who see *Toledot Yeshu* as more reliable than the Gospels which they dislike so passionately, make a conscious or subconscious decision to remove from their translation a text that would lend credibility to the claim of Matthew (2.1) and Luke

1. Mk 6.45-52. Cf. the translation of Foote and Wheeler (p. 26) where no attempt is made to deviate from the Latin.

(2.4-7) that Jesus was born in Bethlehem, a claim concerning which critical scholarship has long had serious doubts.[1]

The Depiction of Yeshu and his Contemporaries

Yeshu's opponents in *Toledot Yeshu* are generally portrayed as the חכמים or חסידים or זקנים. The opposition is occasionally described as being unanimous. Yet the translations attempt to magnify and perhaps to redefine the extent of the opposition.

For example, when the Sages encouraged Rabbi Judah to go and confront Yeshu, the Hebrew records that they all agreed (ויענו כולם; p. 12). Wagenseil's Latin goes one step further, *Tum una omnes voce clamare* (= E.L.G. [p. 9]: 'Then they all with one voice cried'). Or when Queen Helena, who was sympathetic to Yeshu, summoned the Sages, the Hebrew simply reads (p. 19): ותשלח אל חכמי ישראל. E.L.G.'s translation (p. 14) claims that she 'summoned the whole Senate of the Israelites'.[2]

In fact, E.L.G.'s translation is interested not only in exaggerating the extent of the opposition, but also in portraying it as stemming from official circles. The last citation mentions the opposition to Yeshu from a Jewish 'Senate', an idea finding no basis in the Hebrew or the Latin (and presumably not in history, either). There are numerous references to a Jewish 'Council', unsupported by the Hebrew or Latin sources.[3] There are many references to the Scribes and the Elders, always capitalized.[4] E.L.G. wishes to portray the opposition to Yeshu as having come from organized established power

1. See, e.g., R.E. Brown, *The Birth of the Messiah* (Garden City, NY: Doubleday, 1977), especially 'Appendix III: Birth at Bethlehem', pp. 513-16. On p. 513, there, Brown cites the words of C. Burger in *Jesus als Davidssohn* (Göttingen: Vandenhoeck & Ruprecht, 1970), p. 104: 'The overwhelming evidence to the contrary has made the thesis that Bethlehem was *not* the historical birthplace of Jesus the *communis opinio* of New Testament scholarship'. On doubts about the details of the narrative surrounding Jesus' birth already in the eighteenth century, see Thomas Paine, *The Age of Reason*, Part II (Buffalo: Prometheus, 1984), pp. 146-51.

2. Wagenseil's Latin reads: *iubet igitur adesse Sapientes Israëlitarum.*

3. E.g. E.L.G., p. 6: 'one of their Council', translating Wagenseil's *quidam ex Sapientibus* (p. 12; the Hebrew reads אחד מן החכמין).

4. Wagenseil inconsistently capitalizes such words as *Senes, Sapientes* or *Seniores.*

groups among the Jews, despite the fact that his sources do not make that claim. Again one may see this phenomenon as part of the attempt to harmonize *Toledot Yeshu* and the Gospels.

But the most interesting change that E.L.G. makes in the description of the rabbinical opposition to Yeshu is that he very often calls those rabbis Pharisees. There is not one consistent Latin word that E.L.G. translates as 'Pharisees'. Sometimes it is *senes* (Hebrew: זקנים).[1] At other times it is *pii* or *religiosi homines*.[2] So it is not that E.L.G. mistakes one Latin word as meaning Pharisees. It is rather his desire to implicate the Pharisees as persecutors of Jesus. It is curious to note that E.L.G. is then following the pattern that modern scholars have attributed to the Gospel writers themselves who may have taken sources that spoke about some form of Jewish opposition to Jesus and changed those sources into condemnations specifically of the Pharisees.[3]

Similarly one detects a pattern of attempting to make Queen Helena (a figure who has many similarities to either Pilate's wife or to the Pilate of the Gospels) look even more pro-Yeshu than the Hebrew and Latin texts would suggest. Once, after arguing with the rabbis about Yeshu, Queen Helena, according to the Hebrew text, acceded to their request (p. 10; גם לדבר הזה אשמע לכם). In E.L.G.'s English (p. 8) her opposition to the rabbis continues and her response turns into, 'Nevertheless I require you to bring him to me'.[4] On one other occasion when she continued to dispute with the rabbis, her words of opposition (p. 19) מה אוסיף עוד לדבר עמכם become even stronger in E.L.G.'s English: 'How shall I disprove your words' (p. 15).[5]

So as E.L.G. shifts more blame onto the Pharisees, he tries to make the secular authorities in Yeshu's Judea look better than the Latin and Hebrew texts would require. Again one can sense a similarity between

1. E.L.G., p. 6.

2. Both translations of the Hebrew חסידים. See E.L.G., pp. 15 and 12 respectively.

3. See, e.g., the chapter on 'Jesus and his Compatriots', in P. Winter's *On the Trial of Jesus* (rev. and ed. T.A. Burkill and G. Vermes; Berlin: de Gruyter, 1974), pp. 158-89.

4. Wagenseil's Latin (*etiam in ista re vobis obsequar*) is a faithful rendition of the Hebrew and cannot be seen as the source of E.L.G.'s mistranslation.

5. Again Wagenseil's Latin (*quid ego frustra vobiscum sermonem commuto*) is a more faithful rendition of the Hebrew.

his writings and those of the Gospel writers who are seen by many scholars not only to have shifted more blame for the persecution and death of Jesus onto the Pharisees but also to have whitewashed Pilate, the secular authority figure in first-century Judea.[1]

Conclusion

Toledot Yeshu, a Jewish anti-Christian work, can be and has been translated in two very different polemical ways. Foote and Wheeler use the opportunity of translating this work to further the goal of attacking the Christian Gospels, a goal rather similar to the original intent of *Toledot Yeshu* itself. Wagenseil and E.L.G. take a very different approach. They look down on this Jewish work as pornographic literature that should not be translated in full and they often highlight and exaggerate the extent of magic and superstition in it. Yet that is not the primary way in which they use the work polemically. Paradoxically, while seeing the work as a perfidious, devilish, superstitious fabrication, they still try to present it as supporting and proving the veracity of the Gospel accounts of Jesus. In other words, these translators find a number of different ways of using the translation of a Jewish anti-Christian work as a vehicle for furthering the cause of Christianity.

1. See, e.g., the chapter entitled 'Pontius Pilate in History and Christian Tradition', in Winter's *Trial*, pp. 70-89.

GLEANINGS FROM THE BIBLICAL AND TALMUDIC LEXICA IN LIGHT OF AKKADIAN

Shalom M. Paul

To Professor Nahum Sarna—a gentleman and scholar
דבר בעתו מה־טוב (משלי טו:כג)

1. *1 Samuel 24.13 and ARM I, 5.10—'As the Ancient Proverb Says'*

The employment of the substantive 'dog' (Akk. *kalbu*, Heb. כלב) as a term of self-disparagement and as an invective is well known from both Mesopotamian and biblical sources.[1] This expression of insignificance and abasement is further intensified when one refers to himself or is referred to by others as a 'dead dog'. Compare the following from neo-Assyrian and neo-Babylonian epistolary literatures:[2]

> *lapnu mār lapni kalbu mītu anāku*, 'I was a poor man, son of a poor man, a dead dog' (ABL 1285.13-14).

1. See D. Winton Thomas, '*Kelibh*, "Dog": Its Origin and Some Usages of it in the Old Testament', *VT* 10 (1960), pp. 410-27, who also cites the examples found in the Lachish Letters, 2.4; 5.4; 6.3. The Akkadian evidence can be found in *CAD*, K, p. 72. For another example not cited there, cf. *kīma kalbi da'ati ul tašāli*, 'You did not care for me any better than for a dog!'; F.R. Kraus, *Briefe aus dem Istanbuler Museum* (AbB, 5; Leiden, 1972), no. 160, 6-9.

2. The citations are all taken from *ABL* (= R.F. Harper, *Assyrian and Babylonian Letters* [London and Chicago, 1892–1914]). *ABL* 1285 has now been collated and re-edited by S. Parpola, 'The Forlorn Scholar', in *Language, Literature and History: Philological and Historical Studies Presented to Erica Reiner* (ed. F. Rochberg-Halton; New Haven, 1987), pp. 257-78. Instead of *anāku*, Parpola (p. 260 l. 14) reads *[qul-l]u!-lu*, 'a vile person'.

> *ša kalbi mīti mār la mamma anāku šarru bēlâ uballiṭanni*, 'I, who was a dead dog, the son of a nobody, the king, my lord, gave me life' (ABL 521.6-7).
>
> *kalbāni mītūtu anīni šarru bēlī uballiṭannâši*, 'We were dead dogs; the king, my lord, gave us life' (ABL 771.5).
>
> *manna anīni kalbāni mītūtu ša šarru šumani idû*, 'Who are we? Dead dogs whose names the king knows' (ABL 454.18; cf. also ABL 831.5; 992, r. 15; 1289, r. 4).

In the Bible, this canine epithet appears three (or four) times. After David, out of respect for his deceased friend Jonathan, extends the hospitality of the court to his son, Mephibosheth, the latter disparagingly says of himself, 'What is your servant, that you should show regard for a dead dog (הכלב המת) like me?' (2 Sam. 9.8). Abishai, son of Zeruiah, defending the abused honor of David against the verbal vilification of Shimei, son of Gera, vehemently exclaims, 'Why let that dead dog (הכלב המת) abuse my lord, the king? Let me go over and cut off his head!' (2 Sam. 16.9). Another instance of this phrase is preserved only in the Septuagint's translation of 2 Kgs 8.13. When Elisha predicts to Hazael the brutal punishments which the latter will inflict upon Israel, Hazael replies, 'But how can your servant, who is a mere dog (LXX: ὁ κύων ὁ τεθνηκώς, 'a dead dog') perform such a mighty deed?'

The fourth example is attested in 1 Sam. 24.14, when David cries out to King Saul, 'Against whom has the king of Israel come out? Whom are you pursuing? A dead dog (כלב מת)? A mere flea?' This emotional outburst is preceded by David's self-vindication that he never wronged Saul nor had he ever harbored any thoughts of violence or treachery against him (v. 11). He solemnly declares, 'May the Lord judge between you and me! And may he take vengeance upon you for me, but my hand will never touch you' (v. 12).

David then cites 'the ancient proverb (משל הקדמֹני): "Wicked deeds come from wicked men!"' (v. 13). This is the sole instance in the Bible where an aphorism is referred to in this manner, and it has been conjectured that משל הקדמֹני should actually be read משל הקדמנים (the final *mem* having been erroneously omitted by haplography caused by the *mem* beginning the next word, מרשעים), 'the proverb of the ancients'—a reading now attested in 4QSam^{a}, [הקד]מוניים.[1]

Some three decades ago I noted that this very same expression also appears once in Mari, where it, too, is followed by the citation of a pertinent proverb. In a letter from Šamši-Adad I, king of Assyria, to his son, Yasmaḫ-Adad,[2] the king introduces a maxim[3] by saying, *kīma tēltim ullītim ša ummāmi*, 'As the ancient proverb which says'. The Akkadian is not only the exact interdialectal semantic and cognate equivalent of כאשר יאמר משל הקדמני in Samuel,[4] but it also helps to confirm the Masoretic Hebrew text, which speaks of 'the ancient proverb' and not 'the proverb of the ancients'.

2. *The Symbolic Gesture of 'Seizing the Hem of a Cloak' in Zechariah 8.23*

In an eschatological vision the prophet Zechariah foresees a time when many nations and peoples will acknowledge the universal supremacy and authority of the God of Israel:[5] 'In those days, ten men[6] from nations of every tongue will take hold—they will take hold of every

1. See P.K. McCarter, *I Samuel* (AB, 8; Garden City, NY, 1980), p. 382.

2. ARM, I, 5.10.

3. For the interpretation of this proverb, see A. Finet, 'Citations littéraires dans la correspondance de Mari', *RA* 68 (1974), pp. 44-45; A. Marzal, *Gleanings from the Wisdom of Mari* (Studia Pohl, 11; Rome, 1976), pp. 15-23; W.L. Moran, 'Puppies in Proverbs—From Šamši-Adad I to Archilochus?' in *Eretz-Israel*, 14 (H.L. Ginsberg Volume; ed. M. Haran; Jerusalem, 1978), pp. 32*-37*.

4. After this note was written, I was happy to discover that C. Cohen ('New Akkadian Evidence for the Meaning and Etymology of the Term "Mashal" in the Bible', in *Y.M. Grintz Memorial Volume* [Tel-Aviv, 1962], pp. 319 and 323 n. 51 [Hebrew]) refers to an oral communication from Moshe Held, who also compared the expression in the Mari letter to this verse in Samuel. Subsequently I discovered Held's own written remarks which appeared in 'Marginal Notes to the Biblical Lexicon', in *Biblical and Related Studies Presented to Samuel Iwry* (ed. A. Kort and S. Morschauser; Winona Lake, IN, 1985), p. 95.

5. Compare similarly Isa. 2.2-3; 45.14-15, 22-25; 56.6-7; 66.23; Mic. 4.1-2; Zech. 14.9, 16.

6. The symbolic nature of the number ten representing a complete number has been recognized by most commentators. See, in addition to the bibliography usually cited in commentaries, Y. Avishur, 'The Forms of Repetition of Numbers Indicating Wholeness (3, 7, 10)—in the Bible and in Ancient Semitic Literature', *Beer-Sheva* 1 (1973), pp. 1-55 (Hebrew).

Jew by a corner of his cloak and say, "Let us go with you, for we have heard that God is with you"' (Zech. 8.23).[1] The Hebrew expression החזיק בכנף, 'to take hold of a corner/the hem of a cloak', is a symbolical gesture of a suppliant to a superior,[2] whose significance has not been definitively clarified in this passage. Whereas Rudolph, quoting Horst, terms it a 'rechtssymbolischer Ausdruck', which designates 'des Ersuchens um ein Schutzverhältnis,[3] Meyers and Meyers,[4] citing McCarter,[5] interpret this act as one of 'supplication, submission, importuning'. Meyers and Meyers further remark that the 'taking hold of the hem. . . conjures up a picture of rapprochement, submission, loyalty. . . By taking hold of the garment, the non-Yehudite signifies his willingness to accept the supremacy of the God of Israel'.[6] What, then, is the exact nuance of this phrase—supplication, importuning, submission, acceptance, loyalty?

Although neither Meyers nor McCarter cite any ancient Near Eastern textual documentation, the latter relies on a study of Brauner, who, in an article devoted to 1 Sam. 15.27, concludes from a comparison of both the Akkadian (*sissikta ṣabātu*) and Aramaic (אחז בכנף) interdialectal semantic and cognate equivalents of החזיק בכנף that the expression refers to 'supplication' or to 'submission to a superior'.[7] (In a later study, Brauner adduces another Aramaic example as well as

1. *NJPSV* (= *The New Jewish Publication Society of America: The Prophets* [Philadelphia, 1978]), p. 882.

2. This was totally missed by D.L. Petersen, *Haggai and Zechariah 1–8* (OTL; Philadelphia, 1980), pp. 318-20 and not dealt with at all by E. Lipiński, 'Recherches sur le livre de Zacharie', *VT* 20 (1970), pp. 42-46. The latter assumes that this verse refers to the diaspora Jews and not to the foreign nations. For a correct critique of this view, see W. Rudolph, *Haggai, Sacharja 1–8; Sacharja 9–14; Maleachi* (KAT, 13.4; Gütersloh, 1976), p. 153. For a brief review of the various symbolic aspects relating to the hem of a garment, see R.A. Veneer, 'Hem', in *IDBSup*, pp. 401-402.

3. Rudolph, *Haggai, Sacharja 1–8*, p. 152.

4. C.L. Meyers and E.M. Meyers, *Haggai, Zechariah 1–8* (AB, 25b; Garden City, 1987), p. 441.

5. McCarter, *I Samuel*, p. 268. (In a typographical error, Meyers and Meyers, *Haggai, Zechariah*, p. 441, incorrectly cite p. 208.)

6. Meyers and Meyers, *Haggai, Zechariah*, pp. 441-42.

7. R.A. Brauner, '"To Grasp the Hem" and 1 Samuel 15.27', *JANESCU* 6 (1974), pp. 35-38. The quotes are found on pp. 37-38.

one from Ugaritic.)[1] The three texts which he cites, as well as additional ample documentation, should all be interpreted, however, not merely as submission but as an act of declaring allegiance to the god whose hem of the garment is grasped.

> *[asḫur]ki aš'ēki*[2] *sissiktaki aṣbat kīma sissikti ilija u ištarija*, 'I [turned to] you and sought you. I grasped your hem (i.e. was loyal to you) as if it were the hem of my own god and goddess'.[3]
>
> *sissikti ilūtišu rabīti aṣbat ašte'â ašrātešu*, '(When Marduk entrusted the rule of Assyria to me), I grasped the hem of his divine majesty (i.e. pledged allegiance). I sought his shrine'.[4]
>
> *sissikti Sin šar ilāni aṣbatma*, 'I grasped the hem of Sin, king of the gods (night and day)'.[5]

Although many more citations can be quoted,[6] one more will suffice:

> *aššum sissikti Marduk bēlija ṣabtākuma Marduk bēlī jâti irammannima*, 'Because I grasped the hem of Marduk, Marduk, my lord, loves me'.[7]

This concept of allegiance and attachment to a god or a king can be further substantiated by the parallel Akkadian expressions *qannam ṣabātu*, 'to grasp the hem', and *qaran ṣubāti ṣabātu*, 'to grasp the hem of a garment':[8]

1. R.A. Brauner, 'Aramaic and Comparative Semitic', *Gratz College Annual of Jewish Studies*, VI (Philadelphia, 1977), pp. 25-33. See esp. pp. 25-27. For comments, see below p. 248 n. 3.
2. For the verbs *saḫāru* and *še'û*, which often are paired together, see M. Held, 'Two Philological Notes on Enūma Eliš', in *Kramer Anniversary Volume: Cuneiform Studies in Honor of Samuel Noah Kramer* (ed. B.L. Eichler; AOAT, 25; Neukirchen–Vluyn, 1976), p. 233.
3. E. Ebeling, *Die akkadische Gebetsserie "Handerhebung" von neuem gesammelt und herausgeben* (Berlin, 1953), p. 30.7 (= L.W. King, *Babylonian Magic and Sorcery* [London, 1896], p. 4.29).
4. M. Streck, *Assurbanipal und die letzten assyrischen Könige bis zum Untergang Niniveh's* (VAB, 7; Leipzig, 1916), p. 262.27.
5. C.J. Gadd, 'The Harran Inscriptions of Nabonidus', *AnSt* 8 (1958), 46.i.17; cf. also 46.i.12; 48.ii.23.
6. See *CAD*, S, p. 324, d, which also translates the expression 'referring to the hem of the god's garment' as 'a gesture of confidence and allegiance'.
7. S.K. Langdon, *Die neubabylonischen Königsinschriften* (VAB, 4; Leipzig, 1912), 110.iii.25 and 142.ii.7.
8. See *CAD*, Q, p. 84, c, from where the quotes are taken. For a thorough study

> *kurbi ana RN ṣābit qanniki*, '(Ishtar), pronounce your blessings over Sargon who grasps your hem'.[1]

> *ištu ūmim ša qaran ṣubātija iṣbatu matima ina mātišu*[2] *kaspam. . . mimma ul alqut*, 'Ever since he grasped the hem of my garment [i.e. gave me his allegiance], I have never exacted any silver (cattle, sheep or barley) from his country'.[3]

> *ana qabê mātija qaran ṣubāt bēlija aṣbat bēlī qātī la inappaṣ*,[4] 'At the request of my land, I grasped the hem of my lord's garment; may my lord not reject me'.[5]

> *šumma qaran ṣubāt RN uwaššaruma qaran ṣubāt šarrim šanîm iṣabbatu ina ālāni u eperī it [taṣṣ]i*, 'If he lets go of the hem of Abban's garment and takes hold of the hem of another king's (i.e. exchanges his allegiance), he for[feits] his cities and territories'.[6]

And one more felicitous quote:

> *ṣabtākuma kî tīri ina qannīka*, 'I am attached to your hem like a courtier' (i.e. loyal as a dog).[7]

of these terms, see M. Malul, '"*Sissiktu*" and "*Sikku*"—their Meaning and Function', *BiOr* 43 (1986), pp. 19-35, and 'Studies in Biblical Legal Symbolism—A Discussion of the Terms *kanaph, ḥéq*, and *ḥoṣen/ḥeṣen*, their Meaning and Legal Usage in the Bible and the Ancient Near East', *Shnaton* 9 (1985), pp. 191-210 (Hebrew). His volume, *Studies in Mesopotamian Legal Symbolism* (AOAT) was not available to me. According to Malul, *qannu/qarnu ṣubāti* is not the 'hem of a garment' but rather the 'horn-corner of a garment'; and *sissiktu/sikku* refers to an 'undergarment covering one's private parts'. He also discusses *sīqu*, especially in the personal name *Ukāl-sīqi-Aššur*, 'I am/he is holding the *sīqu* of Assur'. For *sikku*, see also *CAD*, S, pp. 254-55; and for *sīqu*, *CAD*, S, p. 305.

1. J.A. Craig, *Assyrian and Babylonian Religious Texts*, I (Leipzig, 1895), 54.iv.18.

2. Note the paronomasia of *matima* and *mātīšu*.

3. The citation is taken from the Shemshara letter quoted in *In Memoriam Eckhard Unger. Beiträge zu Geschichte, Kultur und Religion der Alten Orients* (ed. M. Lurker; Baden-Baden, 1971).

4. For the idiom *qātam napāṣum*, 'to refuse, reject, push back', see *CAD*, N, I, p. 286.

5. J.-R. Kupper, *Correspondance de Baḫdi-Lim, préfet du palais de Mari* (ARM, 6; Paris, 1954), 26, r.8′-9′, p. 42.

6. D.J. Wiseman, 'Abban and Alalah', *JCS* 12 (1958), 126.47-48.

7. Ebeling, *Handerhebung*, p. 92, lines 9-10.

This same meaning applies to the Old Aramaic אחז בכנף.[1] In the inscription from Zenjirli which Bar-Rakib erected to his father, Panammuwa II, the son remarks upon the loyalty of his father to Tiglath-pileser III,[2]

פי אחז בכנף מראה מלך אשור ר[ב]

'He grasped the hem of his lord, the [great] king of Assyria'.[3]

In conclusion, the expression in Zech. 8.23 fits very well into the same context as the above and refers accordingly to a symbolic gesture of loyalty.[4]

1. Cited by Brauner, '"To Grasp the Hem"'.
2. H. Donner and W. Röllig, *KAI*, I (Wiesbaden, 1962), 215.11, p. 40. *Idem*, *KAI*, II (Wiesbaden, 1964), p. 227, note to line 11, refers to this as an 'Ausdruck des Vasallenverhältnisses'. Cf. also B. Landsberger, *Sam'al* (Ankara, 1948), p. 69 n. 178, 'Anhänglichkeit an die Gottheit'; and C.-F. Jean and J. Hoftijzer, *Dictionnaire des inscriptions sémitiques de l'ouest* (Leiden, 1965), p. 10, entry 2, under אחז, 'il s'est soumis à son seigneur, il s'est mis sous la protection de son seigneur'. The inscription is written in Samalian Aramaic. See J.C. Greenfield, 'The Dialects of Early Aramaic', *JNES* 37 (1978), p. 94.
3. The expression 'to seize the hem of a garment' also has specific legal connotations in Mesopotamian texts. See *CAD*, S, p. 17, 2′, á. So, too, *sikka ṣabātu*, 'to grasp the hem'. See Malul, 'Studies in Biblical Legal Symbolism'. See also *CAD*, S, pp. 254-55. For *qaran ṣubāti ṣabātu*, see *CAD*, Q, p. 83, b, 1′. (Thus n. 1 on p. 31 of Brauner's 'Aramaic and Comparative Semitic' should be made more explicit. The idiom *sikka ṣabātu* is not the same as the others discussed in this article. For its legal significance, see also H. Petschow, 'Gewand(saum) im Recht', *RLA*, III [Berlin and New York, 1957–71], pp. 320-21.) For its appearance in prayers and royal inscriptions, see W. Mayer, *Untersuchungen zur Formensprache der babylonischen 'Gebetsbeschwörungen'* (Studia Pohl: Series Maior V; Rome, 1976), pp. 147-49, and M.-J. Seux, *Épithètes royales akkadiennes et sumériennes* (Paris, 1967), p. 327 n. 330.
4. The interpretation of the Aramaic expression אחד בכנפי לבשך in Ahiqar XI.171-172 still remains to be solved. Though it definitely should not be forced to comply with the meanings discussed above in this article, *contra* Brauner, 'Aramaic and Comparative Semitic', p. 26, there still remain two possible options. J.M. Lindenberger, *The Aramaic Proverbs of Ahiqar* (Baltimore and London, 1983), pp. 174-75, following J. Halévy, 'Les nouveaux papyrus d'Eléphantine', *RevSém* 20 (1912), p. 75, opts for a legal context, i.e., taking the garment and holding it as a pledge. This approach has been duly criticized by J.C. Greenfield, 'Two Proverbs of Ahiqar', in *Lingering Over Words: Studies in Ancient Near Eastern Literature in Honor of William L. Moran* (ed. T. Abusch, J. Huehnergard and P. Steinkeller;

3. *Song of Songs 8.2: A Sexual-Textual Nuance*

The poetic ambiguity of the verb תלמדני in Song 8.2 has baffled commentators in regard to both its referent and the exact nuance of its meaning. The verbal form may be interpreted grammatically either as a third-person feminine singular, referring to the young woman's mother just previously mentioned in the verse—'I would lead you, I would bring you to the house of my mother; *she will teach me*'—or it may be understood as a second-person masculine singular, referring to her lover whom she arduously and avidly addresses in vv. 1-2a—'If only you were my own true brother that sucked my mother's breast, then I could kiss you when I met you in the street. . . I would bring you to the house of my mother; *you will teach me*'. An additional problem is presented by the LXX, V, and P, which, instead of rendering the verb תְּלַמְּדֵנִי, all reflect the Hebrew clause, ואל חדר הורתי 'and to the chamber of her who bore me', thus harmonizing this verse

Atlanta, 1990), pp. 195-201, who, in the course of his study of this idiom in Ahiqar, concludes that this 'familiar expression' is employed there 'in a neutral manner, that is, without necessarily implying any of its current meanings'. He interprets the lines to mean 'that if a wicked man tries to get control of your possessions, do not wrangle with him, but turn to Shamash, the god of justice' (p. 198). It is interesting to note that the same sequence of grabbing one's garment and then leaving it behind in the hands of the person who grabbed it is found both in Ahiqar, אחד בכנפי לבשך . . . שבק בידה and in Gen. 39.12, ותתפשהו בבגדו . . . ויעזב בגדו בידה (note the Aramaic Targum's translation, ואחדתה בלבושה ושבקה ללבושה בידה, where the exact same two verbs appear as in Ahiqar, אחד, שבק ביד, within, of course, entirely different contexts). The Ugaritic example cited by Brauner, 'Aramaic and Comparative Semitic', p. 26, from *CTA* 6, col. 2.9-11, has also been noted by E.L. Greenstein, '"To Grasp the Hem" in Ugaritic Literature', *VT* 32 (1982), pp. 217-18: *tiḫd·m[t] bsin·lpš·tšṣq[nh] bqṣ all*, 'She (Anat) grabs Mot by the hem of (his) garment, holds [him] tight by the edge of (his) robe'. (For Ugar. *s'n* and its Akkadian etymological equivalent, *sūnu*, see Malul, '"*Sissiktu*" and "*sikku*"', p. 24 n. 25, p. 26 n. 43.) Though Greenstein does not cite Brauner, they both conclude that this is a gesture of supplication. See already T.H. Gaster, *Thespis* (New York, 2nd edn, 1961), p. 220, note. However, in the light of the continuation of this tablet it becomes obvious that Anat is threatening Mot and not supplicating him. So, too, Greenfield, 'Two Proverbs of Ahiqar', p. 197 n. 12; and Malul, 'Studies in Biblical Legal Symbolism', p. 207.

with the similar one found in 3.4. Partially relying on these ancient versions, several exegetes are prone to emend the verb to תֵּלְדֵנִי[1] or יְלָדַתְנִי,[2] 'who bore me' (cf. 6.9; 8.5). Pope, who accepts the emendation תלדני, further assumes 'that a parallel to 8.2a is missing', and restores a conjectured stich, 'to the chamber of her who bore me' (obviously influenced by, but not citing, the versions).[3] Gordis, on the other hand, cleverly conjectures that maybe תלמדני was written by a scribe who mistook the substantive הורתי (3.4) as being derived from the root ירה, 'to teach', rather than from הרה, 'to bear', and 'then incorporated his erroneous synonym into the text'.[4]

However, once the sexual-textual nuance of the verb למד is correctly understood within the sensuous context of the text, all the above become superfluous.[5] Gerleman was on the right track when he observed, 'Der Zusammenhang lässt ahnen, dass "lehren" hier einen erotischen Hintersinn hat'.[6] Although his reference to the problematical verse in Jer. 13.21 is extremely dubious, and his alleged Egyptian parallel from the Turin papyrus has been contested by Keel (who nevertheless supports the erotic interpretation),[7] his insight can now be corroborated by resort to Akkadian. In both Old Assyrian and Old Babylonian texts the verb *lamādu* (the interdialectal etymological and

1. G. Kuhn, *Erklärung des Hohen Liedes* (Leipzig, 1926), pp. 50-51; W. Rudolph, *Das Buch Ruth, Das Hohelied, Die Klagelieder* (KAT, 17.1-3; Gütersloh, 1962), p. 178; E. Wurthwein, *Die Fünf Megilloth: Ruth, Das Hohelied, Esther* (HAT, 18; Tübingen, 1969), p. 66.

2. A. Ehrlich, *Randglossen zur hebräischen Bibel*, VII (Leipzig, 1914), p. 17.

3. M. Pope, *Song of Songs* (AB, 7c; Garden City, NY: Doubleday, 1977), pp. 653, 659. M.V. Fox (*The Song of Songs and the Ancient Egyptian Love Songs* [Wisconsin, 1985], p. 166), on the other hand, cites the versions and also favors restoring the phrase here.

4. R. Gordis, *The Song of Songs and Lamentations* (New York, 1974), p. 98.

5. Compare also the suggestion of J.N. Epstein to interpret the verb from one of the meanings of this root in Mishnaic Hebrew and Syriac, 'to join', in *Introduction to Tannaitic Literature* (ed. E.Z. Melamed; Jerusalem and Tel-Aviv, 1957), p. 474 (Hebrew).

6. G. Gerleman, *Ruth, Das Hohelied* (BKAT, 18; Neukirchen–Vluyn, 1965), pp. 212-13. He attaches this verb to the following clause, interpreting it 'als Vordersatz eines Bedingungssatzes: wenn du mich "lehrst," werde ich dir zu trinken geben'.

7. O. Keel, *Das Hohelied* (Zürcher Bibelkommentar AT, 18; Zurich, 1986), p. 240 and n. 165.

semantic cognate of Heb. למד) also has the meaning, 'to know sexually'.[1] Cf., for example, the Laws of Hammurapi 154.69, 'If a man had had intercourse (*iltamad*) with his daughter. . . '; LH 155.75, 'If a man has chosen a bride for his son, and his son has had intercourse with her (*mārušu ilmassi*). . . ' (cf. also 156.6).[2] Thus, the fantasizing wishes of the young female to be 'taught' by her lover,[3] to whom she will respond in kind by offering her own erotic mixtures of libations (see the continuation of this verse),[4] turn out to be none other than a 'lesson' in the discourse of intercourse.[5]

4. *Daniel 9.27: A Reflex of Legal Terminology*

In an article pertaining to Dan. 6.8 it was shown that לתקפה אסר was an Aramaic reflex of Assyrian legal terminology.[6] Aramaic תקפה, the *pa'el* infinitive of תקף, is the interdialectal semantic equivalent of the Assyrian verb *dunnunu*. This verb evinces a semantic development similar to its nominal form, *dannatu* (cf., too, Aram. דנת, which is a loan translation), which, from its basic root meaning, 'strength', comes to mean a 'legitimate, valid, binding document' (so, too, its

1. Compare similarly both Heb. ידע and Akk. *idû*. For the latter, see *CAD* I/J, p. 28.

2. For additional examples, see *CAD*, L, pp. 55-56.

3. Compare the Hebrew commentary to the Song of Songs written by an anonymous thirteenth-century French exegete whose work is brimful with penetrating and important insights into the understanding of the book. It was edited by H.J. Matthews, 'An Anonymous Commentary on the Song of Songs', in *Festschrift zum 80en Geburtstag Moritz Steinschneider's* (Leipzig, 1896), pp. 164-85. Commenting on the meaning of תלמדני, he adds a mere two words, משפט החושקים, 'the manner of lovers' (p. 83).

4. R.E. Murphy, *The Song of Songs* (Hermeneia; Fortress-Augsburg, 1990), p. 189, caught the nuance, but not the exact meaning, '. . . where he would "teach" her to prepare for him a drink of wine and pomegranates [which]. . . must symbolize the delights of love. . . '

5. This would add, along with Heb. עלה = Akk. *elû*, 'to mount' (Gen. 31.10, 12) and Heb. ללכת אל = Akk. *ana*. . . *alāku*, 'to have intercourse with', yet another verb to the biblical terminology for copulation. See S.M. Paul, 'Two Cognate Semitic Terms for Mating and Copulation', *VT* 32 (1982), pp. 492-94.

6. See S.M. Paul, 'Dan. 6, 8: An Aramaic Reflex of Assyrian Legal Terminology', *Bib* 65 (1984), pp. 106-10. The quotations and documentation are all taken from that article.

Nabatean calque, חקף, which helps explain, in turn, Heb. חקף in Esth. 9.29). The technical legal meaning of the verb *dunnunu* is attested as early as Old Assyrian, *tuppūšu ludanninma*, 'Let him make his tablets binding', and continues into neo-Assyrian times, for example, *adê ina muḫḫišu issikunu udanninuni iškununi*, 'And concerning whom he has made the treaty binding upon you'. The Aramaic expression חקפה אסר is none other than the cognate equivalent of Assyrian *riksa dunnunu*, in which the nouns אסר and *riksu* represent terms for 'obligatory bonds', and the verbs חקף and *dunnunu* signify 'ratification'—hence 'to make a document legally binding and valid'.

It can be shown that yet another reflex of this idiom makes its appearance in the book of Daniel. At the very end of ch. 9, where the persecutions of Antiochus Epiphanes IV and his profanation of the Temple during the last 'week of years' are being described to Daniel, v. 27 commences with the statement, 'For one week he [i.e. Antiochus] will הגביר ברית with the many'. The exact nuance of this expression, however, has not been thoroughly understood. Hebrew הגביר[1] is the cognate semantic equivalent of Akkaddian *dunnunu* and Aramaic הַקֵּף[2] and, in the present context of a ברית, 'covenant', shares with them the legal meaning of 'binding'.[3] Thus, 'He contracted a legally binding covenant with the many', which apparently refers to the relations of the Greek king with the Hellenizers of that period as

1. Except for this occurrence, the *hiph'il* of Heb. גבר appears elsewhere only in Ps. 12.5, in an entirely different context. The Akkadian and Aramaic verbs appear in the D-form and *pa'el* respectively.

2. If one were to accept the intriguing suggestion of H.L. Ginsberg, that the Hebrew chapters of the second part of Daniel (8–12) are a translation from an Aramaic original, one might venture to suggest that the expression קים יתקף was the *Vorlage* of Heb. הגביר ברית. For Aram. קים as the translation of Heb. ברית, cf., e.g., *Tar. Onk.* to Gen. 9.9, 11. Interestingly enough, R.H. Charles (*A Critical and Exegetical Commentary on the Book of Daniel* [Oxford, 1929], *ad loc.*) actually made this exact same proposal, based on the double sense of קים, 'covenant' and 'statute'. A. Lacocque, *The Book of Daniel* (Atlanta, 1979), p. 198, in turn, assumes that the latter was the intention of the author and concludes that Heb. ברית is 'an erroneous but not a corrupt translation from the original Aramaic'. Since he did not recognize, however, the legal force of the verb, he was led to interpret the expression incorrectly as 'proclaiming a harsh law against the multitude'.

3. There is therefore no need to resort to any of the many proposed emendations; for a listing, see J.A. Montgomery, *The Book of Daniel* (ICC; Edinburgh, 1964), p. 389.

echoed in 1 Macc. 1.11-14.

5. *Hebrew* מהלך *and Akkadian mālaku*

One of the many terms investigated in A. Hurvitz's monograph on the linguistic relationship between Ezekiel and the priestly source was Hebrew מהלך.[1] He clearly demonstrated that this late substantive[2] replaces an earlier term, דרך, in narrative descriptions (cf., e.g. Num. 9.10; 11.31; 33.8 as contrasted to Jon. 3.3, 4; Neh. 2.6), is often present in postbiblical sources (cf., e.g. *m. Ma'as. Š.* 5.2; *m. Roš. Haš.* 1.9; *t. Pes.* 8.3), and is found at times in Targumic Aramaic as the translation for Hebrew דרך (cf., e.g. *Targ. Onk.* to Exod. 3.18 and Deut. 1.2). Its employment in Ezek. 42.4, though also of late vintage, is to be separated, however, from the above, for in that verse it functions as a technical term, meaning 'areaway, pathway'.

What was not pointed out in Hurvitz's study and has been generally overlooked in most modern commentaries is that Hebrew מהלך is the etymological and semantic cognate equivalent of Akkadian *mālaku* (both being derived from the verb 'to go', Akk. *alāku*, Heb. הלך), which bears the same identical meanings:[3]

1. For the usage in Ezek. 42.4 pertaining to the Temple complex, compare the passage in a text from the time of Nebuchadrezzar, a contemporary of Ezekiel, 'I improved greatly the way to the sanctuary and the pathway to the temple (*mālak bīti*)'.[4] Compare also the statement in one of Darius's inscriptions, 'A house which is situated in the pathway to the temple of Mār-bīti (*ina mālaka ša bīt Mār-bīti*).[5]

2. In Neh. 2.6, when Nehemiah requests to be sent to Jerusalem in order to rebuild it, Axtaxerxes, the Persian king, asks, 'How long will

1. A. Hurvitz, *A Linguistic Study of the Relationship between the Priestly Source and the Book of Ezekiel* (Cahiers de la Revue Biblique, 20; Paris, 1982), pp. 91-94.

2. The substantive appears four times in the singular and once in the plural, Zech. 3.7; the latter is not dealt with in this note.

3. See *CAD*, M, I, pp. 158-59, from which all the citations are taken. See also Held, 'Two Philological Notes in Enūma Eliš', p. 238, who notes the various usages of *mālaku* as a physical road or course, but does not make reference to its biblical counterpart.

4. Langdon, *Die neubabylonischen Königinschriften*, 128.iii.55; cf. also 158.vi.38.

5. J.N. Strassmaier, *Inschriften von Darlus, König von Babylon* (Leipzig, 1887), 379.10, 33; cf. 378.1; 428.2.

be מהלכך ('your trip', 'journey', lit. 'your going') and when will you return?' Somewhat similar, Akkadian *mālaku* also means 'march, marching, advance, course', literally 'one's going'. Compare 'He saw from afar the advance (*mālak*) of my campaign';[1] and 'The enemy will intercept the course (*mālak*) of my troops'.[2]

3. The Akkadian noun, moreover, has the additional meaning of 'distance', which is expressed in units of time. Compare 'For a distance (*mālak*) of one month and twenty-five days I devastated the provinces of Elam';[3] 'Where lands are situated at a distance (*mālak*) of seven days out in the middle of the Western Sea';[4] 'There was a distance (*mālak*) of one day between them'.[5] This, of course, is identical to Jon. 3.3-4, 'Nineveh was an enormously large city, a three days' walk (מהלך) across. Jonah started out and made his way into the city the distance of one day's walk (מהלך). . . '

One further passage, though extremely problematical, may be considered in this connection. In Isaiah 35, the prophet rhapsodically proclaims the future deliverance of the people from exile. Through the desert, transformed into a fertile and well-watered land, there will run a 'highway (מסלול ודרך) which shall be called the "Sacred Way".[6] No one unclean shall pass along it; and it למו הלך דרך' (v. 8). Driver has very plausibly suggested combining the letters of the first two words, reading למהלך דרך, 'and it shall be a processional road'.[7] This very same meaning is also attested in Akkadian: compare 'I stand up like a healthy tree at the gate of the processional roads' (*mālakāni*)';[8]

1. F. Thureau-Dangin, *Une relation de la huitième campagne de Sargon* (TCL, 3; Paris, 1912), p. 82.

2. R.C. Thompson, *Cuneiform Texts from Babylonian Tablets* (CT, 20; London, 1904), 26.5.

3. Streck, *Assurbanipal*, 56.vi.77; cf. 24.iii.2.

4. D.G. Lyon, *Keilschrifttexte Sargon's, Königs von Assyrien (722–705 v. Chr.)* (Assyriologische Bibliothek, 5; Leipzig, 1883), 14.28.

5. D.J. Wiseman, *Chronicles of Chaldaean Kings (626–556 B.C.) in the British Museum* (London, 1956), 72, r. 19.

6. For highways bearing special names, cf. *CAD*, Ḫ, p. 108.

7. G.R. Driver, 'Glosses in the Hebrew Text of the Old Testament', in *L'ancien testament et l'orient* (Orientalia et Biblica Lovaniensia, 1; Louvain, 1957), p. 126. On such roads, see W. Andrae, *Alte Feststrassen im Nahen Osten* (Stuttgart, 1964).

8. O.R. Gurney and J.J. Finkelstein, *The Sultantepe Tablets*, I (London, 1957), 360, r. 16. See K. Deller, 'Neuassyrisches aus Sultantepe', *Or* 34 (1965), p. 466, who also cites M. san Nicolò, *Babylonische Rechtsurkunden* (Munich, 1951), p. 43

'At sunrise and sunset he (Marduk) placed the *lumāšu*-stars and granted them (?) a path (*ḫarrānu mālaku(?)]*').[1] The last two Akkadian words (if the proposed restoration is correct) would also be the exact equivalent, but in reverse order, of Hebrew מהלך דרך.

6. *'To Throw' = 'To Put On' Jewelry and Wearing Apparel*

One final lexical note is the interesting semantic development which occurs in several Semitic verbs whose basic meaning is 'to throw' and then, by extension, 'to put on' jewelry as well as other wearing apparel. (Cf. English 'to throw' > 'to throw on' = to put on hastily, and German *werfen* ['to throw'], *ich warf mich in meine Kleider*, 'I threw on my clothes'.) Only a few selected examples for each verb will be cited.

1. Akkadian, *nadû*:
   a. 'Several craftsmen wrapped in a *ṣibtu*-garment and having put on (*nadû*) two belts.'[2]
   b. 'He placed on (*iddi*) her neck a *irimmu*-necklace.'[3]
   c. 'May the *maninnu*-necklace be placed around (*nadi*) my brother's neck for a hundred thousand years.'[4]
   d. 'She (Ninsun) placed on (*ittadi*) the neck of Enkidu *indu*-jewelry.'[5]
2. Akkadian, *ramû*:
   a. 'She is sumptuously arrayed; *irimmu*-jewelry is placed on (*ramû*) her head.'[6]
3. Akkadian, *karāru*:

n. 8, for this same meaning.

1. J.A. Craig, *Assyrian and Babylonian Religious Texts*, I, 31.9, cited also in *CAD*, L, p. 245, meaning 2. See *CAD*, M, I, pp. 158-59, meaning 3, for additional examples.

2. *CAD*, N, I, p. 82, *nadû*, 2, 4′, where other examples are cited. Cf. also *CAD*, M, II, p. 46, *mēzeḫu*, b).

3. *CAD*, I/J, p. 117, *irimmu*; N, I, p. 82, 9′.

4. *CAD*, N, I, p. 82, 9′.

5. *CAD*, N, I; *CAD*, I/J, p. 110, *imdu*, 3.

6. *CAD*, I/J, p. 177, *irimmu*. For other examples (though rare), see *AHw*, p. 952, *ramû* II, 1).

a. 'You place around (*takarrar*) her shoulders (lit., 'her neck') a *ḫullānu*-garment.'[1]
b. 'They cut the seal cylinders from their necks and put them on (*ikterrū*).'[2]
c. 'The king should wear these bandages around (*likrur*) his neck.'[3]
d. 'You put it like a seal around (*taktararšu*) your neck.'[4]

4. Aramaic, רמי (= Akk. *ramû*):
a. '(Rabbi Aqiba said to his wife, Rachel), "If I could only afford it, I would attire you (רמינא) with a Jerusalem of Gold".'[5]
b. 'Rabbah put on (רמי) fine shoes for prayer, saying, "Prepare yourself to meet your God"' (Amos 4.12).[6]

5. Ugaritic, *ndy*
a. The Ugaritic evidence is present but ambiguous. The corresponding verb *ndy* appears four (and most likely five) times in *CTA* 17, col. 1, lines 4, 5, 14, 15 (16?) (Aqhat), where it describes the putting on or the 'throwing off' of a garment.

1. *CAD*, K, p. 448, *kišādu*, 1 ; p. 208, *karāru* A, c), 1′.
2. *CAD*, K, p. 448, 1′.
3. *CAD*, K; *CAD*, M, II, p. 14, *mêlu*.
4. *CAD*, K, p. 208.
5. *B. Ned.* 50a. For the mural crown called 'Jerusalem of Gold', see S.M. Paul, 'Jerusalem—A City of Gold', *IEJ* 17 (1967), pp. 259-63; and 'Jerusalem of Gold—A Song and an Ancient Crown', *BARer* 3 (1977), pp. 38-41.
6. *B. Šab.* 10a.

ELEPHANTINE ARAMAIC CONTRACTS AND THE PRIESTLY LITERATURE

Bezalel Porten

In 1981 I published a study on 'Structure and Chiasm in Aramaic Contracts and Letters'.[1] Aramaic conveyances are narratives which move from past (Transaction), to present (Investiture), to future (Guarantees): I gave you this property; it is yours; no one shall take it away from you.[2] I selected nine documents for stylistic analysis (*TAD* B2.3, 2.7, 2.10, 2.11; 3.4, 3.5, 3.10, 3.11, 3.12)[3] and noted that the Transaction section was characterized by key word repetition, chiasm and inclusion. In the light of recent studies[4] it is now possible to expand our understanding of stylistics in Aramaic contracts and demonstrate their contribution to a fuller understanding of biblical conveyances, specifically Numbers 18. In his commentary to that chapter Jacob Milgrom raises a question already asked by Yochanan Muffs in 1975:[5] 'Why is the account of the priestly emoluments in Num. 18.8-19 appended to the story of Korah?' Both answer with the

1. In J.W. Welch (ed.), *Chiasmus in Antiquity* (Hildesheim), pp. 169-82.

2. 'Structure and Chiasm', pp. 169-70.

3. *TAD* = B. Porten and A. Yardeni, *Textbook of Aramaic Documents from Ancient Egypt I Letters* (= *TAD* A) II. *Contracts* (= *TAD* B) (Jerusalem; Academon, 1986, 1989).

4. J. Milgrom, *The JPS Torah Commentary: Numbers* במדבר (Philadelphia, 1990) and M. Paran, דרכי הסגנון הכוהני בתורה *(Forms of the Priestly Style in the Pentateuch: Patterns, Linguistic Usages, Syntactic Structures)* (Jerusalem, 1989). Milgrom's lucid commentary clarifies the meaning of numerous technical terms and Paran's discussion exposes the many stylistic features that characterize the priestly literature.

5. 'Joy and Love as Metaphorical Expressions of Willingness and Spontaneity in Cuneiform, Ancient Hebrew, and Related Literatures', in J. Neusner (ed.), *Christianity, Judaism and Other Greco-Roman Cults, for Morton Smith at Sixty* (Leiden: Brill 1975), III, p. 18. Unfortunately, Milgrom does not cite Muffs.

citation of a midrash from *Sifre Numbers* 117. As summarized by Milgrom, the midrash relates that

> a king gave a field to his favorite without a deed. Someone contested the gift. The king then wrote a deed and recorded it. Thus after Korah contested Aaron's right to the priesthood, God wrote down the deed and recorded it. That is why the list of priestly perquisites is appended to the story of Korah.

To be sure, Moshe Weinfeld had already asserted in 1970 that 'the holy donations assigned to the Aaronide priesthood are formulated in the manner of royal grants', citing Num. 18.8, 19.[1] To acknowledge common or similar formulary is one thing; but to maintain, as does the midrash, that God 'writes, seals, and registers' a deed is another. Is there any basis for the rabbinic contention that Num. 18.8-19 is an actual deed or modelled on one? A positive answer is to be found in the structure of the Aramaic conveyances analyzed earlier. These bear striking resemblance to the structure of the Numbers passage and demonstrate that the latter was indeed patterned on a written contract. Moreover, just as the Aramaic deeds serve to illuminate Numbers, so other features in the priestly code serve to illuminate the Aramaic deeds. The most elaborate of the deeds is *TAD* B3.10 and I shall present this as a paradigmatic example for purposes of comparison.

We are concerned with the first two parts, which may be outlined as follows:

1a. Bequest I (lines 2-3)

אנה עשתת לכי בחיי ויהבת לכי קצת מן ביתי I thought of you in my lifetime and gave you part of my house

1b. Pedigree (3)

זי זבנת בכסף ודמוהי יהבת which I bought for money and whose value I gave.

1c. Bequest II (3-4)

יהבתה לכי I gave it to you (description).

1. 'The Covenant of Grant in the Old Testament and in the Ancient Near East', *JAOS* 90 (1970), p. 201.

2a+b. Measurements (5-8)

זנה משחת ביתא זי אנה יהבת לידהוישמע ברתי ברחמן	This is the measurements of the house which I gave Jehoishma my daughter in affection;
זנה משחת ביתא זי אנה ענני יהבת להוישמע ברתי	This is the measurements of the house which I, Anani, gave Jehoisma my daughter:

3. Boundaries (8-11)

והא תחומי ביתא זי אנה ענני יהבת לידהוישמע ברתי	And behold the boundaries of the house which I, Anani, gave Jehoishma my daughter:

4. Investiture I (11)

זילך הי אנתי שליטה בה	It is yours; you have right to it.

5. Bequest III (11-12)

ביתא זנה זי משחתה ותחומוהי כתבן בספרא זנה אנה ענני בר עזריה יהבתה לן ברחמן	This house whose measurements and boundaries are written in this document—I, Ananiah son of Azariah, gave it to you in affection.

6. Investiture II (13-15)

אף שליטא אנתי . . .	Moreover, you have right to . . .
אף שליטא אנת . . .	Moreover, you have right to . . .
אף שליטא אנתי . . .	Moreover, you have right to . . .

7. Bequest IV (15-18)

זנה זנא ביתא זי תחומוהי ומשחתה כתיבן ומלוהי כתיבן בספרא זנה אנה ענני יהבתה לידהוישמע ברתי במותי ברחמן לקבל זי סבלתני ואנה ימין סב . . . אף אבה יהבת לה במותי	This {this} house whose boundaries and measurements are written and whose words are written in this document—I, Anani, gave it to Jehoishma my daughter at my death in affection bccause she supported me . . . Moreover, I gave it to her at my death.

The contract contains several stylistic features which are paralleled in the biblical Priestly Code, several in Numbers 18:

1. Refrain-like repetition (nine times) of the key word יהב, 'give' in a variety of combinations—'I gave to you', 'whose value I gave', 'I gave it to you', 'which I gave to Jehoishma my daughter in affection', 'which I, Anani, gave to Jehoishma my daughter', 'which I, Anani,

gave to Jehoishma my daughter', 'I, Anani son of Azariah, gave it to you in affection', 'I, Anani gave it to Jehoishma my daughter at my death in affection', 'I gave it to her at my death'. This phenomenon is well attested in the Priestly Code, particularly in Leviticus 1–15 where key expressions recur in varying verbal combinations (e.g. Lev. 1.9, 13, 17; 5.6, 10,13; 6.2, 5, 6).[1]

2. Clause 1c repeats the verb 1a at the same time that it details the description of the property being bequeathed. This expansive style is paralleled in what Meir Paran called 'circular *inclusio*' (מעגולת), i.e. a reduplication of members in a rhythmic manner, a feature prevalent in a single verse as well as in units of varying length. Rather than making a statement with a single verb and, where required, multiple subjects, objects, or modifiers, the writer repeated the verb twice, thrice, or as often as necessary in order to highlight each one of the nominal, adjectival, or adverbial elements. The repetition would regularly appear in chiastic sequence and usually in a verbal *qṭl-yqṭl* pattern. Moreover, I would add, the repetitions are not random but serve a compositional function; e.g., as introductory verses of four of the five pieces of Tabernacle furniture (Exod. 25.11, 18, 29, 31):

וצפית אתו זהב טהור	And you shall overlay it with pure gold;
מבית ומחוץ תצפנו	inside and outside shall you overlay it.
ועשית שנים כרבים זהב	And you shall make two cherubs of gold;
מקשה תעשה אתם	of hammered work shall you make them.
ועשית קערתיו וכפתיו וקשותיו ומנקיתיו...	And you shall make its bowls and its ladles and its jars and its jugs...;
זהב טהור תעשה אתם	of pure gold shall you make them.
ועשית מנרת זהב טהור	And you shall make a menorah of pure gold;
מקשה תעשה המנורה	of hammered work shall the menorah be made.

Aramaic, of course, does not have the *qṭl-yqṭl* formation.

3. Clauses 2 and 3 are expansive. Occasionally they are terse—הוה משחתה, 'Its measurements are' (*TAD* B2.3:3-4) or משחת ביתא זך, 'Measurements of that house' (*TAD* B.2.4:4); הא תחומוהי,'Behold its measurements' (*TAD* B2.10:4; cf. 3.11:3) or אלה תחומי ביתא זך, 'These are the measurements of that house' (*TAD* B2.7:13, 3.7:5)—and the measurements and boundaries may (*TAD* B2.10 [reverse inclusion]; 3.11) or may not (*TAD* B2.7; 3.7) be part of an inclusion. But frequently the scribe felt it necessary to expand the Measurement and/or

1. See Paran, *Priestly Style*, pp. 175-78.

Boundary clauses and incorporate them into the *inclusio*. The more expansive he was, the more he could distribute the various elements among the different clauses. Thus Clause 1a has בחיי, 'in my lifetime'. Clause 2a has ברחמן, 'in affection', and Clause 2b adds ענני, 'Anani'. The enclosing Clause 5 retains ברחמן, 'in affection' and adds בר עזריה, 'son of Azariah'. Enclosing Clause 7 reverses the basic verb–object word order of Clause 1 (זנה ביתא...יהבתה לך ויהבת לכי... ביתי), reverses the order of Clause 5 (משחתה ותחומוהי——→תחומוהי ומשחתה), retains ברחמן, drops בר עזריה, adds for the first time the correlative במותי, 'at my death,' and explicates עשתת לכי, 'I thought of you' from Clause 1a (see also *TAD* B3.5:5-12; cf. B3.12:15-22).[1] Such distribution of elements was a deliberate feature of style and not a matter of adding what had been forgotten (cf. *TAD* B3.11:2-8 [the addition in the reverse inclusion of פסשרת, 'aftergift']). Among the many examples of an inclusio enclosing a complete unit we may cite Num. 18.8-19:[2]

I. Opening Statement

a	ואני הנה נתתי לך את משמרת תרומתי לכל קדשי בני ישראל	And I behold gave you charge of my dedications, all the holy sacrifices of the Israelites.
b	לך נתתים למשחה	To you I gave them as perquisite,
c	ולבניך לחק עולם	and to your sons as eternal due.

II. Closing Statement

a	כל תרומת הקדשים אשר ירימו בני ישראל לידוה נתתי לך	All the holy sacrifice dedications which the Israelites will dedicate to the Lord—I gave you
b	ולבניך ולבנתיך אתך לחק עולם	and your sons and your daughters with you as eternal due.
c	ברית מלח עולם הוא לפני יהוה לך ולזרעך אתך	An eternal covenant of salt it is before the Lord for you and for your seed with you.

Clause IIa in the Numbers passage reverses the verb–object word

1. See Porten, 'Structure and Chiasm', pp. 170-71.
2. See Paran, *Priestly Style*, p. 152.

order of Ia and adds the prepositional clause אשר ירימו. Clause IIb omits the statement נתתים למשחה from Ib, repeats ולבניך לחק עולם from Ic and inserts ולבנתיך אתך between the two terms. The additions make v. 19 an inclusion not only to v. 8 but also to v. 11. Clause IIc substitutes ולזרעך for ולבנתיך ולבניך of IIb and adds ברית מלח עולם.[1]

4. Clauses 2a+b in *TAD* B3.10 are virtual duplicates; why are two almost identical clauses necessary to introduce the measurements? First of all, it should be noted that clause 2a introduces the adverb ברחמן, 'in affection', which elsewhere is also not found in the opening clause (*TAD* B3.5:4, 5.5:3). Clause 2b omits ברחמן but adds ענני, i.e. the duplicated sentence omits one item while it adds a clarifying detail to the subject of the verb. Similar duplication is found in Exod. 30.13-14. A description, like ours beginning with the demonstrative pronoun (זה = זנה), the second sentence omits the amount contributed but adds the age of the contributors:[2]

זה יתנו כל העבר על הפקדים	This is what everyone who passes by the numbered ones shall give:. . .
. . .מחצית השקל תרומה ליהוה	half the shekel, dedication to the Lord.
כל העבר על הפקדים	Everyone who passes by the numbered ones,
מבן עשרים שנה ומעלה	from twenty years old and up,
יתן תרומת יהוה	shall give a dedication of the Lord.

Other features of the Aramaic documents with parallels in the priestly literature will be treated in conjunction with an analysis of Num. 18.8-19. We have already seen how this unit is demarcated by an inclusion similar in structure to that of *TAD* B3.10:2-18. Let us

1. In his English summary, Paran (*Priestly Style*, pp. xii-xiii) describes this type of inclusion as follows: 'The most unique and interesting of the compositional characteristics of the pericopes is revealed in what we call "closing deviation". The priestly writers tend to construct the pericopes in an ordered manner based upon the principle of a single motif being altered intentionally at the end of a pericope. . . The actions are thus enumerated one after another without any digression. In the final sentence, however, the writer makes a sharp deviation by changing the order of the words. He places the verb in the middle of the sentence or at its end, thereby informing the reader that the matter with which he has been dealing is herewith concluded'. Chiasm, introversion, and inclusion are also presented by Milgrom, *Numbers*, pp. xxii-xxx, as major structural devices in both the legal and narrative portions of the book of Numbers.

2. See Paran, *Priestly Style*, p. 66 The couplet itself is in fact part of a triad whose thrice-repeated key expression is נתן תרומה ליהוה.

now turn to the other features which characterize the donation as evidenced by the Elephantine contracts:

1. The opening verse bears all the elements of the opening sentence(s) in the contracts—(a) the perfect tense verb נתתי parallels Aramaic יהבת; (b) למשחה parallels ברחמן; (c) ולבניך ולבנתיך אתך[1] parallels וזי בניך (מן) אחריך, 'and your children's after you' (*TAD* B2.3:9; 2.7:7-8; 2.10:9; 2.11:7; 3.4:12; cf. 3.5:5; 3.11:9; 3.12:23); (d) לחק עולם parallels (ו)עד עלם, '(from this day and) forever' (*TAD* B2.3:9; 2.7:16; 2.10:9; 3.4:11; 3.5:4-5; cf. 3.11:8; 3.12:22-23); (e) with its expansive addition in the conclusion of אשר ירימו בני ישראל, 'which the Israelites will dedicate' the parallel to the pedigree clause, זי זבנת בכסף ודמוהי יהבת, 'which I bought for silver and whose value I gave', is made explicit.

The generic term for conveyance in Hebrew and Aramaic is the respective verb for 'give'. Attached to it is an adverbial phrase or an auxiliary verb to indicate the nature of the conveyance, e.g. ברחמן for a bequest, זבן or בכסף for a sale (*TAD* B3.4:3, 10; 3.12:3, 12, 25, 29; Gen. 23.9), and here למשחה, 'as a perquisite'.[2] Complete ownership and title last forever and are hereditary. In the Aramaic documents these two features are attached to the Investiture clause ('It is yours from this day and forever and your children's after you'); here they appear already in the Transfer clause. The origin of a conveyance and the alienor's right to transfer it were vital and wherever possible the contract indicated pedigree (*TAD* B.2.7:3, 6-7; 3.5:3-4; 3.12:3-4, 12).[3]

2. The second verse is a blending of the Investiture clause (זילך הו, 'It is yours') and the 'Boundary/Measurement' units which delineate the conveyance and are introduced by the demonstrative pronoun in the singular (ד/זנה [*TAD* B3.5:8; 3.10:5; 3.11:33; 12:6, 15; 3.12:8, 16]) or in the plural (אלה [*TAD* B2.7:13; 3.4:7]).[4] The pronoun is also

1. See comment of Milgrom, *Numbers*, *ad loc.* who proposes the translation 'that are after you'.

2. See comment of Milgrom, *Numbers*, *ad loc.*

3. See B. Porten and H.Z. Szubin, '"Abandoned Property" in Elephantine: A New Interpretation of Kraeling 3', *JNES* 41 (1982), pp. 124-26.

4. The demonstrative pronoun is a recurrent introductory word of description in the priestly literature (Exod. 25.2-3 [יקחו לי תרומה. . . וזאת התרומה אשר תקחו], 'Let them take for me a dedication. . . And this is the dedication which they shall take'—comparable to Elephantine 'I gave you a house. . . This is the measurements of the

used in an apportionment of slaves documents to indicate the share each party gets—והא זנה חלקא זי מטאך בחלק, 'And behold, this is the portion which came to you as a portion. . . (And behold this is the portion which came to me a portion)' (*TAD* B2.11:3, 5). This same partitive feature is present in the verse זה יהיה לך מקדש הקדשים מן האש, 'This will be yours from the most holy sacrifices from the fire'. The most holy sacrifices are divided between deity and priesthood; God receives the whole holocaust and parts of other offerings and the priests receive the parts to be delineated. This chiastic verse is a fine example of priestly style wherein the final element in a repetitive list is expanded:[1]

זה יהיה לך מקדש הקדשים מן האש	This will be yours from the most holy sacrifices from the fire:
כל קרבנם	every offering of theirs—
לכל מנחתם	every meal offering;
ולכל חטאתם	every purification offering;
ולכל אשמם אשר ישיבו לי	every reparation offering which they restore to me—
קדש קדשים לך הוא ולבניך	as most holy sacrifices it is yours and your sons.

3. The third verse (Num. 18.10) is comparable to what the Aramaic document designated מלוהי, 'its words', i.e. specific stipulations, in this case enumerated rights to the house's common property (Investiture II where the recurrent phrase is אף שליטא אנתי, 'Moreover, you have right to. . . '). In the Numbers passage those rights are essentially concerned with the who and where of eating:

> 'In a most holy place you shall eat it; every male may eat it'
> 'Every pure person in your house may eat it' (18.11, 13).

4. Verses 9 and 10 describe the most holy sacrifices, that which is 'offered' (קרבנם);[2] vv. 11-18 detail the holy sacrifices, that which is 'given' (מתנם). Verse 11 begins like v. 9 with a combination of demonstrative and possessive pronouns, continues with the same type

house I gave you']; Lev. 6.7, 13, 18; 11.2; Num. 7.84, 8.4, 28.3, 34.2) and occurs at the heading of the Elephantine Collection Account to introduce the names of the Contributors ('This is the names of the Jewish force who gave silver to YHW. . .' [*TAD* C3.15 = Cowley No. 22]).

1. See Paran, *Priestly Style*, pp. 220-21, *contra* Milgrom, *Numbers*, *ad loc.*
2. For this term see Paran, *Priestly Style*, pp. 292-94.

of transfer clause as in v. 8, and concludes with a stipulation on eating. I would take the second two clauses as parenthetical and find the continuation of 11a in vv. 12-15:

זה יהיה לך מקדש הקדשים. . . כל קרבנם	This will be yours from the most holy sacrifices from the fire: every offering of theirs—
לכל מנחתם	every meal offering,
ולכל חטאתם	every purification offering
ולכל אשמם אשר ישיבו לי . . .	every reparation offering which they restore to me . . .
וזה לך תרומת מתנם . . .	And this is yours of their dedication gifts: . . .
כל חלב יצהר	every fat of oil
וכל חלב תירוש ודגן...לך נתתים	and every fat of wine and grain . . . to you I gave it;
בכורי כל אשר בארצם . . . לך יהיה. . .	first fruits of everything which is in their land . . . yours it will be;. . .
כל חרם בישראל לך יהיה	everything proscribed in Israel yours it will be;
כל פטר רחם לכל בשר... יהיה לך...	every first issue of the womb of every flesh . . . will be yours . . .

To all of the enumerated items there is attached either the Transfer verb נתן or the Investiture affirmation לך יהיה with the final one in chiastic reversal, יהיה לך. In three instances there is also the addition of a pedigree clause— אשר יתנו ליהוה for the three items of 'fat'; אשר יביאו ליהוה for the first fruits; and אשר יקריבו ליהוה for the first issue of the womb.

5. Verses 15b-18 stipulate two limitations on the first-born offerings, each introduced by the adverbial conjunction אך, 'but'. The key word in each of the limitations is פדה, 'redeem'—but you *must* redeem the first-born human and you *may* redeem the first-born impure animal; but you *may not* redeem the first-born sacrificial animal.[1] The term אך is a common feature of the priestly literature, both as a term of limitation (Lev. 11.4, 21, 36; 21.23; 27.26, 28; Num. 1.49; 18.3; 26.55; 31.22-23; 36.6) and of emphasis (Exod. 31.13; Lev. 23.27, 39).[2] Its Aramaic equivalent להן appears in similar double

1. For clarification of the stipulations see Milgrom, *Numbers*, *ad loc.*
2. See Paran, *Priestly Style*, p. 224.

capacity, with the precise nuance occasionally uncertain. In each case it clarifies the verb שלט 'control, have right to':

(a) 'That plot build up. . . and dwell herein with your wife. But (להן) that house—you do not have right (שליט) to sell it or give (it) affectionately to others but (להן) it is your children by Mibtahiah my daughter (who) have right (שליטן) to it after you'. Should Mibtahiah repudiate you, 'she does not have right (שליטה) to take it and give it to others but (להן) it is your children by Mibtahiah (who) have right (שליטן) to it in exchange for the work which you did' (*TAD* B2.4:5-10). The first appearance of להן is restrictive but the two subsequent occurrences are emphatic.

(b) 'But (להן) if you die at the age of 100 years, it is my children whom you bore me (that) have right (שליטן) to it after your death. . . Another person. . . shall not have right (ישלט) to the whole house, but (להן) (only) my children after you' (*TAD* B3.5:16-20). The contract had already stated at the beginning that the house 'is yours from this day forever and your children's, whom your bore me, after you' (lines 4-5). The initial להן is therefore not so much a limitation as it is a clarification, i.e. your children and my children are the same children. The subsequent להן serves the same emphatic function here as in *TAD* B2.4.

(c) 'But (להן) Jeho(ishma) does not have right (שליטה) [to] ACQUIRE another husband be[sides] Anani. And if she do thus, it is hatred; they shall do to her [the law of ha]tred' (*TAD* B3.8:33-34). Taken as a limitation upon the previous clause, this clause would mean that Jehoishma would lose rights to her deceased husband's property should she remarry.[1] But application of the 'law of hatred' would be most strange in reference to a deceased spouse. The sequential balance of clauses (death of husband [lines 28-32]; prohibition against taking another husband [lines 33-34]; death of wife [lines 34-36]; prohibition against taking another wife

1. See R. Yaron, 'Aramaic Marriage Contracts: Corrigenda and Addenda', *JSS* 5 (1960), pp. 68-69; M.A. Friedman, *Jewish Marriage in Palestine: A Cairo Genizah Study* (Tel-Aviv, 1980), I, pp. 393-94, 427-28.

[lines 36-37]) makes it more likely that we have here the emphatic use of להן.

6. The last verse of the unit (v. 18) is another Investiture clause phrased as a chiastic inclusion:

ובשרם יהיה לך	But their meat will be yours;
כחזה התנופה וכשוק הימין	like the breast of elevation offering and like the right thigh
לך יהיה	yours it will be.

The word order יהיה לך forms an inclusion with the beginning of the reference to the first-born (v. 15) whereas the order לך יהיה links the meat offering up with the first fruits and proscribed objects (vv. 13-14).

7. The Elephantine contract discussed above contained a motivational clause which indicated that bequest was made in consideration of old-age support (Bequest IV).[1] The section immediately following the priestly emoluments (Num. 18.20-24) deals with the reward of the tithe for the Levites חלף עבדתם אשר הם עבדים את עבדת אהל מועד, 'in exchange for the work which they are doing, the work of the Tent of Meeting' (Num. 18.21).[2] The identical clause is found in an Elephantine contract granting usufruct to a son-in-law. He acquires certain rights to the property חלף עבידתא זי אנת עבדת, 'in exchange for the work which you did' (*TAD* B2.4:10). The 'work' of the Levites and the son-in-law were considered true 'consideration' for their respective grants. The priests, we are told, received their emoluments למשחה, 'as perquisite'. But for what? Though outside the framework of the formal donation, Num. 18.1-17 forms something of a preamble to that donation and serves the same role as the old-age clause in the Aramaic contract. The key phrase in that unit is משמרת שמר, 'discharge a charge', literally, perform guard duty.[3] The Levites guarded on the outside and the priests on the inside, and in exchange, as it were, for their משמרת המזבח and משמרת הקדש they received משמרת תרומתי, 'charge of my dedications' (Num. 18.8). The key word in Num. 18.1-

1. See B. Porten and H.Z. Szubin, 'An Aramaic Deed of Bequest', in N.M. Waldman (ed.), *Community and Culture*, pp. 189-91.

2. For this meaning see the excursus in Milgrom, *Numbers*, pp. 343-44

3. See discussion by Milgrom, *Numbers*, p. 147; Paran, *Priestly Style*, pp. 286-87.

7, משמרת, is also the literary and legal link to 18.8-19.

Clearly, the structure and terminology of Num. 18.8-9, taken together with its preface 18.1-7, are comparable to that of the Aramaic conveyances, particularly *TAD* B3.10, and warrant the rabbinic assertion that it was the equivalent of a duly redacted contract. Conversely, many of the features of *TAD* B3.10 and other conveyances find their parallels in the priestly literature. In my earlier stylistic study I followed the lead of Reuven Yaron in showing how the priestly 'diagnosis pattern' (e.g. Lev. 13.3, 10-11, 23, 37, etc; 20.14; Num. 35.17) which he had detected in two documents of wifehood (*TAD* B3.8:37, 42; 6.4:8) was woven into the Guarantees section of four Elephantine conveyances (*TAD* B.2.3:15-18; 2.7:11-12; 3.10:21-22; 3.11:15-17).[1] Yaron had concluded that there was 'a clear link between the papyri and biblical sources'. The diagnosis pattern 'is obviously modelled on P, and the conclusion is that this, or some of the material contained in it, must have been known to the scribe' of *TAD* B3.8 and 6.4, Mauziah son of Nathan.[2] We now see that the connection between the papyri and P was not limited to a single feature or a single scribe. The conveyances discussed herein were drawn up by five different scribes, both Jewish and Aramean, over a period of almost sixty years (Attarshuri son of Nabuzeribni [459 BCE; *TAD* B2.3; 2.4] and his grandson Nabutukulti son of Nabuzeribni [410 BCE; *TAD* B2.11], Nathan of Ananiah [446 BCE; *TAD* B2.7] and his son Mauziah son of Nathan [434–416; *TAD* B2.10; 3.5], and Haggai son of Shemaiah [437–402; *TAD* B3.4, 10-12]). Either the Arameans had access to Israelite or Judahite priestly literature or else the style of that literature was not limited to writings originating only in the land of Israel.

As far as biblical parallels are concerned, we may cite three features and terms which show that links to the papyri spanned all strata of biblical Hebrew:

1. In the realm of linear measurements and monetary notations the contracts resemble late Hebrew and biblical Aramaic and differ strikingly from P:

1. See Porten, 'Structure and Chiasm', pp. 172-74.

2. See 'Aramaic Marriage Contracts from Elephantine', *JSS* 3 (1958), pp. 34-35; *Introduction to the Law of the Aramaic Papyri* (Oxford, 1961), pp. 110-12.

עשר אמות ארך הקרש	Ten cubits is the length of the plank
ואמה וחצי האמה רחב הקרש	and a cubit and half the cubit the width of the plank (Exod. 26.16).
ארך היריעה האחת שמנה ועשרים באמה	The length of one curtain is eight and twenty by the cubit
ורחב ארבע באמה	and the width is four by the cubit (Exod. 26.2).
ארכה. . . אמן 13 ופשך 1	And its length. . . is cubits 13 and handbreadth 1;
פתי. . . אמן 11	width. . . is cubits 11 (*TAD* B2.3:4-5).
ארכו. . . אמות עשרים	Its length. . . is cubits twenty
ורחבו אמות עשרים	and its width is cubits twenty (2 Chron. 3.8).

In the Aramaic contracts and in contemporaneous biblical texts, the designation 'length' or 'width' always comes first and the numeral follows the measure. In P the numeral precedes the measure and both, in turn, may be preceded or followed by the 'length'/'width' designation, depending upon the construction[1] (see, too, the late text Zech. 5.2). Similar contrast is to be found in monetary designations:

חמשים שקל כסף	Fifty shekel silver (Lev. 27.3).
חמשה שקלים כסף	Five shekels silver (Lev. 27.6).
כסף כרשן 10	Silver karsh 10 (*TAD* B2.3:21 *et al.*).
וכסף מנים חמשת אלפים	And silver maneh five thousand (Ezra. 2.69).
כסף ככרין מאה	Silver talents a hundred (Ezra 7.22).
כסף שקלים ארבעים	Silver shekels forty (Neh. 5.15).

In P the numeral precedes the weight and both precede the metal. In Elephantine and in contemporaneous biblical texts the order is exactly reversed.

2. As noted, the Investiture clause in *TAD* B3.10:11 consisted of the compound clause זילך הי אנתי שליטה בה, 'it is yours; you control (= have right to) it'. This same combination occurs in two biblical passages and in a medieval Aramaic passage, all in relation to God, and all poetic or semi-poetic. It would be tempting to say that they were borrowed by the papyri from divine enthronement terminology but it is more likely that the lyrical assertions of enthronement are borrowing the terse terminology of private legal contracts:

1. See Paran, *Priestly Style*, pp. 323-24.

כי ליהוה המלוכה ומשל בגוים	For the kingship is the Lord's and he controls[1] (= rules) the nations (Ps. 22.29).
לך יהוה הממלכה...	The kingdom, Lord, is yours. . . and you
ואתה מושל בכל	control (= rule over) all (1 Chron. 29.11-12).
אנת הוא שליט על כלא	You are he who controls (= rules over) all.
אנת הוא דשליט על מלכיא	You are he who controls (= rules over) kings
ומלכותא דילך היא	and the kingship is yours (Zohar *Vayakhel).*

3. The Guarantees section of the contracts is characterized by the key expression לא יכ(ה)ל, 'not able' in the sense of 'not entitled to do something'. The alienor assures the alienee that neither he nor anyone else related to him can challenge the alienee's newly acquired ownership of the property (e.g. *TAD* B2.7:8-11; 3.4:12-19; 3.5:12-16; 3.10:18-21, etc.).[2] This same term, whether in second person or third person, occurs eight times in legal prohibitions in D (Deut. 12.17; 16.5; 17.15; 21.16; 22.3, 19, 29; 24.4), which are usually rendered by *Targum Onqelos* as לית לך רשו, 'you do not have permission to'. Yet the phrase did not originate with D since it is found once with the same meaning in early Hebrew (Exod. 33.20) and in the first person in the narratives of P (Num. 22.18; 24.13) and other books (Judg. 11.35; 1 Kgs 13.16; Jer. 36.5).[3]

Thus, despite a concentration of stylistic and structural features that link the Elephantine contracts with P, other features either disassociate the contracts from P or demonstrate links with other strata of biblical literature. The three dominant features common to P and to the papyri (chiasm, inclusion, and variant repetition) are to be found throughout biblical prose and poetry and in other ancient literatures.[4] These features were common to the laws and to the narratives in P. While

1. In early biblical Hebrew מושל appears in the same legal context as in the Aramaic papyri, i.e. 'have right to do something' (Exod. 21.8); see E.Y. Kutscher, *Hebrew and Aramaic Studies* (Jerusalem, 1977), p. 43 (= *JAOS* 74 [1954], p. 239).

2. For fuller discussion see Porten, 'Structure and Chiasm', pp. 172-77.

3. The second-century Tannaitic sage Joshua son of Korḥa maintained that the expression in Josh. 15.63 was of similar legal import—'they could have done so, but they were not allowed to' because of the covenant made with them by Abraham (*PRE* ch. 36 and Rashi *apud* Deut. 12.17).

4. See J.W. Welch (ed.), *Chiasmus in Antiquity* (Hildesheim, 1981) and my studies on the Solomon narrative (*HUCA* 38 [1967], pp. 93-128) and the scroll of Ruth (*Gratz College Annual of Jewish Studies* 7 [1978], pp. 23-49).

many priestly laws are esoteric, the narratives certainly are not. It is the common style of both that we find reflected in the Elephantine contracts. None of the terms examined here was a technical term whose usage was confined to the legal realm. All were common words which took on a specific meaning in a legal context. Designed to be legal documents, the Elephantine contracts were written as narratives by scribes learned in literary and legal tradition and privy to the terminology of different schools. Conversely, as we read the legal parts of P in the light of the papyri, we should develop an appreciation for their narrative style.

In conclusion we may cite one more biblical passage, a narrative which reiterates the root נתן, 'give' in the manner discussed above. It is the sale of the burial plot in Hebron by Ephron to Abraham. He says to him in three statements

השדה נתתי לך	The field I gave to you,
והמערה אשר בו לך נתתיה	and the cave which is in it to you I gave it;
לעיני בני עמי נתתיה לך	in the eyes of the sons of my people I gave it to you (Gen. 23.11).

Instead of one long sentence—'I gave you the field and its cave in the presence of my people'—Ephron/the narrator breaks up the statement into three, wherein each one adds a detail and the verb/indirect object are reversed in the second statement. The legal situation is the same as in Numbers 18 and TAD B3.10—a conveyance. Stipulations, contract, narrative—three different kinds of text but the repetitive, chiastic *inclusio* style is the same.

PHARISEES AND SADDUCEES IN *PESHER NAḤUM*

Lawrence H. Schiffman

Ever since its discovery in Qumran Cave 4, scholars have realized that the significance of *Pesher Naḥum* (4QpNah) goes way beyond its value for understanding the Qumran sect and its ideology.[1] Indeed, it is the contemporizing form of the biblical exegesis (better, eisegesis) which we designate as *pesher*[2] which makes these texts such important sources of historical information.

In the case of 4QpNah its significance is heightened because of the important information contained in this text regarding the history of the Pharisees and Sadducees, certainly the most important groups of Jews in Hasmonean times.[3] Clearly, a restudy of this document is

1. For bibliography, see M.P. Horgan, *Pesharim: Qumran Interpretations of Biblical Books* (CBQ Monograph Series, 8; Washington, DC: Catholic Biblical Association, 1979), pp. 158-59 and E. Schürer, *The History of the Jewish People in the Age of Jesus Christ*, III.1 (ed. G. Vermes, F. Millar and M. Goodman, with M. Black and P. Vermes; Edinburgh: T. & T. Clark, 1986), p. 433. On the language and the biblical text underlying 4QpNah, see J. Maier, 'Weitere Stücke zum Nahumkommentar aus der Höhle 4 von Qumran', *Judaica* 18 (1962), pp. 215-28.

2. On this genre of biblical interpretation see D. Dimant, 'Qumran Sectarian Literature', in *Jewish Writings of the Second Temple Period* (ed. M. Stone; CRIANT II.2; Philadelphia: Fortress Press, 1984), pp. 505-508.

3. See J.D. Amoussine, 'Éphraïm et Manassé dans le Péshèr de Nahum (4 Q p Nahum)', *RevQ* 4 (1963–64), pp. 389-96; J.D. Amusin, 'The Reflection of Historical Events of the First Century B.C. in Qumran Commentaries (4Q161; 4Q169; 4Q166)', *HUCA* 48 (1977), pp. 134-46; D. Flusser, 'כת מדבר יהודה והפרושים', *Molad* 19 (1961), pp. 456-58; *idem*, 'פרושים צדוקים ואיסיים בפשר נחום', *G. Alon Memorial Volume* (Tel Aviv, 1970), pp. 133-68. It goes without saying that this study will not deal with the many allusions to these sects in other Qumran sectarian texts. Further, the important issue of the relationship of the Essenes of Philo and Josephus to the Dead Sea sect will remain beyond the scope of this paper. As is well known, most scholars see the tri-partite array of groups in this text as equivalent to

necessary at this point in history of Dead Sea Scrolls research, in view of the recently announced, and soon to be published, 4Q *Miqṣat Ma'aseh Ha-Torah* (4QMMT),[1] which has given us a wealth of information on the halakhic views of the Pharisees and the Sadducees in Hasmonean times and in the years immediately preceding.[2] It is now certain as well that the *Temple Scroll* (11QT) also contains numerous laws of Sadducean origin and that it often polemicizes directly against Pharisaic views which were known beforehand in rabbinic literature, either as attributed to the Pharisees or to later tannaim.[3] All this has given an impetus to the use of the scrolls to reconstruct the history of the Pharisees and the Sadducees in the Hasmonean period. It is to this effort that the present study seeks to contribute.

1. *Date and Authorship*

That 4QpNah is a 'sectarian' text, one authored by a member or members of the Qumran community which transmits the teachings and ideology of that community, is certain. This is the case with all the *pesharim* found at Qumran. Indeed, the very nature of the exegesis found in this literature seems to be unique to the sect, although similar contemporizing interpretations exist in the New Testament.

The script of the manuscript of 4QpNah has been described as reflecting a 'formal' type, dating from the end of the Hasmonean

that of Josephus. Accordingly, they see this text as confirming the identity of the sect as Essenes. In my view, the term 'Essene' must be seen as encompassing a variety of groups of which the Dead Sea sect may be one.

1. E. Qimron, and J. Strugnell, 'An Unpublished Halakhic Letter from Qumran', in *Biblical Archaeology Today* (ed. J. Amitai; Jerusalem: Israel Exploration Society, 1985), pp. 400-407, and a different article with the same title, *Israel Museum Journal* 4 (1985), pp. 9-12 and Plate I.

2. See L.H. Schiffman, 'The Temple Scroll and the Systems of Jewish Law of the Second Temple Period', in *Temple Scroll Studies* (ed. G.J. Brooke; Sheffield: JSOT Press, 1989), pp. 245-51; Y. Sussmann, 'חקר תולדות ההלכה ומגילות מדבר יהודה—הרהורים תלמודיים ראשונים לאור מגילת מקצת מעשה התורה"', *Tarbiz* 59 (1989–90), pp. 11-76.

3. L.H. Schiffman, 'The New Halakhic Letter (4QMMT) and the Origins of the Dead Sea Sect', *BA* 55 (1990), pp. 64-73; *idem*, '*Miqṣat Ma'aseh Ha-Torah* and the *Temple Scroll*', *RevQ* 14 (1990), pp. 435-57.

period to the beginning of the Herodian.[1] This paleographic dating is extremely important because it is essentially confirmed by the *terminus ad quem* created by the contents. Here we find a detailed description of the events surrounding the invasion of the Hasmonean kingdom by Demetrius II Eukerus (95–88 BCE) as well as perhaps the events of the rule of Salome Alexandra (76–67 BCE).[2] These events bring us sufficiently close to the end of the Hasmonean dynasty (63 BCE) to indicate that the text was composed at the latest shortly thereafter. Hence, our preserved manuscript would be most reasonably dated from shortly before to shortly after the Roman conquest.[3]

We cannot rule out the possibility that parts of this text pre-existed the invasion in question. We do know that some Qumran works circulated in varying recensions, which seem to testify to the growth of those compositions as a whole over time. Yet in this case, because we are dealing with a sustained interpretation of the biblical book of Nahum, it seems most reasonable to expect composition to have occurred at one time.[4]

2. *The Pharisees*

The text is unfortunately fragmentary at the beginning, so that it picks up with the interpretation of Nah. 1.3 in column II of the manuscript. After some references to the כתיים, clearly an allusion to the Romans, the text continues in 4QpNah 1-2.2.7-8 to comment on Nah. 1.4:

> ופרח ל[ב]נון היא[עדה דורשי החלקות ואנשי עצ]תם ואבדו מלפני[עדה]
> בחיר[י אל.

1. J. Strugnell, 'Notes en marge du volume V des *Discoveries in the Judaean Desert of Jordan*', *RevQ* 7 (1970), p. 205.
2. Horgan, *Pesharim*, pp. 161-62.
3. Contrast the attempt to maintain a date well within the Roman period for the events described in the *pesher* in G.R. Driver, *The Judaean Scrolls, The Problem and a Solution* (Oxford: Basil Blackwell, 1965), pp. 289-93.
4. For an estimate of the size of the entire scroll and the contents of the columns which were not preserved, see Horgan, *Pesharim*, p. 160.

> *And the flower of Le[ba]non* is [the congregation of the interpreters of smooth things[1] and the people of] their [coun]cil.[2] And they will be destroyed from before [the congregation of] the chosen one[s of God.[3]

Already here we see the basic motifs of the sectarian polemic against the Pharisees. They are identified by the *pesher* with 'the flower of Lebanon'. The full citation from the end of Nah. 1.4 is ופרח לבנון אמלל, 'and the flower of Lebanon withers'.[4] Our text takes this clause to indicate that the Pharisees are to be destroyed (ואבדו). The difficult אמלל has been explained by the *pesher* as indicating destruction.

While it is true that crucial parts of these lines are restored, there is little question, as we will see below, that the Pharisees are intended. While it is tempting to address here, at the outset, the significance of the expression 'interpreters of smooth things', methodological considerations make it appropriate to deal with it only in a context which is not restored. We should note that in this passage, even with its lacunae, it is certain that Nah. 1.4 is seen as prophesying the destruction of a group of opponents of the 'chosen one[s of God]', a term for the Qumran sect.

The Pharisees appear in a political context as 4QpNah relates the story of the invasion of Demetrius III Eukerus. In 4QpNah 3-4.1.2-3 there is an interpretation of of Nah. 2.12b:

> [פשרו על דמי]טרוס מלך יון אשר בקש לבוא ירושלים בעצת דורשי החלקות.
> [Its interpretation concerns Deme]trius,[5] king of Greece,[6] who sought to enter Jerusalem on the advice of the interpreters of smooth things.[7]

1. The restoration is that of Horgan, *Pesharim*, p. 170 who suggests two alternatives: עצת דורשי החלקות and ממשלת דורשי החלקות.

2. So Horgan who added the initial ו to the restoration suggested by J.M. Allegro, *Qumrân Cave 4, I (4Q158-4Q186)* (DJD, 5; Oxford: Clarendon Press, 1968), p. 37. Strugnell,'Notes', p. 206, restores בני אשמ]תם. This reading seems too short, however.

3. Restoration of this line is with Horgan, *Pesharim*, p. 170.

4. For MT לבנון the lemma has לבנן in line 5, yet the *pesher* in line 7 agrees with MT.

5. Restored with Allegro, *Qumran Cave 4*, p. 38. It is also possible to read דמי]טריס which is the view of Haberman and Yadin (Horgan, *Pesharim*, p. 173).

6. For this phrase see Dan. 8.21; cf. 10.20, 11.2.

7. For this expression, see עדת דורשי החלקות בירושלים, 'the congregation of the interpreters of smooth things in Jerusalem', mentioned in 4QpIsa[c] 23.2.10, cf. 1QH

This interpretation is based on the identification of Demetrius with the lion mentioned in Nahum. Whereas the MT has אריה לביא, 'lion and lion's breed',[1] 4QpNah has a variant text in the lemma, ארי לבוא, 'the lion to come'.[2] This reading was the basis for the interpretation that Demetrius (the lion) sought 'to enter' Jerusalem, which is identified with the מעון אריות (MT to Nah. 3.12) which, in turn, had already been explained by the *pesher* as מדור לרשעי גוים, 'the dwelling place of the evil ones of the nations', in line 1.[3]

Demetrius is termed here 'king of Greece', but, of course, he was king of Seleucid Syria. As we know, his invasion of the Hasmonean state of Alexander Janneus (103–76 BCE) was brought about by Jewish intervention.[4] I will return to this aspect below.[5] For now, it is important to examine the designation our text uses for the Pharisees. The Hebrew expression דורשי החלקות is actually a pun.[6] It begins with חלקות, literally 'smooth things', i.e. 'falsehoods', which appears in Isa. 30.10, Ps. 12.3-4 and 73.18 and Dan. 11.32. This word is intended here as a play on the word הלכות, a term attested otherwise only later, which refers to the Pharisaic-Rabbinic laws. While the noun חלקות appears in Isaiah with דבר, 'to speak', it appears here, as well as in other sectarian documents, with דרש, which by this time meant 'to interpret'.[7] Accordingly, the expression דורשי החלקות is a designation

2.15, 32 (Horgan, *Pesharim*, p. 173).

1. So NJPS.

2. Many scholars read לביא in the lemma (Horgan, *Pesharim*, p. 172; Strugnell, 'Notes', p. 207) in which case the *pesher* would have based its interpretation on the frequent confusion of ו and י in Qumran and other contemporary manuscripts.

3. Following A. Dupont-Sommer, 'Le Commentaire de Nahum découvert près de la Mer Morte (4Q p Nah): Traduction et notes', *Semitica* 13 (1963), p. 57; Horgan, *Pesharim*, p. 172.

4. See the discussion of this episode in F.M. Cross, *The Ancient Library of Qumran and Modern Biblical Studies* (Garden City, NY: Doubleday, 1961), pp. 122-27.

5. The events are summarized in E. Schürer, *The History of the Jewish People in the Age of Jesus Christ*, I (ed. G. Vermes, F. Millar and M. Black, with P. Vermes; Edinburgh: T. & T. Clark, 1973), pp. 223-24. See especially, pp. 224-25 n. 21, which refers to 4QpNah.

6. See the analysis of Maier, 'Weitere Stücke', pp. 234-37.

7. See L.H. Schiffman, *The Halakhah at Qumran* (Leiden: Brill, 1975), pp. 54-60.

for the Pharisees who, in the view of the sect, are false interpreters of the Torah who derive incorrect legal rulings from their exegesis. It is these false legalists who brought Demetrius to attack Janneus.

Despite all the information he provides on the question of Alexander Janneus's relations with Pharisees and Sadducees, we have only a hint in Josephus that the enemies of Janneus who provoked Demetrius were Pharisees. Josephus discusses this episode in *War* 1.4.1–6.4 (§§85-131) and *Ant.* 13.13.5 (§§372-416). In both these descriptions he tells us only of opposition by the 'Jews' who initiated the revolt against him and called in Demetrius. As a result some of them were executed at the end. Thus, we have no direct claim in Josephus that the Pharisees played a leading role in these affairs.

But in both accounts we hear at the beginning that Janneus angered the populace at the Sukkot festival. This led to his initial slaughter of his own citizens. Whereas the account in *War* 1.4.3 (§§88-89) is quite sketchy, *Ant.* 13.13.5 (§§72-74) gives us two reasons for the conflict. First, 'as he stood beside the altar and was about to sacrifice, they pelted him with citrons'. *Etrogim*, used to fulfil the biblical command of the four kinds (Lev. 23.40), were thrown at him for what in this account is an unknown reason. Secondly, his priestly legitimacy was challenged by those who said that 'he was descended from captives and was unfit to hold (priestly) office'.

Both of these accusations have parallels in tannaitic materials, and these will allow us to confirm the information in 4QpNah to the effect that the Pharisees were indeed the opponents of Janneus who, according to our text, took the lead in the revolt and in inviting Demetrius into the country. In the case of the pelting of Janneus with citrons, there is a parallel in *m. Suk.* 4.9. There it is related that once a priest poured out the water libation on his feet and as a result was pelted by the people with their citrons (ורגמוהו כל העם באתרוגיהן). That this priest is to be identified with Alexander Janneus, about whom little factual detail was remembered in the tannaitic period, is certain.[1] But it is important to note that the issue of the water-drawing ceremony was a long-standing debate between the Pharisees and the Sadducees. Janneus's reason for pouring the water on his feet was to demonstrate publicly his disdain for the Pharisaic approach which

1. Cf. C. Albeck, ששה סדרי משנה, סדר מועד (Jerusalem: Mossad Bialik; Tel Aviv: Dvir, 1954), p. 477.

required a special water libation during Sukkot. The revolt which began in the aftermath of this event would naturally have been led by Pharisees and, therefore, we can accept as historical this new detail which 4QpNah supplies in its account.

Josephus mentioned a second reason for popular objection to Janneus: there was a challenge to his priestly legitimacy. This very same challenge appears in two other places. The well-known *baraita*' describing Janneus's confrontation with the Pharisees in *b. Qid.* 61a has the Pharisees say to him, 'It is enough for you to have the crown of kingship. Leave the crown of priesthood to the descendents of Aaron', to which the comment is added, 'for they were saying that his mother had been captured in Modiin'. A parallel accusation appears in *Ant.* 13.10.5 (§§291-292), where it is made by a certain Eleazer to John Hyrcanus (134–104 BCE) in the context of his confrontation with the Pharisees.

Now there is little question that these two confrontations are one and the same, but critical scholarship has been unable to fix with certainty the date and the Hasmonean high priest to which the story ought to refer. For our purposes it is important to note that the Pharisaic opposition to Janneus is again confirmed in this detail. Again, we have every reason to believe that they are the opponents left unidentified in Josephus's account of the war with Demetrius.

Interpreting the end of Nah. 2.13, the text explains in 4QpNah 3-4.1.6-8:

> פשרו על כפיר החרון [. . .]מות בדורשי החלקות אשר יתלה אנשים חיים [. . .]
> בישראל מלפנים כי לתלוי חי על העץ [י]קרא.
>
> Its interpretation concerns the Lion of Wrath [. . .] death to the interpreters of smooth things, for he hung men alive [. . .] in Israel from of old, for one hung alive on a tree shall [he] be called.

This passage indicates that as a result of their participation in the revolt, the Pharisees were crucified by Janneus. This exegesis already assumes the identification of Janneus as the Lion of Wrath which appears in line 5 (restored), interpreting Nah. 2.13a.[1] He has literally fulfilled the words of this verse; he 'filled his lair[2] with prey[3] and his

1. Cf. Horgan, *Pesharim*, p. 175.
2. The scroll has חורה for MT חריו.
3. The occurrence of this word above in line 4 is most probably a scribal error, not a double *pesher*.

den[1] with torn flesh'. At the end of the passage, direct reference is made to Deut. 21.22-23. It seems most likely that the language of this text is being used but that the explicit mention of hanging men 'alive' is meant to distinguish Janneus's cruel crucifixion from the practice commanded in Deuteronomy.[2]

The account in this passage fits exactly with that of Josephus who discusses 800 crucified by Janneus. *War*. 1.4.6 (§97) simply terms them 'captives' while *Ant*. 13.14.2 (§380) calls them 'Jews'. Our text, however, informs us that the victims of the reign of terror which Janneus engaged in after he forced Demetrius to withdraw were his erstwhile Pharisaic enemies.

We first encounter the designation 'Ephraim' for the Pharisees in line 12 of the same column, but there is no real context preserved. A more complete sense of the use of this term, no doubt a pun on פרושים, 'Pharisees', can be gleaned from the following column. In an interpretation of Nah. 3.1, הוי עיר דמים כלה כחש פרק מלאה, 'Ah, city of crime,[3] utterly treacherous, full of violence', 4QpNah 3-4.2.2 states:

> פשרו היא עיר אפרים דורשי החלקות לאחרית הימים אשר בכחש ושקר[ים י]תהלכו.
> Its interpretation: it is the city of Ephraim, the interpreters of smooth things in the end of days who live by falsehood and lie[s].

Here again the Pharisees appear as false interpreters of the law. It seems most likely that the 'city' of Ephraim does not refer to some actual city, but rather to the Pharisaic community as a whole. Indeed, the word עיר is simply a reflection of the Hebrew of Nah. 3.1. Further, in equating the verse with its interpretation, the sect took דמים, 'crime' (literally, 'blood'), to refer to the Pharisees, so that Ephraim replaces 'violence.' The difficult פרק מלאה is taken by the

1. The scroll has ומשונתו for MT ומענתיו.

2. I cannot accept the suggestion of Y. Yadin ('Pesher Nahum [4Q pNahum] Reconsidered', *IEJ* 21 [1971], pp. 1-12; cf. *idem*, *The Temple Scroll* [Jerusalem: Israel Exploration Society, 1983] I, pp. 373-79) that our text approves of crucifixion as a means of punishment. This would be the case even if 11QT 64.6-13 did allow this punishment for informers. For the vast literature on crucifixion in these two texts, see Horgan, *Pesharim*, pp. 176-79. See especially J.M. Baumgarten, *Studies in Qumran Law* (Leiden: Brill, 1977), pp. 172-82. Note also M.J. Bernstein, '*Midrash Halakhah* at Qumran? 11Q Temple 64.6-13 and Deuteronomy 21.22-23', *Gesher* 7 (1979), pp. 145-66, and 'כי קללת אלהים תלוי (Deut. 21.23): A Study in Early Jewish Exegesis', *JQR* 74 (1983), pp. 21-45.

3. 4QpNah has הדמים for MT דמים.

pesher to refer to the way of life of the Pharisees. It is possible that the choice of the verb יתהלכו may have been conditioned by its cognate הלכה, 'religious law, way of life', which lies behind the pun חלקות.[1] The reference to the end of days refers to the sectarians' own view that they were living on the verge of the dawn of the eschaton, in the 'last days'.[2] It was this period of the end of days about which, in the view of the sect, Nahum had actually prophesied.

We have already encountered the use of חלקות, 'smooth things', to indicate the teachings of the Pharisees which the sectarians considered false. Yet here there are added terms to make the same point, כחש and שקרים. The *pesher*, in fact, substitutes the hendiadys כחש ושקרים for the biblical כחש, no doubt for emphasis. Indeed, overall the claim of the sect against the Pharisees was that they falsely interpreted Scripture, a matter to which we will return below.

Turning to the exegesis of Nah. 3.1b-3,[3] 4QpNah 3-4.2.4-6 expounds:

> פשרו על ממשלת דורשי החלקות אשר לוא ימוש מקרב עדתם חרב גוים שבי ובז
> וחרחור בינותם וגלות מפחד אויב ורוב פגרי אשמה יפולו בימיהם ואין קץ לכלל
> חלליהם ואף בגוית בשרם יכשולו בעצת אשמתם.
>
> Its interpretation concerns the domain of the interpreters of smooth things from the midst of whose congregation there will not depart the sword of the nations, captivity, plunder and strife,[4] and exile because of fear of the enemy. For many guilty corpses will fall in their days, and there will be no end to the total of their slain. And they will even stumble over their decaying flesh because of their guilty council.

1. The authors of our document seem to have regarded the unmentioned term הלכה as derived from the verb 'to go', and understood it to mean 'way of life'. For the alternative derivation from the Aramaic הלך, a land tax (cognate to Akkadian *ilku*), see S. Lieberman, *Hellenism in Jewish Palestine* (New York: Jewish Theological Seminary, 1962), p. 83 n. 3.

2. I cannot agree with Horgan, *Pesharim*, p. 182, who explains that 'the interpretation is shifting from a historical thrust to an eschatological focus'. The sect saw its own history and its own times as eschatological. For this notion, see 4QMMT C, 21-23.

3. The numerous differences with MT found in this citation are discussed in Horgan, *Pesharim*, pp. 182-83.

4. Following Horgan, *Pesharim*, p. 183, who notes this usage in post-biblical Hebrew, as opposed to Deut. 28.22, 'feverish heat'. See E. Ben Yehuda, מלון הלשון העברית (New York: T. Yoseloff, 1959), III, p. 1755, where all the examples cited are medieval.

The description in Nahum of the city (Nineveh) is taken here to apply *in toto* to the Pharisees. Certain modifications of the language of the biblical material are especially significant. The text adds the idea of the עדה, 'congregation', i.e. the community of the Pharisees who in some way have banded together. This means that they are perceived as a party, not simply as isolated individuals who interpret the law. The sword of the verse has become the 'sword of the nations', the non-Jews, with whom the Pharisees conspired to overthrow Alexander Janneus. Despite the sect's dislike for this ruler and disagreements with him, they still condemn the Pharisees for turning to the Seleucids.[1] In the process of interpreting the verse, the *pesher* also adds allusions to the 'exile for fear of the enemy', a matter to be taken up below. The substitution of חלליהם for the biblical גויה is intended to avoid a term which can also be used for living bodies.

Extremely interesting is the manner in which the text deals with Nahum's וכשלו בגויתם (the *ketiv* is יכשלו).[2] This clause literally means, 'they will stumble over their (own) bodies', since the destruction will leave so many corpses. Our author interprets it to mean that the Pharisees will transgress in matters pertaining to their bodies, such as sexual prohibitions, as a result of their guilty council.

The use of ממשלת does not imply that the Pharisees were ruling.[3] Rather, it refers to their 'domain', similar in meaning to the term גורל, 'lot', in Qumran usage.[4] This passage clearly refers to the aftermath of the war with Demetrius, rather than to some period of Pharisaic rule such as probably took place in the days of Salome Alexandra, the wife of Alexander Janneus and her successor.

The text notes that even after the war with Demetrius and his expulsion, the Pharisees were still pursued by destruction and were forced to flee. Further, the text describes the slaying of large numbers

1. Cf. the prohibition on informing to a foreign nation in 11QT 64.6-9.

2. The lemma's text, ונויתם, is certainly an error since the pesher has בגוית (Horgan, *Pesharim*, p. 183).

3. Alternatively, the text has been taken to refer to the period during the reign of Salome Alexandra when the Pharisees returned to power. See Amusin, 'Historical Events', pp. 143-45; A. Dupont-Sommer, 'Lumières nouvelles sur l'arrière-plan historique des écrits de Qumran', *Eretz-Israel* 8 (Sukenik Volume, 1967), pp. 25*-36*.

4. Cf. J. Licht, 'המונח גורל בכתביה של כת מדבר יהודה', *Bet Miqra* 1 (1955–56), pp. 90-99.

of their comrades. All this the author blames on the plot hatched by the Pharisees to overthrow Janneus with the help of the Seleucids.

This picture corresponds closely with that of Josephus. *Ant.* 13.14.2 (§§379-383)[1] describes the manner in which Janneus dealt with his Jewish enemies who had allied themselves with him in order to expel their erstwhile ally Demetrius. He captured and killed the most powerful of them in what Josephus considers a cruel manner, crucifying them, as we have already seen. Then his remaining opponents fled the country and remained in exile for as long as he lived. There can be no question that these are the events described in our text, except that here the opponents of Janneus are correctly identified as the Pharisees.

The account continues as the text interprets Nah. 3.4[2] in 4QpNah 3-4.2.8-10

> פשר[ו ע]ל מתעי אפרים אשר בתלמוד שקרם ולשון כזבידם ושפת מרמה יתעו רבים מלכיה[ם]שרים כוהנים ועם עם גר נלוה ערים ומשפחות יובדו בעצתם נ[כ]בדים ומוש[לים] יפולו [מז]עם לשונם.
>
> [Its] interpretation [con]cerns those who lead Ephraim astray, in whose teaching (*talmud*) is their falsehood, and whose lying tongue and dishonest lip(s) lead many astray, [their] kings, officers priests, and people, with the proselyte who converts [literally, 'joins']. They shall destroy cities and clans with their plot; nob[l]es and rul[ers] shall fall because of the [insol]ence of their speech.[3]

The text now centers on the leadership of the Pharisaic party. The verse being interpreted speaks of the harlotry and magic with which the harlot (herself having already gone astray) led others to harlotry and magic. It is this aspect which called forth for the author the Pharisaic leadership which had, in the view of the sect, led others astray with false interpretations. Whatever the actual meaning of the verb found in MT as המכרת and in the lemma in 4QpNah as הממכרת, it is clear that the *pesher* took it in the sense of 'ensnares', an explanation which seems to require emendation to הכמרת.[4]

According to the biblical text, 'nations' and 'families' are ensnared by the harlot. These terms are expanded considerably by the *pesher*

1. Cf. *War* 1.4.6 (§§96-98).
2. For textual differences with MT in the lemma, see Horgan, *Pesharim*, pp. 183-84.
3. Restored with Dupont-Sommer, 'Le Commentaire', pp. 58, 77; cf. Strugnell, 'Notes', p. 207.
4. Cf. Horgan, *Pesharim*, pp. 183-84.

which takes גוים as referring to 'nobles, eminences' (= גאים), who are the kings, officers, and priests.[1] The משפחות are taken to refer to the people, the proselytes and the various cities and clans of the Jewish people as well as their leaders. All of these are said to have been victimized by the insolent teachings of the Pharisees.

From this text it is certain that there is a distinction to be made between those who actually expounded the law themselves and their followers. The leaders are apparently able to influence even members of the aristocracy. We also hear that they influenced the common people, עם, as well as proselytes. This statement is significant in that it dovetails with Josephus's statement (*Ant.* 13.10.6 [§298]) about the popularity of the Pharisees among the common people. This is probably a correct statement, although we cannot be certain whether it applied at all times, nor can we gauge the extent and ramifications of this popularity.[2]

At this point we learn of the content of the lies described above. They refer specifically to the תלמוד of the Pharisees.[3] We ought not to be surprised at this point to learn that such a *talmud* existed.[4] We have already seen that laws existed which were generally termed הלכות and that the use of the term דרש implied that the Pharisees used midrashic exegesis in analyzing biblical texts. Together with the method of logical deduction known as *talmud*,[5] these approaches were the mainstay of later tannaitic and amoraic learning, and our text indicates that these components existed already for the Pharisees. This *talmud* was the method of logical analysis which must have already been part of the intellectual equipment of Pharisaic endeavor, and it was regarded as false by the Qumran sectarians, just like the exegesis and the laws of the Pharisaic tradition.

1. For this list, but including also the prophets, see Jer. 2.26 and 32.32 where they appear with third person plural possessive suffixes, as in our text.

2. Amusin, 'Historical Events', p. 145. On the Pharisees in Josephus, see J. Neusner, *From Politics to Piety: The Emergence of Pharisaic Judaism* (Englewood Cliffs, NJ: Prentice Hall, 1973), pp. 49-66.

3. The extensive bibliography on this term is reviewed in Horgan, *Pesharim*, p. 184.

4. See B.Z. Wacholder, 'A Qumran Attack on the Oral Exegesis? The Phrase אשר בתלמוד שקרם in 4Q Pesher Nahum', *RevQ* 5 (1964–66), pp. 575-78.

5. See Rashi to *b. Suk.* 28a, s.v. תלמוד, in the uncensored Venice edition. Later editions, as a result of Christian censorship, substitute גמרא in this passage.

The author of our text continues his polemic against the Pharisees and tells us that in the end of days the evil of their ways will become manifest and those whom they have led astray (the 'simple ones of Ephraim') will leave those who have led them astray. These Pharisaic followers are then expected, in the sectarian understanding of the prophecies of Nah. 3.5, to rejoin the true House of Israel, thought by the sect to be itself (4QpNah 3-4.2.1-8). These dreams of the sect, of course, were never realized. Since they tell us little about the Pharisees in the author's time, or beforehand, I omit detailed consideration of these passages from this study.

3. *Sadducees*

This document also gives us some information about the Sadducees. It appears that, had the text survived in its entirety, there would have been more information; the preserved text effectively breaks off in the middle of discussing this group. I will first gather these data and analyze them, and then discuss their connection to the Sadducean background of the founders of the Qumran sect and their halakhic traditions.

Towards the end of the preserved portion of the scroll, the author turns to the Sadducees, who are designated by him as 'Manasseh'. He most probably chose this term in apposition to Ephraim, which was recommended as a term for the Pharisees by its similar consonants. Interpreting Nah. 3.8a, 4QpNah 3-4.3.9-10 describes them and their aristocratic leaders:

> פשרו אמון הם מנשה והיאורים הם גד[ו]לי מנשה נכבדי ה[עיר המחזק]ים את מ[נשה].
>
> Its interpretation is (that) Amon,[1] they are Manasseh, and the rivers are the magnates of Manasseh, the honored ones of the [city who suppo]rt[2] Ma[nasseh].

To understand this point, careful attention must be paid to the biblical text being interpreted. The text in Nah. 3.7 regarding Nineveh and

1. Although MT has מנא אמון, the lemma in 4QpNah has מני, 'from', here meaning 'than' (reading with Allegro, *Qumran Cave 4*, p. 39 and Horgan, *Pesharim*, p. 188). That this is the correct reading rather than מנו = phonetic spelling of מנא) is most likely in view of the omission of נא from the *pesher*.
2. Restoring with Horgan, *Pesharim*, p. 188.

its destruction was interpreted by the *pesher* to refer to the prophesied devastation of the Pharisees. It is then that the biblical prophet turns to Nineveh and asks her whether she is really better than No-Amon (Thebes), which had been destroyed only shortly before by the Assyrians (in 663 BCE). In context, therefore, the *pesher* is arguing that we can be certain that the Pharisees (= Nineveh) will be destroyed because of the destruction of the Sadducees which had taken place previously.

This interpretation presumes that the Sadducees had met their match and been weakened before the Pharisees.[1] Indeed, to a great extent Hasmonean priestly power came at the expense of their Sadducean predecessors. Yet in our text we learn additional facts about the Sadducees in the author's day or earlier. The magnates of the Sadducees were the honored ones of the city, that is, the aristocracy, religious and economic. The very same claim was made by Josephus based on his experience of later Judean society (*Ant.* 13.10.6 [§298]),[2] and this claim seems to be borne out by our text and can be taken as fact. These aristocrats were 'supporters' of Manasseh. This indicates that besides the Sadducees themselves various others connected with the upper classes supported this group even while not being full-fledged members. Indeed, this same situation seems to be described above for the Pharisees.

Interpreting Nah. 3.9,[3] 4QpNah 3-4.4.1 explains

> פשרו הם רשע[י מנש]ה בית פלג הנלוים על מנשה.
>
> Its interpretation is that it is the evil [ones of Manass]eh,[4] the House of Peleg, who have joined Manasseh.

Here we again hear about the followers of the Sadducees, termed the House of Peleg, literally 'division', who have joined the Sadducees. From this designation we can already see that they are regarded as a group of evildoers within the Sadducean camp. The interpretation is

1. Cf. Amusin, 'Historical Events', p. 144.
2. For parallels, see E. Schürer, *The History of the Jewish People in the Age of Jesus Christ*, II (ed. G. Vermes, F. Millar and M. Black, with P. Vermes; Edinburgh: T. & T. Clark, 1979), pp. 404-405.
3. According to Carmignac's placement of the fragments; J. Carmignac, É. Cothenet and H. Lignée, *Les Textes de Qumran, traduits et annotés*, II (Paris: Letouzey & Ané, 1963), p. 92; cf. Strugnell, 'Notes', p. 210.
4. Restored with Horgan, *Pesharim*, p. 189.

probably based on the end of the verse, 'Put and the Libyans, they were your helpers'. Presumably, the *pesher* understands the House of Peleg, equivalent to Put and Libya, as the helpers, i.e. associates of Manasseh who are the Sadducees. These again are supporters or 'retainers'. Apparently, large groups of Jews had allegiance to the teachings of these groups without full membership.

To a great extent our understanding of this passage is dependent on the identity of the House of Peleg. This term also occurs in the *Zadokite Fragments* (CD 20.22). The passage is only preserved in the medieval manuscript B: מבית פלג אשר יצאו מעיר הקדש וישענו על אל בקץ מעל ישראל וטמאו את המקדש ושבו עד אל, 'from the House of Peleg who left the holy city (Jerusalem) and were dependent on God, during the period of the transgression of Israel when they defiled the Temple; but they (i.e. the House of Peleg) returned to God'. This parallel gives the distinct impression that the House of Peleg is the sect. After all, they are the ones who, when transgression set in, when the Temple was taken over by Hasmoneans, left and formed a sect dedicated to returning to God.

But if we were to restore the text differently, and accept the reading רשע]י יהוד[ה, 'the evil [ones of Jud]ah', it would allow us to see this as a reference to evil members of the sect who attached themselves to the Sadducees.[1] In any case, this difficult phrase is likely to remain a matter of debate.

In the interpretation of Nah. 3.10,[2] 4QpNah 3-4.4.3 states:

> פשרו על מנשה לקץ האחרון אשר תשפל מלכותו ביש[ראל. . .] נשיו עילוליו וטפו ילכו בשבי גבוריו ונכבדיו בחרב [יובדו].
>
> Its interpretation concerns Manasseh in the final period (end of days) when his kingdom will be brought low in Is[rael. . .] Its women, children, and infants, will go into captivity. Its mighty ones and honored ones [will perish][3] by the sword.

Nah. 3.10 speaks of the destruction of No-Amon. It tells us that the city went into captivity, that her children were slaughtered, that her honored men were distributed by lot as spoil of war and that her nobles were led off in chains. This fate, according to the *pesher*,

1. J. Licht, 'דפים נוספים לפשר נחום', *Molad* 19 (1961), p. 455.
2. For textual differences with MT, see Horgan, *Pesharim*, p. 190.
3. Restored with Horgan, *Pesharim*, p. 190. Strugnell and, apparently, Carmignac: יפולו.

refers to the overturning of the power of the Sadducees, they who are indeed the 'honored men' and 'nobles' of Israel. The text specifically mentions Israel so as to apply the prophecies directed at No-Amon to the Jewish people.

This text sees the Sadducees as effectively a kingdom, or dominion, which will be destroyed. The text continues to describe the exile of the women and children of the Sadducees, and the slaughter of their elite at the sword.

The final preserved material relevant to our study appears in 4QpNah 3-4.4.5-6, commenting on Nah. 3.11:[1]

> פשרו על רשעי א[פרים] אשר תבוא כוסם אחר מנשה.
>
> Its interpretation concerns the evil ones of E[phraim] whose cup (of destruction) will come after that of Manasseh.

This excerpt is important only in that it understands the destruction of the Sadducees to precede that of the Pharisees, a notion we saw already above. The author interprets Nah. 3.11 as saying to the Pharisees: you too will be overcome and have to flee the enemy, now that the Sadducees have been devastated. To be sure the author(s) of this document had distinctive and consistently worked out ideas on the fate which the Sadducees and then the Pharisees would experience. Unfortunately for this study, little else is preserved of 4QpNah and we hear no more here about the text's views on the two major sects of Jews of the Second Temple period.

This treatment of the Sadducees, describing them as an aristocratic group augmented by supporters or retainers, is totally negative. Although the details of the sect's judgment of this group do not appear here, it is clear that certain specific misdeeds, like those of the Pharisees, led the Qumran sect to expect the utter destruction of the Sadducees in the now dawning eschaton. In short, the Sadducees are here seen as the villains.

It is difficult at first glance to reconcile this image with our conclusion relating to the Sadducean character of the founders of the sect and the halakhic traditions of the group. Why does 4QpNah condemn so roundly the very group from which the sect seems to have emerged?

The answer to this question lies in the complex historical processes

1. For textual differences with MT, see Horgan, *Pesharim*, p. 190.

which affected both the sect and the Sadducees in the years between the founding of the group c. 152 BCE, and the composition of this text, some time after 63 BCE. In the case of the Qumran sect, the evidence of the initial section of the *Zadokite Fragments* (*Damascus Covenant*) indicates that the teacher of righteousness, who developed the basic sectarian stance of the group, only entered the picture after the initial break had already taken place (CD 1.10-12).[1] Over time, the sect became increasingly radicalized and isolated, while at the same time adopting the apocalyptic messianism and ethical dualism which became its hallmarks. For this reason, it began to look at the Sadducean way from which it had emerged as improper, while still retaining the substratum of Sadducean law which if had brought into the sect in the early years.

In the case of the Sadducees, the processes of change also help to explain the problem. The sect was formed by Sadducees who represented the 'lower clergy', and who, therefore, were not Hellenized to a great extent. More Hellenized Sadducees played an increasing role in the Hasmonean dynasty over time. Both Josephus and the *baraita'* recorded in the Babylonian Talmud testify to a sharp break with the Pharisees which took place, as we have mentioned, either under John Hyrcanus or Alexander Janneus. By the time of this break, the Sadducees in Jerusalem, as well as their Maccabean colleagues, had come a long way since the days when Jonathan the Hasmonean had instituted adherence to Pharisaic law in the Temple and its service. Now the Sadducees had gained control. It is these Hellenized Sadducees whom our text condemns. Opposition to them comes not from the legal traditions they espouse, but rather from their having strayed from the strict adherence to the Torah required by the sectarians.

1. This picture is not changed by the additional lines which in the Qumran manuscripts precede the text preserved on p. 1 of the medieval copy. See B.Z. Wacholder and M. Abegg, *A Preliminary Edition of the Unpublished Dead Sea Scrolls: The Hebrew and Aramaic Texts from Cave Four* (Washington, DC: Biblical Archaeology Society, 1991), p. 1 (4QD^a 1, 1-17) and p. 4 (4QD^b 2, I, 1-14).

Conclusion

4QpNah testifies to the nature of the Pharisees and Sadducees in the period of Alexander Janneus. During his tenure he was seriously challenged by the Pharisees while the Sadducees drew closer to him. From the examination of this document we have been able to confirm the general outlines of the picture of these groups presented in Josephus as well as to gain new details about the episode of Demetrius III Eukerus's invasion of Judea.

Although little of the text's critique of the Sadducees survives, we can at least observe their aristocratic character. Yet of the Pharisees so much more can be said. We learn here of the role of halakhic midrash in their method of deriving law, as well as of a system of logical deduction termed *talmud*. We hear much about the manner in which the leadership of this group allegedly leads the people astray, indicating that they did indeed have a considerable following among the people. For both the Pharisees and Sadducees we hear of the 'retainers', those followers who were at the outer fringes of the power elite but who were themselves part of the group in one way or another. In general, we realize that no group of Jews in this period could be expected to embrace such large numbers of people. Rather, they functioned by teaching and influencing, a process in which the Pharisees indeed excelled.

When taken together with 4QMMT and other texts, we can sketch a history of the fortunes of these two groups in the Hasmonean period. In the early days of the dynasty, the Pharisees were allied with the Hasmoneans and their views were dominant. At some point, the break in relations took place and this led to the re-entry of the Sadducees who now were associated with the much more Hellenized Hasmoneans. The Pharisees tried the ultimate power play, perhaps driven by genuine religious motives, but it backfired, leading to execution and exile for many of them. Presumably, the aristocratic Sadducees described in our text then retained power and their rulings were now observed in the Temple in place of the Pharisaic views put into effect in the early Hasmonean period. Finally, and after the period described in our text, we hear of a *rapprochement* between Salome Alexandra (76–67 BCE) and the Pharisees.

The picture I have painted admittedly differs only in details from that of Josephus and rabbinic sources. For a generation now scholars have complained that we have no contemporary accounts of the Pharisees and Sadducees from the Hasmonean period. In the Dead Sea Scrolls, it turns out, we do have these sources, and they verify the essential historicity of the later accounts. Both for the ideological and religious issues and for those of political history the information of our later sources is confirmed by the *Pesher Naḥum*.

PENITENCE, PRAYER AND (CHARITY?)

Menahem Schmelzer

The triad, תשובה, תפלה, צדקה, is familiar to the Jewish worshipper from the liturgy of the Days of Awe. It is found in the liturgical poem, ונתנה תקף, which is recited according to the present Ashkenazi rite on both days of Rosh ha-shanah as well as on Yom Kippur.[1] The full sentence, in which these three nouns are found, reads:

> ותשובה ותפלה וצדקה מעבירין את רוע הגזרה
> and repentance, and prayer and charity remove the evil decree.

This statement reaches back (over the rather long section beginning with the words בראש השנה) to the closing words of the first paragraph of the poem:

> ותכתוב את גזר דינם
> and you will inscribe their decree

All commentators point to a passage in *Bereshith Rabba* as the source of the statement. We read there:[2]

> ר׳ יודן בשם ר׳ לעזר: שלשה דברים מבטלין את הגזירה ואילו הן: תפילה וצדקה ותשובה ושלשתן בפסוק אחד: ויכנעו עמי אשר נקרא שמי עליו ויתפללו (דה״ב ז יד), הרי תפילה, ויבקשו פני (שם שם), הרי צדקה היך דאת אמר אני בצדק אחזה פניך (תהלים יז טו), וישובו מדרכם הרעה (דה״ב שם), הרי תשובה וכו.

> R. Yudan in the name of R. Eleazar: Three things annul the decree: Prayer, *sedaqah* and repentance. We learn this from one and the same verse: 'When My people, who bear My name, humble themselves, pray' (II Chronicles 7.14): this means prayer, 'and seek My face' (*ib.*) this is

1. The poem was originally for Rosh ha-shanah only. It is not found for Yom Kippur in the old French and German rites. See *Mahzor le-yamim noraim*. I. *Rosh ha-shanah* (ed. D. Goldschmidt; Jerusalem, 1970), pp. 169-71, esp. the variant reading to line 1. See also *op. cit.*, II, Introduction, pp. 41-43.
2. *Bereshith Rabba* 44.12 (ed. Theodor-Albeck), p. 434 and parallels.

> *sedaqah*, as it is written 'Then I, *be-ṣedeq*, will behold Your face' (Psalms 17.15) 'and turn from their evil ways' (*ib.*): this is repentance, etc.

This saying of R. Eleazar is quoted in various contexts in rabbinic literature. Its original setting seems to be in connection with astrology or dreams; *gezerah* means one's fate as determined by stars or foretold by dreams. In *Bereshith Rabba* R. Eleazar's words are recorded immediately following the assertion that Abraham, the patriarch, was a prophet and not an astrologer, and that the stars had no power over him. In *Koheleth Rabba* (and in its parallels), R. Yudan's statement is quoted in connection with the verse:

> There is much dreaming and futilities and superfluous talk, but you should fear God (Eccl. 5.6): Rabbi says: if you dreamt difficult dreams and had difficult and contradictory visions and (or) you are scared because of them, hasten to do three things and you will be saved, as stated by R. Yudan in the name of R. Eleazar, three things annul bad decrees, etc.[1]

In both sources, then, the *gezerah* is not the result of actions by man, but rather of superhuman or unconscious forces. To counteract these forces, the Rabbis urge the individual to resort to three things, which, for sure, will act as an antidote to ill fate destined by astrology or predicted by dreams.

There is, however, a third midrashic context, in which R. Eleazar's saying appears. In the *Tanhuma* the triad is recommended as an antidote to the evil inclination, the *yeṣer ha-ra*^{c}[2]. Thus, in the *Tanhuma*, the belief in the effectiveness of the triad shows affinity for the liturgical theme, as it appears in the hymn ונתנה תקף. The statement becomes appropriate for the Days of Awe: sin (caused by the evil inclination) results in an unfavorable, severe divine decree. This decree may be annulled and atonement may be attained by employing the three things recommended by R. Eleazar. Here it is the evil inclination, and not the stars or dreams, that determines man's fate.

In the Babylonian Talmud, R. Yitzhak, suggests four remedies for averting the severe decree:

1. *Midrash Koheleth Rabba* on Eccl. 5.6.
2. *Tanhuma, Noah*, paragraph 8.

צדקה, צעקה, שינוי השם, שינוי מעשה
ṣedaqah, crying out (prayer), of name, change of deed.[1]

The original context of R. Yitzhak's statement is not indicated, but it is likely that he said it in connection with averting destiny declared upon an individual by the stars, and not brought upon himself by his evil deeds. Otherwise it would be difficult to explain why שינוי השם would be considered useful to change the divine judgment.

Three of R. Yitzhak's four things match the triad of R. Eleazar. צעקה (crying out) obviously corresponds to תפלה, as does שינוי מעשה (changing of deed) to penitence (תשובה). צדקה is the same in both sources. Still, there is an important difference: in R. Yitzhak's statement the prooftext for צדקה is וצדקה תציל ממות (Prov. 11.4, But *ṣedaqah* saves from death), while, as we recall, R. Eleazar's prooftext is Ps. 17.15, 'Then I, *be-ṣedeq*, will behold Your face'. We shall return to this discrepancy below. It is obvious that various strains are discernible in these traditions about *gezerah* or *gezar din*. They include destiny determined by stars, foretold by dreams, caused by the evil inclination or declared in God's annual judgment of human beings according to their deeds. The recommended acts to avert fate resulting from any of the above, however, always include prayer, penitence and *ṣedaqah*. That these matters are commingled in the various sources indicate the complexity of the concept of destiny on the New Year in Ancient Israel and in rabbinic Judaism. It is obvious that the change of year brings with it a change of fate. At first, this fate was probably conceived as determined by astrology, and only later by the individual's good (or evil) ways.[2] It would be interesting to attempt to trace the evolution of this concept in the literature, but let us instead turn our attention to some other matters relating to the occurrence of the triad in the liturgy of the Days of Awe.

In R. Eleazar's homily, based on 2 Chron. 7.14, the sequence of the

1. *B. Roš. Haš.* 16b.

2. See N.H. Snaith, *The Jewish New Year Festival: Its Origins and its Development* (London, 1947), esp. pp. 73ff; 165ff; 217f. The various meanings of *gezerah* are also discussed in traditional Jewish sources, see, e.g. Samuel Ashkenazi, *Yefeh Toar*, a commentary on *Bereshith Rabba* (Fuerth, 1692, reprint Jerusalem, 1989), f. 262b. In his comments on our passage, he differentiates between גזר דין דראש השנה and גזירות המערכה, the latter meaning destiny determined by the constellations.

triad is: first תפלה, followed by צדקה, and concluded by תשובה. Whether by design or by chance, the sequence of words in the *Tanhuma*, is different. Here we find תשובה, תפלה, צדקה. It is in the order of the *Tanhuma* which has found its way into the liturgical hymn, ונתנה תקף. We recall that it is also the *Tanhuma* that connects the three to the evil inclination. Since ונתנה תקף follows the order of the *Tanhuma*, and not that of the other sources, and, furthermore, since in the liturgical setting of Rosh ha-shanah judgment of sins (caused by evil inclination) plays such a central role, it is plausable to suggest that the anonymous author of ונתנה תקף used the *Tanhuma* (or a source similar to it) as his inspiration.

The deviation from the sequence of the three things as enumerated in the original midrashic exegesis did not escape the attention of medieval liturgists. On the other hand, in modern times the issue has been forgotten completely. No trace of it is left in present liturgical practice, and for that matter, it is hardly even mentioned in scholarly literature.[1] A cursory examination of just a few medieval and early modern manuscripts as well as printed *mahzorim* yields some interesting information relating to a debate among Rabbis concerning the proper sequence of the triad. In some *mahzorim* we find small letters above the three words, indicating a different order.[2] The text in these sources looks like this:

ב	א	ג
וצדקה	ותפלה	ותשובה

There is no doubt that the superimposed letters try to restore the order of the original homily, as derived by R. Eleazar from the biblical verse. Still, in no *mahzor* was the conventional sequence changed in the body of the text itself. It was only some commentator, owner or scribe who indicated the 'correct' sequence by superimposing letters, thereby disapproving of the order as normally found in ונתנה תקף. The sources also give explicit explanation for the graphic signs. It is

1. W. Bacher, *Die Agadah der palaestinischen Amoraer*, II (Strassburg 1896), p. 13, n. 3 refers to the different sequence in the *u-netanneh tokef.* Bacher's observation is quoted by Theodor in his *Minhath yehuda* to *Bereshith Rabba*, top of p. 435.

2. Ms. Oxford, Opp. 166, Neubauer, Catalogue, 1160, f. 49a; JTS, Ms. 4843, f. 85b; *Mahzor*, Prague 1522-25 (printed), I, for *mussaf* for first day of Rosh ha-shanah.

reported in the name of Rabbi Abraham Klausner (Austria, 14–15th century):

וכת' הרא"ק שיש לומר ותפלה וצדקה ותשובה כסדר הפסוק ואין לשנות כלל.[1]

Rabbi Abraham Klausner wrote: one must say ותפלה וצדקה ותשובה, according to the order of the verse (2 Chron. 7.14), and one should not change this at all.

On the other hand, Rabbi Jacob Moellin (the Maharil; Germany, 14–15th century) advocates the conventional order. Since he is aware of the weighty argument against the common reading, which is based on the original sequence of the Midrash, he has to defend the prevalent practice and find justification for it. Accordingly, he advances the following explanation:

ותשובה ותפלה וצדקה ודלא כסדר הקראי ואמר ותשובה ותפלה ר"ל ע"י יתשובה הקדומה לתפלה ולצדקה על דרך נירו לכם ניר (ירמ' ד ג).[2]

תשובה, placed before the two others, alludes, according to Maharil, to the need of 'preparing the ground' for the effectiveness of תפלה וצדקה. As if תשובה would be needed to break the untilled ground (Jer. 3.4) so that sowing (and not amidst thorns) may follow.

The controversy about the proper order of the words cannot be documented before the 14th–15th centuries. Therefore, it should be assumed that the appearance of superimposed letters in older *mahzor* manuscripts indicates later additions.[3]

The origin of another tradition in connection with this triad may be explained as a result of the controversy concerning its proper

1. Handwritten marginal note in the printed *Mahzor*, Prague, 1522-1525, see previous note. This remark is not found in *Minhagim* of Rabbi Abraham Klausner (ed. Y.Y. Dissen; Jerusalem, 1978).

2. See *Sefer Maharil; Minhagim shel R. Yaakov Moellin* (ed. Sh. Y. Spitzer; Jerusalem, 1989), pp. 294-95.

3. That the suggestions for changing the order are late may also be seen from the comments of R. Moses Mat (Poland, 16th cent.). In his *Matteh Mosheh* (Cracow, 1591), 144a, paragraph 819 (in later editions: 818) he writes:

ואומר ונתנה תוקף ואח"כ ותשובה ותפילה וצדקה. כך נמצא בכל המחזורים, חדשים גם ישנים. רק חדשים מקרוב באו אומרים ותפילה וצדקה ותשובה על פי המדרש, אמר ר יודן וכו ונראה דאין לשנות כלל כמו שכתב בדרשות מהרי"ל וזה לשון מהרי"ל שגגה היא ביד המגיהים את הספרים של הצבור וכו . . . ומי יודע מה היא כוונת המסדר ואפשר שהיה כוונתו על דרך הנעלם סוד . . . לכן אין לשנות. וכן ראיתי כל רבותיי נוהגים . . . וכל המשנה ידו על התחתונה.

sequence. Worshippers are familiar with the way תשובה ותפלה וצדקה appear in the printed editions of most *mahzorim*. Above each of the words, in smaller type, a kind of identification appears. It looks likes this:

צום	קול	ממון
תשובה	תפלה	צדקה

This phenomenon is, of course, quite odd. There is no other passage in the prayerbook with a similar attempt of definition. Why the superimposition of these 'explanations'? It is suggested here that the placing of the three words on top of the original triad is connected with the issue of its sequence, namely that the three superimposed letter-numerals that originally indicated the 'proper' sequence ultimately evolved into the three superimposed words. In at least two printed commentaries to ונתנה תקף, we read:

ומהר״י היה אומ׳ ותשובה ותפלה וצדקה ודלא כסדר הפסוקים ושקולים זה כזה דכל א׳[חד] בני׳[מטריא] קל״ו: צו״ם קו״ל ממו״ן[1]

Mahari, probably identical with Maharil, justified the deviation of the liturgical text from that of the midrashic one in the following ingenious way: since the numerical value of three words, which are 'synonymous' with the original three words of the triad, comes to the same amount, it does not actually matter in what order one recites them; ignore the superimposed *letter-numerals*, which try to tell you that the sequence is wrong. Pay attention, instead, to the superimposed *words* and their numerical value. Since it is the same for all three, 136 for צום and קול as well as for ממון there is no need to worry about the sequence of תשובה ותפלה וצדקה. Apparently, the previous explanation, about 'preparing the ground' was found wanting, and, therefore, a supplemental reason, based on *gematria*, was advanced.

The identification of צדקה as ממון (money) seems natural. After all, the word means giving charity in rabbinic and post-rabbinic parlance. This is how the word, as it appears in the midrashic passage and in ונתנה תקף, is universally understood. There is only one possible

1. *Mahzor* (Cracow, 1585) f. 21a and *Mahzor* (Venice, 1600), with commentary *Hadrath kodesh*, f. 72b. The same comment is found in a marginal manuscript note in the copy of a *Mahzor Ashkenaz* (Salonika, 1555–1556), the verso of quire 8.1, in the Library of JTS, 1758.2. In this *Mahzor* one also finds the superimposed letters over the three words.

exception: a passage in Solomon ibn Gabirol's *Kether Malkhuth*. This religious poem was intended as a private devotion for Yom Kippur. In it we read:

> קטנתי מכל החסדים ומכל האמת אשר עשית את עבדך...כי נתת בי נפש קדושה...וביצרי הרע חללתיה...יצרי האכזר נצב על ימיני לשטני . . . וכמה פעמים יצאתי להלחם עמו וערכתי מחנה עבודתי ותשובתי ושמתי מחנה רחמיך לעמתי לעזרתי: כי אמרתי: אם יבוא יצרי אל המחנה האחת והכהו- והיה המחנה הנשאר לפליטה. וכאשר חשבתי, כן היה: והנה גבר עלי, והפיץ חילי, ולא נשאר אלי, כי אם מחנה רחמיך.[1]

> I am unworthy of all the mercies and of all the truth that Thou hast dispensed to Thy servant. . . for Thou hast put a holy soul in me. . . and with my evil imagining I profaned it. . . my cruel temper stands firm by my right hand. . . how many times did I go forth to fight against him and order the company of my worship and my penitence, putting the company of Thy mercies before me to help me. For I said: if my temper 'comes to the one company and smites it, then the other company which is left shall escape'. And as I thought, so it was. For he prevailed over me, and scattered my warriors, and nothing remained to me but the company of Thy mercies.[2]

It seems that this passage alludes to R. Eleazar's statement. The three 'companies' are worship, penitence and God's mercy. They are the ones that are mobilized against the evil inclination (evil imagining or temper, in the above translation). In the *Tanhuma*,[3] too, the triad serves as an antidote against the evil inclination. It seems plausible to suggest that ibn Gabirol's source is the *Tanhuma*. Ibn Gabirol, however, understood צדקה in R. Eleazar's statement as God's mercy and not as the giving of charity. This can easily be done if one understands the word according to one of its many biblical nuances. While in rabbinic literature צדקה denotes charity, in the Bible it may mean many things, including God's love, compassion, mercy, etc.[4]

However, a question remains: is it appropriate to interpret צדקה,

1. Paragraph 36 (Y.A. Seidmann; Jerusalem, 1950), pp. 76-78.

2. Solomon ibn Gabirol, *The Kingly Crown* (trans. B. Lewis; London, 1961), p. 58. See also R. Loewe, *Ibn Gabirol* (New York, 1990), pp. 150-51.

3. See above, p. 292 n. 2.

4. See the various biblical dictionaries. See also A. Hurvitz, 'The Biblical Roots of a Talmudic Term: The Early History of the Concept צדקה (=charity, alms)', in *Mehkarim be-lashon* (Jerusalem, 1987), pp. 155-60. I am grateful to David Marcus for calling this paper to my attention.

occurring in a midrash, in its biblical sense? Let us now take a look at the midrash again. Two of the phrases in 2 Chron. 7.14 easily support their rabbinic exegesis: ויתפללו: הרי תפלה and וישובו מדרכם הרע: הרי תשובה. These are very simple, straightforward 'midrashim'. This is not so, however, in the case of the third phrase: ויבקשו פני: הרי צדקה. Indeed, for this exegesis the midrash needs a prooftext: היאך דאת אמר אני בצדק אחזה פניך (תה' יז טו). לבקש פני ה means to seek the face of God, that is, to gain God's attention and favor;[1] in other words, to seek God's mercy. Therefore, צדקה, as the rabbinic exegesis of ויבקשו פני, may be interpreted by Ibn Gabirol as mercy in the abstract sense, and as God's mercy.[2] That צדקה and רחמים are equated is known from the Babylonian Talmud: חסד זו גמילת חסדים רחמים זו צדקה, but there צדקה clearly means the giving of charity.[3] In the statement by R. Eleazar, as interpreted by Ibn Gabirol, it refers to God's mercy. Possibly, this could have been the original intent of the midrashic passage as well.

Now the prooftext makes sense, too. Ps. 17.15 (אני בצדק אחזה פניך) was chosen to 'prove' that ויבקשו פני means צדקה in the sense of God's mercy. If one would want to bring a prooftext to indicate that צדקה means charity, Prov. 10.2 (וצדקה תציל ממות) would be more to the point. This is, indeed, the prooftext in R. Yitzhak's statement, quoted above,[4] and it serves to demonstrate the merit of charity in rabbinic literature.[5]

Through this interpretation, Ibn Gabirol lends a new dimension to the midrashic statement and to its liturgical derivation. Man can do two things to combat the *gezerah* (in Ibn Gabirol's understanding, the machinations of the evil inclination): engage in worship (תפלה = עבודה) and repent. If these two fail, one can only rely on God's mercy. Although the giving of charity is a great and meritorious deed,

1. See C.L. Mayers and E.M. Mayers, *Haggai, Zechariah 1–8*, (AB, 25B; New York, 1987), p. 438.

2. It may be just a coincidence, but it is interesting to note that in a poem by Yonnai for Rosh ha-shanah (*The Liturgical Poems of Rabbi Yannai* [ed. Z.M. Rabinovitz; Jerusalem, 1987], p. 199, line 13) we read ותרועה מפרשת צדקה מבקשת. The sense of the line is that Israel seeks צדקה (from God). Does the midrashic passage, ויבקשו פני: הרי צדקה, reverberate here? Does Yannai understand the passage in the Midrash in the same way as Ibn Gabirol?

3. *B. B. Bat.* 10a.

4. See above, p. 293 n. 1.

5. E.g. in *b. Šab* 156b.

it is not in the same category as prayer and penitence. One could argue that some other deed could easily be substituted for charity, but not for prayer and penitence. Instead of singling out just one good deed, we would rather expect a more general category, such as for example the frequently used מעשים טובים, as in the expression תשובה ומעשים טובים.[1] In light of the above, Ibn Gabirol's treatment of the passage provides a better understanding of the original intent of R. Eleazar.

Ibn Gabirol's surprising interpretation should not be attributed to poetic license alone; he may have possessed a tradition according to which the word צדקה in the passage in *Bereshit Rabba* (and parallels) referred to God's mercy and not to the giving of charity. Ibn Gabirol's *Kether Malkhuth* is the only surviving testimony of this interpretation.

1. E.g. in *m. Ab.* 4.11; 4.17; *b. Ber.* 17a; *b. Šab.* 32a, etc.

YIṢḤAḲI: A SPANISH BIBLICAL COMMENTATOR WHOSE 'BOOK SHOULD BE BURNED', ACCORDING TO ABRAHAM IBN EZRA*

Uriel Simon

The great scholarly interest in Yiṣḥaḳi stands in inverse proportion to our meager knowledge about him. Eight times he is mentioned by Abraham Ibn Ezra, and in each instance his opinions are rejected. This consistent censure by such a linguist and biblical scholar as Ibn Ezra seems to have diminished Yiṣḥaḳi's status and contributed to his consignment to oblivion. His work—the *Book of the Yiṣḥaḳi*—has been lost, even though it was written in Hebrew; except for the passages quoted by Ibn Ezra, no other citation has survived nor has any other information about him reached us. In the fourteenth century R. Joseph ben Eliezer, the most outstanding of the supercommentators on Ibn Ezra's Pentateuch commentary, attempted to identify him on the basis of his name and disparaging appellation. Ibn Ezra, in the section of the introduction to his standard Pentateuch commentary that discusses the 'first method', rejects the wordy and discursive style of 'R. Isaac who wrote two whole books from "in the beginning" (Gen. 1.1) until "the heavens and earth were completed" (Gen. 2.1), and still did not complete his work, because of his excessive loquacity'. On this R. Joseph notes: 'This is R. Isaac ben Yashush the Spaniard; (in his commentary on Gen. 36.32) he calls him the "prater Yiṣḥaḳi" and at the beginning of his commentary on Daniel (1.1.) R. Abraham said that this scholar wrote ten books on grammar'.[1] Clearly this three-termed equation cannot stand up to criticism. First, there is no doubt

* Translated by Lenn J. Schramm through the generosity of the Leib Merkin Chair for the Study of the Commentaries of R. Abraham Ibn Ezra and his Contemporaries, Bar Ilan University.

1. *Ṣafnat Pa'ne'aḥ* (ed. D. Herzog; Cracow, 1912), I, p. 10.

that the first R. Isaac mentioned is the physician and philosopher R. Isaac ben Solomon Israeli (Kairouan [Tunis], tenth century), whose writings on the creation story have been lost, except for the 'Treatise on Let the Waters Bring Forth', which certainly fits Ibn Ezra's characterization of his style. Secondly, we must not identify Yiṣḥaḳi, with no accompanying epithet, with R. Isaac Ibn Yashush, the eleventh-century physician and grammarian who lived in Spain and all of whose writings are lost, because Ibn Ezra's two certain references to him are favorable and employ his full name.[1] The third term in the equation—the identification of Yiṣḥaḳi with the proponent of lexical substitution, attacked by Ibn Ezra in his long commentary on Daniel (1.1), lacks even the element of a common name and rests entirely on the fact that Ibn Ezra sometimes calls him 'the prater', just as he designates Yiṣḥaḳi (see *Ṣafᵉnaṯ Pa'ne'aḥ* on Gen. 36.32). This identification, which gives more color and detail to the otherwise shadowy figure of Yiṣḥaḳi, has received broad support from scholars, but I have examined and refuted their arguments elsewhere.[2] Also based on this erroneous identification is Ezra Fleischer's attractive hypothesis that Yiṣḥaḳi is the author of the unique work known as *Ha-shᵉ'eloṯ ha-'atiḳoṯ*, many passages of which have survived in the Cairo Geniza.[3] In another inquiry I have demonstrated that Ibn Ezra's sharp attack on Yiṣḥaḳi cannot be understood literally, since he employed no less vituperative expressions with regard to authors whom he esteemed, such as Sa'adiah Gaon and Jonah Ibn Janāḥ.[4] In the present article I shall attempt to answer the question: what is the baleful phenomenon, represented by Yiṣḥaḳi, that Ibn Ezra assaults so harshly? The inquiry

1. See *Mozne Leshon Haqqodesh* (Hebrew Grammar) (ed. W. Heidenheim; Offenbach, 1791), fol. 2a, and *The Second Recension on Genesis* in A. Weiser (ed.), *The Torah Commentaries of R. Abraham Ibn Ezra* (Hebrew) (Jerusalem, 1976), I, p. 165.

2. U. Simon, 'Who was the Proponent of Lexical Substitution whom Ibn Ezra Denounced as a Prater and Madman?', in B. Walfish (ed.), *Frank Talmage Memorial Volume*, I (Haifa, in press).

3. E. Fleischer, 'The Nature of *ha-šᵉ'eloṯ ha-'atiḳoṯ* and the Identity of their Author', *HUCA* 38 (1967), pp. 1-23 (Hebrew section). A detailed treatment of Fleischer's arguments cannot be given here.

4. U. Simon, 'Ibn Ezra's Harsh Language and Biting Humor: Real Denunciation or Hispanic Mannerism?', in F. Díaz Estetan (ed.), *Abraham Ibn Ezra and his Age* (Madrid, 1990), pp. 325-34.

has a twofold goal: gaining an acquaintance with Yiṣḥaḳi's exegetical method (the approach reflected in his presentation of questions and the method reflected in the answers he provides thereto), and adding a few lineaments to the image of Ibn Ezra himself, in the reflected light of his disagreement with his predecessor.

I begin by reviewing all of Ibn Ezra's references to Yiṣḥaḳi. Since a uniform attitude toward Yiṣḥaḳi emerges from all of Ibn Ezra's *oeuvre*, with no evidence of any evolution or development, we can ignore chronology and cite these references in the order of increasingly severe criticism of Yiṣḥaḳi.

1. *The Five Issues Discussed in Eight Places in Ibn Ezra's Writings*

a. *The Gloss on bᵉnei šeṯ (Num. 24.17) as a Synonymous Parallelism for 'the Brow of Moab'*

In Yiṣḥaḳi's opinion, in this verse the word *šeṯ* does not refer to the third son of Adam, but is rather a common noun meaning 'buttocks', used here in the broader metonymous sense of 'pudenda' (as in Yiṣḥaḳi's ostensible proof text: 'with bared buttocks—to the shame [lit, nakedness] of Egypt' [Isa. 2.4]). According to this interpretation, *bᵉnei šeṯ* means 'children of incest' and refers to the descendants of Lot's daughters; thus it is a synonymous parallel for Moab that also includes the Ammonites. This gloss may well have been original with Yiṣḥaḳi, since it is to be found neither in Menaḥem's *Maḥberet* (s.v. *š.t*) nor in Ibn Janāḥ's *Shorashim* (s.v. *š.w.t.*). Ibn Ezra does not reject it out of hand, but characterizes it as 'far-fetched'; he does not believe it possible to extend the meaning of *šet* to a woman's private parts, because the derivation of this noun shows that it refers specifically to the buttocks or fundament of a man, just as *šaṯoṯ* (Ps. 11.3; Isa. 19.10) are the foundations of a building.

b. *The Two Errors in the Epithet 'ha-Yiṣḥaḳi': The Definite Article with a Proper Noun and the Possessive Suffix*

Proper nouns have three specific properties, set forth by Sa'adiah Gaon in three prohibitions: (1) they cannot take a prepended definite article ('the Jacob'); (2) they cannot be pluralized ('Jacobs'); and (3) they cannot be used to support a construct case ('Jacob our family') or take a possessive suffix.[1] It is likely that Sa'adiah assumed that his rules allow exceptions, since in his commentary on Psalms he interprets *'al mut la-ben* (Ps. 9.1) as a reference to the musician 'Ben' (mentioned in 1 Chron. 15.18), which here does have the definite article attached. Dunash, for his part, argues that prefixing the definite article to a proper noun is indeed legitimate, and not merely exceptional, for the construction is frequent in Scripture (e.g. *ha-Levanon, ha-'ai, b^e^nei ha-Yiṣhar*). Even if there is no support for the construct and pluralization of proper nouns in biblical Hebrew, these too can be permitted by analogy with the use of the definite article, and because they are permissible in Arabic (*Teshuvot*, §104).

R. Jonah Ibn Janāḥ, too, rejects in principle attaching a definite article to a proper noun, but is not unaware that it is occasionally found in Scripture—e.g. *ḥaṣi ševet ha-Menašeh* (Deut. 3.13), *ha-Aravnah ha-Y^e^vusi* (2 Sam. 24.16), *w^e^-Zevaḥ w^e^-Ṣalmunna' ba-Ḳarḳor* (Judg. 8.10)—and that in Arabic, too, one can say *far'on Musi* = Moses's Pharaoh.[2]

In Ibn Ezra's opinion, however, what is permissible in Arabic is not allowed in Hebrew, because the holy tongue is more consistent in its insistence on the special character of proper nouns. To prove this he explains and resolves, through grammatical or exegetical methods, all the passages that his predecessors deemed legitimate exceptions.[3] But whereas he shelters the reputations of Sa'adiah and Ibn Janāḥ and does not mention them by name when he disputes their positions, he heaps scorn on Yiṣḥaḳi:

> The one who calls his book the *Book of the Yiṣḥaḳi* erred too. He believed that such a book would be attributed to a man named Isaac. The meaning is not this, however, but rather that the author is among the sons of Isaac. And were it correct to say 'the Yiṣḥaḳi', he should have called it

1. Quoted by Dunash ben Labrat, *Sefer Tešuḇoth 'al Rabbi Sa'adiah Gaon* (ed. R. Schroeter; Breslau, 1866), p. 29, §104.

2. Jonah Ibn Janāḥ, *Sefer ha-riḳmah* (Hebrew Grammar) (trans. Judah Ibn Tibbon; ed. M. Wilensky; Jerusalem, 2nd rev. edn, 1964), I, pp. 250-51, 376 (Hebrew).

3. Abraham Ibn Ezra, *Sefer Yesod Diḳduḳ* (Hebrew Grammar) (ed. N. Allony; Jerusalem, 1985), pp. 172-72; *idem*, *Sepher Haschem* (The Book on the Tetragrammaton) (ed. G.H. Lippmann; Fürth, 1834), fol. 3b. Cf. also his commentaries on Gen. 2.8; Num. 13.22 and 21.28; Deut. 6.16; long commentary on Exod. 3.15; Isa. 15.1 and 60.14; Zech. 1.8; Ps. 9.1; Job 2.11: Ruth 1.1; Eccl. 12.8.

'the Yiṣḥaḳi Book' [with two definite articles in Hebrew]. Hence he made two serious mistakes at the very beginning of his work (*Sefer Ha-shem*, fol. 3b).

Ibn Ezra applies similar language to Dunash ben Labrat: 'This is a grave error'; 'hence he made two errors'.[1] Clearly, however, the lack of comprehension that Ibn Ezra finds in Yiṣḥaḳi's mistakes is more serious, and, what is more, they figure prominently in the very title of his book. This means that, unlike Sa'adiah and Ibn Janāḥ, Yiṣḥaḳi considered that such proper-noun constructions are normal rather than exceptional or marginal. We learn that his name really was Isaac, since this is how Ibn Ezra refers to him in his commentary on Job 42.16 (according to all the textual evidence: seven MSS and the *editio princeps*) and in his commentary on Gen. 36.31 ('rightly is he called Isaac'). But all the other references speak of 'the Yiṣḥaḳi', evidently in order to ridicule one who presumed to gloss Scripture but whose lack of understanding of its language is reflected even in his appellation.

We will not be far from the mark if we assume that Ibn Ezra's harsh criticism of Yiṣḥaḳi was intended not only to protect his readers from incorrect use of proper nouns, but also to detract from Isaac's status as a philologist and to undermine his authority as an exegete. This is precisely what Ibn Ezra did in his critique of Karaite scriptural exegesis:

It is not enough for these who lack understanding / and have no faith / to the point that they remove a word from its meaning / since they are ignorant of grammar / and have never heard of it in their country.[2]

c. *The Identification of Job with Jobab ben Zeraḥ King of Edom.*

The one who said that [Job] is the same as Jobab son of Zeraḥ of Boṣra (Gen. 36.33) may have seen this in a dream, for he has nothing on which to base himself, neither in the words of the prophets nor on what our Sages have taught (comm. on Job 1.1; cf. comm. on Gen. 36.32).

Ibn Ezra does not cite any of Yiṣḥaḳi's proofs, except for the similarity in Hebrew of the names *Iyyov* and *Yovav*. It may be surmised

1. Abraham Ibn Ezra, *Sefat Yeter* (Defense of Saadiah Gaon) (ed. G.H. Lippmann; Frankfurt am Main, 1843), §85; *idem*, *Sefer Tsachoth* (Hebrew Grammar) (ed. H. Lippmann; Fürth, 1827), fol. 36a.

2. Introduction to the *Second Recension on Genesis*, in Weiser (ed.), *Torah Commentaries*, I, p. 138.

that Yiṣḥaḳi also buttressed his identification of these two personages with the similarity between the names of Job's three friends and those of three other Edomites mentioned in Genesis, as Tur-Sinai did in our own century: Eliphaz the Temanite with Eliphaz, Esau's oldest son and the father of Teman (Gen. 36.4 and 11); Bildad the Shuhite with Bedad father of Hadad (Gen. 36.35); and Zophar the Naamathite with Esau's son Zepho (Gen. 36.11).[1] In any case, Ibn Ezra maintains that this identification is merely the fruit of an overwrought imagination, since it has no basis in the plain meaning of the 'words of the prophets' (i.e. the Pentateuch and the Prophetic books, of which Job is one)[2] nor any foundation in 'what our Sages have transmitted' (i.e. in the oral law). He castigates the identification of Job with Jobab king of Edom as a vain dream, because such an identification is simultaneously quasi-homiletical and quasi-historical. What is permitted the talmudic Sages in their homiletical glosses is forbidden to someone who claims to be a commentator on the plain meaning, that is, someone whose method is philological and historical.

d. *The Identification of the Prophet Hosea with Hosea son of Elah, King of Israel.*

> This is Hosea, one of the honored prophets of the Lord. The Yiṣḥaḳi spoke waywardly (*sarah*) in his book about him, when he said that he is the son of Elah and that Be'eri is Elah, on the basis of what he found written: 'at Beer-elim her wailing' (Isa. 15.8). But Elah is not Elim; the addition of a letter changes the name, as in 'Ziph and Ziphah' (1 Chron. 4.16). What is more, it is not in accordance with the rules of the holy tongue to say that an individual is the son of a city; this can be said only collectively, as in 'daughter of Zion' (Isa. 1.8); [the appropriate construc-

1. N.H. Torczyner (Tur-Sinai), *The Book of Job* (Hebrew) (Jerusalem, 1941), pp. 17-18. On pp. 541-42 he offers two items that attest to the antiquity among the Jews of the identification Job = Jobab: (1) the Septuagint additions to the end of Job, where we read, 'his name was formerly Jobab'; (2) in the pseudepigraphical *Testament of Job* (2.1) we read: 'Now I used to be Jobab before the Lord named me Job' (J.H. Charlesworth [ed.], *The Old Testament Pseudepigrapha* [Garden City, NY: Doubleday, 1983], I, p. 840).

2. Even though Ibn Ezra suggests that Job may not have been originally written in Aramaic (comm. on Job 2.11) and even though he realizes that its main characters, except for Elihu, are not Israelites (see on 1.1; 2.11; 32.2), he ascribes a 'small prophecy' to Eliphaz (comm. on 4.16) and full prophetic revelation to Job himself (comm. on 42.5).

> tion] is an attributive adjective, as in 'the Shimronite'. These two facts forced him to say as follows: first, that he found in Chronicles 'his son Beerah—whom King Tillegath Pilneser of Assyria exiled—was chieftain of the Reubenites' (1 Chron. 5.6), and he was the father of this prophet. Second, he glossed '[The Lord. . .] punished Jacob for his conduct' (Hos. 12.3) as applying to our father Jacob, who deprived Reuben of his birthright; but the meaning is not what he thought it was.
>
> Apparently he forgot what is written about Hosea son of Elah: 'He did what was displeasing to the Lord' (2 Kgs 17.2). The Yiṣḥaḳi said that he took a prostitute to wife, but he is blind and did not see the text: 'When the Lord first spoke to Hosea, the Lord said', so that he was not rebelling against God's word, which heaven forbid! Thus Hosea son of Be'eri is not Hosea son of Elah, just as Hanoch is the name of four different people in the Pentateuch, and [there are] Saul of Rehoboth-on-the-river and Saul son of the Canaanite and Saul son of Kish, and many others like this (comm. on Hosea 1.1).

In his gloss on Deut. 13.6, Ibn Ezra derives *sarah* from *sorer u-moreh* 'wayward and defiant'; hence when he uses the word in dismissing the identification of the prophet with the sinful king he is castigating Yiṣḥaḳi as speaking rebellious words that exceed the bounds of what is permissible from a theological point of view. After the denial of theological legitimacy comes a refutation of the philological basis. Evidently Yiṣḥaḳi held that Be'er and Elim are two names for the same place (like 'Bela' which is Zoar' [Gen. 14.2]), which have been combined into the compound name 'Beer-elim' (like 'Ḥamath Zobah'—2 Chron. 8.3, which combines Ḥamath [2 Kgs 14.28] and Zobah [1 Sam. 14.47]). Beer-elim was on the Moabite border east of the Jordan, as indicated by the reference to it in Isaiah's pronouncement of Moab (15.8); its location was in fact the cornerstone of Yiṣḥaḳi's argument, as will be seen below.

Disputing Yiṣḥaḳi's view of similar names as variations on the same name, Ibn Ezra argues that they are in fact distinct. His proof is that the names Ziph and Ziphah differ only by the addition of one letter, but their appearance side by side in a single verse proves that they refer to different persons. It seems, however, that Yiṣḥaḳi's method was that of consonantal substitution, subsequently developed by Ibn Janāḥ, who explained the two names of the king of Judah—Aviyah and Aviyam—as resulting from the interchange of the two consonants *heh* and *mem* (*Riḳmah*, p. 111), just as he attributed variations such as Hadar/Hadad, Dodanim/Rodanim, and Deuel/Reuel to the interchange of the consonants *daled* and *resh* (*Riḳmah*, p. 107). Hence on this question, too, it is Ibn Ezra rather than Yiṣḥaḳi who adopts the exceptional position, since, unlike Ibn Janāḥ, Ibn Ezra accepts the interchange only of the weak letters *alef, heh, waw*, and *yod*, the consonants *samekh* and *sin*, and to a limited extent, the consonants *mem, nun*, and *taw*.[1]

The identification of the son of Elah with the son of Be'eri rests on another erroneous assumption—namely, that the word *ben* can denote the relationship of a man to his city of residence. Ibn Ezra dismisses this possibility out of hand, contending that 'daughter of Zion' is no proof, because this expression refers to all the residents of Jerusalem and not to a single Jerusalemite (see his gloss on Isa. 47.1: 'daughter of—like community of').

According to Ibn Ezra, two factors propelled Yiṣḥaḳi to his far-fetched conclusion that prophet and king were one. The first is appropriate to his historical method and desire to uncover the biographical substance of biblical personages. Hence he is enthralled by the possibility of identifying the father of the king-prophet on the basis of the information in 1 Chron. 5.6 about B'erah son of Ba'al, prince of the tribe of Reuben, exiled by Tiglath Pileser III when he conquered Transjordania in 733–32 (roughly ten years before Hosea son of Elah was taken prisoner by Shalmaneser V, as recounted in 2 Kgs 17.4). The identification of Be'eri, father of the prophet, with Be'erah the Reubenite prince was not new with Yiṣḥaḳi; Ibn Ezra seems to have forgotten that its source is a midrash found in *Pesiḳta de-Rav Kahana*. According to this midrash, God rewarded Reuben for trying to return Joseph to his father Jacob by promising him:

> By your life, your descendant will return Israel to their Father in the heaven. And who is this? Hosea as is written 'the word of the Lord that came to Hosea son of Beeri', and it is also written 'his son Beerah' (1 Chron. 5.6). Why was he called Be'erah [and not Be'eri, as he is designated in the superscription to the book of Hosea]? Because he is the well-spring [*be'erah*] of the Torah.[2]

Yiṣḥaḳi viewed this midrash as stating the literal meaning (in this he was preceded by the Karaite exegete Yefet ben Ali [Arabic commen-

1. *Mozne Leshon Haqqodesh*, fol. 15a-16b; *Sefer Tsachoth*, fol. 24a.
2. *Pesikta de Rav Kahana* (ed. B. Mandelbaum; New York: Jewish Theological Seminary, 1962), II, pp. 356-57.

tary on Hos. 1.1], and later followed by Abarbanel in his commentary on Hos. 1.2). By supplementing the identification of Be'eri and Be'erah with that of Be'eri and Elah, he was led to the extremely far-fetched hypothesis that 'the son of Be'eri' means both 'a citizen of the town of Beer-elim' as well as 'the son of Be'eri the prince' (so called after his place of residence).

Yiṣḥaḳi's second motive, too, is historical—the chance to offer a political explanation of the prophet Hosea's statement (12.3-4) that the Lord is repaying our father Jacob for the sin of wrestling with his brother in their mother's womb and with the angel at Peniel. Ascribing the reproof to the king-prophet Hosea, son of Elah the Reubenite, leads to an analogical understanding of this passage: the injustice done by Jacob to his son Reuben by depriving him of his birthright is similar to that previously perpetrated on his older brother Esau and the name change he extorted by wrestling with the angel. Thus Yiṣḥaḳi took from the midrash only the identification of Be'eri with Be'erah, while rejecting both its theological assumptions and the positive image of the prophet and his father presented in it. Ibn Ezra merely asserts that this is not a reasonable interpretation of Hos. 12.3-4; in his commentary *ad loc.*, too, he feels no need to argue with Yiṣḥaḳi's idea that Hosea was fighting to defend the status of the tribe of Rueben.

The sins of Hosea son of Elah are not detailed in the book of Kings; Scripture even finds merit in him: 'He did what was displeasing to the Lord, though not as much as the kings of Israel who preceded him' (2 Kgs 17.2). Perhaps Yiṣḥaḳi grounded his rationalistic-historicist view of the prophet as a king prophesying so as to promote the limited interests of the royal house on the assumption that the sin of the last of the kings of Israel was not idolatry but rather taking a prostitute to wife. On this count Ibn Ezra censures Yiṣḥaḳi as 'blind', since Scripture states explicitly that Hosea married this woman in compliance with a divine command; hence clearly he did not do so this in obedience to his urges. This stubborn blindness to an explicit text is supplemented by Yiṣḥaḳi's obliviousness to the fact that Scripture is replete with different persons bearing the same name. Yiṣḥaḳi's bold innovations are totally groundless from both the philological and exegetical points of view, just as he had spoken 'waywardly' from a theological perspective. For a master of the *peshat* and firm believer like Ibn Ezra, the two are interlinked.

e. *The Identification of Hadar and his Wife Mehetabel with Hadad the Edomite and his Wife the Sister of Tahpanes*

> *Four generations.* Here the prater Yiṣḥaḳi erred when he said that a generation is 35 years. We see that from Adam to Noah there were ten generations, and also that Heman lived in the time of David, even though David was eleven generations after our father Jacob and Heman twice that (comm. on Job 42.16).

> *And these are the kings*: Some say that this section was written prophetically. But Yiṣḥaḳi wrote in his book that this section was written in the time of King Jehoshaphat and explained the generations as he wished. Rightly is he called Yiṣḥaḳi, for all who hear will laugh (*yiṣḥaḳ*) at him. He said that Hadar (v. 39) is the same as Hadad the Edomite (1 Kgs 11.14), and that Mehetabel is 'the sister of Tahpenes' (1 Kgs 11.20). But heaven forbid that it be as he said about the time of Jehoshaphat; his book should be burned! Why was he astonished that as many as eight kings reigned? There were twice as many kings of Israel, and the years of these kings are close to the years of the kings of Israel. There were also more kings of Judah than kings of Edom until the time of Moses. The truth is that 'before any king reigned' refers to Moses, king of Israel, as is written—'he was king in Jeshurun' (Deut. 33.5) (comm. on Gen. 36.32).

Yiṣḥaḳi's computation on the basis of the figures in Job 42.16 is correct in and of itself ($4 \times 35 = 140$). His error lies in his hasty conclusion that in Scripture the average length of a generation is 35 years. Ibn Ezra's first argument is that for the ten generations from Adam to Noah the average duration of a generation is four times higher ($1556 \div 10 = 155$, according to Gen. 5). His second argument is that in the lapse of time that saw 11 generations in the tribe of Judah (from Judah son of Jacob to David, according to Ruth 4.18-22), the tribe of Levi went through 22 generations (from Levi son of Jacob to Heman the musician, a contemporary of David, on the basis of 1 Chron. 6.18-23). At first sight it is surprising that Ibn Ezra invoked the antediluvian patriarchs, since their long lives explicitly exceeded those of all later people. It seems, however, that he referred to them because the dispute is not only chronological (the average duration of a generation) but also philological (the dictionary meaning of *dor* in biblical and talmudic language). As Ibn Ezra states in his commentary on Gen. 15.16:

> Most commentators have misinterpreted 'generation'. The Sages said 'ten generations' (*M. Avot* 5.2); we also find 'to the thousandth generation'

> (Deut. 7.9), and, in Job (42.16), 'four generations'. In my opinion *dor* should be understood to mean 'dwell'—'than dwell (*dur*) in the tents of the wicked' (Ps. 84.11; its duration is the time that a man dwells on earth, and some are short and some are long.

The words 'most commentators have misinterpreted' indicate that on this question, too, Yiṣḥaḳi's linguistic and thematic point of departure correspond to a common and broadly accepted opinion.

What is more, even though Ibn Ezra does not say so explicitly, it is extremely likely that Yiṣḥaḳi shared another common error, according to which there is astronomical support for the chronological index derived from Job 42.16 (one generation = 35 years on average). Ibn Ezra deals with this in his gloss on 'to the thousandth generation' (Deut. 7.9); because of variant readings there, however, it is not clear whether he is conducting an anonymous dispute with Yiṣḥaḳi or with the other scholars who, as we know, also held this opinion:[1] 'He [many MSS: they] erred who said that in 36,000 [years] the zodiac will return [to its original orientation], because it has been found [that it moves] one degree in seventy years. "Thousand" means "without end".' Unlike Ibn Ezra, who holds that here a thousand is a large number meaning forever (see also the short commentary on Exod. 20.6), the advocates of the other opinion believe that here thousand is to be understood literally and refers explicitly to the end of the world, when the covenant between God and his believers will lapse in any case. In their view the end of the universe is intrinsic in its structure, as can be demonstrated from an astronomical phenomenon about which Ibn Ezra is somewhat more forthcoming in his commentary on 'Therefore we are not afraid though the earth reels, though mountains topple into the sea' (Ps. 46.3): 'Because the zenith shifts from degree to degree and from constellation to constellation, the natural philosophers said that a time will come when the dry land will return to the sea and the sea to dry land'. R. Joseph ben Eliezer, who cites this statement of Ibn Ezra's in *Ṣafnat Pa'ne'aḥ* on Gen. 8.22, explains them as follows:

> Ptolemy made instruments and investigated the locations of the seven planets and the location of each of the stars in the eighth sphere, of which

1. See Saadiah Gaon, *The Book of Beliefs and Opinions* (trans. S. Rosenblatt: New Haven, 1948), 1, 3; Abraham bar Ḥiyya, *La obra Sefer Ḥešbon Maḥlekot ha-Koḵabim* (ed. J.M. Millás Vallicrosa; Barcelona, 1959), ch. 17, p. 101.

as is known there are 1022, and found that these stars are moving from west to east, one degree every hundred years. He said that in this way the zenith of the planets moves [. . .] A sphere has 360 degrees, so 360 times 100 is 36,000 years, after which time the sphere will return to its original state.

This computation of the end of the world (100 years × 360 degrees equals 36,000 years) is based on what is known today as the precession of the equinoxes, namely the earlier occurrence of the equinoxes in each successive sidereal year because of a slow retrograde motion of the equinoctial points along the ecliptic. The phenomenon was discovered by Hipparchus around 125 BCE; according to his computations, the rate of precession is one degree per century, and this value was accepted by Ptolemy (second century CE), the father of medieval astronomy. The Arab astronomers, however, disagreed with this computation, as Ibn Ezra explains in the *Letter of the Sabbath*: 'The argument is about the movement of the constellations of the zodiac; the ancients said that this motion is one degree per century, while the moderns say in 66 years, and some say in 70 years'.[1] In this controversy he opted for the view of the Arab astronomers[2] and was totally convinced that they were right. Hence he relied on the fact that 'it has been found [that it moves] one degree in seventy years' (comm. on Deut. 7.9, cited above; see also his commentary on Amos 5.8) to refute the impressive correlation between the (erroneous) astronomical computation and (erroneous) exegetical conclusion based on Job 42.16. For if the zodiac will return to its starting point after only 25,200 years (70 years × 360 degrees), one cannot derive from 'to the thousandth generation' that the average duration of a generation is 35–36 years (since 25,200 ÷ 1000 is 25).

Among all of those who misinterpreted the word *dor* 'generation', Ibn Ezra mentions only Yiṣḥaḳi and even tags him with the pejorative epithet 'the prater'. Even if he did so as part of his effort to undermine the man's authority as a reliable scriptural exegete, there must have been another more specific motive—namely, that Yiṣḥaḳi had used the chronological index derived from Job 42.16 in order to reach

1. *Letter of the Sabbath* (ed. M. Friedlaender), *Transactions of the Jewish Historical Society of England* 2 (1894–95), p. 65.

2. A. Ibn Ezra, *K^eli ha-N^eḥošeṯ* (ed. Z.H. Chen-Tob [Edelmann]; Koenigsberg, 1845), ch. 29, p. 31.

far-reaching conclusions concerning both the era of the Edomite kings enumerated in Gen. 36.31-39 and the date of composition of that section.

At the beginning of his commentary on Gen. 36.31, Ibn Ezra offers anonymously, and with no explicit reservations, the gloss found in *Gen. R.* 3.2 and in Rashi's commentary here, according to which Moses is listing prophetically the names of the Edomite kings and the places of their origin until the time of Saul, first king of Israel. At the end of his gloss, however, he confidently offers the explanation he prefers, namely, that the past tense of the passage (reigned, died) is not a prophetic but a true past, because 'before any king reigned over the Israelites' can refer to Moses (on the basis of 'there was a king in Jeshurun'), and thus the reference is to Edomite kings who had preceded him. Yiṣḥaḳi, too, rejected the prophetic interpretation; Ibn Ezra makes clear why he had not assumed that the Edomite kings preceded Moses: he 'explained the [duration of the] generations as he wished', that is, according to the chronological constraints imposed by his arbitrary understanding of the word 'generation'. If the average length of a generation is indeed 35 years, the eight kings of Edom reigned for 280 years; but according to the biblical chronology, only 200 years or so elapsed from the death of Esau until the Exodus from Egypt. Hence Yiṣḥaḳi offers his own original solution, based on his method of identifying bearers of similar names: the last of the kings of Edom, here called Hadar (and, in 1 Chron. 1.50, Hadad [!]). is the same as Hadad the Edomite who fled to Egypt when Edom was conquered in the time of David. Yiṣḥaḳi found support for this identification, which from a purely phonetic point of view agrees with Ibn Janāḥ's theory of consonantal substitution (*Riḳmah*, p. 107), in the fact that of all the kings of Edom only Hadar's wife is mentioned, namely 'Mehetabel daughter of Matred daughter of Mei Zahav' (Gen. 36.39)—an impressive name most appropriate to the otherwise anonymous sister of Queen Tahpenes given in marriage to Hadad the Edomite. This identification requires that we not understand 'before there reigned a king of the Israelites' in the sense of 'before the reign of the [first] Israelite king' (i.e. Saul), but in a totally different sense—'before there reigned [in Edom] an Israelite king', i.e. David, as we read in 2 Sam. 8.14: 'He stationed garrisons in Edom—in all of Edom he stationed garrisons—and all the Edomites become vassals of David'.

If this is the case, however, why did Yiṣḥaḳi not date the list of Edomite kings to the era of David or Solomon instead of to the reign of Jehoshaphat? Evidently he was impressed by the similarity between the language in Genesis (as he understood it to refer to an Israelite king in Edom) and what is recorded about the time of Jehoshaphat—'There was no king in Edom; a viceroy acted as king' (1 Kgs 22.48)—and even more so from the fact that in the time of Jehoshaphat the Judean viceroy was in fact called 'the king of Edom' (2 Kgs 3.9). By Yiṣḥaḳi's method, the roster of kings could be dated any time between David, who put an end to the Edomite kingdom, and Jehoshaphat, but not later, since during the reign of his son Joram 'the Edomites rebelled against Judah's rule and set up a king of their own' (2 Kgs 8.20). If Yiṣḥaḳi preferred to date its composition to the lower bound of that period, perhaps it was a stylistic element that carried the day for him—namely, the fact that the list does not speak of a viceroy, as under David, but of a king, as in the time of Jehoshaphat.

Ibn Ezra does not refute the identification, but ridicules it by a scornful pun on Yiṣḥaḳi's name. After rejecting the religious legitimacy of ascribing this passage to a later date, he takes the trouble to undermine the chronological basis upon which Yiṣḥaḳi founded the identification and late-dating. Ibn Ezra offers two decisive proofs against Yiṣḥaḳi's method: according to the figures in 2 Kings, the total regnal years of the 16 kings of Israel from Jeroboam son of Nebat until Hosea son of Elah (omitted from this reckoning are three kings who reigned for less than a year—Zimri, Zechariah and Shallum) add up to 241 years; hence there is no difficulty in assuming that eight kings ruled in Edom in the only 200 years that elapsed from the death of Esau until the time of Moses. What is more, in those same 241 years no fewer than 13 kings (Rehoboam to Hezekiah) reigned in Judah.

The rejection on principle of Yiṣḥaḳi's interpretation, summarized by 'his book should be burned', is most astonishing when we hear it from Ibn Ezra. The problem presented with great clarity by R. Joseph be Eliezer, who also tried to answer it:

> In my opinion he said this because, if it was written in the time of Jehoshaphat, an entire section was added to the Pentateuch, and the Torah said 'you shall not add anything' (Deut. 4.2). Someone might argue that R. Abraham himself hinted, at the beginning of the book of Deuteronomy (1.2), that later prophets added words and even verses to the Pentateuch!

> The answer is that adding a word or verse to explain what Moses wrote, for the sake of additional clarity, is not the same as adding an entire section; a word or a verse is a commentary, but an entire section is an addition (*Ṣaf*ᵉ*nat Pa'ne'aḥ* on Gen. 36.31).

But this distinction does not stand up to scrutiny. The 'mystery of the twelve' on which Ibn Ezra bases his commentary on Deut. 1.2, when he wishes to ascribe a later date to Deut. 1.1-5, refers to the last 12 verses of the Pentateuch (as is proven by *Ṣaf*ᵉ*nat Pa'ne'aḥ ad loc.*), which Ibn Ezra holds were written 'prophetically' by Joshua (see his commentary on Deut. 34.1 and 6). It is difficult to accept that the 13 verses of the list of Edomite kings are an entire section but the 12 verses full of information on the death of Moses are merely commentary. The same applies to Num. 21.1-3, about which Ibn Ezra writes: 'Many said that Joshua wrote this section, and their proof is "king of Arad, one" (Josh. 12.14), and also that the Judahites called the place Ḥormah (see Judg. 1.17), but their claim is groundless'. He goes on to demonstrate why 'their claim is groundless' and offers an alternative explanation, but does not argue that assigning a post-Mosaic date to the composition of 'this section' is invalid in principle.

Another way to resolve the contradiction between what Ibn Ezra allowed himself but forbade Yiṣḥaḳi is to assume that he is not being totally candid when he says 'his book should be burned'. The leading advocate of this method is Samuel David Luzatto, who wrote to Joseph Samuel Reggio as follows:

> If we turn to the other side, and investigate Abraham Ibn Ezra with regard to his understanding and honesty, what shall we say when we see his deviousness to make himself pious in the eyes of his readers, saying, 'see how pure I am', when he somersaults in his schemes, while his thoughts contradict his words.[1]

Luzatto finds this lack of candor in three areas: (1) in his vigorous attacks on the Karaites, intended merely to cover over his clandestine agreement with many of their opinions; (2) in his pronouncements that one must interpret the text in accordance with the cantillation signs, despite his many glosses in which he deviates from the syntax they indicate; (3) his repeated rejection, on theological grounds, of the method of lexical substitution, while he himself claimed (albeit allusively) that there are passages in the Pentateuch that were added

1. *Kerem Ḥemed* 4 (1839), letter 20, pp. 135-36.

several generations later and that half the prophesies of Isaiah were written in the Babylonian exile. Solomon Judah Rappaport and Joseph Samuel Reggio came to Ibn Ezra's defense against this weighty charge in their letters to Luzatto;[1] I too have been persuaded of his sincerity in his disputes with the Karaites[2] and his insistence on adherence to the cantillation signs.[3] Why, then, will he not allow Yiṣḥaḳi to do with regard to Gen. 36.31-39 what he himself does with regard to certain sections in the Pentateuch and the second half of the book of Isaiah?

2. *Yiṣḥaḳi: A Pretentious but Unqualified Peshat Commentator*

The philological *peshat* must be sharply distinguished from the homiletic *derash*, but must also be defended against the pretentious *peshat* and its misinterpretations. *Peshat* and *derash* are differentiated in principle and by definition, but incorrect and deceptive *peshat* must be refuted *ad hoc*, because it stems from the faulty application of the method. Ibn Ezra does this whenever he rejects a gloss that seems wrong to him, and with greater force and vigor when, in his opinion, the gloss evidences a fundamental lack of understanding. A fine example of this is what he has to say about the sons of Haman in the second recension of Esth. 9.7:

> *And Parshandata*—There was a commentator in Spain who glossed Parshandata as a commentator [*paršan*] on the law [*dat*]; but this is nonsense, because the name in Persian. [. . .] Similarly he said that Aridata is the lion [*ari*] of the law [*dat*]. What would he say about Parmashta and the others?

In the standard commentary *ad loc.* he attributes this opinion—which, judging by its exegetical merits and philological level could have come from the pen of Yiṣḥaḳi—to 'Spanish scholars'; as we have seen, there were many others who shared Yiṣḥaḳi's views. The methods he applied were widespread and accepted. Even if some of his

1. S.J. Rappaport, *Iggerot* (Przemysl, 1885), letter 1, pp. 4-7; letter 2, pp. 19-20, 22-26; letter 3, p. 51; *Kerem Ḥemed* 4 (1839), letter 21, pp. 147-54.

2. U. Simon, 'The Exegetic Method of A. Ibn Ezra, as Revealed in Three Interpretations of One Biblical Passage' (Hebrew), *Bar Ilan* 3 (1965), pp. 100-11.

3. U. Simon, 'Ibn Ezra and Kimḥi: Two Approaches to the Masoretic Text' (Hebrew), *Bar Ilan* 6 (1968), pp. 224-26.

conclusions were extremely far-fetched and out of the mainstream, it seems that Ibn Ezra attacked him chiefly as the outstanding representative of amateur *peshat*, which must be castigated lest the seeming cover up the genuine. In this vein Ibn Ezra demurs sharply at an erroneous gloss on 'thigh muscle' (Gen. 32.33), which combines philological and anatomical ignorance:

> *Gid ha-našeh*—The well-known meaning [viz., the femoral tendon or sciatic nerve] is in accordance with the tradition of our Sages; none doubt this except those lacking in knowledge of the language and of nature [reading with MS Cambridge 46 and MS Paris 176], who explain that it is the male organ and gloss *našeh* as derived from *našim* [women].

Unless his target here is a Karaite opinion, those lacking in knowledge of language and nature can only be the plain-meaning commentators who follow the method of Yiṣḥaḳi and dare to question the Talmudic tradition on the basis of preposterous arguments.

The damage caused by false learning is great. Because the public at large lacks the tools to distinguish it from genuine knowledge, Ibn Ezra sees himself duty-bound to correct such errors and to ridicule the deceiver. This is his aim when he says of Yiṣḥaḳi that 'all who hear will laugh at him', and also when he attacks pseudo-scholars in his other field of expertise, astronomy and the Hebrew calendar. After exposing the erroneous calculations of 'those who are wise in their own eyes' and the damage caused among the Christians by their false astronomical predictions, he concludes:

> I have gone on at length because one of the learned men of our generation asked me to explain [intercalation] to him on one foot and got angry at me when I remained silent. I gave him good counsel, namely, that he should fast and humbly entreat the omnipotent God to create for him a pure heart and endow him with a new spirit, to pour on him a spirit of wisdom, until he knows all the sciences by himself, without spending years in study—something He has not done for any human being since He created man on earth. Perhaps the Lord will hear his prayer and create for him this great wonder and miracle—to be second to Balaam's ass.[1]

Hence we should not be surprised that Ibn Ezra would not allow an unqualified commentator to do what he himself did. Yiṣḥaḳi's book should be burned not because it ascribes post-Mosaic authorship to one section of the Pentateuch, but because the hypothesis was offered with

1. *Letter of the Sabbath*, ch. 2, pp. 71-72.

philological and also apparently theological recklessness. Whereas Ibn Ezra merely hinted, in terms comprehensible only to the erudite, at the possibility of post-Mosaic authorship in cases of genuine exegetical imperatives, while stressing that such additions, too, are of divine inspiration, Yiṣḥaḳi offered such a solution to what Ibn Ezra viewed as a non-existent difficulty and proposed far-fetched identifications on the basis of philological, historical and chronological arguments that Ibn Ezra considered weak. Hence he is merely a prater, and 'all who hear will laugh at him'.

FRAGMENTS OF A PSALMS SCROLL FROM MASADA, MPS^{b} (MASADA 1103–1742)

Shemaryahu Talmon

The excavation of Masada, led by the late Yigael Yadin, yielded a considerable number of inscribed materials, among them remains of 16 documents written in the square Hebrew alphabet, and one papyrus fragment penned in ancient Hebrew characters. Yadin published in full the extant fragments of a Ben-Sira Scroll,[1] and a fragment of the שירות עולות השבת,[2] a composition which was already known from finds in the Qumran Caves.[3]

Six additional items, some quite extensive, stem from copies of biblical books: Leviticus, Psalms (two scrolls each), Deuteronomy and Ezekiel. Seven other small pieces which evidently come from non-biblical compositions cannot be confidently identified.[4] Yadin recorded them in his excavation report,[5] but it was not given him to publish them in full. Their publication was entrusted to me within the framework of the comprehensive edition of the Masada discoveries.[6]

1. Y. Yadin, *The Ben Sira Scroll from Masada* (Jerusalem: IEJ and the Shrine of the Book, 1965).

2. C. Newsom and Y. Yadin, 'The Masada Fragment of the Qumran Songs of the Sabbath Sacrifice', *IEJ* 34 (1984), pp. 77-88.

3. J. Strugnell, 'The Angelic Liturgy at Qumran—4QSerek Širot 'Olat Haššabbat', *VTSup* 7 (1960), pp. 318-45; and C. Newsom, *Songs of the Sabbath Sacrifice: A Critical Edition* (Atlanta, GA: Scholars Press, 1985).

4. Most recently, another unnumbered sliver of parchment turned up which measures 5.6 × 2.4 cm. It contains a few letters in three partial lines.

5. Y. Yadin, 'The Excavation of Masada 1963–64', *IEJ* 15 (1965), pp. 79-82; 103-105 = 'מצדה', *Yedict* 29 (1965), pp. 115-17.

6. For a preliminary publication of the non-biblical items, with the exception of the above mentioned piece which was brought only recently to my attention, see: S. Talmon, 'קטעי כתבים כתובים עבריה ממצדה', *Eretz-Israel* 20 (1989), pp. 278-86; 'קטע ממגילה חיצונית לספר יהושע ממצדה', in *Shai le-Ḥayyim Rabin: Asufat Meḥqere*

In the present study I discuss a small fragment of a Psalms scroll which contains almost the full text of Psalm 150 and will be designated MPs^{b}.[1] Yadin did not mention this item in his initial report,[2] although in a paper read at the annual meeting of the Israel Exploration Society in 1966, he referred in passing to 'fragments of Psalms'.[3] He then explicitly mentioned the document under review in the entry 'Masada' in the *Encyclopedia of Archaeological Excavations in the Holy Land*:[4]

> a small fragment discovered in casemate 1103, north of the Snake Gate Path. The scroll [lege: fragment] contains nearly the entire Psalm 150, and is also identical with the Masoretic Text. The blank space to the left of the text shows that it was the last Psalm on the parchment, corresponding to the Masoretic Text and (was) unlike the Septuagint and Psalms Scroll from Qumran.[5]

Description

MPs^{b} consists of two small pieces of parchment of a light-brown hue, (a) and (b), which could be comfortably fitted together, although at the joint one line is presumably missing.

Each fragment contains four largely preserved lines of text. With the blank spaces at their tops frag. (a) is 2.5 cm high and 4.5 cm long. while frag. (b) measures 2.0 × 7.5 cm. Taking into account the missing first line, which held only the superscription הללויה, Psalm 150 would have taken up about 5 cm of the height of the last column of the scroll.

Lashon li-Khevodo bi-melot lo Shiv'im we-Hamesh (ed. M. Goshen-Gottstein, S. Morag and S. Kogut; Jerusalem: Academon Press, 1990), pp. 147-57.

1. The siglum MPs^{a} has been reserved for the fragments of a larger Psalms scroll from Masada (1107-1742) which in Yadin's report (ibid. 103-104) is said to contain Pss. 81.6–85.10. This should be corrected to Pss. 81.3 (or possibly 81.2)–85.6. See for the present G.W. Nebe, 'Die Masada-Psalmen-Handschrift M1039-160 nach einem jüngst veröffentlichten Photo mit Text von *Psalm* 81.2–85.6', *RevQ* 53 (1989), pp. 89-97 (with bibliographical information).

2. See above, p. 318 n. 5.

3. 'קומראן ומצדה', *Yediot* 30 (1966), p. 126.

4. Ed. M. Avi-Yonah; Jerusalem: Masada, 1975, II, pp. 811-12.

5. The reference is evidently to 11QPs^{a}, edited by J.A. Sanders, *The Psalms Scroll of Qumrân Cave 11* (11QPs^{a}) (DJD, IV; Oxford: Clarendon Press, 1965).

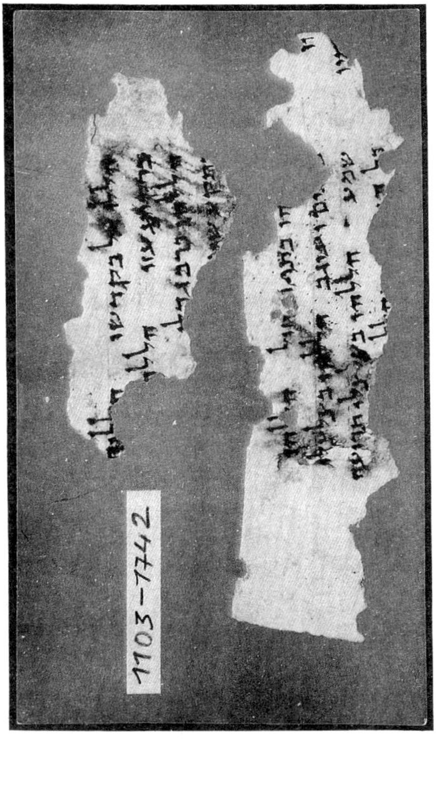

Fragments of a Psalms Scroll from Masada, MPs[b]

The written lines are 3.8–4 cm wide. Where fully preserved, the right-hand margin amounts to 0.9–1.1 cm. The blank width of leather to the left of the written column is considerably broader, measuring 1.9–2.1 cm. The rugged edges of frag. (a), all round, as well as the right-hand and lower edges of frag. (b), were evidently caused by the decomposition of the material, whereas the straight upper and left-hand edges of frag. (b) possibly resulted from breakage of the dry parchment or from willful tearing.[1] But the evenness of the left-hand edge of the partly preserved sheet, which may have contained four or five columns of text, could possibly be explained by assuming that originally another length of parchment had been stitched on to it, serving as the handle sheet of the scroll.[2] Some faint traces of needle holes can yet be discerned.

There are no vertical dry rulings. Horizontal dry rulings, 0.4 cm apart, run through the right-hand margin into the preceding column but end at the left-hand side of the last column. This seems to imply that the resulting blank stretch of parchment was in fact part of the handle sheet.

The expertly executed, regular lettering evinces the hand of a trained scribe. The letters are consistently 1.5 mm high, with the exception of ל which measures 0.4 cm, and equally broad, except for the 1.0 mm 'thin' letters ו, ז, י. All letters hang from below the line, as was the custom, with only the heads of ל protruding above the line.

The fully extant penultimate line, l. 9 of the restored text, and the preceding line, l. 8, of which the first letter—ב of במנים—is partly preserved, together with almost all remaining letters including the last, help in determining that, as said, the width of the written column was 3.8–4 cm. The restored l. 5 in which I count 16 letters or 18 spaces would be the shortest line of the extant text if, as is suggested,[3] the word בכנור was written in the presumably missing l. 6 at the joint of (a) and (b). But if בכנור was the last word in l. 5, this line would be the longest, holding 21 letters or 25 spaces.

1. A comparable situation obtains with regard to the Masada fragment 1063–1747. See Talmon, 'קטעי כתבים', pp. 279-280.

2. This is clearly the case with the fragment of a Deuteronomy scroll from Masada (MDeut, 1043/1-4).

3. See below.

Date

The fall of Masada in 73 CE provides the definite *terminus ante quem* for the dating of MPs^b, as for all other documents discovered there. The actual date can be further lowered since there is no reason to assume that the scroll was written at Masada. Rather, it can be postulated that it was in the possession of a fugitive who fled to the fortress before the Roman army effectively cut it off from the hinterland, or that it was brought to the site at an even earlier date which, however, cannot be historically determined.

Epigraphical data suggest that MPs^b was written in the last half-century BCE. In terms of the developments of the Jewish scripts charted by F.M. Cross,[1] the script of MPs^b can be defined as 'late Hasmonaean or early Herodian' (c. 50–25 BCE), especially on the strength of the letters ג, ל, פ, צ, ק, ש.[2] However, its identification as an 'early Herodian formal script' (c. 30–1 BCE) cannot be ruled out.[3]

The Text

As said, the conjoined fragments (a) and (b) contain practically the entire text of Psalm 150. In addition, beyond the right-hand margin at ll. 8 and 9, the letters חו and קיו of the corresponding line endings of the preceding column are still visible. They can be identified as the remains of the words רוחו and ח]קיו in Psalm 147 vv. 18 and 19.[4]

1 [הלליה]
2 הללו אל בקדשו הללוה[ו]
3 ברקיע עזו הללה[ו בגברתיו]
4 הללהו ברב גדלו [הללהו]
5 בתקע שפר [הללהו בנבל]
6 [וכנור]

1. See F.M. Cross, 'The Development of the Jewish Scripts', in *The Bible and the Ancient Near East. Essays in Honor of W.F. Albright* (ed. G.E. Wright; Garden City, NY: Doubleday, 1961), pp. 133-202.

2. Cross, 'Development', p. 138, chart no. 3.

3. Cross, 'Development', chart no. 4.

4. As will be shown, these two line-endings beyond the right-hand margin of the last column enable us to restore conjecturally the entire preceding column which presumably held Psalms 147 and 148. In consequence, the upper part of the last column must have contained Psalm 149 above Psalm 150.

[הלל]הו בתף ו[מ]חול הללהו	7	
ב[מ]נים ועוגב הללהו בצלצלי	8	[רו]חו
שמע הללהו בצלצלי תרועה	9	ח]קיו
כל ה[נשמה ת]הלל [יה הללויה]	10	

The preserved text of Psalm 150 is identical with the MT except for one recurrent spelling variant: whereas the MT exhibits consistently the plene spelling הללוהו[1] as does 11QPs^{a},[2] MPs^{b} has the defective spelling הללהו. Only in l. 2 the barely discernible head of a ו between ל and ה suggests the reading הללוהו. On the other hand, MPs^{b} exhibits the plene spelling עוגב (l. 9), like 11QPs^{a},[3] herein concurring with a branch of the MT tradition, represented by L (see BHS), whereas another branch, represented by A, preserves the defective spelling עגב.[4]

More important, MPs^{b} agrees with MT and the ancient Vss against two variant readings in 11QPs^{a}: MT 150.3 = MPs^{b} l. 5 and Vss—בתקע שופר, 11QPs^{a}—בתקוע; 150.6 MT = MPs^{b} l. 10 and Vss—כל הנשמה (sing.), 11QPs^{a}—כל הנשמות (pl.). These variants underscore both the close affinity of MPs^{b} with MT and its textual divergence from the practically contemporaneous Qumran scroll (11QPs^{a}).[5]

Text Division

MT accentuates the poetic structure of Psalm 150 by arranging the text in hemistichs,[6] alternatively closed by the mid-sentence divider *'etnaḥ* or the sentence divider *pāsēq*. This structure, termed לבנה על גבי לבנה by the Masoretes,[7] is reproduced in BH(S) from L. It is even more pronounced in A where, however, in v. 5 the narrow blank space

1. Both L(eningrad) and A(leppo). Ginsburg does not register any variants.
2. See 11QPs^{a} pl. XVI, Sanders, *Psalms Scroll*, p. 47.
3. See Sanders, *Psalms Scroll*.
4. Ginsburg reads עגב in his text, but records that other mss have the plene spelling עוגב: ס"א ועוגב מלא.
5. See below.
6. The oldest example of the stichic arrangement of a poetic text is an Aramaic funeral inscription of unknown provenance from the 5th or 4th century BCE. See H. Donner and W. Röllig, *Kanaanäische und Aramäische Inschriften* (Wiesbaden: Harrassowitz, 1966–1969), nr. 269; J.C.L. Gibson, *Textbook of Syrian Semitic Inscriptions*. II. *Aramaic Inscriptions* (Oxford: Clarendon Press, 1975), nr. 24.
7. 'One brick atop the other.'

between the hemistichs is effectively closed because of the especially large number of letters which had to be accommodated in this line.

The scribe of MPs[b] wrote the text continuously, viz not as לבנה על נבי לבנה. But he highlighted the poetic structure by leaving a blank space of two or three letters where the MT marks an *'etnah* or a *pāsēq*. Thus, like some Pentateuch and Psalms fragments from Qumran, MPs[b] attests to the antiquity of the Masoretic punctuation and cantillation tradition whose roots are shown to reach down into the Second Temple period.

The mostly empty line at the joint of frags. (a) and (b), between ll. 6 and 7 (vv. 3 and 4), which presumably contained only the word וכנור at its beginning,[1] effectively divides the psalm into two strophes. The exceptionally large blank appears to equal a *pārāšāh petûḥāh* in the Masoretic system of text divisions.[2] However, no such subdivision of Psalm 150 is preserved in the main MT witnesses.

In this context it is worth pointing out that 11QPs[a] does not exhibit either the strophic division of MPs[b] or the poetic arrangement in hemistichs which is even more accentuated in the columnar structure of MT.[3] These prominent scribal features were possibly applied only in copies of biblical writings, especially of the book of Psalms. Their absence from 11QPs[a] may therefore buttress the proposition that that MS is a copy of an extra-biblical compilation of songs which the Qumran Covenanters used in their prayer service,[4] rather than a copy of the biblical book of Psalms, as proposed by its editor.[5]

Reconstituting the Last Two Columns of MPs[b]

In view of the fact that the text of Psalm 150 and MPs[b] is to all intents and purposes identical with MT, it may be presumed that this was the

1. See above.
2. See J.M. Oesch, *Petucha und Setuma* (ObO, 27; Göttingen: Vandenhoeck & Ruprecht, 1979), pp. 290, 321ff.
3. Similarly, Psalm 136 is written in 11QPs[a] as a running text, whereas MT (L and A) presents it in the columnar arrangement.
4. See M.H. Goshen-Gottstein, 'The Psalms Scroll (11QPs[a])—A Problem of Canon and Text', *Textus* 5 (1966), pp. 22-23; S. Talmon, 'Pisqah Be'emṣa 'Pasuq and 11QPs[a]', ibid. 11-21 = *idem*, 'Extra-Canonical Hebrew Psalms from Qumran—Psalm 151', *WQW*, pp. 244-272.
5. See Sanders, *Psalms Scroll*.

case with the entire book of Psalms. Therefore, the preserved end-letters of two lines beyond the right-hand margin of the last column which contains Psalm 150, provide the basis for proposing a tentative reconstruction not only of this column but also of the preceding one.

In the space between the words רו]חו and חק]יו which can be restored beyond the margin opposite ll. 8-9 of our fragment, the text יזלו מים מגיד דבריו ליעקב (Ps. 147.18-19) must be inserted. From here it follows that the line in the penultimate column which ended with חק]יו contained 24 letters or 29 spaces. The three letters קיו protrude into the margin beyond רו]חו, the last word in the preceding line which therefore may possibly have been one or two spaces shorter. In any case, we cannot be far off the mark in assuming that a line in the penultimate column, in which Psalms 147 and 148 must be accommodated, contained on the average 27-28 spaces, allowing for a vacillation between 25-30 spaces per line. Thus the lines in this as presumably in all preceding columns were a fraction longer than the lines in the last column. The difference was probably caused by the hemistich structure of Psalm 150 which imposed upon the scribe a shorter line-length. In the obviously conjectural reconstruction of the last two columns of MPs[b] proposed below, ll. 8 and 9 of Psalm 150 correspond to ll. 22 and 23 of Psalm 147, while l. 24, the last but one line of Psalm 147 corresponds to the closing lines of Psalm 150. It follows that the bottom part of the last column was left blank; this indicates that the text of the scroll indeed ended here.

We can thus establish that the portion of text of Psalm 147 which preceded the short section demarcated by the words רו]חו and חק]יו (vv. 18-19), took up 22 lines at the top of the penultimate column. This section, together with the last clause of v. 19, ומשפטיו לישראל, and v. 20 of Psalm 147, extended over four lines. On the strength of these calculations I conclude that the bottom part of the column was taken up by the text of Psalm 148 which presumably filled 20 lines. It follows that the penultimate column of MPs[b] contained altogether 44 lines[1] which was probably the standard column format of the scroll.[2] The upper part of the last column, above the 10 lines of Psalm 150, held 14 lines of the text of Psalm 149. As a result, Psalms 149 and 150

1. Unless a blank line separated one psalm from the other. If that was the case, the column would have held 45 lines.

2. With the exception of the last column which, as said, was evidently shorter.

combined took up 24 lines, exactly paralleling the 24 lines of Psalm 147 in the upper part of the preceding column, with the last line of that psalm being written opposite the top of the blank portion of the last column.

The height of the scroll can be assessed by the following considerations. As said, the ten lines of the text of Psalm 150 cover approximately 5 cm. Therefore the 44 (or 45) lines of a fully written-out column would measure about 22-23 cm. With top and bottom margins of about 1.5 cm each, MPs[b] would have stood to a height of about 25-26 cm which was presumably a standard measure.[1]

The Reconstituted Text[2]

1 הללו יה
2 כי טוב זמרה אלהינו כי נעים נאוה
3 תהלה בונה ירושלם יהוה נדחי
4 ישראל יכנס הרפא לשבורי לב ומחבש
5 לעצבותם מונה מספר לכוכבים לכלם
6 שמות יקרא גדול אדונינו ורב כח
7 לתבונתו אין מספר מעודד ענוים יהוה
8 משפיל רשעים עדי ארץ ענו ליהוה
9 בתודה זמרו לאלהינו בכנור המכסה
10 שמים בעבים המכין לארץ מטר
11 המצמיח הרים חציר נותן לבהמה לחמה
12 לבני ערב אשר יקראו לא בגבורת
13 הסוס יחפץ לא בשוקי האיש ירצה
14 רוצה יהוה את יראיו את המיחלים
15 לחסדו שבחי ירושלם את יהוה
16 הללי אלהיך ציון כי חזק בריחי
17 שעריך ברך בניך בקרבך השם גבולך
18 שלום חלב חטים ישביעך השלח
19 אמרתו ארץ עד מהרה ירוץ דברו
20 הנתן שלג כצמר כפור כאפר יפזר
21 משליך קרחו כפתים לפני קרתו מי
22 יעמד ישלח דברו וימסם ישב רוחו

הללו יה
שירו ליהוה שיר חדש תהלתו בקהל
חסידים ישמח ישראל בעשיו
בני ציון יגילו במלכם יהללו שמו
במחול בתף וכנור יזמרו לו כי
רוצה יהוה בעמו יפאר ענוים
בישועה יעלזו חסידים בכבוד
ירננו על משכבותם רוממות אל
בגרונם וחרב פיפיות בידם לעשות
נקמה בגוים תוכחת בל אמים
לאסר מלכיהם בזקים ונכבדיהם
בכבלי ברזל לעשות בהם
משפט כתוב הדר הוא לכל
חסידיו הללו יה
הללו יה
הללו אל בקדשו הללוהו
ברקיע עזו הללהו בגבנרתיו
הללהו כרב גדלו הללהו
בתקע שופר הללהו בנבל
וכנור
הללהו **בתף ומחול הללהו**
במנים ועוגב הללוהו
בצלצלי

1. The other Psalms scroll from Masada (MPs[a] 1039-160) stands to a height of 25.5 cm. The height of several Qumran scrolls is in that very same range.

2. My thanks go to Galen Marquis for assistance in setting up the reconstructed text and for some stylistic improvements.

23 יזלו מים מגיד דברו ליעקב חקיו
24 ומשפטיו לישראל לא עשה כן לכל
25 גוי ומשפטים בל ידעום הללו יה
26 הללו יה
27 הללו את יהוה מן השמים הללהו
28 במרומים הללהו כל מלאכיו
29 הללהו כל צבאיו הללהו שמש וירח
30 הללהו כל כוכבי אור הללהו
31 שמי השמים והמים אשר מעל השמים
32 יהללו את שם יהוה כי הוא צוה
33 ונבראו ויעמידם לעד לעולם חק נתן
34 ולא יעבור הללו את יהוה מן הארץ
35 תנינים וכל תהמות אש וברד שלג
36 וקיטור רוח סערה עשה דברו ההרים
37 וכל גבעות עץ פרי וכל ארזים החיה
38 וכל בהמה רמש וצפור כנף מלכי ארץ
39 וכל לאמים שרים וכל שפטי ארץ
40 בחורים וגם בתולות זקנים עם נערים
41 יהללו את שם יהוה כי נשגב שמו
42 לבדו הודו על ארץ ושמים וירם קרן
43 לעמו תהלה לכל חסידיו לבני
44 ישראל עם קרבו הללו יה

שמע הללוהו בצלצלי תרועה
כל הנשמה תהלל יה הללו יה

A TALMUDIC PARALLEL TO THE PETITION FROM YAVNEH-YAM

Jeffrey H. Tigay

My friendship with Nahum Sarna spans thirty years, from the time I was his student at the Jewish Theological Seminary through our recent collaboration on the *JPS Torah Commentary*. It was my good fortune to meet him in a setting where I was able to learn from his personal qualities no less than his scholarly ones. It is a privilege for me to acknowledge his friendship and scholarly inspiration and to join in this expression of esteem and good wishes.

In the Hebrew letter from Yavneh-Yam, near Kibbutz Palmahim, published by Joseph Naveh in 1960,[1] the petitioner complains to an official that although he had finished his work properly, his garment was seized by his superior, one Hashabiahu b. Shobai. Naveh and subsequent writers on the inscription have explained the seizure in the light of passages in the Bible which refer to the distraint of garments for non-payment of debts. According to Naveh, the petitioner was 'one of many reapers who were apparently working in the governor's

1. J. Naveh, 'A Hebrew Letter from the Seventh Century BC', *IEJ* 10 (1960), pp. 129-39 (= *KAI* 200; *ANET*, p. 568). The most recent (grammatical) study of the inscription is M. Weippert, 'Die Petition eines Erntarbeiters aus Mesad Hashavyahu und die Syntax althebräischer erzahlender Prosa', in E. Blum *et al.*, *Die Hebräische Bibel und ihre zweifache Nachgeschichte (Festschrift. . . Rendtorff)* (Neukirchen–Vluyn: Neukirchener Verlag, 1990), pp. 449-66. For bibliography see D. Pardee *et al.*, *Handbook of Ancient Hebrew Letters* (SBLSBS, 15; Chico, CA: Scholars Press, 1982), pp. 16-20; R.W. Suder, *Hebrew Inscriptions. A Classified Bibliography* (Selinsgrove: Susquehanna University Press, 1984), pp. 62-63; Weippert, 'Petition', p. 458 n. 19. I am grateful to Jonas C. Greenfield for the reference to Weippert's article and for several helpful suggestions about the present study.

service. It seems that the charge was one of idling. . . '[1] F.M. Cross, on the other hand, argued that the petitioner was more likely a small farmer or sharecropper who owed the military establishment part of his crop. Cross reasoned that

> if [the petitioner] were merely a conscripted laborer, or hireling, it is difficult to see why a pledge was taken; other forms of retaliation, non-payment of wages, corporal punishment or confinement, or an increased work load, would appear more appropriate.[2]

J. Milgrom held that the petitioner was a defaulting debtor whose creditor had pursued him into the field to distrain his garment. Milgrom reasoned,

> That Hosaiah was in fact a creditor may be inferred from the plaintiff's plea that even if he is not innocent (of Hosaiah's claim) the garment should be returned. . . an expectancy that is plausible only in the light of the pentateuchal law of distraint, Exod. 22.25-26. Indeed, if the complainant were not a debtor what would lead him to expect the return of the garment?[3]

Like Milgrom, Naveh and Cross also accommodated their views to the biblical laws. To Naveh, 'it seems likely that the debt in this case was simply [the petitioner's] quota of work'. To Cross, on the other hand, 'the taking of the garment implies the claim of a creditor', that is, one owed a material obligation and not merely a labor quota.

The biblical laws about the seizure of garments are certainly pertinent to the inscription. Creditors in at least some cases had a right to take property from their debtors to induce them to repay their debts. So far as is known, in Israel pledges were neither taken nor specified at the time of the loan. Rather, the lender had a lien on the debtor's possessions. If the debtor defaulted, the creditor would receive or distrain (Heb. חבל, עבט)[4] some of his property, choosing what to take

1. Naveh, 'Hebrew Letter', p. 135; cf. A. Lemaire, *Inscriptions Hébraïques*. I. *Les Ostraca* (Paris: Cerf, 1977), pp. 264, 267-68.

2. F.M. Cross, 'Epigraphic Notes on Hebrew Documents of the Eighth–Sixth Centuries BC: II. The Murabba^{c}at Papyrus and the Letter Found Near Yabneh-Yam', *BASOR* 165 (1962), p. 46.

3. J. Milgrom, *Cult and Conscience* (Leiden: Brill, 1976), p. 96 n. 349.

4. Rashi, Exod. 22.25; Loewenstamm, ?ערב = עבט, *Leš* 25 (1960–61), pp. 111-14; Milgrom, *Cult and Conscience*, pp. 95-98, 102-104.

either in agreement with the debtor or at his own discretion.[1] Since the property seized was sometimes of little value to the creditor (according to the Torah, the creditor could not even sleep in a seized night-garment but had to return it to the debtor every night!), its function was evidently not to satisfy the debt but to pressure the creditor to repay by depriving him of something important to him.

Since borrowers were usually impoverished, they would often have few possessions left apart from clothing and necessary household items, thus limiting the creditor's choice of objects to distrain. Clothing is mentioned in several passages.[2] The aim of the Torah's laws about distraint is to ensure that in such circumstances, the creditor's legitimate right to force repayment is subordinated to the survival and dignity of the debtor. Accordingly, the creditor may not take a handmill, which is necessary for making food (Deut. 24.6), he may not take a widow's garment (v. 17), if he takes a poor man's night-cover he must return it every evening (vv. 12-13; Exod. 22.25-26), and he may not invade the debtor's house to seize an object for distraint but must wait outside while the debtor brings it to him (Deut. 24.10-11).[3] These restrictions considerably reduce the creditor's

1. Cf. Josephus, *Ant.* 4.268-70; A.E. Cowley, *Aramaic Papyri of the Fifth Century BC* (Oxford: Clarendon Press, 1923), no. 10.9-10, 17; E.G. Kraeling, *The Brooklyn Museum Aramaic Papyri* (New Haven: Yale University Press, 1953), no. 11.9-11. See Milgrom, *Cult and Conscience*, pp. 94-104; I.L. Seeligmann, 'Lending, Pledge and Interest in Biblical Law and Biblical Thought', in *Studies in Bible and the Ancient Near East Presented to Samuel E. Loewenstamm* (ed. Y. Avishur and J. Blau; Jerusalem: E. Rubinstein's Publishing House, 1978), I, pp. 183-205 (Hebrew); J.J. Rabinowitz, הלואה, in אנציקלופדיה מקראית 2.813-16; B.L. Eichler, 'Loan', in *Harper's Dictionary of the Bible* (San Francisco: Harper & Row, 1985), pp. 571-72.

2. Exod. 22.25-26; Deut. 24.12-13, 17; Amos 2.8; Prov. 20.16; 27.13; Job 22.6. The Jewish Ketubbah stipulates that a wife may collect her marriage settlement from all of her husband's possessions, 'even from the cloak on (his) shoulders' (Maimonides, הלכות יבום, 4.33). Kraeling, *Brooklyn Museum Aramaic Papyri*, no. 11.11, also mentions clothing among objects that may be seized in satisfaction of a debt. In the latter cases, as in Amos 2.6, the clothing is not necessarily a night-wrap of relatively little value.

3. Similarly, Job criticizes those who distrain the widow's ox and the Laws of Hammurabi forbid the distraint of oxen and grain. See Job 24.3; Laws of Hammurabi 113, 241 (see G.R. Driver and J.C. Miles, *The Babylonian Laws* [Oxford: Clarendon Press, 1955], 1.210, 214-15).

leverage in securing repayment, but they are consistent with the Bible's position that loans to the poor are acts of charity that may well turn into outright gifts.

The Yavneh-Yam inscription, with its complaint about distraint for alleged nonfeasance, is the earliest evidence we have that garments might be seized for reasons other than default on a loan. There is also evidence from the talmudic period to the same effect.[1] Talmudic sources describe one or two cases that are in some respects strikingly similar to the case described in the inscription. Translations follow; for clarity, I have substituted pertinent names for the pronouns that appear in the text. According to the Palestinian Talmud:

> R. Nehemiah was a potter. He gave some of his pots to a man who broke them, and R. Nehemiah took his cloak. The man went to R. Yose b. Haninah who said: 'Go tell him (that Scripture says) "Follow the ways of the good" (Prov. 2.20a)'. He went and told him, and R. Nehemiah gave him back his cloak. R. Yose b. Haninah asked the man, 'Did he pay you your wages?' The man said, 'No.' R. Yose b. Haninah said: 'Go tell him (that the rest of the verse says) "And keep to the paths of the just" (Prov. 2.20b'. He went and told him and he paid him his wages.[2]

A similar account appears in the Babylonian Talmud and in Yalqut Shimoni. The version in the Yalqut, which is clearest and seems to be closest to the original, is as follows:

> Rabbah bar bar Hannah hired some porters to carry a jug of wine for him. They broke it and he took their cloaks. They went before Rav (d. 247). He said to Rabbah bar bar Hannah, 'Go and give them their cloaks'. Rabbah bar bar Hannah asked, 'Is this the law?' Said Rav, '(As Scripture says), "Follow the ways of the good" (Prov. 2.20a)'. They then stood and cried out to Rav, saying, 'We are poor and we worked for him the entire day; we are hungry and have nothing to eat'. So Rav said to Rabbah

1. While I was preparing this paper for publication, Mayer Rabinowitz, Librarian of the Jewish Theological Seminary of America, kindly called my attention to S.Y. Friedman's recent volume תלמוד ערוך. פרק השוכר את האומנין. בבלי בבא מציעא פרק ששי (Jerusalem: The Jewish Theological Seminary of America, 1990). There (p. 414) I found that Friedman had already noted the similarity of the passage to the Yavneh-Yam inscription, and that S.J. Berman had noted it earlier (see below, p. 125 n. 4).

2. *Y.B.M.* 6 end (p. 10a). The text is cited from the Escorial manuscript published in E.M. Rosenthal and S. Lieberman, *Yerushalmi Neziqin* (Jerusalem: Israel Academy of Sciences and Humanities, 1983), p. 69.

bar bar Hannah, 'go pay them their wages'. Rabbah bar bar Hannah asked, 'Is this the law?' Said Rav, '(As the rest of the verse says), "And keep to the paths of the just" (Prov. 2.20b)'.[1]

Legally the porters in these cases were liable for the damage they caused.[2] Their employers distrained their cloaks. The sages to whom the porters appealed did not deny that they were liable,[3] but advised their employers, who were sages, to forgo their rights under the circumstances, in keeping with Prov. 2.20 as understood by those sages.[4]

It is clear that the employers distrained the porters' cloaks as surety for the loss the porters caused. As in the case of the biblical laws, it is not clear whether the cloaks were valuable enough to offset the loss or whether they were held simply to pressure the porters into making good the loss.[5] One group of commentators, in fact, holds that the employers' purpose was simply to pressure the porters into appearing in court so that their liability could be determined.[6]

Since R. Yose b. Hanina was an *amora* of the second generation in Israel, the incident reported in the Palestinian Talmud implicitly took place in Israel during the third century CE, some nine centuries later

1. Yalqut to Prov. 2.20 (sec. 832), cf. the parallel passage in *b. B.M.* 83a. For variants see Friedman; E.E. Urbach, חז"ל.פרקי אמונות ודעות (Jerusalem: Magnes, 1971), p. 291. Much of the information that follows is based on Friedman, pp. 413-22.

2. See *b. B.M.* 82b-83a and 99b; Friedman, p. 420.

3. In a paraphrase of the account of the Babylonian Talmud in a medieval ethical treatise, Rav begins his response to the question 'Is this the law?' by saying: 'Legally they should pay you for the jug, but. . . ' (Israel Al-Naqawa, *Menorat Ha-Maor* [ed. H.G. Enelow; New York: Bloch, 1932], p. 167).

4. The most important variant to the account in the Babylonian Talmud is the addition of 'Yes' at the beginning of Rav's answers to one or both of Rabbah bar bar Hannah's questions, 'Is this the law?' (the variant appears in the printed editions and in some manuscripts; see above, n. 1; against it see Urbach, p. 291; Friedman, p. 418; it is also absent in the Meiri *ad loc.*). This reading implies that supererogation (לפנים משורת הדין) is, in the circumstances in question, not only advisable but obligatory. See Friedman, p. 417 n. 387; Urbach, pp. 291-92; M. Silberg, *Principia Talmudica* (Jerusalem: Hebrew University Students' Press, 1964), pp. 127-31; S.J. Berman. '*Lifnim Mishurat Hadin* II', *JJS* 28 (1977), pp. 191-92; E. Berkovits, *Not in Heaven* (New York: Ktav, 1983), pp. 27-28.

5. For the subject in general see M. Elon, 'Pledge', *EncJud*, XIII, pp. 636-44.

6. Ritva in שיטה מקובצת (New York: M.P. Press, 1972), *ad loc.*; Nachmanides, חדושי הרמב"ן, II (New York: Feldheim, 1960), *ad loc.*

than that reported in the Yavneh-Yam letter. The same century is implied for the Yalqut/Babylonian Talmud version by the fact that Rav probably is the correct reading of the name of the sage to whom the porters appealed in it. That version may imply a Babylonian locale, but there is room for doubt.[1] Complicating matters even further is the fact that the stories are similar enough to have suggested to several scholars that they are really two versions of a single incident; which is the original is debated. Hence it is not certain whether the incident or incidents parallel to that reported in the Yavneh-Yam letter took place in Israel or Babylonia or both.

Our main interest in these passages lies in the fact that an employer distrained the cloaks of laborers whose negligent performance of their duty had caused him financial loss. The laborers, the employer and the sage to whom they appeal play roles parallel to those of the petitioner, of Hashabiahu b. Shobai, and of the officer in the Yavneh-Yam letter. The parallels are not precise enough to resolve the difference of opinion between Naveh, Cross and Milgrom. In fact, they are partly compatible with each view. In that they involve hired laborers (as Naveh holds regarding the Yavneh-Yam inscription), they show that distraint of garments was not practiced only against defaulting debtors. However, they neither confirm nor disprove that garments might be distrained for simple non-performance of duty. Since in these cases the laborers destroyed their employers' goods, they show that garments might be distrained for a specific material obligation, as Cross and Milgrom hold. Clearly, however, they do not relate to farmers or sharecroppers or defaulting debtors.

Despite the fact that this issue remains unresolved, the talmudic case, or cases, shows that garments might indeed be distrained for either negligence or misfeasance in situations other than default on a loan, and they show that the case described in the Yavneh-Yam letter was not anomalous.

1. The main manuscript traditions identify the employer as Rabbah bar Rab Huna or Rabbah bar bar Hana, both Babylonian *amoraim*, which would locate the incident in Babylonia. One group of readings, however, identifies him as Rabbah bar Hanna, who was associated with Rav in both Israel and Babylonia (see 'Rabbah bar Hana', *EncJud*, XIII, p. 1441), which means that the incident could have taken place in either land. See Friedman, pp. 414-17.

THE PUBLISHED WRITINGS OF NAHUM M. SARNA

a. Books

A Syllabus of Biblical History; College of Jewish Studies (Pittsburgh, 1953).

Understanding Genesis, Jewish Theological Seminary (New York: McGraw Hill, 1966).

A New Translation of the Book of Psalms (co-authored with M. Greenberg and J. Greenfield; Philadelphia: Jewish Publication Society, 1973).

The Book of Job. A New Translation according to the Traditional Hebrew Text with Introductions (co-authored with M. Greenberg and J. Greenfield; Philadelphia: Jewish Publication Society, 1980).

The Writings (Kethubim). A New Translation of the Holy Scriptures (co-authored with M. Greenberg and J. Greenfield; Philadelphia: Jewish Publication Society, 1982).

Exploring Exodus: The Heritage of Biblical Israel (New York: Schocken Books, 1986).

Commentary to Genesis (Philadelphia: Jewish Publication Society, 1989).

Commentary to Exodus (Philadelphia: Jewish Publication Society, 1991).

b. Articles

'Some Instances of Enclitic-*m* in Job', *JJS* 6 (1955), pp. 108-10.

'Ethanim, Job 12 19', *JBL* 74 (1955), pp. 272-74.

'A *Crux Interpretum* in Job 22 3', *JNES* 15 (1956), pp. 118-19.

'Epic Substratum in the Prose of Job', *JBL* 76 (1957), pp. 13-25.

'The Biblical Period', in *Study Guide to Great Ages and Ideas of the Jewish People* (ed. L. Schwartz; New York: Hadassah Education Department, 1958).

'The Interchange of the Prepositions *beth* and *min* in Biblical Hebrew', *JBL* 78 (1959), pp. 310-16.

'From Wellhausen to Kaufmann', *Midstream* (Summer, 1961), pp. 64-74.

'Yehezkel Kaufman and Biblical Scholarship', *Jewish Chronicle* (London), 12 Jan. 1962, p. 19.

'The Psalm for the Sabbath Day (Psalm 92)', *JBL* 81 (1962), pp. 155-68.

'The Library of the Jewish Theological Seminary of America', *Jewish Book Annual* 21 (1963–64), pp. 53-59.

'Psalm 89: A Study in Inner Biblical Exegesis', in *Biblical and Other Studies: Brandeis University Studies and Texts*, I (ed. A. Altmann; Cambridge, MA: Harvard University Press, 1963), pp. 29-46.

'Ashkenazim', 'Sephardim', in *Encyclopedia International* (Grollier, 1963).

'The Mythical Background of Job 18', *JBL* 82 (1963), pp. 315-18.

'Ezekiel 8 17: A Fresh Examination', *HTR* 57 (1964), pp. 347-52.

'Cultural Influences on Biblical Israel (Psalm 19)', *Hadassah Magazine* 47.7 (March, 1966), pp. 9, 31-32.

'Psalm XIX and the Near Eastern Sun-god Literature', in *Proceedings of the Fourth World Congress of Jewish Studies* (Jerusalem, 1967), pp. 171-75.

'Prolegomenon' to M. Buttenwieser, *The Psalms* (New York: Ktav, 1969), pp. xxiii-xxxviii.

'The Bible and Judaic Studies', in *The Teaching of Judaica in American Universities* (ed. L.A. Jick; New York: Ktav, 1970), pp. 35-42.

'Hebrew and Bible Studies in Medieval Spain', in *The Sephardi Heritage* (ed. R.D. Barnett; London: Vallentine and Mitchell, 1971), pp. 323-66.

'Ṣaphon' (Hebrew), in *Encyclopedia Miqraith* (Jerusalem, 1971), VI, cols. 747-51.

'An Obscure Chapter in Jeremiah in the Light of the Babylonian Chronicle and Rabbinic Tradition' (Hebrew), in *Haguth Ivrith Be'Amerika* (Tel Aviv: Yavneh, 1971), pp. 121-30.

'The Order of the Books', in *Studies in Jewish Bibliography, History, and Literature* (ed. C. Berlin; New York: Ktav, 1971), pp. 407-13.

'Bible' (Hebrew), in *Encyclopedia Ivrith* (Jerusalem, 1972), XXIV, cols. 281-83, 286-89.

Articles contributed to *Encyclopedia Judaica* (1972): Aaron, Aaronides, Abihu, Abimelech, Abraham, Acrostics, Amraphel, Asenath, Bible, Bible Canon, Boaz, Dothan and Abiram, Delilah, Genesis, Gershom, Gideon, Hallelujah, Hur, Ichabod, Isaac, Jacob, Jael, Jephthah, Jochebed, Joseph, Nadab, Orpah, Patriarchs, Psalms, Rebekah.

'Zedekiah's Emancipation of Slaves and the Sabbatical Year', in *Orient and Occident* (ed. H.A. Hoffner; Neukirchen: Neukirchener Verlag, 1973), pp. 144-49.

'Biblical Literature, section II', 'O.T. Canon, Text, and Versions', in *Encyclopedia Britannica* (Macropedia, 1973 edition), II, pp. 881-95.

'Introduction to the Early Spanish Pentateuch Manuscript (Toledo, 1241)' (Jerusalem: Makor, 1974).

'Abraham Geiger and Biblical Scholarship', in *New Perspectives on Abraham Geiger* (ed. J.J. Petuchowski; New York: Ktav, 1975), pp. 17-30.

'The Chirotonic Motif on the Lachish Altar', in *Investigations at Lachish* (ed. Y. Aharoni; Tel Aviv, 1975), pp. 44-46.

'Concerning the Problem of the Ordering of the Biblical Books' (Hebrew), *Shnaton, An Annual for Biblical and Near Eastern Studies* I (1975), pp. 197-203.

'Biblical Studies: Some Recent Publications', *Association for Jewish Studies Newsletter* 14 (June, 1975), pp. 12-13.

'Rehab' (Hebrew), in *Encyclopaedia Miqraith* (Jerusalem, 1976), VII, cols. 328-29.

'Paganism and Biblical Judaism', in *Great Confrontations in Jewish History* (ed. S.M. Wagner and A.D. Breck; Denver: University of Denver, 1977), pp. 3-20.

'Abraham in History', *BARev* 3.4 (Dec. 1977), pp. 5-9.

'Rachel' (Hebrew), in *Encyclopaedia Ivrith* (Jerusalem, 1978), XXX, cols. 980-81.

'The Abortive Insurrection in Zedekiah's Day (Jer. 27–29)', *Eretz–Israel* 14 (1978), pp. 89*-96*

'The Divine Title *'abhir ya'ăqôbh'*, in *Essays on the Occasion of the Seventieth Anniversary of the Dropsie University* (Philadelphia, 1979), pp. 389-96.

'The Psalm Superscriptions and the Guilds', in *Studies in Jewish Religious and Intellectual History Presented to Alexander Altmann* (ed. S. Stein and R. Loewe; University of Alabama, 1979), pp. 281-300.

'The Biblical Sources for the History of the Monarchy', in *World History of the Jewish People* (ed. A. Malamat; Jerusalem: Massada Press, 1979), IV.1, pp. 3-19.

'The Last Legacy of Roland de Vaux', *BARev* 6.4 (1980), pp. 14-21.

'The Anticipatory Use of Information as a Literary Feature of the Genesis Narratives', in *The Creation of Sacred Literature* (ed. R.E. Friedman; Berkeley, CA: University of California Press, 1981), pp. 76-82.

Šemeš' and '*Tehillim*' (Hebrew), in *Encyclopaedia Miqraith* (Jerusalem, 1982), VIII, cols. 182-89, 438-62.

'The Decalogue', in *The Solomon Goldman Lectures: Perspectives in Jewish Learning* (ed. N. Stampfer; Chicago, 1982), III, pp. 1-9.

'Genesis Chapter 23: The Cave of Machpelah', *Hebrew Studies* 23 (1982), pp. 17-21.

'The Modern Study of the Bible in the Framework of Jewish Studies', in *Proceedings of the Eighth World Congress of Jewish Studies* (Jerusalem, 1983), pp. 19-27.

'Understanding Creation in Genesis', in *Is God a Creationist? The Religious Case Against Creation-Science* (ed. R.M. Frye; New York, 1983), 155-75.

'The Ravishing of Dinah: A Commentary on Genesis, Chapter 34', in *Studies in Jewish Education in Honor of Louis Newman* (ed. A.M. Shapiro and B.I. Cohen; New York: Ktav, 1984), pp. 143-56.

'Unusual Aspects of Biblical Exegesis During the Middle Ages' (Hebrew), in *Thought and Action: Essays in Memory of Simon Rawidowicz* (ed. A.A. Greenbaum and A.L. Ivry; Tel Aviv, 1982), pp. 35-42.

'Exegesis, Jewish', in *Dictionary of the Middle Ages* (ed. J.R. Strayer; New York: Charles Scribner's Sons, 1984), IV, pp. 538-42.

'Hebrew Language, Jewish Study of', in *Dictionary of the Middle Ages* (ed. J.R. Strayer; New York: Charles Scribner's Sons, 1985), VI, pp. 128-29.

'Authority and Interpretation of Scripture in Jewish Tradition', in *Understanding Scripture* (ed. C. Thoma and M. Wyschogrod; New York: Paulist Press, 1987), pp. 9-20.

'Hebrew in the University' (Hebrew), *Hadoar* 66.38 (1987), pp. 17-19.

'Biblical Literature: Hebrew Scriptures', in *The Encyclopedia of Religion* (ed. M. Eliade, New York: Macmillan Publishing Company, 1987), II, pp. 152-73.

(together with J.D. Sarna) 'Jewish Bible Scholarship and Translations in the United States', in *The Bible and Bibles in America* (ed. E.S. Frerichs; Atlanta, GA: Scholars Press, 1988), pp. 83-117.

'Israel in Egypt: The Egyptian Sojourn and the Exodus', in *Ancient Israel: A Short History* (ed. H. Shanks; Washington, DC: Biblical Archaeology Society, 1988), pp. 31-52.

'Genesis 21 33: A Study in the Development of a Biblical Text and its Rabbinic Transformation', in *From Ancient Israel to Modern Judaism. Intellect in Quest of Understanding. Essays in Honor of Marvin Fox* (ed. J. Neusner, E.S. Frerichs and N.M. Sarna; Atlanta, GA: Scholars Press, 1989), I, pp. 69-75.

'Ancient Libraries and the Ordering of the Biblical Books', Library of Congress, Center for the Book, 1989.

'Writing a Commentary on the Torah', University of Cincinnati, Judaic Studies Program, 1990.

'Legal Terminology in Psalm 3 8', in *Sha'arei Talmon: Studies in the Bible, Qumran, and the Ancient Near East Presented to Shemaryahu Talmon* (ed. M. Fishbane and E. Tov; Winona Lake, IN: Eisenbrauns, 1992), pp. 175-81.

'Exodus, Book of', in *Anchor Bible Dictionary* (New York: Doubleday, 1992), II, pp. 689-700.

c. Book Reviews

L.I. Honor, *The Book of Kings, I*, *Conservative Judaism* 10.2 (Winter, 1956), pp. 54-56.

S. Moscati, *The Semites in Ancient History*, *JBL* 79 (1960), pp. 288-89.

J. Morgenstern, *The Message of Deutero-Isaiah*, *Jewish Social Studies* 26 (1964), pp. 42-43.

J.A. Sanders, *The Psalms Scroll of Qumran Cave 11 (11QPs*^{a}*)*, *Conservative Judaism* 20.4 (1966), pp. 63-66.

S.E. Loewenstamm, *The Tradition of the Exodus in its Development*, *JBL* 85 (1966), pp. 244-46.

O. Eissfeldt, *The Old Testament: An Introduction*, *Conservative Judaism* 22.1 (1967), pp. 63-86.

M. Noth, *The Laws in the Pentateuch*, *Jewish Social Studies* (July, 1968), pp. 175-76.

J. Mann, *The Bible as Read and Preached in the Old Synagogue (vol. 2)*, *JBL* 87 (1968), pp. 100-106.

E.L. Sukenik Memorial Volume: Eretz Israel, VIII, *JBL* 87 (1968), pp. 462-64.

Y. Aharoni and M. Avi-Yonah, *The Macmillan Bible Atlas*, *Conservative Judaism* 23.3 (Spring, 1969), pp. 91-93.

I. Yeivin (ed.), *Genizah Bible Fragments with Babylonian Massorah and Vocalization* (Jerusalem: Makor, 1973), *Association for Jewish Studies Newsletter* No. 10 (January, 1974), p. 10.

S. Schechter, *Documents of Jewish Sectaries*, Prolegomenon by J.A. Fitzmyer, 1970, *JAOS* 94 (1974), pp. 515-16.

F.M. Cross, *Canaanite Myth and Hebrew Epic*, *Int* 29 (1975), pp. 75-78.

G.J. Botterweck and H. Ringgren (eds.), *Theological Dictionary of the Old Testament*, I, *Association for Jewish Studies Newsletter*, No. 17 (June, 1976), pp. 17, 22.

D.A. Robertson, *Linguistic Evidence in Dating Early Hebrew Poetry*, *JBL* 95 (1976), pp. 126-29.

M. Sokoloff, *The Targum to Job from Qumran Cave XI*, *IEJ* 26 (1976), pp. 51-153.

M. Weinfeld, *Justice and Righteousness in Israel and the Nations*, *JAOS* 107 (1987), pp. 144-45.

L. Greenspoon, *Max L. Margolis: A Scholar's Scholar*, *JQR* 82 (1992), pp. 557-58.

JOURNAL FOR THE STUDY OF THE OLD TESTAMENT

Supplement Series

33 LAW AND THEOLOGY IN DEUTERONOMY
J.G. McConville
34 THE TEMPLE SCROLL:
AN INTRODUCTION, TRANSLATION & COMMENTARY
Johann Maier
35 SAGA, LEGEND, TALE, NOVELLA, FABLE:
NARRATIVE FORMS IN OLD TESTAMENT LITERATURE
Edited by George W. Coats
36 THE SONG OF FOURTEEN SONGS
Michael D. Goulder
37 UNDERSTANDING THE WORD:
ESSAYS IN HONOR OF BERNHARD W. ANDERSON
Edited by James T. Butler, Edgar W. Conrad & Ben C. Ollenburger
38 SLEEP, DIVINE AND HUMAN, IN THE OLD TESTAMENT
Thomas H. McAlpine
39 THE SENSE OF BIBLICAL NARRATIVE II:
STRUCTURAL ANALYSES IN THE HEBREW BIBLE
David Jobling
40 DIRECTIONS IN BIBLICAL HEBREW POETRY
Edited by Elaine R. Follis
41 ZION, THE CITY OF THE GREAT KING:
A THEOLOGICAL SYMBOL OF THE JERUSALEM CULT
Ben C. Ollenburger
42 A WORD IN SEASON:
ESSAYS IN HONOUR OF WILLIAM MCKANE
Edited by James D. Martin & Philip R. Davies
43 THE CULT OF MOLEK:
A REASSESSMENT
G.C. Heider
44 THE IDENTITY OF THE INDIVIDUAL IN THE PSALMS
Steven J.L. Croft
45 THE CONFESSIONS OF JEREMIAH IN CONTEXT:
SCENES OF PROPHETIC DRAMA
A.R. Diamond
46 THE BOOK OF JUDGES:
AN INTEGRATED READING
Barry G. Webb
47 THE GREEK TEXT OF JEREMIAH:
A REVISED HYPOTHESIS
Sven Soderlund
48 TEXT AND CONTEXT:
OLD TESTAMENT AND SEMITIC STUDIES FOR F.C. FENSHAM
Edited by W. Claassen

49 THEOPHORIC PERSONAL NAMES IN ANCIENT HEBREW:
A COMPARATIVE STUDY
Jeaneane D. Fowler

50 THE CHRONICLER'S HISTORY
Martin Noth
Translated by H.G.M. Williamson with an Introduction

51 DIVINE INITIATIVE AND HUMAN RESPONSE IN EZEKIEL
Paul Joyce

52 THE CONFLICT OF FAITH AND EXPERIENCE IN THE PSALMS:
A FORM-CRITICAL AND THEOLOGICAL STUDY
Craig C. Broyles

53 THE MAKING OF THE PENTATEUCH:
A METHODOLOGICAL STUDY
R.N. Whybray

54 FROM REPENTANCE TO REDEMPTION:
JEREMIAH'S THOUGHT IN TRANSITION
Jeremiah Unterman

55 THE ORIGIN TRADITION OF ANCIENT ISRAEL:
1. THE LITERARY FORMATION OF GENESIS AND EXODUS 1–23
T.L. Thompson

56 THE PURIFICATION OFFERING IN THE PRIESTLY LITERATURE:
ITS MEANING AND FUNCTION
N. Kiuchi

57 MOSES:
HEROIC MAN, MAN OF GOD
George W. Coats

58 THE LISTENING HEART:
ESSAYS IN WISDOM AND THE PSALMS
IN HONOR OF ROLAND E. MURPHY, O. CARM.
Edited by Kenneth G. Hoglund, Elizabeth F. Huwiler, Jonathan T. Glass and Roger W. Lee

59 CREATIVE BIBLICAL EXEGESIS:
CHRISTIAN AND JEWISH HERMENEUTICS THROUGH THE CENTURIES
Edited by Benjamin Uffenheimer & Henning Graf Reventlow

60 HER PRICE IS BEYOND RUBIES:
THE JEWISH WOMAN IN GRAECO-ROMAN PALESTINE
Léonie J. Archer

61 FROM CHAOS TO RESTORATION:
AN INTEGRATIVE READING OF ISAIAH 24–27
Dan G. Johnson

62 THE OLD TESTAMENT AND FOLKLORE STUDY
Patricia G. Kirkpatrick

63 SHILOH:
A BIBLICAL CITY IN TRADITION AND HISTORY
Donald G. Schley

64 TO SEE AND NOT PERCEIVE:
ISAIAH 6.9-10 IN EARLY JEWISH AND CHRISTIAN INTERPRETATION
Craig A. Evans

65 THERE IS HOPE FOR A TREE: THE TREE AS METAPHOR IN ISAIAH
Kirsten Nielsen

66 SECRETS OF THE TIMES:
MYTH AND HISTORY IN BIBLICAL CHRONOLOGY
Jeremy Hughes

67 ASCRIBE TO THE LORD:
BIBLICAL AND OTHER STUDIES IN MEMORY OF PETER C. CRAIGIE
Edited by Lyle Eslinger & Glen Taylor

68 THE TRIUMPH OF IRONY IN THE BOOK OF JUDGES
Lillian R. Klein

69 ZEPHANIAH, A PROPHETIC DRAMA
Paul R. House

70 NARRATIVE ART IN THE BIBLE
Shimon Bar-Efrat

71 QOHELET AND HIS CONTRADICTIONS
Michael V. Fox

72 CIRCLE OF SOVEREIGNTY:
A STORY OF STORIES IN DANIEL 1–6
Danna Nolan Fewell

73 DAVID'S SOCIAL DRAMA:
A HOLOGRAM OF THE EARLY IRON AGE
James W. Flanagan

74 THE STRUCTURAL ANALYSIS OF BIBLICAL AND CANAANITE POETRY
Edited by Willem van der Meer & Johannes C. de Moor

75 DAVID IN LOVE AND WAR:
THE PURSUIT OF POWER IN 2 SAMUEL 10–12
Randall C. Bailey

76 GOD IS KING:
UNDERSTANDING AN ISRAELITE METAPHOR
Marc Zvi Brettler

77 EDOM AND THE EDOMITES
John R. Bartlett

78 SWALLOWING THE SCROLL:
TEXTUALITY AND THE DYNAMICS OF DISCOURSE
IN EZEKIEL'S PROPHECY
Ellen F. Davies

79 GIBEAH:
THE SEARCH FOR A BIBLICAL CITY
Patrick M. Arnold, S.J.

80 THE NATHAN NARRATIVES
Gwilym H. Jones

81 Anti-Covenant:
Counter-Reading Women's Lives in the Hebrew Bible
Edited by Mieke Bal

82 Rhetoric and Biblical Interpretation
Dale Patrick & Allen Scult

83 The Earth and the Waters in Genesis 1 and 2:
A Linguistic Investigation
David Toshio Tsumura

84 Into the Hands of the Living God
Lyle Eslinger

85 From Carmel to Horeb:
Elijah in Crisis
Alan J. Hauser & Russell Gregory

86 The Syntax of the Verb in Classical Hebrew Prose
Alviero Niccacci
Translated by W.G.E. Watson

87 The Bible in Three Dimensions:
Essays in Celebration of Forty Years of Biblical Studies in the University of Sheffield
Edited by David J.A. Clines, Stephen E. Fowl & Stanley E. Porter

88 The Persuasive Appeal of the Chronicler:
A Rhetorical Analysis
Rodney K. Duke

89 The Problem of the Process of Transmission in the Pentateuch
Rolf Rendtorff
Translated by John J. Scullion

90 Biblical Hebrew in Transition:
The Language of the Book of Ezekiel
Mark F. Rooker

91 The Ideology of Ritual:
Space, Time and Status in the Priestly Theology
Frank H. Gorman, Jr

92 On Humour and the Comic in the Hebrew Bible
Edited by Yehuda T. Radday & Athalya Brenner

93 Joshua 24 as Poetic Narrative
William T. Koopmans

94 What Does Eve Do to Help? And Other Readerly Questions to the Old Testament
David J.A. Clines

95 God Saves:
Lessons from the Elisha Stories
Rick Dale Moore

96 Announcements of Plot in Genesis
Laurence A. Turner

97 THE UNITY OF THE TWELVE
Paul R. House

98 ANCIENT CONQUEST ACCOUNTS:
A STUDY IN ANCIENT NEAR EASTERN AND BIBLICAL HISTORY WRITING
K. Lawson Younger, Jr

99 WEALTH AND POVERTY IN THE BOOK OF PROVERBS
R.N. Whybray

100 A TRIBUTE TO GEZA VERMES:
ESSAYS ON JEWISH AND CHRISTIAN
LITERATURE AND HISTORY
Edited by Philip R. Davies & Richard T. White

101 THE CHRONICLER IN HIS AGE
Peter R. Ackroyd

102 THE PRAYERS OF DAVID (PSALMS 51–72):
STUDIES IN THE PSALTER, II
Michael Goulder

103 THE SOCIOLOGY OF POTTERY IN ANCIENT PALESTINE:
THE CERAMIC INDUSTRY AND THE DIFFUSION OF CERAMIC STYLE
IN THE BRONZE AND IRON AGES
Bryant G. Wood

104 PSALM STRUCTURES:
A STUDY OF PSALMS WITH REFRAINS
Paul R. Raabe

105 ESTABLISHING JUSTICE
Pietro Bovati

106 GRADED HOLINESS:
A KEY TO THE PRIESTLY CONCEPTION OF THE WORLD
Philip Jenson

107 THE ALIEN IN THE PENTATEUCH
Christiana van Houten

108 THE FORGING OF ISRAEL:
IRON TECHNOLOGY, SYMBOLISM AND TRADITION IN ANCIENT SOCIETY
Paula M. McNutt

109 SCRIBES AND SCHOOLS IN MONARCHIC JUDAH:
A SOCIO-ARCHAEOLOGICAL APPROACH
David Jamieson-Drake

110 THE CANAANITES AND THEIR LAND:
THE TRADITION OF THE CANAANITES
Niels Peter Lemche

111 YAHWEH AND THE SUN:
THE BIBLICAL AND ARCHAEOLOGICAL EVIDENCE
J. Glen Taylor

112 WISDOM IN REVOLT:
METAPHORICAL THEOLOGY IN THE BOOK OF JOB
Leo G. Perdue

113 PROPERTY AND THE FAMILY IN BIBLICAL LAW
Raymond Westbrook
114 A TRADITIONAL QUEST:
ESSAYS IN HONOUR OF LOUIS JACOBS
Edited by Dan Cohn-Sherbok
115 I HAVE BUILT YOU AN EXALTED HOUSE:
TEMPLE BUILDING IN THE BIBLE IN THE LIGHT OF MESOPOTAMIAN
AND NORTH-WEST SEMITIC WRITINGS
Victor Hurowitz
116 NARRATIVE AND NOVELLA IN SAMUEL:
STUDIES BY HUGO GRESSMANN AND OTHER SCHOLARS 1906–1923
Translated by David E. Orton
Edited by David M. Gunn
117 SECOND TEMPLE STUDIES:
1. PERSIAN PERIOD
Edited by Philip R. Davies
118 SEEING AND HEARING GOD WITH THE PSALMS:
THE PROPHETIC LITURGY FROM THE SECOND TEMPLE IN JERUSALEM
Raymond Jacques Tournay
Translated by J. Edward Crowley
119 TELLING QUEEN MICHAL'S STORY:
AN EXPERIMENT IN COMPARATIVE INTERPRETATION
Edited by David J.A. Clines & Tamara C. Eskenazi
120 THE REFORMING KINGS:
CULT AND SOCIETY IN FIRST TEMPLE JUDAH
Richard H. Lowery
121 KING SAUL IN THE HISTORIOGRAPHY OF JUDAH
Diana Vikander Edelman
122 IMAGES OF EMPIRE
Edited by Loveday Alexander
123 JUDAHITE BURIAL PRACTICES AND BELIEFS ABOUT THE DEAD
Elizabeth Bloch-Smith
124 LAW AND IDEOLOGY IN MONARCHIC ISRAEL
Edited by Baruch Halpern and Deborah W. Hobson
125 PRIESTHOOD AND CULT IN ANCIENT ISRAEL
Edited by Gary A. Anderson and Saul M. Olyan
126 W.M.L.DE WETTE, FOUNDER OF MODERN BIBLICAL CRITICISM:
AN INTELLECTUAL BIOGRAPHY
John W. Rogerson
127 THE FABRIC OF HISTORY:
TEXT, ARTIFACT AND ISRAEL'S PAST
Edited by Diana Vikander Edelman
128 BIBLICAL SOUND AND SENSE:
POETIC SOUND PATTERNS IN PROVERBS 10–29
Thomas P. McCreesh

129 THE ARAMAIC OF DANIEL IN THE LIGHT OF OLD ARAMAIC
Zdravko Stefanovic
130 STRUCTURE AND THE BOOK OF ZECHARIAH
Michael Butterworth
131 FORMS OF DEFORMITY:
A MOTIF-INDEX OF ABNORMALITIES, DEFORMITIES AND DISABILITIES IN TRADITIONAL JEWISH LITERATURE
Lynn Holden
132 CONTEXTS FOR AMOS:
PROPHETIC POETICS IN LATIN AMERICAN PERSPECTIVE
Mark Daniel Carroll R.
133 THE FORSAKEN FIRSTBORN:
A STUDY OF A RECURRENT MOTIF IN THE PATRIARCHAL NARRATIVES
R. Syrén
135 ISRAEL IN EGYPT:
A READING OF EXODUS 1–2
G.F. Davies
136 A WALK THROUGH THE GARDEN:
BIBLICAL, ICONOGRAPHICAL AND LITERARY IMAGES OF EDEN
Edited by P. Morris and D. Sawyer
137 JUSTICE AND RIGHTEOUSNESS:
BIBLICAL THEMES AND THEIR INFLUENCE
Edited by H. Graf Reventlow & Y. Hoffman
138 TEXT AS PRETEXT:
ESSAYS IN HONOUR OF ROBERT DAVIDSON
Edited by R.P. Carroll
139 PSALM AND STORY:
INSET HYMNS IN HEBREW NARRATIVE
J.W. Watts
140 PURITY AND MONOTHEISM:
CLEAN AND UNCLEAN ANIMALS IN BIBLICAL LAW
Walter Houston
141 DEBT SLAVERY IN ISRAEL AND THE ANCIENT NEAR EAST
Gregory C. Chirichigno
142 DIVINATION IN ANCIENT ISRAEL AND ITS NEAR EASTERN ENVIRONMENT:
A SOCIO-HISTORICAL INVESTIGATION
Frederick H. Cryer
143 HOUSES AND THEIR FURNISHINGS IN BRONZE AGE PALESTINE:
DOMESTIC ACTIVITY AREAS AND ARTIFACT DISTRIBUTION IN THE MIDDLE AND LATE BRONZE AGES
P.M. Michèle Daviau
144 AMONG THE PROPHETS:
ESSAYS ON PROPHETIC TOPICS
Edited by P.R. Davies and D.J.A Clines

145 THE SPEECHES OF MICAH:
A RHETORICAL-HISTORICAL ANALYSIS
Charles S. Shaw
146 THE HISTORY OF ANCIENT PALESTINE FROM THE PALAEOLITHIC PERIOD TO ALEXANDER'S CONQUEST
Gösta W. Ahlström
147 VOWS IN THE HEBREW BIBLE AND THE ANCIENT NEAR EAST
Tony W. Cartledge
148 IN SEARCH OF 'ANCIENT ISRAEL'
Philip R. Davies
149 PRIESTS, PROPHETS AND SCRIBES; ESSAYS ON THE FORMATION AND HERITAGE OF SECOND TEMPLE JUDAISM IN HONOUR OF JOSEPH BLENKINSOPP
Eugene Ulrich, John W. Wright, Robert P. Carroll and Philip R. Davies (eds)
150 TRADITION AND INNOVATION IN HAGGAI AND ZECHARIAH
Janet A. Tollington
151 THE CITIZEN-TEMPLE COMMUNITY
J.P. Weinberg
152 UNDERSTANDING POETS AND PROPHETS; ESSAYS IN HONOUR OF GEORGE WISHART ANDERSON
A.G. Auld
153 THE PSALMS AND THEIR READERS; INTERPRETIVE STRATEGIES FOR PSALM 18
D.K. Berry
154 MINHAH LE-NAHUM: BIBLICAL AND OTHER STUDIES PRESENTED TO NAHUM M. SARNA IN HONOUR OF HIS 70TH BIRTHDAY
M. Fishbane and M. Brettler (eds)